BRECKNOCK

MONMOUTH

Trevithick's Engine

Aberdare

Merthyr Tydfil

POWYS

Caersalem

Rhondda

Miner resting

Bridgend

Llantrisant

THE VALE

CARDIFF

Llantwit Major

St Nicholas

St Fagans

Point light

Aberthaw
Bell buoy

BARRY

Flat Holm

Some small harvest

Some small harvest

THE MEMOIRS OF
GLYN DANIEL

THAMES AND HUDSON

BY THE SAME AUTHOR:

The Three Ages

A Hundred Years of Archaeology

The Prehistoric Chamber Tombs of England and Wales

Lascaux and Carnac

The Megalithic Builders of Western Europe

The Prehistoric Chamber Tombs of France

The Idea of Prehistory

The Hungry Archaeologist in France

New Grange and the Bend of the Boyne (with S.P.Ó Ríordáin)

Man Discovers his Past

The Origins and Growth of Archaeology

The First Civilizations

Megaliths in History

A Hundred and Fifty Years of Archaeology

A Short History of Archaeology

The Cambridge Murders

Welcome Death

Endpapers. Front: Glamorgan, by Leslie Illingworth,
from Stewart Williams, *Glamorgan Historian*, 1968.
Back: the Pas de Calais region, specially
drawn by H.A. Shelley.

Frontispiece: drawing of Glyn Daniel by Robert Tollast,
by kind permission of the Master and Fellows of
St. John's College, Cambridge.

Calligraphy by Will Carter

Filmset in Great Britain by Servis Filmsetting Limited, Manchester
Monochrome illustrations printed by BAS Printers Limited, Over Wallop, Hampshire
Text printed and bound by Butler and Tanner Limited, Frome, Somerset

CONTENTS

Cogitavi dies antiquos et annos aeternos (Psalm 77:5)

*I have considered the days of old: and the years
that are past (Coverdale)*

PREFACE

IN THE EARLY SIXTIES, when I was travelling one Sunday morning from Cambridge to Aarhus, Walter Neurath met me at King's Cross, gave me lunch, and put me on the Scandinavian Express at Liverpool Street. We were then intimately concerned with the *Ancient Peoples and Places* series which we had created in 1956. I must have been in good form at lunch, because as we drove eastwards from Soho he asked me if one day I would put down in writing some of the stories I had told him.

A quarter of a century later I have done so – those and many more. Alas, Walter is dead, as are so many of my friends, foes, and acquaintances mentioned in these pages. The present Master of Balliol in his half-autobiography *A path from Rome* says: 'I have not yet reached the advanced age which seems to confer on autobiographers the privilege of making free, in this way, with the past of others.' I have, though I am sure that my recollections – I have written a journal for forty years but no diary, although I have my Cambridge Pocket Diary and my desk diaries for all these years – do not coincide with those of many others. My stories involving Stuart Piggott are slightly different in his memory: and I describe the different views that Sir David Attenborough and I have about the Julian Huxley land-snail story – if Julian were alive he would certainly have yet a third version! I am sure that Sir David Wilson, Dorothy de Navarro, Grace Thornton and Basil Megaw have different versions of the Chadwick-de Navarro stories that I retell. And I am also sure Enoch Powell has a different recollection, if he recollects it at all, of the dinner party in the Imperial Gymkhana Club, Delhi in December 1945. But then these personal recollections are what history is made of: what we all thought we did and said and heard at the time. My journals are contemporary and explicit.

I am grateful to my publishers, Frank Collieson of Heffers, and most especially my wife, Ruth, for their careful and helpful editing and copy-editing of this manuscript which was typed and retyped by Mrs Eva Cousins with her usual care and efficiency. Brian Hope-Taylor gave permission for his drawing to be reproduced, and Arthur Shelley drew for us a map of the Pas-de-Calais to balance Leslie Illingworth's map of Glamorgan. The Master and Fellows of St John's College gave permission to reproduce the page from Siegfried Sassoon's *Picture Show* with its autographed page to W.H. Rivers Rivers and the drawing of me by Robert Tollast. Eadward Langhorne, my brother-in-law, readily gave permission to reproduce some of his excellent photographs.

CHAPTER ONE

Growing up in South Wales

THE CURRENT EDITION of *Halliwell's Television Companion* gives my date of birth, surprisingly, as *circa* 1900. I may be, as *The Sunday Times* recently described me, 'the grand old man of archaeological television' (sadly, the real grand old man of archaeological television, Sir Mortimer Wheeler, is no longer with us). But I am not *circa* eighty-six; there is no uncertainty about the date or the place of my birth. I was born on 23 April 1914 in the schoolhouse of Lampeter Velfrey in what was then Pembrokeshire and is now part of Dyfed. My father, John Daniel, was the village schoolmaster: he had been married to my mother, Mary Jane Edmunds, in 1913. I was their first and, as it turned out, their only child.

Lampeter Velfrey is a very small village between Narberth and Whitland. I have seldom met, outside Dyfed, anyone who was born or bred in Lampeter Velfrey, with the exception of the late Colonel Robin Humphreys, mine host of the Antelope in Eaton Square, who made of that public house, in the 1960s, such a fine place for eating and drinking. Many is the time we have drunk a glass together and wondered whether our Nonconformist ancestors in West Wales were turning and twisting with rage in their graves as we twisted and tasted our glasses of Graves and Beaujolais.

My birth was registered at Narberth which was, in days of old, the capital of the kings or princes of Dyfed. When that great seventeenth-century Welsh antiquary, Edward Lhuyd, who was the second keeper of the Ashmolean Museum in Oxford, was asked why he spelt his name in such an odd way – it is the name Lloyd – he used to say proudly, 'Because I am an Ancient Briton'. I share his pride: I too am an Ancient Briton. In the old days when, travelling in France, one had to fill in a *fiche* when staying in a hotel, I always put 'Gallois' as my nationality and 'Pays de Galles' as my country of birth. As likely as not the *patron* or *patronne* would look at my short, stocky, sturdy figure and murmur, 'Oui, oui, Gallois, le rugby n'est-ce-pas et les chants sacrés?' Those are about the only things the average Frenchman knows about

9

the Welsh: that they play rugby very well and often beat the French at this game, frequently to the accompaniment of crowds singing hymns like 'Cwm Rhondda' or doggerel verse like 'Sospan Fach'.

My father was a Carmarthenshire man brought up in the family farm of Glynadda near Alltwalis, ten miles north of Carmarthen on the road to Pencader. There are many Daniels in Carmarthenshire and Cardiganshire. The only distinguished member of the Carmarthen Daniel clan that I know about is John Daniel, the printer (*circa* 1755–1823). He was the son of a south Carmarthenshire farmer who, after seven years' apprenticeship with John Ross in Carmarthen, went to London where he worked for the king's printers, returning to Carmarthen and setting up business there in 1784. He came to be regarded as one of the best Welsh printers of his time, and was the first person in Wales to print music in staff notation. He it was who printed the earliest issues of the *Carmarthen Journal* which began its life on 3 March 1810.

When my father's father, William, was in the prime of life he had farmed a large property called Glynadda and I was given the very common Welsh Christian name of Glyn because of that family farm. I never knew my maternal grandmother except through the memories of her children, some photographs and a painting – he never spoke of her himself. They had five children: two girls, Rachel and Elizabeth, and three boys, John (my father), Henry and David. My aunts Rachel and Lizzie married prosperous Carmarthenshire farmers and I grew up in my holidays in their farmyards with their children. Uncles Henry and David served in the 1914–18 war and, when demobilized, refused to go back into the accepted pattern of small farming. Henry became a successful garagist at St Clears; David was trained as a chemist and became first a very successful manager for Boots and then, when his deafness became considerable, ran his own business. David had a great sense of humour which never deserted him: I loved him for that and for the fact that he always gave me chocolate-coated toffees.

My mother came from Nantymoel in the Ogmore Valley in what was then north Glamorgan: she was Mary Jane Edmunds and my second Christian name, Edmund, came from my mother's maiden name. My mother's family were Cardigan people: her father had moved from his family farm at a time of agricultural recession and the opening up of the South Welsh coal mines. He was a miner. My father and mother met when they were teachers together in a school near

Pontypridd; and they were married in Bridgend. After the first five years of my life in south Pembrokeshire doctors advised that my mother should go and live in a drier climate and we moved to Llantwit Major in the middle of the Vale of Glamorgan where I was brought up and lived until I went to Cambridge as an undergraduate in 1932.

I am therefore a South Welshman through and through – my roots being in Carmarthenshire, Cardiganshire, Pembrokeshire and then Glamorgan. I like to think that I am descended from the ancient British tribe of the Demetae who gave their name to Dyfed, although I lived my childhood and adolescence in the territory of the Silures whom Tacitus described so well. I am proud, too, that my ancestry combines those characteristic essentials of Welsh life: farming, mining and education. When I first met Cyril Fox, Director of the National Museum of Wales, he asked me slightly nervously about my family and parentage, wondering perhaps what sort of young man he was dealing with, an undergraduate from St John's College, Cambridge, on vacation. I told him my father was the headmaster of the village school at Llantwit Major and my family were Carmarthen farmers. His face beamed and he clapped me on the shoulder. 'Excellent,' he said, 'good yeoman stock like myself and O.G.S. Crawford and Stuart Piggott. Backbone of England, dear boy – and of Wales.'

My parents must naturally bear the responsibility, even of a diminished kind, for the fact that I, a staunch Welshman and Ancient Briton, was born on St George's Day, 23 April, although what could be a nicer time for a birthday, the spring moving into early summer, and how grand to share one's birthday with William Shakespeare (it is also curiously enough the day on which he died), as also with the nineteenth-century Welsh poet John Ceiriog Hughes. Hughes was a schoolmaster in North Wales. I had to study and learn his poetry when I was at school in Barry and indeed had to recite one of his poems at a School Eisteddfod. I spent so much time and effort on memorizing this short poem about a mountain brook that I have never forgotten it, and suddenly when I am alone the lines come tumbling back through my head with the force and freshness of the river itself:

> *Nant y Mynydd groew, loew,*
> *Yn ymdroelli tua'r pant,*
> *Rhwng y brwyn yn sisial ganu,*
> *O na bawn i fel y nant!*

11

Mountain stream, bright and happy,
Rushing down towards the valley,
Singing sweetly through the heather,
How I wish I was like the brook!

I collect saints, as I collect the labels of bottles of wine I have drunk,
and with saints and quarter birthdays the year is broken up by not less
than twelve special feast days. St David is the patron saint of Wales; St
Edmund King and Martyr belongs to my second Christian name; St
Illtud presides over Llantwit Major, where I spent my childhood; and
St John over the college in which I have spent my adult life in
Cambridge. The accident of my birth on St George's Day provided
me with an extra saint.

My Cambridge college is dedicated to St John the Evangelist and
his day, as most people know, is 27 December. It used to be our main
feast day at which we admitted new Fellows, and indeed for many
years the St John's festivities went on for the twelve days of Christmas.
But very gradually their festivities – which I describe later in this book,
as recounted to me by E.J. Rapson – came to an end, and even St
John's Night was an unsuitable day for our major feast of the year.
This was transferred to 6 May by adopting to ourselves St John *ante
Portam Latinam*. In Rome in the first century AD St John narrowly
escaped being boiled in oil. He is a good saint to have, and very
suitable for an academic occasion, being patron of all those who deal
with books – printers, editors, engravers and binders – as well as those
who have to do with wine – *tonnelliers* and *vignerons*.

There are several saints' days for the different St Daniels. St Daniel
the prophet has his day on 21 July. I like the entry about him in my
French *Dictionnaire des Saints de tous les jours*, published by Robert Morel
and written by Father Philippe Rouillard of the Abbey of Wisques –
only half a dozen miles from where I now write at Zouafques in the
Pas-de-Calais – with a surprising and revealing appendix on miracles
by Pierre Teilhard de Chardin SJ: 'spécialiste de l'interprétation des
songes, auteur de prophéties énigmatiques, et ami des lions.' It says
nothing of the St Daniel whose feast day is 21 November (I am always
delighted when this dark moment of November comes round to have
Edmund on the 20th and Daniel on the 21st) and again nothing about
St Daniel of North Italy whose day is 3 January. This third Daniel is
my particular favourite because it is in his village in the Trentino that
the best smoked ham is made – better than Parma, Bayonne or

Strasbourg. *Prosciutto San Daniele* is surely one of the greatest delights of European gastronomy, and whenever I walked down Old Compton Street, as I used to do almost every other week from the British Museum, Thames and Hudson and Foyles to my club in Pall Mall, I would stop in Parmigiano Figli to buy a dozen slices of St Daniel's ham, and slaver as the wafer-thin slices were cut for me.

The Welsh have few genuine ancient surnames: most are single Christian names, some of which go back to pre-Christian times like Pwyll (present Powell), Lhwyd (now Lloyd, a colour name: it is the word for grey), Llewellyn, Dillwyn, Madoc, Rhys and Cadwallader (there seemed to me recently more Cadwalladers in the Philadelphia 'phonebook than in Wales); but more generally they are from the Bible, such as David, Daniel, Elias, John (Jones comes from this, and so does Evans from the Welsh form Ioan) and James; and many come from the Norman occupation of Wales, such as William, Hugh/ Hughes or Morgan. It is because of these single names that so many Welsh people were known familiarly and generally by locational or occupational names such as Davies the Shop, Williams the Pincers (the local dentist), Evans the Death (the local undertaker). My grandfather was always known as Daniel Crossvale from the farm he lived in in his retirement from Glynadda, and my great friend in the village of Alltwalis was Tom y Gôf – Tom the Blacksmith: I still after all these years do not know his surname.

The name Daniel is a very convenient one for Continental travel: in France there is only confusion as to whether it is my surname. 'Tiens,' they say, 'Daniel comme le prénom! Curieux!', and as often as not I find myself down as M. Daniel Glyn. It is just as easy in Italy, and Signor e Signora Danieli get along very well. One day, for the hell of it, I am going to book a table for lunch or dinner in the Royal Danieli Hotel in Venice, give my name as Professore Danieli and when I get there say that naturally we will begin our meal with *Prosciutto San Daniele*: a childish and amusing prospect!

I have very few real recollections of my first five years in Pembrokeshire and suspect that much of what I now recollect, or think I recollect, of those early years comes from stories told me by parents, friends or relatives. I was born and brought up in the headmaster's house which was next to and physically adjoined the small village school where he reigned, assisted by a dear lady, Miss Coles, who became a great friend and patron of mine. There was a square hole in the wall between our garden and the playground and I used to wriggle through this and get into the back of the classroom. My father didn't formally approve of this but Miss Coles would keep me quiet with chocolates and so, lonely in the house, I really started going to school before I was two and soon learned the difference between Bat, Hat, Mat and Cat. Then there came a horrid day when I found I was older and fatter, and I got stuck in the hole in the wall. I lay there struggling for what seemed hours but was only until the mid-morning break, and was then rescued by Miss Coles and some senior boys and pushed or pulled through the hole. Thereafter I was allowed to go formally to school as an ordinary pupil and was reading well before I left Lampeter Velfrey at the age of five.

I do remember that I had a special cupboard in the kitchen dresser where I kept my toys and I was taught to put them tidily back there when I had finished. Then I was given a kitten and solemnly put it back in the cupboard when I had finished playing with it. Its pained cries brought my mother to the rescue and I began to learn the difference between inanimate and animate objects. The same lack of basic understanding of nature bedevilled my first efforts at gardening. My father, always a very good and very keen gardener, thought that from an early age I should have a plot of ground to cultivate. This seemed a good idea: I planted seeds and in due course green shoots and eventually flowers appeared. But this was not what I wanted. Suddenly my parents were electrified by my assiduous attendance to my garden. There was one row that I constantly visited, waiting for results. In the end I burst into childish sobs. What was the matter? I had planted a row of broken up Marie biscuits! 'Why won't my biscuit trees grow? I sobbed. 'It isn't fair.'

I don't know whether I was obsessed by food at that early age, but one day an old farmer friend found me half-a-mile from home walking in the direction of Whitland Station carrying my father's umbrella. 'Where are you going?' he asked. 'To London,' I said. 'They don't give me enough to eat at home.' 'It's a long way to London. Come up beside me in the cart.' And later he delivered a sleepy boy back to his distracted parents who gave him a good meal and put him to bed.

My first experience of the sea was from Lampeter Velfrey. We went on a Sunday School outing – a large jolly party of boys and girls and some parents and teachers in a 'gambo', a horse-drawn waggon, along the leafy August lanes to Amroth and Saundersfoot. There I saw the sea for the first time in my life.

Although I remember accurately little of my life in Lampeter Velfrey my memories of Llantwit Major are very clear from the moment I came to live there in 1919. I was lucky to be brought up in the Vale of Glamorgan, the most southerly part of Wales, and in one of the most interesting and historical villages in western Britain, the village now known as Llantwit Major. Its original Welsh name was Llanilltud Fawr, which means 'the church of St Illtud the Great'. This small village, as it was in the 1920s, some twenty miles west of Cardiff, nestles in a hollow two miles from the Severn Sea. A few miles away, between the village and Cardiff, was the famous chambered long barrow of Tinkinswood excavated by John Ward in 1913, a year before I was born; and a mile from that site the cromlech, or free-standing megalithic chamber, of St Lythans which became the frontispiece of Mortimer Wheeler's *Prehistoric and Roman Wales* (1925), and which does, in fact, show traces of its original long mound. North of the village was a group of Bronze Age round barrows, one of which was excavated by W.F. Grimes, and others during the last war by Cyril Fox. Fox's excavations were caused by the construction of an airfield at Llandow, and it was these excavations that eventually inspired him to write *Life and Death in the Bronze Age*.

These last excavations were years later than my childhood. When I was a schoolboy the Llandow round barrows were places to walk to and wonder about. So were the remains of the Roman villa at Caermead, and the splendid promontory hillforts of the Early Iron Age at Llantwit Major itself ('The Castle Ditches'), and Nash and Porthkerry.

St Illtud was one of the great early fathers of the Celtic Church and his monastery at Llantwit Major attracted many famous men like St Samson, St Cadoc and perhaps Gildas. But, alas, no traces of the fifth/sixth-century monastery survive: only the Norman and post-Norman church, but it contains pre-Norman Celtic crosses of great beauty and interest. On the hill to the seaward of the church is a gatehouse, and in the fields behind it are tumps and tussocks and hillocks which I used to walk over and wonder whether they could be the remains of St Illtud's monastery. V.E. Nash-Williams's excavations of 1952 showed that they were only medieval buildings connected with the gatehouse, perhaps leading to a monastic grange.

The Vale was rich farming country and we were proud when William Board, whose fields lay behind our house, won the top Smithfield award with his black Aberdeen Angus cattle. The *Life of St Illtud* has an interesting passage about the Vale in early days: 'This territory is meet to be cultivated and there is none more fertile throughout the country. Tilled, it abounds in harvests; it is seen to be flowing with honey and fragant flowers . . . Italy is fertile . . . this is more abundant and more temperate.'

The first money I ever earned was from very minor agricultural activities. My father's assistant master lived in a flat in a large farmhouse outside the village and I used to visit him and read his books, especially the illustrated version of H.G. Wells's *Outline of History*. One day the farmer, Thomas Leyshon, asked me if I would like to earn a few shillings helping him drive his sheep from distant fields back to the farm. This I did, although the real work was naturally done by two splendid dogs; I went home with half a crown in my pocket.

Even more exciting was winning a prize. The *Western Mail* set a competition for children under fourteen to write not more than three hundred words on how they would spend £2 if they were given it. I spent a long time over my entry and sent it in without showing it to my parents. Imagine their surprise, and my delight, when a week later they opened the paper and discovered I had won first prize – and the prize was £5, untold wealth, or so it seemed to me then.

Llantwit Major was full of fascinating people. There was Mrs Williams who lived in Court House in a very grand manner. She was supposed to be very 'county' and to have never forgiven herself for marrying beneath her, one of the village grocers. I was made to visit her once a week, when she lent me her copy of the *National Geographic Magazine*. I was required to bring it back the following week and was questioned kindly but sharply on my views of all the articles. Then there was Morgan Rees, the prosperous farmer of Plymouth Farm who kept open house in his wonderful Elizabethan farmhouse: one never knew whom one would meet there – often it would be Daniel Hopkin, a local boy who became MP for Carmarthen. Morgan seemed a confirmed bachelor but delighted us all by marrying Lilian Morgan, sister of one of my father's schoolteachers. In the last twenty years when I have revisited the Vale I have often stayed with his widow (as I write, alas, I have heard of her death). Mrs Morgan Rees dispensed the lavish hospitality I always associated with Plymouth Farm and was a mine of information about the old days in the Vale.

I knew only two of my grandparents. My mother's father died before I was born and so did my father's mother. So I knew only Mrs Edmunds, a widow living in a terrace house in the colliery town of Nantymoel, and William Daniel, in his old age a small farmer in Alltwalis. I was devoted to both of them and they to me. Neither of them spoke any English, which is proof positive that I was a fluent Welsh speaker in my childhood and adolescence.

From a very early age I was sent up alone from Llantwit Major to Nantymoel at Christmas-time. Four or five days before Christmas I was saddled with what seemed to me then two enormous bags of goodies. I travelled to Bridgend and then crossed from the Vale of Glamorgan terminal over the bridge under which the West Wales to London expresses thundered and down to the Ogmore Valley line. Life was full of pleasant kindly porters and officials and they appreciated I was a curiosity. 'I am taking Christmas to my grandma,' I once said; 'Then you must travel first class,' said the ticket-inspector, and I sat in lonely splendour all the way from Bridgend to Nantymoel. They had telephoned ahead and the stationmaster met me. He knew my grandmother well and had known my grandfather. 'Thomas Edmunds was a very good man,' he said, 'very religious. Yes, very religious. Perhaps too religious. But an excellent deacon at Bethesda.'

My grandmother would have been waiting at the front door from the moment the train came in. She embraced me and always said the same thing. 'You're growing up, boy, and you're getting to look more and more like your grandfather.' Perhaps these curious single visitations every Christmas (and the exercise lasted for more than ten years) were some clever ploy of my mother's to give me confidence in myself, and to give her mother a special happiness in seeing her only grandson whom she might see resembling – as indeed I did – her husband's Cardigan peasant stock.

Our visits were always the same. My bags of goodies were opened and accepted and then we sat down, grandma and me, to midday dinner. There was always a fine dish of home-made soup, then roast beef, Yorkshire pudding, roast potatoes, and because she knew they were my favourite vegetable, a purée of swedes and turnips, which was, I suppose, an old Cardigan farmhouse dish.

Then there would be apple tart and cream and, of course, tea drunk all through the meal. Looking back on it, with no clear memory of the conversations, I wonder at these midday dinners between a growing boy of seven to seventeen and an old lady of seventy to eighty. She must have been a loving and accommodating person. When we had finished our meal we washed up and then she gave me a pound: 'Spend it, boyo, before you go home.' And I went down into the town while she put her feet up and had a much-earned siesta. I knew where to go: to the one bookshop, and I always knew what I wanted to buy. There was a series called *The Child's Illustrated Guide to . . .* and year after year I bought these books about Dickens, Scott and many another. Then after a large tea I would catch the train down to Bridgend, cross the bridge, take the Vale of Glamorgan train, and a very sleepy boy was collected by his father at Llantwit Major.

On one of my visits there was an icy stillness at the Nantymoel railway station and no one smiled or greeted me. I walked up to Station Road. There were people standing at the doors of their houses. My grandmother was crying when I got to her house and it was half an hour before I realized what had happened. A man had been killed in the colliery during the night. My grandmother took me to the door as they carried his body up to his house only five doors away from us. It was the first time I was faced with death.

As I grew older, on my Christmas visits I went for long walks up above the colliery town of Nantymoel to the hills, right up to Bwlch-y-clawdd and the wonderful view down into the Rhondda Valley. Looking down at the north Glamorgan valleys, so changed as cultural landscapes since the Industrial Revolution, one can never forget the evocative picture of Richard Llewellyn's writing in *How Green was my Valley*. How green and beautiful they must have been, and how delightful the high valley road still is!

My Nantymoel grandmother had four children: my mother, her two sisters (both of whom I was always told died of TB), and her brother Tom. Thomas Edmunds went into the Baptist ministry and was a most successful preacher and pastor, first in Aberystwyth, then in Birmingham, and finally in Leicester. Perhaps I inherited through him what is rudely called the Welsh gift of the gab. When I was an undergraduate I went to stay with him and my aunt in Leicester and heard him preach. He was brilliant, clear, persuasive, with a curious touch of arrogance. When in Cambridge I talked to his friend and admirer T.R. Glover, who said, 'Your Uncle Tom knows what's right for the world and is happy to tell the world that. This is why he packed over a thousand every Sunday into his chapel in Birmingham.' I once asked Uncle Tom, as I was finishing being a research student and was about to start lecturing, what advice he had about addressing an audience, large or small. His reply was at that time astonishing. 'Treat them like cabbages,' he said. 'Think of a field of cabbages in front of you but remember they are not all cabbages. One or two will get your message: and that's worth all the effort.'

I wish I had known him better. He read everything, had an astonishing library and was supposed to be writing a critical work on Christianity in relation to all other religions. He was a friend of the Reverend J.F. Bethune-Baker – the 'Bath Bun' as he was called – who was Professor of Divinity and a Fellow of Peterhouse. I once sat next to him at dinner and, rather nervously, asked him about Tom Edmunds. 'A great man,' he said; 'ought to have been a don. Wasting his time preaching to Nonconformist audiences, most of whom can't understand what he is saying.' I said something about his book and his interest in my interests – archaeology, anthropology, *The Golden Bough*. The Bath Bun looked at me sadly. 'He'll never finish his great book,' he said. 'None of us ever do. Remember that before you get too old to do no more than regret your past.'

I was devoted to my paternal grandfather and so, I understand, was he to me, describing me agreeably as his favourite grandchild. When he died he was not a rich man, but he left me £200 in his will – a very considerable sum in the thirties – with the message that I should buy a piano or a motor car. I bought a baby grand Bechstein which is still with me. William Daniel was a kind, careful, quiet, saintly man and for many years when holidaying in Alltwalis I shared his bedroom in the small Crossvale Farm. We seemed to have jumped the generation gap and I talked more freely to him as a schoolboy and undergraduate than to my parents.

He was the senior deacon in the chapel at Alltwalis and, as I grew older, on Sunday mornings I was allowed to help him cut up the bread for the communion service into little squares and prepare the communion wine. He was a strict teetotaller but always took a glass of the communion wine before we set out to chapel. He became interested in the fact that I was much concerned with playing organs, and I often had to accompany the hymns when the organist, my cousin Hannah, could not be there. The Welsh have a great tradition of repeating the last verse over and over again, particularly when they have heard a good sermon and the *hwyl* is on them. This made playing the large harmonium at Alltwalis very difficult: one never knew when the hymn was over. Suddenly some deeply moved deacon or member of the congregation would start up again and we were back to another round of 'Cwm Rhondda' or 'Aberystwyth'.

He always knelt down by his bedside before going to sleep and prayed out loud for many minutes. It was first a kind of confessional: he said all the things he had been doing during the day and often talked of private details such as the arrival of a calf, or the condition of the pigs, or his worry that the cows had broken into a far field and were eating buttercups which would affect the taste of his butter. There was always a reference to his wife and the fact that he would see her soon in the other world, in which he had an unquestioning belief, and there was always thanks for being alive and enjoying life. It was a simple, sincere, total faith which I took for granted at the time, but now look back on as the testimony of one good man in a world full of evil and doubts.

He went to bed early and got up early: it may well be that my habit of early rising – and I do get up most days at five-thirty or six – goes back to my farm upbringing in Carmarthenshire. He would take a quick cup of tea and a slice of bread and cheese and then go out to the byres, barns and fields returning around eight o'clock for a proper breakfast of eggs and bacon. He taught me where to go in September to get mushrooms. Is there anything more lovely than wild field mushrooms from the hill meadows of Wales, unless it be the black truffles of Dordogne, the *cêpes* of the Causses, or the white truffles of Piedmont? He taught me where to go in July to collect wild strawberries, and in August the best blackberries and blueberries. He taught me to milk a cow; to assist in the birth of calves; and to look after the horse that every Wednesday went round and round in the farmyard working the mechanism that turned the churn in the barn and made butter.

The routine on the farm was an unalterable one. Monday was washing day. On Tuesday the washing was ironed and crempogau (pancakes) were made. His housekeeper, Mary Ann, was a superb pancake-maker and I sat in the wash-house watching her making them on the gridiron over an open fire, and being given – too often I am sure – little pancakes to taste. Then the great pile would be carried into the house for our midday meal and to be eaten cold in the evening. Wednesday was the day for making butter and we were all up early for the horse and for the operations in the dairy. Thursday was reserved for special operations such as cheese-making and killing a pig. My Aunt Elizabeth used to come over from her own farm: she was a cheese-maker of repute and I have the most vivid memory of her excellent cheese. It was, I suppose, in classificatory terms a kind of Caerphilly but firmer and more tasty than most Caerphilly. It was nearer to the excellence of Cantal – one of my favourite French cheeses. Friday was baking day for bread, and Saturday was of course market day.

I rode with my grandfather in his horse and trap the eight miles to Carmarthen market, laden with eggs, butter, chickens and cheese. The market transactions took no time: old Mr William Daniel's products were well known for their excellence and were bought up by stall-holders within a few minutes of arriving. Then we did our shopping and it was always the same: a leg of lamb, a large dollop of laver-bread and a great bag of cockles. We then bought a copy of the *Carmarthen Journal* and drove home, the little cob horse going more slowly on the return journey. We would stop on the way to see Uncle Ben or Uncle Henry and be given tea and pieces of a plate-tart of apples. I remember taking my wife to see Uncle Henry in the fifties; he was then ninety-five and deliciously eccentric. 'How do you keep so well?' I asked him. His answer was simple: 'By eating buns all day,' he said.

Saturday night was cockle night. Sunday breakfast was bacon and laver-bread, crisply fried in oatmeal, and Sunday lunch was the lamb. My memory of the food in the Crossvale farmhouse was of simple excellence: it was peasant food such as one meets in farmhouses and small family restaurants in France today. The beams of the kitchen were hung with hams and at any time of the day it was possible to have a rasher of ham or bacon grilled in the Dutch oven before the fire and some fried eggs. What more could one want, with beautiful home-made *cawl*, the Welsh vegetable and meat soup, home-made bread and butter, cheese, Welsh cakes and plate-tarts? When my father got up early he would catch trout in the stream that ran through our fields, and the memory of them grilled at breakfast-time is exquisite after all these years. I early got to enjoy the products of the pigs, although when a pig was to be killed I would go for a long walk to avoid hearing its anguished cries. Have there ever been nicer things to eat than spare-ribs grilled in the Dutch oven and the faggots made by Mary Ann? And have there ever been better teas than those taken in the sloping hill-fields during hay-making, the tea poured out of large tin cans that I used to lug up from the farm kitchen, and baskets of Welsh cakes, *bara brith*, and fruit tarts?

The path behind the farm led up into the woods and there was one small cottage at the edge of the woods. It was a single-storey wattle-and-daub house, black with smoke: what I would now call a typical Neolithic long house. It had hardly any windows. One day outside the front door I met two black cats and spoke to them. The door opened and there was a frightening old woman: she was exactly how witches were portrayed in my story books, and for a moment I wanted to run away. Then she spoke: 'You're from Crossvale, aren't you? You're William Daniel's grandchild, and you are called after Glynadda. Come in.' Fearful, I went into the darkened house. There were more cats, an open hearth and smoke everywhere. 'I'm Liza,' she said, and made me a cup of tea and gave me some biscuits. One of the cats came and sat on my lap. I went away, my fear gone, and every holiday I called on Liza and talked to her and her cats. One day my grandfather said to me, 'You have made friends with Liza. That's a good boy. She likes you. Will you do something for me?' And he used to give me parcels of food and vegetables from the garden to take to her. It was all arranged very surreptitiously: 'You mustn't let Mary Ann or your father know about this,' he said. It was a secret between us; and I found it exciting to have a secret of this kind with my grandfather. I thought he was a kind old man who wanted to help an impoverished old woman living in a cottage on his land. So for many years I visited Liza in her dark Neolithic cottage, took her parcels, drank tea, ate biscuits and cultivated and was cultivated by her many cats. As I grew older and went up to Cambridge as an undergraduate I began thinking critically about her and decided she was some strange survival from prehistoric times. She really was the kind of person who would have been living in the same sort of house in the same place five thousand years ago.

There were only four focal points in the small hamlet which was Alltwalis: the chapel, the pub – the Masons' Arms – the village shop and the smithy. The rest was the farms themselves spread out on either side of the valley. The village shop was run by a second cousin of mine:

I adored it, and he let me stand behind the counter and help him from the age of eight onwards. John Davies was a great man; he was an auctioneer as well as a shopkeeper, and I knew I had grown up when one day he went away to an auction and asked me to run the shop for the afternoon. It was one of the proudest days of my life and, as I measured out flour and rice and sold packets of Quaker Oats and cornflakes, I decided there and then that I wanted to be a shopkeeper. John Davies once said to me when I was an undergraduate reading archaeology in Cambridge, 'There is a very odd thing on the mantelshelf in the Masons' Arms: I think it is in your line of business.' I was then eighteen but, knowing my grandfather's strong disapproval of drink, had to creep into the pub full of excuses. The 'odd thing' was a lovely polished stone axe, found in a field nearby. They gave it to me to give to the National Museum of Wales and I published a note about it in *Archaeologia Cambrensis*. But I had not the courage to give my grandfather an offprint or explain what I had done.

When I was not walking the hills or serving in the shop, I was in the smithy across the road and Tom y Gôf was one of my great friends and mentors. It is said that one remembers the sounds of the past more than anything else, and for me there is one sound that is unforgettable – that of the newly forged horseshoe, red-hot and livid, being put out through the window of the smithy and plunged into the trough of cold water outside; the sizzling and the smoke and the faces of the patient horses are part of my life. I sat in the corner of the smithy for hours on end and Tom brought me toffees.

My grandfather died when I was an undergraduate and my parents wisely said there was no point in dragging me back for his funeral. But when I was next in South Wales I said I wanted to go and see his grave and pay my last respects to William Daniel. My parents understood: I went alone by train and walked the five miles from the Bronwydd Arms Junction to Alltwalis. I visited the grave and I went round the farm of Crossvale. I walked up the hill to Liza's house. It wasn't there; only a shambles of burnt thatch and wood. I went to Tom y Gôf and we talked about old times. 'What happened to Liza's house?' I asked. 'I was afraid, boyo, you were going to ask me that and I hoped no one would ever tell you.' He then said that Liza had long ago been my grandfather's mistress, and that on the day of his funeral she had set fire to her house and perished in it. 'What happened to the cats?' I asked. 'Two of them stayed with her and died in the fire,' he said, 'one is in Crossvale, one is with us here.' He paused; 'and the fifth,' he said, 'still lives in the house.'

I walked back to Crossvale and up the hill to the burnt ruins of Liza's house and stood among the charred beams looking back down the valley and at my youth. There was a sudden movement behind me and as I turned a black cat moved into the woods from the wrecked cottage. I walked sadly down the hill and turned at the gate of Crossvale Farm; at the top of the hill one of Liza's black cats was sitting looking at me. A cold shiver went down my spine and I went quickly to the Masons' Arms and drank to the memory of my grandfather and Liza and all the good things that had made my life so full and interesting in the Carmarthenshire countryside in my youth.

My father was a deeply religious man with an unquestioning, unwavering faith in God, the existence and resurrection of Jesus Christ and the essential goodness of man. The Daniels had been converted to Nonconformity and the family faith sprang from the Congregational Chapel in Alltwalis. The Edmunds were Baptists but my mother joined my father in worshipping in the Congregational Chapel of Ebenezer in Llantwit Major where my father was a deacon, a lay preacher and in charge of the music.

I was a very regular attender at Ebenezer. My father preached very well and with conviction and enthusiasm. Any competence I may have had in later life in speaking and lecturing must in part go back to the inspiration and example of my father as well as my Uncle Tom, though I have no doubt that it owed something too to the excellent example of teaching provided by men like David Williams, Clifford Darby and Miles Burkitt, whom I shall introduce in a later chapter.

Apart from Ebenezer in Colhugh Street in Llantwit Major there was another small chapel called Bethesda Fro, Bethesda in the Vale. This had been built in 1807 in the countryside two or three miles from Llantwit Major. It was founded by Thomas Williams, a well-to-do farmer who was a Calvinistic Methodist, but left them for a while on the question of doctrine.

The owner of the farm at Eglwys Brewis had two daughters. One of them married a strict Church of England parson who was vicar of the church. The other married a minister who preached wherever he could find men and women to listen to him. He was prohibited from preaching in Eglwys Brewis church but he went on preaching outside it, from the steps of the granary of the farm. This went on for a while until his wife decided that she would have a building constructed where he could preach in comfort and with dignity. She approached Sir Isaac Redwood of Orchard House, Boverton, who was deeply interested in Nonconformity. He gave a piece of land to the Independents of Glamorgan so that they could build a chapel, and gave a substantial sum of money towards its construction. This was the man who entertained Thomas Carlyle when he came to South Wales to gather material for the life of Captain Sterling that he was writing – the Sterling who lived at Llanblethian and who started the foreign column in *The Times*.

For a while the people of the Vale would listen to the parson in the church and then walk on to Bethesda Fro to hear the alternative preacher. They ultimately left the church and formed at Bethesda a new sect known as the Glamorgan Methodists. Thomas Williams was ordained minister and John Williams of St Athan was secretary. My father often preached in Bethesda and I played the harmonium there. Thomas Williams was one of the great Welsh hymnologists and my father loved lecturing on the Welsh hymn writers who were a remarkable group of people. I liked walking on a Sunday morning to Bethesda Fro with my father when he took the service there and then home through the lanes to Llanmaes and our Sunday lunch.

I took a Sunday School class at Ebenezer and played the harmonium at the evening services and much enjoyed finding voluntaries to play before and after the service from a book I bought in a secondhand bookshop in Cardiff. The evening service over, I would go for a long walk alone down to the sea and home for supper. But I wanted to move on to proper organs. There were two in the village: one in the parish church and the other in Ham House. I got permission to play both these instruments. Every Saturday morning I spent an hour in the parish church and a shilling of my pocket money went to a boy not much younger than me who worked the bellows.

I had been taught to play the piano very badly by an old maid called Miss Sally Hopkins. She was the only music teacher in the village and we all suffered from her inadequacy and her curious habits. She would rap one over the knuckles with a ruler at every mistake, and she talked to herself, apparently recollecting her earlier life. We were told that she had been crossed in love or that her intended husband had been killed in the war: at times she cried and dabbed her eyes with her handkerchief. It was all embarrassing and sad.

The Welsh language survived largely because the Bible was translated into Welsh and the people of Wales met and used their language in their churches and chapels. I take a parochial pride in the fact that two of the great translators, William Morgan, later Bishop of St Asaph, and Edmund Prys, later Archdeacon of Merioneth, were friends and undergraduates together at St John's. There was no Bible in the vernacular in Ireland, and this is why the Irish language nearly died out. I have great sympathy with those who are striving successfully to keep the Welsh language alive, but little with the excesses of Welsh nationalism.

My father's Nonconformist conscience made him a strict teetotaller. Drinking and smoking were evils that must be discouraged in all possible ways. He was not a militant in these matters, nor in anything else: he was a quiet, kind, good man who knew evil when he saw it and would have no truck with it. There was a bottle of sherry in the dining-room cupboard and special visitors who were so inclined were given a glass of sherry and a slice of cake. My father's Nonconformist conscience was strengthened by his social conscience as a schoolmaster. He often said how furious he was – and yet he was never apparently furious – when he saw a village child come to his school with broken and leaking shoes and was told that the family couldn't afford new shoes, yet knew that the father was spending on beer every week in the Swan, the Globe or the White Hart the money that could have bought a pair of shoes. He was a practical Christian and widely respected for his honesty, integrity and good faith.

He was also a fine practical man and could do anything in the house and garden – carpentry, mending fuses, rearing hens, creating a fine ornamental and vegetable garden. It was perhaps because he was so good at all these things himself and impatient of my fumbling efforts that I have never been a success at them. My memory of the vegetables and fruit from our garden remains vivid after half a century: have there ever been such good things as the new potatoes, peas, broad beans, strawberries, raspberries and loganberries that came from our garden when I was a child, or has time enhanced that gastronomic memory? I do not think so, nor is it a hazy childhood memory that reminds me how good, though plain, the food was in our lower middle-class home in South Wales in the twenties. My mother was a good cook by the standards of Welsh home-cooking at the time.

I have no recollection of being lonely as a child. Though an only child, I had plenty of playmates in neighbouring houses and I liked being by myself, reading, inventing games and going for walks on my own. I never had a bicycle and have never learnt to ride one: I must be one of the few Cambridge men deprived of this skill.

And I never had a dog, but a beautiful black-and-white cat to whom I was passionately devoted. I was reading *Twelfth Night* at the time I was given the kitten and christened it Toby. It turned out to be a female and had several litters of kittens, always born in a garden shed in my presence. I also became specially attached to a hedgehog who lived in our garden and fed it with bread and milk. It became tame and came out in the summer afternoons. At first Toby was suspicious of Hodge but they grew to tolerate each other and one of the earliest photographs taken by me with my Box Brownie is of Toby and Hodge sitting side by side on a large box.

One day Toby came home dragging herself along after having walked through fresh tar, and had to be destroyed. I was devastated: it was the first tragedy in my young life, and I wept, unconsoled, for days. I knew that tragedies happened: a school chum had been knocked off his bicycle and killed, a friend's mother had died, and a man I knew vaguely had been drowned. But these were things that happened to other people – not to the Daniels, who lived a comfortable and charmed existence. Or so it seemed to an innocent and unworldly schoolboy of eleven.

CHAPTER TWO

Barry and Cardiff

IN MY ELEVENTH YEAR I made my first move away from the close
childhood intimacy of my family. In 1925 I passed what was then
called the Scholarship Examination (the forerunner of the Eleven
Plus) and moved on from the primary phase of my education in my
father's school to the secondary phase. Those who determined these
matters in the Glamorgan County Education Office in Cardiff said
that the Llantwit Major pupils should go to Cowbridge Grammar
School five miles away, but as there was then no public transport of
any kind from Llantwit to Cowbridge they had, after many delays, to
revise their plans and chose Barry instead; we Vale boys became train
boys, catching the 8.10 each morning to Barry and walking up the hill
to the Barry County School for Boys. For six years I caught that train
from Monday to Friday and never once missed it. Although we only
lived five minutes' walk from the station I always set out a quarter of
an hour before time, and this fear of missing the train built up in me
something which has lasted all my life: I always arrive at stations long
before trains are due to leave.

The Vale of Glamorgan railway no longer exists for passenger
traffic. It used to run from Barry to Bridgend through lovely country.
The journey to Barry took half an hour: we stopped at St Athan (this
was long before RAF St Athan came into existence), then past the
cement works to Aberthaw, on to Rhoose (long before RAF Rhoose or
its present successor, Cardiff airport), and then through Porthkerry
tunnel, over the Porthkerry viaduct and on to Barry, always with fine
views over the Bristol Channel.

The walk uphill to school took nearly half an hour. We were always
last for morning prayers and assembly, and the train boys from the
Vale had special places at the back of the hall. On Mondays,
Tuesdays, Thursdays and Fridays we walked back down the hill to
catch the 5.10 train and were back in our homes at six. The train went
no further than Llantwit Major; occasionally the engine-driver took
one or two of us on the short ride when he disconnected the engine

28

from the front end of the train and manoeuvered it round to the east to go back to Barry. There was always time to read and do our prep on the journeys – how we cursed the darkness of the Porthkerry tunnel – and my Latin was always done with the assistance of Bill Davies, then in the sixth form and later to be Professor of Classics at the University College of Wales, Aberystwyth.

On Wednesdays school stopped at one o'clock and there was longer to wait for the train home. My recollections of the daily walks from school to station are vivid. Our route passed a small reading room set up by the Barry Public Libraries for the benefit of the residents of West Barry. It was of the most enormous benefit to me and I spent ten to fifteen minutes every day and longer on Wednesdays poring through the magazines. For six years or more I read every issue of the *Illustrated London News*, *Graphic* and *Sphere*. I can't say that the archaeological articles particularly enthused me at the time, but how good they were! What did excite me were the detailed reconstruction drawings by G.H. Davis which told us how everything worked.

The highlights of the *ILN*'s contribution to archaeology have been set out in *The Great Archaeologists* by Edward Bacon, who was archaeological editor of the journal for many years. Many years later, when I was writing my *A Hundred Years of Archaeology*, I reflected on the part that journal had played in the dissemination of archaeological interest and the creation of a public for archaeology, long before the television successes of the fifties and after. From its inception the *ILN* had dealt sporadically with all sensational archaeological discoveries. From 1900 when Bruce Ingram took over the editorship it adopted a more considered policy of covering the field of archaeological exploration. I wrote to him asking how this came about and he replied on 16 February 1949 as follows:

As a boy at school, I was taken to Egypt by my father for an extended tour of most of the exploration sites, an experience which made a lasting impression on me. When the control of the paper fell to me in 1900, I made up my mind that there were a great many people who would have been interested if they were to be given an opportunity of seeing what was being done all over the world to throw light upon the civilisation of the past. The difficulty was to combine technical accuracy with an exposition simple enough for the comprehension of the layman, and by that means to stimulate his desire for further publication of a similar character.

A look back over the volumes of the *ILN* for the last eighty years will show how brilliantly Ingram achieved his aims.

Certainly part of my extra-curricular education took place in the Porthkerry reading room and then afterwards, when I was a student at Cardiff, in the Reference Library and Reading Rooms in The Hayes. I had an annual season ticket and during holidays I went into Barry and Cardiff one day a week to go through the illustrated weeklies.

The organization of secondary education in Wales stems from the Elizabethan grammar schools such as Cowbridge, Llandovery and Shrewsbury. The second impetus, and it was a most important one, resulted from the Welsh Intermediate Education Act of 1896. This it was which led to the County or High Schools at Cardiff, Penarth, Caerphilly, Porth, Pengam, Bridgend, Neath, Swansea and Barry; and what remarkable men they produced: Dylan Thomas, Wynford Vaughan-Thomas, Alun Owen, Harry Secombe, Clifford Darby, Richard Llewellyn, Richard Burton – to mention a few in addition to the Barry boys who appear in this chapter. Roy Jenkins went to Abersychan, Neil Kinnock to Pengam, and the Governor of Hong Kong, Sir Edward Youde, was a Penarth boy.

The Boys' School at Barry on the top of the hill was built in 1896: the Girls' School further down in 1913. In my time the headmistress of the Girls' School was a very strict disciplinarian: boys walked on the north side of the road, girls on the south, and woe betide any girl caught speaking to a boy on the way to or from school.

When one reads autobiographies it is only too common to find authors describing their schooldays as heaven or hell. Mine seemed then, as now in reflection, a normal agreeable pattern of life no different from life itself, with ups and downs, triumphs and disappointments, but in no way different except in complexity and variety from my life before I was eleven. This may have been due to the good fortune of having an outstanding man, Edgar Jones, as my headmaster at Barry, and to the fact that his staff was full of dedicated and excellent teachers, and that my schoolfellows were friendly and able and often excitingly challenging in their achievement.

There was corporal punishment administered by the head, and only by him, but it never came my way and I was never bullied nor do I remember others being so treated. I think a day school must in this matter have a great advantage over boarding schools. I remember that on my first journey to Barry by train I and another new boy were made to bend over and were beaten by the other boys using the leather window-straps. But this was an amusing, if painful, initiation ceremony. When years later I was school prefect of the train, I remember a parent complaining to me and to the headmaster that his son had been humiliated and brutally assaulted on his first day travelling to school. Edgar Jones asked me what I had replied to the angry parent. I said that I had told him it was an age-old custom going back to the foundation of the school and the Vale of Glamorgan railway, that it was an initiation rite, an important and unharmful *rite de passage*. The head shared the joke: 'I see,' he said, 'you have extended your human geography studies into anthropology.'

I have often discussed with my contemporaries and friends and with former masters what it was that made Barry County School such a happy and successful institution. We all agreed that it came in great part from the personality and practice of Edgar Jones. He treated everyone from the newest second-form boy onwards as reasonable adults, and as a result we treated him and all the masters as reasonable adults, uncle figures – and indeed the deputy head was always referred to by boys and staff alike as Uncle Tom. But behind the avuncular friendliness was the knowledge of authority and a firm discipline which the head was rarely forced to exercise. It was a pattern which I tried to follow when during the war in India I was in charge of a large RAF unit – with some success and some failure.

But whatever the reality of the Edgar Jones system – if it was a system and not the spontaneous functioning of a generous, imaginative, wise and kind man – we were all devoted to him. He was always affectionately known as 'the Major'. He had indeed been a major in charge of an RA battery on Cold Knap on Barry Island during the First World War and we firmly believed that his battery (some of us himself personally) had sunk a German submarine which had surfaced in the Bristol Channel. This may well have been a school myth: certainly he had an OBE and retained his military title all his life.

A few days after I started at Barry I was overawed to be summoned to see the head. I don't think he interviewed every new boy and I learnt subsequently that he had had a letter from my father. 'You come from a very interesting part of Wales,' he said. 'Have you seen the Castle Ditches?' 'Yes, sir,' I replied, 'I go there every year to pick blackberries.' 'Blackberries,' he snorted: 'do you realize the so-called Castle Ditches are a promontory fort built in pre-Roman times by your Ancient British ancestors? Have you seen the remains of the Roman villa at Caermead?' 'No, sir,' I said. 'Then see you do before you come back to school next week. And get your father to take you to see the cromlechs at Tinkinswood and St Lythans. Do you know what a cromlech is?' I confessed my ignorance and he explained: it was my first acquaintanceship with megalithic monuments, the study of which has occupied a great deal of my lifetime and still does. Curiously enough I discovered, when studying the Pembrokeshire cromlechau, that a possible one in a ruined condition lay in the field next to the schoolhouse at Lampeter Velfrey.

'You will be at a loose end between morning and afternoon school,' he went on, 'when most of the boys go home for their midday dinner. I know you will have your own meal in the school canteen but that only takes twenty minutes. We usually have one boy from each year who assists the kitchen staff and helps with laying the tables and waiting. So I am detailing you to be the boy for this year. So please go and see Miss Powell.' And as I left he said, smiling, 'Your parents tell me you are interested in food.'

And so began my first connection with catering and my association with Miss Powell, the kind efficient lady who ran the school kitchens and produced sixty to a hundred meals a day. Miss Powell approved of me and so I spent Monday, Tuesday, Thursday and Friday of my school lunch breaks in the school cookhouse and dining room, eventually becoming food prefect and organizing the waiting. I enjoyed it, and when the service of school dinners was over, by about one o'clock, I retired to the cookhouse and with Miss Powell and Dinah, her assistant, sat down to our own meal which often consisted of ampler and more interesting portions than the ordinary diners had been given. (My wife, on reading a draft of this chapter, said she now knows for certain where the origins of my generous proportions may be sought!)

The snag was that as the years went by it became more irksome: the menus were always the same and are for ever engraved on the tablets of my memory: Monday was roast beef, Yorkshire pudding, roast potatoes, mashed swedes and jam tart. Tuesday was roast lamb, boiled potatoes, cabbage and spotted dick. Thursday was boiled silverside of beef, dumplings, carrots and fruit salad. Friday was shepherd's pie and treacle tart. I was reminded the other day by an old school friend of a story that went round the school – I am sure it is apocryphal – that when a master once asked for a second helping of treacle tart I said, 'No second helpings even for my favourite masters.'

Miss Powell made a most excellent treacle tart and on Fridays, privately, we had large helpings topped with cream. I formed over the years a close friendship with her: she became a sort of aunt figure for me to whom I brought my problems. Once a term my mother invited her to come and spend the afternoon with us in Llantwit Major and a very special tea was prepared.

When I had left school and was up at Cambridge I used to go back and visit the school occasionally and always called on Miss Powell. She was amused when I told her in 1946 that I had been made Steward of my College and was in charge of the kitchens. 'I'm sure,' she said drily, 'that you will see they have treacle tart on their menus,' and she was right.

There were no compulsory games at school and no Officers' Training Corps. I had never played any team game at Llantwit Major, neither football nor cricket, and am not clear how this came to be. It was suggested at Barry that I might like to play rugger and our sports master – Bud Fisher, who in 1983 celebrated his ninetieth birthday – tried to make me interested. 'You'll make a good scrum half,' he said. I watched one game, mystified, and told Fisher that I thought it too rough for me. 'Ha,' he snorted, 'then you must take up hockey: a game suitable for namby-pambies and girls.' My mother bought me a hockey stick and I played several games with little success and less pleasure or enthusiasm, maybe because no one explained the rules to me: or was it that I really just wasn't interested? I think the real trouble was that organized games demanded being in Barry on Wednesday afternoons or Saturdays and I wanted these days at home to walk about the countryside and enjoy myself. Gradually I persuaded school friends, and later masters, to come to Llantwit Major on Saturday afternoons: we went for long walks along the cliffs and, after mammoth teas prepared by my long-suffering mother, played games like Monopoly until the evening train took them back to Barry. And so I have never played any organized game in my life. Tennis, yes, and squash, and golf – all badly – with great enthusiasm and pleasure, but never any game as a member of a team, until many, many years later I had to play soccer in an Officers-*v*-Airmen match in

33

Delhi. The captain of my team said at the end of the match, 'You seem, sir, to operate according to rules not normal to football as I understand it.'

There was no question that Edgar Jones had assembled a very fine staff and we were excellently well taught. He took Latin himself and for English we had an inspiring teacher, John Francis, whom we all admired because he had published an anthology of verse. As I progressed through the school during my first four years, I had no idea whether I was good or mediocre; but although I was never top of my form I was always somewhere between third and fifth in the end-of-term list. Even so, I was considerably surprised when at the end of my fourth year we took what was then called School Certificate (now O Levels) I passed in all subjects, five with distinction. The surprise of my mathematics master erupted into fury, because he knew I had no aptitude for the subject. I had indeed failed in arithmetic but had distinction in mathematics as a whole. 'The whole examination system is quite monstrous,' he exclaimed, 'if Daniel can have a distinction in mathematics – and he actually had 99 per cent in trigonometry, the highest mark anyone had for years – it makes me want to give up teaching.'

The explanation was a simple one. I had then, and have retained all my life, a kind of parrot memory. It is not an exact memory such as Stuart Piggott enviably has, which enables him to quote correctly and extensively from poets and writers. And it is certainly not the visual memory which some conductors and soloists must have when they memorize scores, or perhaps some actors when they memorize texts. I was always astounded at the virtuoso memory performances of a person like Denis Brogan, whom I once heard quoting a letter from *The Times*: when challenged he said, 'But I know I am right, and if you like I will tell you what the other letters were on that page and what was on the opposite page.'

No, my memory has never been of that exact text-true kind, but it enables me to give an hour's lecture without notes. St John Fisher said of the Lady Margaret Beaufort that she had 'a holding memory' and that is what I have. And yet this is not a sufficient explanation of 99 marks for trigonometry: there must have been a remarkable parrot element present then.

We had assembly and morning prayers every day but Tuesdays and Fridays were special. On Tuesdays when the staff had left the rostrum and the doors were closed, Edgar Jones read his favourite poems to the whole school. He read well, his choice was brilliant, and he had a captive audience for ten to twenty minutes. He read some standard poems like Tennyson's *The Revenge* and Newbolt's *Vitai Lampada*, but mainly modern poems like Ralph Hodgson's *The Bull* and *Miss Thompson went shopping*. He was very fond of Ralph Hodgson and, as well as *The Bull*, read to us *Time You Old Gypsy Man* and *Reason has Moons*. He introduced us to Yeats through *The Lake Isle of Innisfree*, and Walter Savage Landor through *Rose Aylmer*. Then one day he read us Walter de la Mare's *The Listeners*. I think none of us knew it when he began:

> 'Is there anybody there?' said the Traveller
> Knocking on the moonlit door; . . .

We were electrified:

> 'Tell them I came, and no one answered,
> That I kept my word,' he said.

We listened spellbound until the end:

> Ay, they heard his foot upon the stirrup,
> And the sound of iron on stone,
> And how the silence surged softly backward,
> When the plunging hoofs were gone.

We were stunned into silence and as the silence surged backward we burst spontaneously into rapturous and appreciative applause. The Major turned to us as he left the hall and silenced us. 'No,' he said, 'no applause, ever. Not that it spoils the effect of my reading, but if you do it once you may feel you have always to do it and then perhaps once you may not applaud. No, listen, enjoy, but in silence.' Sixth-formers were allowed to leave assembly on Tuesdays because we would have heard some of the readings many times during our first four years. No one did.

And no one left the special post-prayers musical class on Fridays. These were run by Christopher Whitehead, our classics master, who also conducted the school orchestra. For half the time we sang songs from the *National Song Book* but this was interspersed with musical appreciation. Whitehead played gramophone records and explained music on the piano, and so we learnt to appreciate Beethoven's

35

Pastoral, Schubert's Unfinished, Elgar's Enigma Variations, the Hallelujah Chorus, and, perhaps surprisingly, Boelmann's Suite Gothique – the first great organ work I ever heard. I remember how moved I was by Elgar and Boelmann. Many years later when I was a research student working in France I walked out of the Musée des Antiquités Nationales at Saint-Germain-en-Laye at lunchtime, depressed by my morning's work and wondering whether I was getting anywhere in my study of megaliths. I crossed the square and saw the west doors of the church were open. I walked in: it was the end of a marriage ceremony and, as I stood watching the procession, I realized that the organ was playing them out to the glorious Toccata from the Boelmann Suite; the confidence and assurance and happiness of my schooldays was re-established in me and I went contentedly to lunch.

I never learnt to play any orchestral instrument, so the school orchestra was not for me, but the school dramatic society very soon became a part of my life. Membership of this society was by selection, and thought to be a great honour; and so I was alarmed and flattered when I was summoned for an interview with Mr Carpenter who ran the school plays. Pegleg Carpenter, as he was cruelly called by the boys, was our second French master and had a wooden leg – the result, we firmly believed, of some heroic action in the Great War. Apparently approving of my potentialities as an actor he sent me for a further interview with his colleague in the Girls' School – my first visit to that forbidden kingdom. All went well and I appeared in the next few years in *A Midsummer Night's Dream*, *Twelfth Night* and *As You Like It*.

It was all most exciting, not least the fact that all rehearsals and performances took place in the Girls' School. This was the only official moment when the Boys' School and the Girls' School got together. How much, then, we got together in the rehearsals and intervals, though how little we spoke. I fell in love every year and in the dark corridors and unlit classrooms exchanged passionate kisses and eternal vows with different girls in successive years. I have forgotten those lovely teenage beauties as they have long forgotten me, but the memory of acting in those plays is as vivid as ever. If ever I was turned from a schoolboy into something older it was in those magic moments – so magic at the time and so magic in memory – when, holding hot sticky hands in prompt corners, we watched others say 'If music be the food of love, play on'.

36

In *A Midsummer Night's Dream* I played Quince, and I shall never forget those lines 'Marry, our play is the most lamentable comedy and most cruel death of Pyramus and Thisbe', and as long as I live, when I hear Mendelssohn's music and the flourish of trumpets I shall think that it is time for me, well in advance of Pyramus, Thisbe, Wall, Moonshine and Lion, to come on the stage and say:

> If we offend, it is with our good will.
> That you should think, we come not to offend,
> But with good will.

We were very proud of our performances. Each year the cast was taken by bus to Stratford to see a performance of the play they were doing. The Memorial Theatre had been burnt down and the performance was in a cinema. These were splendid occasions, much looked forward to. We had a tremendous tea before being driven home, tearing the production to shreds and alleging that our interpretation was better, more sympathetic, more understanding. Oh, the delicious arrogance and certainty of youth! But these thoughts comforted us as later we peeled off our beards – agonizing to our adolescent acne.

My parents took me to the Wembley Exhibition – my first experience of London. Even more memorable was when the school organized a trip to Paris – my first experience of France. We went overnight from Southampton to Le Havre. It was a cold March morning as we docked. It was not yet light and a blustering wind blew across the quays. The arrangement with buses had gone wrong and we walked a long distance to the railway station dragging our suitcases and carrying our tennis rackets (we had all been told we could play tennis in the Jardin du Luxembourg. Later we realized that there were no tennis courts in the Luxembourg Gardens and what we were expected to do – and did – was pat-a-ball along the dusty gravel walks!) Few of us had slept on the boat; we were too excited at the prospect of visiting a foreign country. We dozed away in the train with occasional quick glimpses in waking moments of the Normandy countryside. I was wide awake as we approached Paris and was puzzled, as I still am, by the way the railway line crosses and re-crosses the twisting Seine. We caught a glimpse of the Tour Eiffel, which we all knew about, and the Basilique du Sacré Coeur. There was a bus to meet us and we were in the Lycée Louis-le-Grand in the rue Saint-

Jacques in time for breakfast. The bread was crusty and good but there was jam instead of marmalade, and coffee instead of tea, and no bacon, eggs, sausages or potatoes: we were quite hungry by lunchtime.

Our first lunch was a surprise but not a disappointment: there was a cold dish of sausage, sardines, and what I learnt to call pâté, raw vegetables, and then a hot dish of what seemed to us to be under-done beef with chipped potatoes and haricot beans; then cheese; then ice cream. From then on we did not complain of being hungry. Our only complaint was that the meat was under-done, but after three or four days some of us, malleable youths, decided we liked it that way; and perhaps to those early days at the age of twelve I may trace my strong disapproval of over-cooked meat. With our lunch and dinner we were given red wine. Most of us had never drunk wine before: it was rough and tasted at first like nasty vinegar. Some of us might have been given half a glass of sweet sherry at a party; most of us rejected the wine and demanded lemonade.

There was a little café across the road from the front gate of the Lycée where I discovered a *sirop de citron* which seemed to me and my schoolfriends divine. The *patron* was amused to be invaded by British schoolboys and was most helpful: I liked him and he seemed to take an avuncular interest in me. 'You don't like wine?' he said. No, we said in our schoolboy French: it tastes like vinegar. 'Ah,' he said, 'c'est le vin de table du Lycée. Buvez du bon vin.' He went behind the bar and brought back three large glasses full of red wine of a lighter colour than what we were given in the Lycée. 'Avec mes compliments,' he said – and then, surprisingly, 'bottoms up!' It was delicious, and I summoned up courage to ask what it was. It is wine from the Beaujolais, he said. I had my diary with me and I made him write down the word and he added two others: Fleurie, Morgon. 'Demandez toujours le Fleurie ou le Morgon.'

I had fallen in love with Paris and travelled back to Wales with a model of the Eiffel Tower in a glass bottle which when you turned it upside down was engulfed in a snowstorm. I kept it on the mantelshelf in my bedroom and turned it upside down every night before going to bed and said in my prayers that I hoped it would not be long before I was back in Paris.

My prayers, or fate, or what you will, saw that this came about. In 1930 I was in the sixth form and my history master was David Williams – one of the major influences in my life. David, a

Pembrokeshire man, graduated in Cardiff, had been a Commonwealth Fellow in America, and was then snapped up by Edgar Jones
who knew he would only have him for a few years: but those few years
changed the lives of myself and my close school friends Hrothgar
Habakkuk and Bryan Hopkin, of whom more hereafter. Here was a
very learned man who treated us sixth-form boys as serious undergraduates and taught us in a very remarkable way.

He went on to be a lecturer in University College, Cardiff, and then
became Sir John Williams Professor of Welsh History at Aberystwyth. I was devoted to him and he came to spend a day or weekend
with us in Llantwit Major on many an occasion. He got on very well
with my father: they were from the same stock – farmers' boys from
West Wales.

I was very moved when I read the preface of Gwyn Williams's
excellent book *Madoc: the Making of a Myth* (1979) in which he says
'David Williams, a man of wit, industry and style, called himself a
Voltairean Baptist and would clearly have been at home in his chosen
eighteenth century. . . . The history of the Welsh may have been full of
myths, but they have numbered giants among their historians. David
Williams among them was Ysbaddaden (Chief Giant).'

In 1930 David Williams took me aside and told me that the Welsh
League of Nations Society was offering a scholarship of a fortnight in
Geneva to two Welsh schoolboys. All one had to do was to sit an
examination on the work of the League. A fortnight in Geneva
sounded lovely and of course the train from London to Geneva went
through Paris of beloved memory. But, I protested, I knew nothing
about the League and was not particularly interested in it. 'Here,' said
David, 'is a pile of books. Go away and read them. Next Monday we
will begin our class on the League.' Curiously enough I found the
books interesting – particularly those on drug traffic, international
prostitution and racial discrimination. When the examination came I
was delighted there were questions on drugs and prostitution and I
waxed eloquent on these issues, but less fervently on mandates. Four
boys were summoned to Llandrindod Wells as finalists in the
competition and I was one of them. We were all interviewed and I
surprised myself and certainly my judges by the intimate knowledge I
seemed to have about drugs and the white slave traffic. One of my
interviewers said, 'I have given you 100 per cent for your answer on
the white slave traffic. It could not have been bettered. It shows the

most remarkable and adult appreciation of these difficult problems.' I blushed – not because of this praise but because at that time I was never very clear what happened to the women who were taken away to South America.

To my great delight I was selected for one of the two scholarships, but the audience before whom we appeared said what a shame it was that the two other boys were denied a trip to Geneva and immediately subscribed for two more scholarships. Later Dan Evans, a successful businessman in Barry, asked if he could pay for his son to join this party. And so on a Monday in September five young Welsh schoolboys, including a future Archbishop of Wales (Gwilym Williams), and a future Leader of the Welsh Nationalist Party (Gwynfor Evans), set out for Geneva on what was supposed to be a starry-eyed inspection of this great organization which was to rule the world and prevent future wars. I had no illusions about my visit. It was travel; and I would see the Alps and perhaps a glacier.

Our chaperon was the Reverend Gwilym Davies, a retired Nonconformist minister: told he had only a year or so to live, he gave up his ministry and devoted himself to the League of Nations. (He actually lived for many years and died in the fullness of time.) We left Victoria at 2 p.m. and at 8.55 got to the Gare du Nord, where we were met by David Williams and his wife – what a delightful surprise! We went to the Gare de Lyon and stayed the night in the Lyon Palace Hotel. Then David Williams took us to see the Place de la Concorde, the Grands Boulevards and the Opéra, and we had a drink in the Café de la Paix. Next morning the train for Geneva did not leave until 10.10. I got up early and took the bus to the Place Saint-Michel, walked up to the Lycée Louis-le-Grand and took a cup of coffee in the café across the road. The *patron* remembered me. The joys of my first visit to Paris so overcame me that I was nearly late for the train. 'Where have you been?' said Gwilym Davies. 'I went to visit some friends,' I said, and it was true.

I kept an illustrated diary of our journey to Geneva and back: it was a sort of exercise in human geography. 'We travelled up the Seine to Dijon,' I wrote, 'and into the Burgundy country with the vines ripening on the hillsides. Real Swiss country appeared at Bellegarde where the twilight cast strange shadows on the high mountains towering on either side of the Rhône valley, and on the small mountain chalets and village churches and the half-cut lucerne crops.'

We got to the Gare Cornavin at 8.55 and were driven to our billet, a most agreeable *pension*, 44 boulevard des Tranchées. We were registered at the English section of the International Union of League of Nations Societies Summer School at the University of Geneva and went to lectures by Professor Alfred Zimmern and others. I remember my intense embarrassment when, waiting for a lecture to begin, I had my knees up when someone sat down quickly on the seat in front, pinning my trousers; and I didn't have the courage to ask to be released. Many of the lectures were boring but none seemed to last so long as that when I sat with legs suspended in this curious way.

We were taken to the opening of the 11th Assembly, shown round the International Labour Office and introduced (how boring it must have been for them) to Titulesco, Briand, Henderson, Curtius and Lord Cecil. I suppose we were the youth of the world who, as we grew up, would be supporters and defenders of the ill-fated League. Then there were very special 'do's': we were taken to see Madame de Staël's château at Coppet; to the Circus Knie; to an English service in the historic chapel of the Maccabees (part of the Church of Scotland in Geneva); we went up the Salève and came down late in the dark and the rain; and we went to hear Rabindranath Tagore reading his poetry in English and Bengali in the Théâtre de la Comédie. Halfway through Tagore's reading I discovered I was bleeding from my nose: this had never happened to me before and, alarmed, I left and went back to the boulevard des Tranchées: cold compresses and a glass of some powerful herbal brandy (?) sent me happily to sleep.

But gradually the international excitement of the League of Nations palled, and I went to less and less of the lectures and discussion groups (although apparently I took part with distinction in a seminar on drugs and the white slave traffic, and the Reverend Gwilym Davies said how surprised he was at the depth of my knowledge of these curious matters!) and I began to go off on my own. I went to Ferney-Voltaire and looked at the church 'dedicated by Voltaire to God'. I travelled there on the delightful departmental railway and walked back: the customs official on the French/Swiss frontier asked me to take a photograph of him, which I did with my Box Brownie. I sent him a print and he replied thanking me. The schoolchildren were going home from school and seized on an English schoolboy and took me to the Promenade des Crêts where I enjoyed the marvellous vista of the Alps and a clear view of Mont Blanc. I took a steamer trip round the lake and during that day the Graf Zeppelin flew back and forth over Geneva. And I took a whole day's trip to Chamonix and went up the rack-and-pinion railway to see the Mer de Glace and two other glaciers. I sat entranced by these mountains of ice, the tinkling of cowbells around me; and I believed in physical geography.

The magical exciting formative fortnight was soon over. We bought our presents and set off home. I bought a cuckoo clock and a photograph of the Mer de Glace and – my first experience of international skullduggery – was given a bill which I paid, and another much less to show the customs. When we got to Bellegarde our purchases were examined. I showed the alternative bill. 'These clocks is very cheap,' said the customs man. My fortnight had stood me in good stead. 'Mais oui,' I said. 'Je suis un pauvre étudiant gallois' – a phrase Pegleg Carpenter had taught me as useful everywhere. The official shrugged his shoulders and turned to the luggage of the future Archbishop of Wales. To his astonishment and ours his suitcase was stuffed with chocolate – pounds and pounds of delicious varieties. Whether there was a limit or not I do not know but the *douanier* was taken aback. 'Pourquoi?' he asked. Gwilym Williams had, to our intense surprise, an answer. He sat stolidly there and said sweetly, 'C'est pour manger sur le voyage.' The customs officer disappeared to return with two other men of higher rank who looked aghast at the kilos of assorted chocolate in the future archbishop's suitcase. Again they questioned Gwilym, and again he repeated with smiling and confident imperturbability, 'C'est pour manger sur le voyage.' The *douaniers* threw up their hands in renewed incomprehension of the mad English and we fastened up our suitcases and slept through the night to Paris. I got safely home and my cuckoo clock and the Mer de Glace joined my Eiffel Tower snowstorm as trophies of my early travel.

Many years later when Gwilym Williams was headmaster of Llandovery he asked me to his speech day and to give away the prizes. I talked to the boys about many things and told them stories, including the return from Geneva, and the chocolates 'pour manger sur le voyage'. The whole school collapsed in shrieks of mirth, but the headmaster was not amused.

As a schoolboy my interest in geography was developed by B.M. Jones, our geography master, who lived in our village of Llantwit Major. He had been wounded in the 1914–18 war and was often ill. In my third year he had to undergo a severe operation. When he was back home I went to see him frequently and we built up an interesting relationship. He taught me to play chess and I went several evenings a week to talk about geography and play chess for many months in the summer of 1927. I said that I wanted to do geography in the Higher School Certificate and then take a degree in it at a university. I remember saying to my parents that I wanted to be a geography master and play chess with my pupils.

Imagine my distress when B.M. Jones, recovered from his operation, was appointed headmaster of the Grammar School at Hawarden. Yet when the School Certificate results saw me safely into the sixth form and all set for two years' reading for the Higher School Certificate I still wanted to read geography as well as history and English as my three subjects. But no one had read Higher School Certificate geography at Barry before. Ben Jones said he would have taught me with pleasure but he was now running his own school in North Wales – and very well too; we used to visit him often. His replacement was an Aberystwyth graduate called D.J.P. Richards, who was an international runner; and I suspect his athletic prowess had influenced his selection. He readily agreed to take me on, but it was very soon clear that he was a poor teacher and not a very knowledgeable person. He often abandoned the class he was supposed to be giving me and was found in shorts running round the field while I was trying to read through the notes he had taken in lectures at Aberystwyth. After some thought and without consulting my parents or anyone else I asked to see the headmaster. The Major looked kindly over his spectacles and said, 'I know why you have come to see me and I already have a solution to your problem. Mr Richards is overworked and cannot devote the time to you.' His eyes twinkled, 'But Miss Celia Evans, the geography mistress at the Girls' School, has agreed to take you on. You will go to her every Tuesday and Thursday afternoon, but first report to the headmistress.' And so for nearly a year I went to the Girls' School twice a week – which was a matter for amused and ribald comment by the Boys' School. The headmistress turned out not the dragon she was reputed to be, and Celia was enchanting and kind. Her brother, then Director of Education at Erith, had been an inspector of schools and knew my father. She taught me very well, lent me books and encouraged me to go on field walks to see the cliffs at Penarth, the antiquities of the Vale, and to spend the odd afternoon in the geology and archaeology galleries of the National Museum of

Wales. She gave me money for the return fare from Barry to Cardiff and said it came from special educational funds, but I think it came from her own pocket. I was getting on famously and then the blow fell. Four months before the Higher School Certificate examination she broke the news to me that she was leaving Britain and taking up a job in South Africa. 'I want to travel,' she said, 'and live geography. You'll be all right working on your own.' But Edgar Jones had other ideas, and for one day a week I went westwards to Bridgend rather than eastwards to Barry, and was taught by the geography master there, a Mr Eastling, another devoted and kind man, delighted to have a pupil reading for the Higher School Certificate.

And so in the end all went well. There was plenty of encouragement in the sixth form, which was a remarkable one. When I look back on it it seems surprising that a school serving a small area could throw up between 1929 and 1931 a sixth form that produced three knights bachelor, five professors, two vice-chancellors, two Fellows of the British Academy, an economic adviser to the Government and the Director of the International Meteorological Office. We were certainly kept on our mettle and not allowed to become too closely embedded in our subjects. We were divided into Arts sixth and Science sixth, but every Wednesday at twelve-thirty we came together and were addressed by a master on some special subject. David Williams spoke on the buildings of Paris and life in an American university. Uncle Tom gave us four talks on philosophers which few of us understood. Edgar Jones himself talked about his annual holidays abroad, introduced us to the cave paintings of Dordogne and the megalithic monuments of southern Brittany, to the buildings of Florence and Siena, and to the French Impressionists and Post-Impressionists. He was by now Chairman of the Archaeology and Art Committee of the National Museum of Wales and a friend of the Misses Davies of Llandinam who eventually gave their great collection of French paintings to the National Museum of Wales.

We lived at Barry County School through six civilized years in a cultivated society which treated us like adults and made us into adults. I owe an enormous amount to that school: the Major, the teaching, the absence of compulsory games, the absence of bullying, the dramatic society, music, and the life-long friendships among staff and boys. All that I owe to Barry and, not least, the Porthkerry Road reading room.

As I type out these words in Cambridge fifty years after I left Barry to start another life at St John's College, I think that it is the good humour and tolerance of my schooldays that now most impress me. Some time in the middle of my six years there was a special trip to see an eclipse: I didn't go but was there to welcome back the weary and bleary-eyed watchers off their bus and into the Assembly Hall for morning prayers. Chris Whitehead had chosen the hymn with care and we all had difficulty in maintaining our composure as we sang:

> Through the night of doubt and sorrow
> Onward goes the pilgrim band,
> Singing songs of expectation,
> Marching to the Promised Land.
> Clear before us through the darkness
> Gleams and burns the guiding light;
> Brother clasps the hand of brother,
> Stepping fearless through the night.

But with one accord and no prompting we all sang 'master' instead of 'brother'. It was that sort of school.

The summer of 1931 came and passed and four of us were awarded State Scholarships on the result of our performance in Higher School Certificate examinations. These were Arthur Bryant, who went to Jesus College, Oxford, to read classics and then out to teach the Welsh colony in Patagonia; David Arthur Davies who went to Aberystwyth to read physics and retired a few years ago, knighted, as Director of the International Meteorological Office; Alan Michell and myself. I wanted to take a degree in geography. Edgar Jones said that the obvious way was to follow in the footsteps of his beloved and gifted son Gareth who went first to Aberystwyth (his father's own University College) and then on as an affiliated student to Trinity College, Cambridge. Alas, the great tragedy in the Major's life came when Gareth, then a correspondent for *The Times*, was murdered by bandits in Manchuria in 1935. I stood behind him with Hrothgar Habakkuk and Bryan Hopkin in the chapel of Trinity when there was a short memorial service.

And so it looked as if I would begin my university career in the 'college by the sea' in H.J. Fleure's department, but my father thought otherwise. He had been for a headmasters' refresher course in Jesus College, Oxford, and the heady Oxbridge spell had enthralled him. I

was to go to Oxford. I wrote to J.N.L. Baker who was Geography
Tutor at Jesus, and he replied saying that the Oxford Honour Course
in geography was unlikely to materialize for two or three years and I
should try Cambridge, where the Geographical Tripos had already
started. I wrote to the Registrar of the University of Cambridge and
had a characteristic letter back from Harrison beginning, 'Your letter
addressed to the Registrar of this University has been opened by me
who hold the office of Registrary'. I learnt later of Harrison's many
pedantries and I believe he was the prime mover in seeing that holders
of Cambridge PhDs (he strongly disapproved of Cambridge having
such a degree) should appear in the lists with their initials and only
senior doctors (holders of doctorates of science, letters, law, music,
divinity or medicine) were allowed to call themselves Dr so-and-so. I
was 'Dr G.E. Daniel' from my PhD in 1938 to 1962 when I took my
LittD and was allowed to be 'Dr Daniel'. I am sure it was Harrison
who was responsible for maintaining the rigid rules for the assembly of
dons in university processions which go: professors who are doctors,
doctors who are not professors, professors who are not doctors!

But he did send me the regulations for the Geographical Tripos
explaining that it was new, that only some colleges had fellows in the
subject and that I should consult the *Students' Handbook to the University
of Cambridge*. This I did in the public library in Cardiff. There was one
young man who had come to live in our village who was a student at St
Catharine's College in Cambridge, and he told me that St Catharine's
was *the* geography college. My father decided we should visit
Cambridge and we spent a week's holiday in 1931 in East Anglia. I
was interviewed by the Senior Tutor of St Catharine's, the Reverend
H.J. Chaytor. I didn't take to him, nor I think he to me, and he seemed
averse to having more geographers in his college. But he listened to my
qualifications, asked me to set it all down in writing with a letter from
my headmaster, and gave the impression he would accept me. 'We
have many successful geographers from Welsh schools such as yours,'
he said, and I heard for the first time the names of H.C. Darby and
Vaughan Lewis.

I reported all this to my father, but I was depressed, partly by
Chaytor and partly by the building of St Catharine's (which I have
since learnt to admire). Next morning I went for a long walk and was
captivated by King's and Trinity, but most of all by St John's. I
walked for the first time, as I have walked now for over half a century,

through the three old courts and across the Bridge of Sighs to the Rickman New Court and through the Backs and paused on the Kitchen Bridge, curiously enough looking up at the river range of the 1699 buildings where I have had a set of rooms for so many years. I don't think I consciously made up my mind there and then; but I went back to my parents and said I wanted to go up to St John's College. We looked in the *Students' Handbook*: it had a Director of Studies in Geography, one J.M. Wordie. I wrote to him setting out my case: he replied before the week was out offering me a place in October 1932. 'But come earlier if you like,' he wrote. 'We have a vacant place for 1931.' That was in a few weeks' time and my father thought otherwise.

It was thus by a curious series of accidents that I went up to St John's College, Cambridge, in 1932 and not to Jesus College, Oxford. Hrothgar Habakkuk and Bryan Hopkin, who followed me to St John's in 1933, would, without doubt, have followed me to Jesus, Oxford, if I had gone there. It is amusing to reflect now that Hrothgar did eventually get there, when in 1967 he was elected Principal of Jesus.

In 1933 a young woman called Ruth Langhorne (whom I was to marry in 1946) went up to Oxford to read the new Honour School of Geography. Had J.N.L. Baker not dissuaded me from going to Oxford we would have been fellow students in the Oxford Department of Geography and, who knows, passed out of each other's lives as undergraduate acquaintances. Time and chance, to my eternal good fortune, happened otherwise.

And so it was that I accepted a place for 1932. But what to do in the meantime? Alan Michell, who was going to Oxford in 1932, reminded me that we had Glamorgan County Scholarships as well as State Scholarships. Why didn't we take up the County Scholarships for one year and spend the time at University College, Cardiff? It seemed a doubtful proposition: we went to the office in Cardiff, where they welcomed us and confirmed we could draw our scholarships and be students for one year.

But what to read? Alan Michell was going to read modern languages at Oxford and so he enrolled for French and German. I discussed my problem with Bill Davies, now a second year student at Cardiff. Geology was clearly one choice and archaeology was a possible second. Bill Davies did not recommend the archaeology course: he said Victor Nash Williams was a dull lecturer, read out the same notes each year, and I could have his set, which offer I accepted. In the event I found the Nash Williams notes a useful introduction – there were hardly any introductions to archaeology in the early thirties – and the list of references to books and articles of great value.

So I returned to the academic registry office in Cardiff and registered for geology. 'No second subject?' asked the clerk; and at that moment I noticed that one could be taught a musical instrument. Here was my great opportunity. 'Yes,' I said, 'I would like to be put down for the organ course.' She permitted herself a moment's hesitation. 'An unusual combination,' she said, 'but there is nothing against it. You know where the Department of Geology is, in Newport Road: report there. As for the organ, write to Dr George Beal at Llandaff Cathedral.'

The Geology Department at Cardiff was a very happy one and the Professor, A.H. Cox, and his two lecturers, all most agreeable people and excellent teachers. They appreciated what I wanted to do and arranged that I went to all the first and second year classes and when I left with their warm wishes to O.T. Jones, the Professor of Geology at Cambridge, they gave me a letter saying I had reached the subsidiary level in geology. I very much enjoyed peering at rock slices through the microscope, and the handling, description and drawing of fossils, and, of course, the lectures on physical geology were invaluable to me when I went up to Cambridge. Then in the Easter vacation we set out in a bus for a long weekend field class in Shropshire: it taught me how such university teaching in the field should and could be successfully organized.

I received during my one year in University College, Cardiff, some of the best teaching in my life; when I eventually came to teach in Cambridge I modelled myself consciously and deliberately on the Department of Geology at Cardiff as it was in 1931–32. I was fascinated by trilobites and I became an *aficionado* of the fossils in the lias limestone of the Vale of Glamorgan. With my newly bought geological hammer I hacked away at the cliffs along the beaches from Southerndown to Penarth, collecting fine examples of *Gryphaea arcuata*, but to my disappointment never found a really good ammonite.

I felt at once that I was going to be happy in the Geology Department; and so I was and made many friends. I began to regret my rash and sudden registration for organ lessons but I wrote and fixed an appointment with Dr George Beal and went out nervously to Llandaff. The organ was playing but stopped as I got to the narrow stairs leading up to the loft. A cheerful voice called down, 'Miss Daniel? Come up.' I climbed the stairs and said, 'It isn't a Miss Daniel.' Dr Beal roared with laughter: and from that moment we got on well together. He soon realized that I was never going to make a good organist: I had been badly taught the piano to begin with and I seemed bad at co-ordinating the pedal work with my hands. But he taught me all about the organ, shared his enormous enthusiasm and knowledge with me and made my Wednesday afternoon half hours in Llandaff as enjoyable as any since. He taught me all the stops and educated me in the great music from Bach to Vierne and Widor. I once asked my genial mentor how this organ differed in its essentials from the organ in the Capitol Cinema in Cardiff which I loved to hear. 'My dear boy,' he said, 'I can make this organ do as well, or as I think as bad, as any cinema organ in Cardiff.' And suddenly Llandaff Cathedral was filled with the most amazing sound. I was enthralled. Then, just as Beal was producing his most dramatic effects, there was a heavy step on the stairs and the top half of an agitated head verger appeared. 'Dr Beal, sir, have you by any chance forgotten the funeral?' 'Certainly not,' said Beal blandly as he leant over the gallery and saw the west door open, and returned to his manuals for suitable accompaniment. I often wonder what the large assembling congregation in the nave made of the music they had heard before.

During my years at Barry and Cardiff and my first years as an undergraduate we had family holidays. There was a strict pattern: two or three weeks with my grandfather in Carmarthenshire, one week in Central Wales, and one week elsewhere chosen by my father – Bournemouth, Cheltenham, Anglesey. I think he chose places he wanted primarily my mother and me, and only lastly himself, to see. I remember all those holidays but most of all those weeks in Llandrindod Wells. We were always in some middle-class boarding house or hotel that provided very good breakfasts and evening meals. The pattern of my days was straightforward. I woke up early and went to the spa, returning with a bottle of saline water which was supposed to, and no doubt did, assist the morning motions of my parents. Then the day was spent walking, getting books out of W.H. Smith's lending library, and playing on the putting and approach courses. I read voraciously in those years, certainly a novel a day – Brett Young,

Hugh Walpole, J.B. Priestley, Agatha Christie, Dorothy Sayers, Ngaio Marsh, and occasionally old novels, particularly those of Harrison Ainsworth.

One day my father came home to tea and said that they had posted him a new teacher called Phyllis Illingworth, trained in Homerton, and the sister of Leslie Illingworth the cartoonist. 'They live at Picketstone,' he said, 'and I suggest you call on them on one of your walks.'

I did so a few days later and so began my lifelong friendship with Leslie Illingworth, the great cartoonist, which I describe at length in a later chapter. The Illingworths lived in a small farmhouse cottage they had bought. Papa Illingworth – a rather crusty old man in his retirement – was a Yorkshireman who had come down to work on the Vale of Glamorgan railway. He had retired early and was now secretary of the Barry Golf Club. He had three children, Leslie, Vivian, who went into the army as an engineer dealing with railways (and died in the 1939–45 war in Italy, not of fighting but of leukaemia) and Phyllis.

I was devoted to them all and they were a family which gave me a different view of life from that of my own family and many in Llantwit Major. Their cottage at Picketstone was only three miles from our house and I walked over to see Leslie frequently – perhaps too frequently, but he never complained: and as the years went on there was no suggestion other than we did many things together. We played tennis, we played golf, but mostly we talked – about everything under the sun as he sat drawing in the converted barn which was his studio, a cartoon for *Punch* or the *Daily Mail* or an advertisement. And when we had tired the sun with talking we would walk the four miles to Cowbridge and drink pints of bitter in the Bear or eat a steak in the Duke of Wellington and, walking home in the moonlight, argue about sex and God, and whether there was going to be another war, and deplore the building of aerodromes at St Athan and Llandow which we felt sure were going to revolutionize the countryside and ruin the peace and quiet of Bro Morgannwg.

In his characteristically amusing, evocative and brilliant preface to *Old Barry in Photographs* (Barry, 1977), Gwyn Thomas refers to the 'ring of villages rich in tranquillity and revered taverns' from which he says 'the Barry Grammar School drew some of its finest talent'; and then goes on to mention Keith Thomas from Llancarfan, and myself, then perpetuating the apocryphal story that I began my archaeological career as a schoolboy by uncovering a tessellated Roman pavement at Llantwit Major.

I certainly came from a village in the Vale rich in tranquillity and revered taverns – the Swan and the Globe and the White Hart are still there, though many have been closed in the last thirty years. From the age of five to eleven Llantwit Major and the Vale of Glamorgan was my world, and Barry a foreign place from which one took Campbell's steamers to Avonmouth and Minehead, Clovelly and Ilfracombe – places with cafés producing lobster and crab salads, and teas with scones, jam and cream. It was also a place for beach picnics, paddling and bathing, and donkey rides, games of pitch-and-putt golf, and wonderful outsize Knickerbocker Glories in ice-cream parlours.

But afterwards it became part of me: Barry and Cardiff are as much a part of me, of my past and my present memory, as is the Vale of Glamorgan.

In the long summer holidays my walks always took me to the sea, to the beaches of Colaugh and Nash and Boverton. There was a small group of teenagers who used to swim in the Bristol Channel in the afternoons. The senior of the group was Bill Davies, who taught me how to swim. Afterwards, drying ourselves in the sun or walking home, we used to argue about everything. Davies was a stern fundamentalist. I, now in the Barry sixth form, and later at Cardiff, was reading widely about the origins of Christianity, comparative religion and man's physical evolution. The books of Arthur Keith, Elliot Smith and James Frazer made me look at Welsh Nonconformist faith in which I had been brought up from a new and external standpoint. I began to ask myself whether it was not merely an accident that I had not been born into a Roman Catholic household in the Cevennes or a Muslim household in Baghdad or a Hindu family in Delhi. Why was the Congregational faith necessarily true and all other religions false? Bill Davies had no doubts; everything outside the chapels of Wales was virtually paganism. We argued a great deal.

It is now five decades and more since I left the Vale of Glamorgan and went up to Cambridge. Is it still such a lovely place, as I look across the Backs to it through time and space? Perhaps not quite, because it has changed and so have I: in the twenties and early thirties I was seeing it intoxicated by the adventure of growing up.

The train journey through the Vale from Llantwit Major to Barry is forever photographed and recorded in detail in my mind – the curve over the Thaw and the distant view of the Leys; the disused pier at Rhoose; the tunnels and the viaduct at Porthkerry – and always the view across the Severn Sea to Somerset and Devon; the ships coming up the Channel; and, when there was fog, the knelling-belling of the Breaksea Lightship and the cold, sinister boom of the foghorn at Nash Point.

I have tried to put something of my feelings for the Vale into my second detective story, which I called *Welcome Death*. It was about two young men (yes, both of them me) who came back to the Vale after the war to find that things were not the same as when they left. I read this book again the other day and when I read the brief account of the train journey from Barry to Llantwit Major, here for me was a moment of truth (though written, as I now remember, in the airport hotel in Basra): and the acrid smoke of the Porthkerry tunnel was in my nose, and the vision of my schoolgirl-schoolboy no good boy-no good girl calf loves on the station platforms of Aberthaw and Gileston still haunts my memory-stained eyes.

I know that there is nowhere I would have preferred to grow up in than the Vale of Glamorgan: it is something intensely powerful in my emotional life. I don't often go back but when I do, and on a summer's day get up early and walk through what is now a very large village and out into the countryside that I walked over and around for so many years, I am possessed by some ineffable peace in which past, present and future are one in some mystical confusion that my reason tells me not to resolve.

What I do know is that if a terrible crisis occurred in my life and I had to be alone to think, I would drive from Cambridge across the South Midlands to Glamorgan, leave my car at Colhugh Beach and walk along the high cliffs to St Donat's Castle, the setting sun in my eyes, the wind from the Atlantic distance blowing in my face, and the grey Severn Sea at my feet. And I would know that if ever again there were to be moments of peace and truth and decision, they would come there, as they came when I was young, the gorse golden around me, the bracken crisp under my feet, the seabirds wheeling around my head.

CHAPTER THREE

Cambridge in the Thirties

THE FIRST MAJOR BREAK in my life came in early October 1932 when I caught my usual 8.10 train from Llantwit Major that had taken me for six years to school in Barry and for one year to university at Cardiff. But on this warm October day I took the express to Paddington, the Inner Circle to Liverpool Street, the train to Cambridge, and was knocking at the door of 53 Bridge Street having taken the first taxi in my life. I was alone and in the Fens: it was foggy. I had left two hundred miles away the comfort, the cherished intimacy and confidence of my childhood and adolescence. I knew nobody in Cambridge. My landlady, Mrs Hayes, helped me unpack and produced a cup of tea. I went round the corner and signed my name in the book in the Porters' Lodge at St John's and walked through the College which had so entranced me the year before and still does. It was dark and cold.

I collected my gown and went into the Hall; early, because I had no idea of what went on. There was one other undergraduate already sitting at one of the long tables. I went and sat next to him. 'Do you mind if I join you?' I asked, 'I am a new boy and know nobody.' 'I am also a new boy and know nobody,' he said. The Hall filled: we stood up for Grace. We sat down and ate what seemed to me a good meal. 'Bit stodgy,' said my new acquaintance, Bob Mitchell. We stood up again for Grace. 'What do we do now?' he asked. 'Go for a walk,' I suggested. In cap and gown we walked all round Cambridge for two hours and then parted to our lodgings. 'Well, at least we each know somebody,' said Bob.

Robert Mitchell was a very fine swimmer and like many swimmers was rather spherical. He became a blue and captained both the Cambridge swimming and water-polo teams: and then swam for Britain in the Olympic and World Games. I have just looked him up in what a BBC reporter once referred to me as 'that useful Whosey Whosey book.' He has been a Greater London Councillor since 1964 and has the Orders of Orange Nassau (Holland), the Star (Afghanistan) and the Rising Sun (Japan). He describes his hobbies as planting trees and watching them grow. Someone once asked me why I knew Bob Mitchell so well. 'Surely,' he said, 'you two have nothing in common?' 'On the contrary,' I said, 'we are allies who share a past.'

Three undergraduates lodged at 53 Bridge Street – myself, someone called W.B. Morrell, and a tall rowing engineer called Crosby Warren who was often intoxicated. My room looked out on to the street and was directly opposite those agreeable hostelries, the Baron of Beef and the Mitre, which have played such a part in the life of St John's College and particularly in that of the thirsty College Choir and its organists and Directors of Music – a quick one during the sermon always helps the final voluntary to go with a swing, bells, *trompeta real* and all. My rooms were on the first floor and underneath was a fruit and vegetable shop run by two elderly dwarves who had to stand on stools to deal with their customers. I was very fond of these nice ladies and was distressed when one Saturday night Crosby Warren came into my rooms, leaned out of the window and hauled up out of the street some of his drunken friends. I was alarmed as my room filled with these characters, and more alarmed when the last one kicked his legs as he was being dragged up and broke the window of the shop below.

My landlady burst into my rooms and demanded to know what was going on. 'When I locked the door at 10 o'clock there were no strangers in this house. Now there are ten men. Out with them. I am ashamed of you, Mr Daniel. I always thought you were a mild, well-behaved person.'

Next day we all had to visit our tutors to explain our behaviour. James Wordie was as blandly distant and unconcerned as he always seemed to be. 'You say the shop under you is run by female dwarves,' he said. 'Strange and intriguing.' It was intriguing, and I went to see them and apologised. They both stood on their boxes and laughed. 'We've always been wanting a reason for retiring,' they said. 'Here it is. We stop today. Please help yourself to anything you want: the Cox's you like are still very good. We couldn't go on no more. Our customers wouldn't like our fruit and veg full of bits of broken glass!'

Bill Morrell was a year older than me, had been at school at The Downs at Colwall and Bootham. He was part of the rich Quaker Society of York that owned newspapers and chocolate factories. Through him I moved into a wide friendship of Boothamites including

Leonard Miall and Frank Thistlethwaite. Bill himself was one of the kindest, most sympathetic and sensible persons I have met: he came and stayed with my parents in South Wales. He went into his family newspapers – the *Nottingham Journal* and the *Birmingham Gazette*; these were part of the Westminster Press Provincial Newspapers of which he was Managing Director from 1965 onwards: he was Chairman of the Press Association 1970–71.

I think we were perhaps a little frightened of some of the Bootham boys. Leonard Miall became President of the Union and editor of *The Cambridge Review* and seemed for a while a person of outstanding charm and ability who would go anywhere. I found him later in the BBC, the glittering prizes gone, and an uncertain ally in my campaign to get archaeology properly presented on television.

Frank Thistlethwaite was a very different Boothamite: charming, courteous, a man of wide interests, a very good pianist, he was a notable figure in the College and in Cambridge in the early thirties. He took firsts in the Historical and English Triposes and was also editor of *The Cambridge Review*, was a Commonwealth Fund Fellow in the University of Minnesota and there married his delightful and vivacious wife Jane. After war service in the Cabinet Office he returned to St John's and after fifteen years as Tutor, Steward, Praelector, went in 1961 to found the University of East Anglia in Norwich, of which institution he was Vice-Chancellor until his retirement in 1980. There was no archaeology in the first courses at the UEA and to encourage the cause I offered to give some lectures on the archaeological evidence for the origins of civilization. They were well attended and there were lengthy, vigorous and valuable discussions. The lectures were eventually broadcast by the BBC and published as *The First Civilizations* (1968, Pelican 1971) and were dedicated to Frank and Jane. It was, I think, the first clear and definite statement of the independent origins of civilizations in many different parts of the world.

In my first years as an undergraduate the Boothamite connection was a source of comfort, friendship and reassurance: but gradually contacts in lectures, in the College, among fellow Welshmen and by playing squash and chess brought a wide circle of friends and acquaintances and the lonely, friendless boy of October 1932 was, thankfully, a thing of the past.

My generation of 1932 – the class of 1935 as it is called in American parlance – was full of interesting and notable persons such as Alan Hodgkin, who retired in 1983 from the Mastership of Trinity, and Mervyn Stockwood who retired a few years ago from the Bishopric of Southwark. In that same 1932 Michaelmas Term in which we came up Anthony Blunt was made a Fellow of Trinity College. Much has been written recently, since his identification as the 'fourth man', and a lurid picture has been painted of intrigue, Communists and Fascists, homosexuality and obsession with politics at Cambridge in the thirties. I seem to have belonged to a very different Cambridge. I never knew Burgess or Maclean, was never approached by Blunt, and had never heard of the Apostles until after the war, although I knew one of its members, Hugh Sykes Davies, both as an undergraduate and increasingly when I became a Fellow. I met John Cornford through Hrothgar Habakkuk and was saddened by the news of his death, but even more saddened that people should want to go and fight in the Spanish Civil War.

I was an apolitical young man: I did not join the Conservative, Labour or Liberal parties and no one asked me to join the Communists. Indeed most of the canvassing in my three undergraduate years was for religious societies and we all shared the joke when the Cambridge University New Testament Society had to change its name because initially it seemed inappropriate for its purpose. I was a member of the Union and attended a few debates but used it mainly for its library and its restaurant. Politics did not interest me at all and, like many of my blind contemporaries, I could not believe that another great war was inevitable. What we had read of the First World War made it seem incredible that civilized Western Europeans could ever embark on such a bloody folly again. We watched the growth of Nazism and Fascism with aloof disgust, not realizing that all Europeans were not civilized and that below the smiling face of the world there sometimes lay horror and cruelty beyond reasonable belief.

We, of course, had endless discussions well into the night over tea and beer, but they were mainly not about politics: they were about religion and God, the nature of man, sex, archaeology and anthropology, films, music. There was one issue on which I was aroused and became politically conscious, and that was the abdication of Edward VIII. Like so many of my generation we were profoundly for him: had he not spent the night after his tour of the Welsh coalfields in the sidings of Llantwit Major Station a few hundred yards from my house? We were pro-the Prince of Wales and hoped against all hope that he would not abdicate and that the Baldwins of the world would be defeated. I travelled home to South Wales in December and walking down the corridor of the Paddington-Fishguard express saw Daniel Hopkin sitting reading papers in a first-class compartment and he summoned me in for a talk. Daniel was a Llantwit boy: his mother had been the caretaker of the school where my father was now headmaster. He was then MP for Carmarthen: starting as a Liberal MP he had moved to Labour and carried his constituency with him. He had great charisma and as two porters on Carmarthen Station once said to me, 'To hell with Labour or Liberal: we want Daniel and that's what we are voting for.' We talked about many things and then the conversation came round to the abdication. I told him my views and those of my contemporaries and asked him his. He paused and then said slowly, 'Boyo, I know how you feel, but he's not a good man. He is not suitable to be king. He is fundamentally lazy. Right now we are all just waiting for him to sober up enough to sign the right documents and say the right things.' I returned shattered to my third-class compartment and that evening sadly retailed to my parents what I had been told.

This chapter, then, portrays a very different Cambridge in the thirties from that recently sensationalized. It is because it is seen through the eyes of a very ordinary secondary-school boy from Wales who lapped up the magic of Cambridge, and is still deeply sensible of it – familiarity has not bred contempt. If he had any ideas of his future when he came up he would probably have thought tentatively in terms of becoming a geography master and trying to inspire in his students an interest in human geography and in the allied aspects of archaeology and anthropology. But between 1932 and 1939 this competent but ordinary schoolboy came into touch with real scholarship in the persons of Miles Burkitt, J.M. de Navarro, H.M. Chadwick and many another, and the doors of a scholarly future opened showing vistas that beckoned him away from modest dreams of schoolmastering. He began to think, especially when he was elected a Fellow of his College in 1938, that there might be a life in which he studied megalithic monuments and the history of archaeology, and taught undergraduates. It was his great good fortune, for which he is eternally grateful, that this life happened.

I was well equipped to read geography. I had been excellently taught in my extra-school episode; my year in the Geology Department at Cardiff had given me a very good grounding in physical geography and I had myself read widely in human geography, archaeology and anthropology. I have often heard it said that scholars who came up to Cambridge from schools like Eton with fine classical sixths found their first year in the university reading for the Classical Tripos disappointing. I felt the same about first-year geography. I wanted to get on and was being taught mainly at a lowish sixth-form level. And with two exceptions the teaching was uninspiring to poor. I was particularly disappointed by the teaching in human geography which was given by Mrs Alison Hingston Quiggin, a charming but slightly vague widow of a Fellow of Caius and teacher of Celtic.

Mrs Quiggin's idea of human geography was to spend a whole lecture describing one primitive community – Eskimos, Bushmen, Australian aborigines, Andaman islanders. It was an introduction to ethnography but on a very elementary level: nowhere in her course was the excitement and inspiration of Brunhes, Vidal de la Blache, or even Fleure. She had curious mannerisms and the tiresomely repeated use of the phrase 'And you have your . . .'. 'And you have your igloos,' she would say when describing the Eskimos. 'And you have your boomerangs,' she said brightly when describing the Australian aborigines. During her lecture on the Lapps she excelled herself: 'And you have your reindeer moss,' she declared and then fishing in a large brown bag brought out a little box and held it aloft triumphantly, 'And here is some reindeer moss.'

I got to know her well in later years and much admired the work she did in the Faculty of Archaeology and Anthropology, especially the short *History of Anthropology* which she wrote with A.C. Haddon; but in my first year she was a wet blanket on my youthful fiery ambitions to become a human geographer.

The two exceptions to the poor geography teachers were Alfred Steers and Clifford Darby. Steers taught physical geography and geomorphology clearly and interestingly. Darby taught historical geography, a subject entirely new to me, brilliantly: he was one of the half-dozen best lecturers I have ever heard. A boy from Neath County School, he had gone up young to St Catharine's, taken a PhD on the Draining of the Fens, and at the youthful age of 22, when I first met him, was a prize Fellow of King's.

Soon I set up a relationship with him similar to that I had in South Wales with Leslie Illingworth: he became an elder brother/young uncle figure and I expect I wasted too much of his time. It had been discovered that I was short-sighted just before I went up to Cambridge: my eyes were tested and spectacles prescribed which were not properly checked and centred. All through my first year I was subject to violent and blinding headaches which prevented me from doing as much reading as I wanted, and late in the evening I would wander about Jesus Green and Midsummer Common wondering what was the matter with me. It was Clifford Darby who suggested I should go to a Cambridge oculist, which I did, and he immediately prescribed new spectacles, which were fine: and the headaches ceased.

I used to complain to Darby about the inefficiency and lack of inspiration in the human geography teaching in the Cambridge Department and it was he who suggested that I might change to the Archaeology and Anthropology Tripos. I knew nothing about it but read its prospectus in the Cambridge *Students' Handbook* and was excited.

My tutor, James Wordie, a geographer of distinction himself, had taken a special interest in me. Early on he asked me to dine with him at home: I well remember the occasion – it was the first time I had worn a dinner jacket, boiled shirt, and stiff collar. I was ill at ease but enjoyed the evening. James was technically my supervisor in geography and I was supposed to do an essay for him each week or so – I remember doing one on the Parallel Roads of Glenroy; but he was too busy with his other many activities to be able to find time to teach undergraduates, and when my supervision hour was due I used to spend most of it waiting in his outer room talking to his secretary, Mrs Eva Cousins, who, curiously enough, became my secretary many years later when Wordie, then Sir James, died. And, indeed, has typed many manuscripts for me, including this book.

He was a fascinating man, gifted in many ways, shrewd and well aware of academic and scientific politics. One day Alec Deer, then a research student at St John's, was travelling by train to Cambridge from Scotland and got into conversation with someone who knew James Wordie in his Glasgow business contexts. 'Yon's a deep subterranean bugger,' he said. So he was, but kind, sympathetic and prepared to spend a great deal of time over his pupils.

I told him how disappointed I was with the teaching in human geography and that I had read the syllabus of the Archaeology and Anthropology Tripos with excitement. He thought for a while and said: 'Yes; change. Read Arch and Anth in your second year, then switch back to Geography Part II in your third. You will then be well equipped to take over Mrs Quiggin's teaching when she retires.' The die was cast, but neither Wordie nor I knew the repercussions or that my move was away from geography for ever.

I was nervous of the examinations at the end of my first year, being unsure of standards. To my surprise I got a first in the qualifying examination for Part I of the Geography Tripos and as top of the list of candidates got a Wright's Prize in College. My parents were delighted, but surprised and a little mystified at my change of Tripos. But they accepted it when they knew it was approved by Wordie and by Darby who had driven over from Neath to have tea with us at Llantwit Major.

Just before the examinations I conceived the idea of going on a week's walking tour in Brittany and asked Clifford Darby to join me. He readily agreed and also to our being joined by a third person, namely Hrothgar Habakkuk, who was then still at Barry County School but was to come up as an undergraduate to St John's in October of that year. Looking back now it seemed a dangerous, almost mad, idea to set out with two people who had not met each other before, one a Fellow of King's and the other a sixth-form schoolboy. They had apparently nothing in common except their friendship with me, and the fact that all three of us were products of South Welsh secondary schools. I need not have worried, it was a great success and we three have remained firm friends ever since.

Hrothgar and I set out in the train from Cardiff to Southampton: I had £10 in my pocket which I had saved during the previous year. We met Clifford off the London train and sailed overnight to St Malo and walked the first day to Cancale where I tasted my first oysters. Then we walked to Dol. It was very, very hot, as most summers seem to have been, at least in recollection, in the thirties. We stopped in a village at what seemed to be a café: it was in fact a large farmhouse with a room in the front where the farm sold its own cider. The farmer took a liking to us and insisted we inspect the farm and his *chais*. He also insisted we should degust, *gratuit*, several of his ciders and his calvados: the first time any of us three had tasted this apple brandy. We went on our way happy and the miles to Dol seemed short.

I had always wanted to see Dol where St Samson came in the sixth century from Llantwit Major, built his cathedral and became bishop of that part of Brittany. We also saw the great menhir to the south of the town and walked on to Mont St-Michel where we rested a day entranced by the site and delighted to try Mère Poulard's famous omelette. Then on foot to Combourg and Dinard and by boat down the river Rance to St Malo and overnight to Southampton. Clifford Darby caught the first train to London and was in Cambridge in time to give the first lecture in a long-vacation course.

I shall not easily forget this train. He had been asked to buy when in France copies of *Ulysses* and *Lady Chatterley's Lover* which were set books for the English Tripos but unobtainable in England. This he did, and it was arranged that we should each smuggle one book in our haversacks, go through the customs separately and re-assemble on his train before it left Southampton. I was first and, nervous and a little tired, slumped down in an empty compartment. When I looked up there was an enormous St Bernard standing in the doorway looking, as it seemed, accusingly at me. I thought in my innocence 'My God they have trained dogs to smell out contraband literature!' And then I saw he was collecting for charity. I have often seen those collecting dogs since – I don't think they exist any more – never without a remembrance of my early fright: and hastily given them some offering as conscience money. Having delivered our smuggled books to Darby, we said goodbye and got into the South Wales train with sighs of relief.

I arrived back home with one shilling in my pocket: we had had a last blow-out at St Malo and eaten *langoustines mayonnaise* and a *sole normande*. Looking back on that week it seems incredible that we had six nights, twelve meals and a lot of beer, cider and wine – it was very hot and we were always thirsty – for £10, but I have just been consulting Whitaker for 1933 and see that in real money the £1 was then worth the equivalent of £6 in France, so our jaunt really cost £60. Those were indeed very good days in which to travel in France.

I spent that long vacation of 1933 reading everything I could about prehistoric archaeology and visiting as many archaeological sites in South Wales as I could persuade my parents to see, and they were indulgent and interested. We visited all the promontory forts from Sudbrook West, Caerleon and Caerwent and the megaliths of the Gower peninsula. Still, when I went to my first lecture in the Museum of Archaeology and Ethnology, I was apprehensive on two grounds: first that I should be out of my depth, and secondly a nagging doubt that I had made a mistake in abandoning geography.

My doubts and fears were soon resolved. The Arch and Anth Tripos course was well designed for beginners and with two exceptions the teaching was inspiringly good. The exceptions were the two Professors, Hodson, Professor of Anthropology, and Minns, the holder of the Disney Professorship of Archaeology.

Hodson was a retired Indian Civil Servant and the first holder of the William Wyse Chair of Anthropology in Cambridge: the great A.C. Haddon had never got further up the academic ladder than a readership in ethnology. Hodson had no idea how to teach and his lectures were a travesty. He made us all use the Royal Anthropological Institute's *Notes and Queries in Anthropology* as a sort of bible or text. We sat waiting in the small lecture room clutching our copies. He would come in bearing his copy and a cup of cold tea. Then we went through this valuable handbook for anthropologists in the field, page by page. Anything he found of interest – the caste system, cannibalism, circumcision, shamanism – would set him off to comment with anecdotes. But one day we turned to a page which had nothing to interest him and he announced to us solemnly, 'Page 120 succeeds page 119: let us turn to page 121.' I suppose it was a good way of making us read *Notes and Queries* but it was very dull.

Equally dull were the lectures of E.H. Minns. A distinguished scholar, he was said to be disappointed that he had not been made either Professor of Slavonic Languages or University Librarian, and accepted the Chair of Archaeology as a third best. He too used his own book *Scythians and Greeks* as a text and had it on his desk as he talked to us. He was totally unable to make the archaeology of South Russia come to life and could find no way of interesting undergraduates. We realized he was contributing nothing to our Tripos courses and his audience dropped to two and sometimes one.

Five years later it was discovered that no one was attending his lectures and I was begged by the Secretary of the Faculty Board to attend. Minns was justifiably surprised to see me, then a senior Research Student. I was the only person in the room. 'Good heavens, Daniel,' said Minns, 'what are you doing here? You didn't pay much attention to my lectures when you were an undergraduate.' I mumbled that I was now more interested in his subject. 'Don't believe it for a moment,' he said. In this uneasy atmosphere we continued for several weeks and suddenly he snapped shut his book and said: 'Daniel, let's give up this farce. Let me tell you some stories. Would you like to know how I killed Gregory Bateson's mother?'

The Batesons lived next door to the Minns family in Wordsworth Grove. Mrs Bateson was old and had a passion for green gooseberries which she was forbidden to eat. One day she begged Ellis Minns to give her some green gooseberries, which he did. This resulted in a tremendous tummy upset: she took to her bed and never left it alive.

After this and other unusual anecdotes the Minns lecture course to me came to an end. Much later he dined as my guest in St John's, sat on the right of Martin Charlesworth, then President of the College, and poured out carping and often vitriolic comments on his colleagues. Martin was equal to that occasion and turned blandly to Minns saying, 'Yours, dear Minns, may be the sort of conversation that is acceptable at the high table of Pembroke. We do not encourage it here.' Minns was nonplussed and silenced. I walked home with him. 'What a rude man Charlesworth is,' he said, and suddenly clutched his breast. 'I'm having a heart attack,' he said. 'Where are my pills?' He sat on the wall outside King's, took his pills and was soon all right again. An alarming evening.

I thought of Minns as an archetype of pedantic don and arid scholar: Grahame Clark and Hrothgar Habakkuk tell me I am quite wrong: that he was a kind, generous, lovable man. But my view was shared by my contemporaries in the class of 1933–4. With the easy contempt of youth we shrugged him off because he did not seem 'passionné de la préhistoire et de l'anthropologie', as we were all becoming under the influence of four excellent men – Driberg, Sayce, Burkitt and de Navarro.

Jack Driberg was exciting and outrageous, a strange and colourful man, though not as strange and colourful as his brother Tom, the politician who many years later was raised to the peerage as Lord Bradwell of Tottenham. He enthralled and entertained us with his accounts of life among East African tribes: we were told that many of his stories were imaginary and that he had been sacked from his job there for some impropriety. We were never clear about what this misdeed was but Alan Watkins in his brilliant piece on brother Tom in his delightful *Brief Lives*, confirms, or at least repeats, the story current in Cambridge in the thirties. 'As a colonial administrator to North-

East Africa' writes Watkins, 'he refused to burn down a village as a punitive measure. He concocted an account of the burning, was discovered in his invention, and was dismissed.' Certainly a brave, if from the point of view of his career, a foolhardy action.

He wrote several very good books: *The Dinka* and *At Home with the Savage* but also a most endearing book called *Engato the Lion Cub* about a lion cub he brought up. Engato used to sleep under his bed and when he grew larger and turned over in his sleep would tip Jack out of bed. Eventually he was too large and adult, and Jack was anyhow leaving East Africa. He deposited him in the zoo at Marseilles but always went to see him when in that city. He would go to the lion's cage and give the whistle he had always used. Immediately the full-grown lion would come and stand at the bars of his cage looking puzzled and curious. This story may also have been one of Jack's inventions but I believed it and tears came to my eyes every time I read it.

He was someone I was looking forward to seeing back in Cambridge after the war but he vanished to the Middle East in the war on secret intelligence missions, became a Muslim, and died under curious circumstances. I met his brother in the fifties on the platform of King's Cross while waiting to board our sleepers for Edinburgh. We were in neighbouring compartments and he was happy to talk about Jack: and delighted to find someone who admired his brother and had enjoyed being taught by him. He gave the impression that he thought Jack was a seedy, second-rate person who had been lucky to pick up a Cambridge lectureship. When I reported all this to John Hutton, then Professor of Social Anthropology at Cambridge, he said sharply, 'I hope the door of your sleeping compartment was double locked.' This was long before I had read Lord Bradwell's autobiography *Ruling Passions*. It was only later that I saw the fascinating photograph of the 1921 sixth form at Lancing which contained Evelyn Waugh, Roger Fulford, Tom Driberg and Max Mallowan. It appears in Evelyn Waugh's *Diaries* and in Max Mallowan's *Mallowan's Memoirs*. I asked Max one day what Tom was like at school. 'Seemed all right to me,' he said, 'but I had no idea then of his specialized proclivities.'

There can be no doubt in my mind that the most stimulating teacher was R.U. Sayce, a Welshman who subsequently left Cambridge to run the Manchester Museum and did nothing of any importance after that. But he brought to us the best of the tradition of the Aberystwyth anthropological and human geography teaching of

H.J. Fleure and his experience as a teacher in South Africa. He taught material culture and physical anthropology and both with clarity and inspiration. I still think his little book *Primitive Arts and Crafts* an invaluable and stimulating introduction to what Georges Montandon calls ergology – the word, perhaps fortunately, never caught on. It was Sayce who introduced me to the notion of skeuomorphism: originally set out by Otis Mason in his long forgotten book *The Origins of Invention*.

He was a kind, unassuming, friendly bachelor – I never knew why he was nicknamed Uncle Lenin. He organized with J.M. de Navarro one of the first Cambridge archaeological field-classes, starting a tradition which I was able to develop later. We set off in a small fleet of cars through central Wales looking at hillforts and churches. One of the cars belonged to de Navarro: it was his father's car which had been shipped over from New York. There his father had been given the great privilege of a police siren and this device remained fixed to the enormous limousine. Sitting in the back there was a strange motion as though one was at sea and at some moments I thought I might be seasick. One Sunday afternoon as we were driving into Barmouth Kenneth Jackson (now Emeritus Professor of Celtic at Edinburgh) clutched me – he was a pale grey, moving to green. 'Stop this car,' he said, 'I am going to be sick.' I knocked on the glass window separating us from the chauffeur, who in bringing the car to a rapid stop set off the American police siren. Kenneth fell out on to the grass verge and was violently sick. As I got out to help him I noticed we were in front of a board bearing the reproving words 'Silence. Sabbatarian observances in progress.' It took a little while before the chauffeur managed to stop the siren and Kenneth was put back safely in the front of the limousine.

Miles Burkitt was another inspired and distinguished teacher. He was himself a Cambridge boy: his father was one of the Professors of Divinity, the first layman to hold a Divinity Chair in the twenties and thirties when there were seven such Chairs.

Miles went to Eton and was very proud of his school, and wore no other tie for the rest of his life. He came up to Trinity, read geology, and was preparing to do research when he met the Abbé Breuil, then on a short visit to Cambridge. Breuil invited him to work with him in Spain and he spent several seasons in the cave-art site of Castillo. The outbreak of war in 1914 put an end to field archaeology: Burkitt was a Quaker and served in a field ambulance unit. After the war A.C.

Haddon asked him to give a course on prehistoric archaeology in the new Tripos just coming into being. Miles was at first paid £10 a year for his course of lectures. He eventually became a fully paid university lecturer and went on teaching until his retirement in 1958. I thought him an admirable teacher and his book *The Old Stone Age* (1933) one of the best possible introductions to Palaeolithic archaeology. He always lectured at 9 a.m. and arrived dressed in a large overcoat (he never wore a gown) with a box of 3¼ by 3¼ glass lantern slides. He never had any notes but was always lucid, clear and interesting. He taught and inspired everyone who came to Cambridge to read archaeology and the list of what he always referred to as 'my brilliant pupils' is a long roster of very distinguished archaeologists – Louis Leakey, Grahame Clark, Desmond Clark, Thurstan Shaw, Charles McBurney, Derek Roe, Gale Sieveking, Clare Fell, Eleanor Hardy, Basil Megaw, Ann Sieveking, to mention a few.

We were all invited out to tea in his house in Grantchester once a week. These were not formal supervisions. We moved after tea into his study and gossiped about prehistory: he sat on a leather-covered fender in front of the fire incessantly smoking cigarettes in a brown cigarette holder. His dear wife Peggy was always at the tea party but vanished during the session in the study. She had been an undergraduate at Newnham and he had snatched her away before she took her degree: the story is, and it has never been denied, that he collected her from Newnham in a taxi with the blinds down to avoid any scandal.

Peggy was a great friend to us all then and through all my life until she died in 1978. She was a brilliant draughtswoman and illustrated all of her husband's books. Some of her drawings are classics of archaeological illustration like the drawing of an Acheulian handaxe which I reproduce here.

Miles was really only interested in the Old Stone Age and when the Cambridge University Press persuaded him to write a successor to *The Old Stone Age*, called *Our Early Ancestors*, it was very poor. He used to say that in his lectures he took his students up on to a high hill, told them about the Palaeolithic and shewed them Julius Caesar in the distance.

His career was a strange one and he was in his old age a saddened and disappointed man. One would have thought that in the early twenties he was one of the topmost archaeologists in Britain. He had introduced the Old Stone Age to Britain as Boyd Dawkins and Lubbock had never done. When Abercromby died and left money to

Drawing of an Acheulian hand-axe by Peggy Burkitt, an example of archaeological draughtsmanship at its best.

Inches   1,   2,   3,

found a Chair of Archaeology in Edinburgh in the twenties, Burkitt was the obvious first holder. He was invited but declined, believing, as he told me later, that Cambridge students were more worthwhile than anyone who might want to read archaeology in Edinburgh. He had also been turned down for a Senior Doctorate and he was never made a Fellow of the British Academy, nor did his own College, Trinity, elect him into a Fellowship. It was all very sad: he turned to public service, became a County Councillor and Chairman of the Cambridge County Council, and did a term as High Sheriff. He once said that he was a member of a hundred committees.

What went wrong in a career that seemed in the twenties so full of distinction and promise? He wrote only one original work of scholarship: and he retreated to the family comforts of Grantchester. When the great Glozel affair (see p. 354) broke in 1927 he was asked to be a member of the International Commission of Enquiry but declined to serve, and Dorothy Garrod replaced him. There was something lacking in his character. In 1967 when Rouffignac was discovered and there was, as there still is, uncertainty about its authenticity, I tried to persuade him to come and see the site with me, but he declined. Why? If you had been in almost at the beginning of the discovery of Palaeolithic art, as he had, would you not have caught the first aircraft to Bordeaux and rushed up to see Rouffignac? I once discussed this with the Abbé Breuil before he had taken a violent

67

dislike to me because I suspected Rouffignac. 'Burkitt' he said, 'Miles Burkitt, c'est un professeur en pantoufles.'

And towards the end of his life when I persuaded him to dine in St John's – somehow he didn't like the collegiate system – he said to me sadly that he was a failure, and when I remonstrated with him and said, 'How can you say you are a failure with all your distinguished pupils?' he said in a sad phrase which I have always remembered, 'I taught them, but they have out-distanced me.' He was my research supervisor for three years and it is not unfair to say that I got very little out of my supervisions except good teas out at Grantchester and a lot of archaeological gossip. I used to walk back from Grantchester to the bus stop in the Barton Road fuming at the waste of time, energy and money.

Roy Rainbird Clarke was born in 1914 in Norwich, the son of W.G. Clarke, a journalist, a keen archaeologist, and one of the co-founders of the Prehistoric Society of East Anglia – the remarkable regional society which in due course gave birth to the Prehistoric Society. From his father Rainbird inherited or was inspired with a passion for archaeology and for East Anglia: and at an early age he edited a new edition of his father's classic book *In Breckland Wilds*. He went up to St John's College, Cambridge, as an undergraduate in the Michaelmas Term of 1932 – the very same term as I went up as a freshman to the same College, and it was in a set of rooms at the bottom of the staircase where I now keep, many years later, as a Fellow of that College, that Rainbird kept. His infectious enthusiasm for archaeology and his ability as an organizer were very soon obvious to all of us. I think we were all a little frightened of him then, because of his efficiency and his confident assurance that he knew what he was doing in life. We were all very impressed when, while he was an undergraduate, he got an article accepted by O.G.S. Crawford and published in *Antiquity* in 1935. It was on 'The Flint Knappers of Brandon' and is still the standard account of this unusual and ancient craft.

He was for a few years in the Taunton Museum and then came back to his native Norfolk, first as Deputy Curator of Norwich Castle Museum, where he was in charge of the archaeological collections, and then as Director of the Norwich Museums. The skill and promise of his undergraduate days remained and developed. He created and ran the Norfolk Research Committee. He was brilliant in telling the people of East Anglia the importance of the antiquities they found and what they should do with them. Tragically he died in 1963 at the early age of forty-nine.

Eleanor Hardy was the daughter of Sir William Bate Hardy, the very distinguished scientist, Fellow of Caius, who lived in a large Edwardian don's house at 5 Grange Road. I never met Sir William, who died in 1933, and we all did what we could do to comfort her and cheer Eleanor during the months when her father was dying. He had been a firm and loud protagonist of the admission of women to the University and during the famous vote of 1921, when he was Senior Tutor of Caius, had hung a banner across from the main building of Caius to St Michael's Court bearing the words 'Cambridge expects every man this day to do his duty.' Sir William Ridgway is reported to have said angrily to its originator, 'I suppose you expect them to come to you saying, "Kiss me Hardy".'

I got to know 5 Grange Road very well. Lady Hardy was the daughter of a former President of Queens' and lived in the thirties a modified version of the sort of Cambridge life so brilliantly portrayed by Gwen Raverat in that enchanting book *Period Piece*. She even had a companion secretary. I was invited to dinner and they were formal occasions. The food and wine were good: two faithful maids served us. The senior, Florence, became a great ally. On one occasion I was the only male present. When dinner was over and the ladies left, I made to follow them but Florence discreetly kept me back, put me to sit at the head of the table, and solemnly produced a decanter of port. There I sat for a quarter of an hour, a solitary owl in a boiled shirt, until she told me it was time to join the ladies. Sitting in the dining room alone I felt I had joined an earlier Cambridge. Lady Hardy was full of stories of her youth and her young married life. I have never ceased to repeat her tale of the curious behaviour of Sir William Pope, Professor of Chemistry. He and his wife gave weekly dinner parties beginning at 7.30 and, in accordance with their views, ending promptly at ten. If the guests showed no signs of going by ten he would leave the drawing room, returning in a few minutes dressed in a nightshirt and nightcap. Looking round the company he would say 'I don't know about you, Lady Pope, but I am going to bed. Goodnight all.'

Gradually I became more and more a part of the Hardy household, dining there once a week, acting as the male member of this matriarchal set-up and playing tennis every Sunday afternoon. Tennis took place not in the Hardy establishment but at the house of the Clays a few doors away. Richard Clay, a small precise man, was head of the printing firm at Bungay and was often difficult to deal with. On one Sunday afternoon, when I arrived early and the girls had not yet appeared, he took me out into the garden puffing a very long cigar. We had little to say to each other and I think he had a healthy distaste for undergraduates. 'It is cooler today,' he said to me, 'the pressure is dropping.' 'Oh, do you think so?' I replied. 'Young man', he said sharply, 'I don't *think* so, I have consulted my instruments.'

When I was in my first year as a research student Terence Powell and I planned an extensive field trip to Brittany, the Vendée and the Loire Valley to visit museums and study megaliths in the field. Eleanor Hardy said she would like to come with us, at least for the week in Brittany, and we, reluctantly, agreed. Her mother then announced that it was not proper that a young girl should travel alone in France with two young men. This was 1936 and we were all 22/23. She must be with us as a chaperon. Terence was in revolt: he had never cared for Lady Hardy – indeed there were very few people he unreservedly approved of. 'That old dragon is trying to get you married to her daughter,' he said. 'Don't fall for it.' Even more reluctantly, we agreed. Lady Hardy had travelled extensively: holidays in Switzerland and the north Italian lakes, scientific congresses with her husband in various parts of the world. But she disapproved of France and the French: dirty, unreliable and often indecent, she said.

We took the night-boat to St-Malo, the train to Rennes and the train on to Auray. I explained that they were to go to our hotel at Carnac but that Terence and I were getting out and going on a very long walk to see the famous *allée couverte* of Essé. I had carefully worked out our route and knew that we got out at a station curiously named Les Corps Nues. When we dismounted from the train Lady Hardy read the name. 'Disgusting,' she said, 'the French are immoral and filthy. I hope nothing strange happens to you on your walk.'

But when we got to Carnac later that day, very tired, she had a bottle of champagne waiting for us, and had ordered a specially good dinner. They had apparently lunched very well and her Francophobia was lessening. 'At least they are good on food and wine,' she said grudgingly.

Eleanor went to study in Sweden and my research kept me travelling all over England and Wales, and to France and Portugal.

The Hardy connection weakened. Then when I became a Fellow and the war came it virtually ceased. Eleanor Hardy married Basil Megaw and they were most happy together while he was in the Isle of Man and then Director of the School of Scottish Studies in Edinburgh, until she died suddenly of a massive heart attack. But the Hardy connection, while it lasted, was lovely: I valued it enormously and in retrospect it gave me a kind of second home in Cambridge and a place away from the College.

Jacquetta Hawkes – 'La Belle Jacquette' as she is often and affectionately called – was not my year. She was an undergraduate generation before me but had been at the Perse Girls' School with Eleanor Hardy and was a kind of legend at school and at Newnham. She was then Jacquetta Hopkins and I often saw her distinguished father, Sir Frederick Gowland Hopkins OM, walking through St John's and along Trinity Street. I did not know her until she had married Christopher Hawkes in 1933: our friendship grew over the years, and after her second marriage to J.B. Priestley my wife and I stayed with them at Alveston and often lunched there. She is a valued member of the Antiquity Trust and I have always admired how, never having had an archaeological job, she has maintained an up-to-date and stimulating approach to the subject, while also achieving a career as a creative writer. Her remark, 'Every generation has the Stonehenge it deserves and wants' has passed into archaeological parlance. Her portrait of Sir Mortimer Wheeler is a sympathetic and distinguished work of biography. She always dressed in a distinctive and arresting way and the hats of La Belle Jacquette were for very long a feature of the archaeological and literary world, as indeed they were of the Aldermaston marches!

Toty de Navarro was an exciting, inspiring, but very exacting teacher. He had been a research Fellow of Trinity in the early twenties: indeed the first Roman Catholic Fellow since the Reformation, and when his Fellowship ran out he had been allowed to stay on in a set of rooms in Nevile's Court. Here he gave his lectures at 5 p.m. two evenings a week. We sat round a table piled high with books and he read out to us, at slightly faster than dictation speed, a wonderful account of the Bronze and Iron Age in Europe distilled from his notes and brought up to date by his constant reading. But he never showed us pictures: there were never any lantern slides, just constant references to illustrations in other books, such as Ebert V, 946. This was Ebert's *Realexikon der Vorgeschichte* which was not readily available to us in our college libraries. I went to his course twice, checking and improving my notes in the second year: I was often in despair in the first year – it was all so detailed and it was assumed I knew exactly what was meant by Montelius IV and Reinecke B. We were taught to very high standards – no harm, but very hard going at the time. But often during the first time I went to his course I walked back to my rooms in St John's, crossing Trinity Great Court in darkness and fog, wondering whether this kind of archaeology was for me.

The great thing about de Navarro was his integrity, devotion and scholarship. He himself wrote little and found writing difficult. He was a perfectionist in writing and lecturing – not that he ever really lectured. He just read out his text around the table. As the Cambridge fogs retreated and spring came to the Backs and the Tripos examinations got nearer he found that to cover the ground he had to lecture more frequently. We had morning lectures: and at the end of one a most startling episode occurred. He was distinctly prudish and we were all puzzled when he kept referring to the River Padus because he did not want to use the word Po in lectures to a mixed audience! He was hoist by his own petard when just about lunchtime on a late May morning in 1935, while he was finishing his lecture, there burst rumbustiously into his rooms Adolf Mahr, head of the National Museum of Antiquities in Ireland. We were all introduced to the great man who puffed clouds of cigar smoke over us. Then Toty said, 'My lecture will be over in a few minutes and I shall take you in to lunch in the Combination Room. What would you like to do in the afternoon? Would you like to talk to some of my students?' He waved a hand around the room. Then came the crash. 'No,' said Adolf, 'I would like to go for a walk to Grantchester as we did last year and see the students fucking in the meadows and in their punts.' Toty was taken aback and we were hastily pushed out of his rooms, rapidly filling with cigar smoke, where no doubt a gentle lecture on English usage took place.

I told this story after the war to a party of Irish friends: they laughed but seemed embarrassed. Then Sean Ó Ríordáin confessed that he and Brian O'Kelly were so infuriated about the appointment of the German, Mahr, as their Director of Antiquities over the head of many suitable Irish and British candidates that they decided to play a wicked trick on him. He had asked that they should teach him a simple Irish phrase which he could use conversationally with Irish speakers he met after wishing them good day and enquiring about their health. They taught him a short phrase and carefully rehearsed him until he was word perfect, but Mahr was constantly surprised at the reception this phrase got and wondered if his accent was at fault. Not at all. The phrase he had been taught was, 'Have you fucked your grandmother recently?'

I next met Adolf Mahr in Dublin and he took me out to a very good lunch in the Hibernian. During lunch, when we were talking about Irish archaeology, he suddenly had qualms about me. The name Daniel puzzled and annoyed him. 'Excuse me,' he said, 'perhaps an impertinent question. Are you a Jew?' I explained to him how Welsh people had surnames which were Christian names and he was reassured. I did not know then – how should I? – that he was an agent of the German government and was to be Gauleiter of Ireland when the Nazis had conquered the British Isles.

José Maria de Navarro (he was always Toty because this was his childhood way of saying his name) was a man who inspired devotion and gave generously of his friendship and learning. A wealthy American, he was a third generation Basque immigrant. His grandfather, we were told, was largely involved in building the New York Elevated Railroad and the first block of flats in the Big Apple – there was until recently a De Navarro 'Hotel' of luxury apartments on the south side of Central Park. His father was married to the famed beauty and actress, Mary Anderson, and they settled in England, living in the very lovely Cotswold house called Court Farm at Broadway.

Here Mary created a salon of literary, musical and stage friends including Barrie, Elgar, Gerald Finzi, Howard Ferguson and many another. The main drawing room in Court Farm was large, looking out on beautiful gardens; it had two grand pianos. On one occasion Mary asked Elgar to play the piano for her. He refused. 'I only play the organ in public where I cannot be seen.' When he next visited the de Navarros he found that an organ had been installed on the gallery.

I often stayed in Court Farm to my great delight. It was my first experience of being in an expensive luxurious establishment with servants. My meagre clothing and toiletries were carefully unpacked and stowed away and when I told my mother I noticed that, without further comment, on future occasions I travelled to Broadway with a larger suitcase beautifully packed with all my best clothes. I well remember my first Broadway visit. I was met at the station by a very large car with a chauffeur and footman who sat me in the back of the car and wrapped a rug around my legs. When we got to Court Farm he unpacked me and assisted me to the front door. It was a dark January evening: suddenly out of the gloom a lady rushed across the road and embraced me. 'Toty, dear,' she said, 'how are you? Haven't seen you for so long!' Then she realized her error – Toty and I were about the same size, his a Basque figure, mine a Breton-Welsh – and fled. Shaken, I went into the house. 'I will deal with your bag,' said the footman. 'Madame suggested you should go straight into tea. There is company.' I straightened my tie, opened the door shewn to me and fell down two steps into a room full of people sitting round a long tea-table. Collecting myself and trying to hide my embarrassment I looked up straight into the familiar and much adored face of George Arliss. He clapped his monocle into his eye and said kindly, 'Good afternoon, I hope you haven't hurt yourself. Madame is waiting to welcome you.'

I think she was very proud of her son's academic prowess and scholarly distinction and thought his pupils were cute and worth encouraging. On another occasion I was travelling with Martin Charlesworth, President of St John's, from Cambridge to South Wales. I was then a research student and we called in at Court Farm on our way west. 'Madame is unwell,' we were told, 'and confined to her room but she would like to see you for a few moments.' We were taken to the foot of a wide staircase. Mary Anderson appeared at the head of the staircase supported by a maid. 'Welcome,' she said, 'you college boys mean a lot to me,' and the interview was over.

I think Toty was dominated, if not frightened, by his mother who was a very forceful character. He certainly did not marry until after her death and then to his gifted colleague, Dorothy Hoare, who survives him, living in Court Farm. During every winter his mother spent some weeks in the Grand Hotel at Ostend and our lectures on Friday evenings had to be cut short so that a taxi could take Toty to catch the Ostend night boat.

His mother once embarrassed Toty by asking if he could arrange a meeting with A.E. Housman, whom he knew well as a Fellow of Trinity where Housman often exercised his sharp tongue on his colleagues. Toty thought it might be a disaster, a meeting between his dominating, tuft-hunting mother and the fame-shirking Housman.

But she longed to meet the author of *A Shropshire Lad* and it had to happen. Housman agreed, and a lunch was arranged in de Navarro's rooms in Trinity: he was, understandably, dreading the occasion when the famous actress would first confront the famous scholar-poet. He could hardly believe his ears when, after effecting the introduction he heard his mother say to Housman. 'Delighted to meet you, Mr Housman. I so seldom come to Cambridge: I live in the Cotswolds, looking out over Bredon and the Malverns. I wonder if you know that part of the world?' There was a cold silence, then at last Housman smiled. 'I used to,' he said, and they became friends.

I did not know A.E. Housman, but I often saw him in Cambridge. He used to go for a walk most afternoons from his rooms in Whewell's Court along the Backs of the colleges, and almost always returned through St John's. It was this daily walk that caused an outburst at T.R. Glover, whom he did not like. They were joint examiners for some prize essay and Glover, meaning to be helpful, said to Housman, 'Don't bother to put it in the post when you have read it: just drop it in my rooms as you pass through St John's on your afternoon walk.' Housman – so Glover told me – was furious. 'How dare you make such a suggestion!' he said. 'You have been spying on me. My private life is my own affair.' And he sent the essay through the post!

De Navarro was a splendid mimic and a born raconteur. He and S.C. Roberts of the University Press, later Master of Pembroke, used to vie with each other in giving the most realistic imitations of H.M. Chadwick. 'Chadders' for the greater part of his life left his dealings with the University Press to de Navarro and S.C. Roberts: and all the years that the Press was publishing the great three-volume work *The Growth of Literature* by Chadwick and his wife Nora the business was conducted by them, often pretending to be Chadwick, so that H.M.C. was for many years a legendary figure in the Press. Then, one day, to everyone's consternation, Chadders decided without warning to visit the Press. Shyly he went into the main editorial office and said nervously, 'I'm Chadwick. I've just called to see how my *Growth* is getting on.' The apparition of reality was too much for the sober editors who stared in amazement, burst into laughter or fled from the room. 'Curious chaps you have working for you,' he said later to S.C. Roberts. 'Are you sure they are all right in the head?'

I wish I had noted down at the time some of the de Navarro stories, but a few I have never forgotten. There was a Fellow of Trinity called

Glaisher who collected porcelain figures and whose collection is now in the Fitzwilliam. Many were displayed in his rooms: one was of a male figure with erect penis. One morning he noticed that his bedmaker had turned it round so that the offending organ could not be seen. Glaisher set it to rights but next morning it had been turned round again. Glaisher set it to rights and told himself I must mention this business to my bedmaker. But he didn't, and every morning of his long life the strange ritual went on. When she arrived in the morning the bedmaker saw that the offending organ was turned away from her gaze and later each morning Glaisher would turn it round so that it looked at him as he ate his breakfast. For thirty-odd years the subject was never mentioned between them. 'She was such a good bedmaker,' he said.

There was in the twenties and thirties a special bedmakers' service in Trinity Chapel once a year and Toty used to tell the story of a Dean of Chapel who had forgotten this in planning his service list. For the bedmakers' annual service he had mistakenly booked a learned Professor of Divinity and omitted to tell him the special nature of his congregation. He announced his text and not casting a glance at the sea of bonnets in front of him began, 'The ontological argument for the existence of the Deity has, I grant you, received but scant attention in recent years from the main exponents of Christian apologetics. . . .' As they crowded out later the bedmakers were heard to say, 'Wasn't he lovely?'

There was no formal college supervision in archaeology and anthropology in the thirties, but by a curious chance there were two Research Fellows of my own College in these subjects, namely Louis Leakey and Gregory Bateson, both now dead. Leakey was the legendary and famous discoverer of early man in East Africa. Gregory Bateson was the anthropologist who eventually became a professor in Stanford and Santa Cruz, California. On paper I was extremely lucky to be taught by two such remarkable men: in practice it was not always successful. Bateson's grandfather, W.H., had been Master of St John's from 1857–81: his father, another William Bateson, was the distinguished biologist, founder of 'genetics' – he coined the word – and defender and advocate of Mendel. William Bateson left Cambridge in 1910 to take up the directorship of the newly founded John Innes Horticultural Institution at Merton, Surrey. A Fellow of St John's from 1883, he lived at Merton House, Grantchester, which I visited frequently when Miles and Peggy Burkitt were living there. Bateson was once Steward of St John's and the story goes that he is responsible for St John's not having a letter box outside it as do most other Cambridge colleges (Trinity now has a sub-post office in lieu). The colleges had their own postal services and their own stamps. When this system was abolished the Government said they would supply pillar boxes for every college. One was set up outside St John's and infuriated William Bateson who gathered together a group of undergraduates, dug up the offending red object, and rolled it down Bridge Street into the river.

Genetically Gregory Bateson ought to have been brilliant if he inherited genes from his father and grandfather: and his aunt was the great historian Mary Bateson. All the anthropologists I trust tell me that he was brilliant and that his book *Naven* is one of the classics of social anthropology. I could not understand it and could not understand what he was trying to teach me: he was impatient of a young man who wanted to be an archaeologist. Archaeology was a form of constipation, he used to say: archaeologists have anal perversions, their bowels are stuffed with useless artifacts. They were not rewarding supervisions: he never asked me to write an essay or answered any of the questions helpfully, and he was outspokenly contemptuous of those who were teaching anthropology, Hodson and Driberg. Only Haddon he approved of. He killed my interest in social anthropology and made me intensely suspicious of that discipline, a suspicion which has been partially but not wholly allayed by my friendship with and respect for Evans-Pritchard, Meyer Fortes, Edmund Leach and Jack Goody. But I still hanker after the wide anthropological vision of E.B. Tylor.

Louis Leakey came up to St John's in curious circumstances and these, and the comical affair of his reading Kikuyu in the Modern and Medieval Languages Tripos Part I, have been well told by himself in the first volume of his autobiography, *White African* (1937), and by Sonia Cole in her perceptive, accurate and sympathetic biography of him entitled *Leakey's Luck* (1975). The story, at first sight extravagant, is quite true and personally confirmed to me by E.A. Benians who admitted Leakey and was his tutor. It is not true, as Oxford denigrators of Leakey used to say, that he actually examined himself in the Cambridge Tripos, and was then nick-named 'the Senior Wangler'.

He was an immensely inspiring and exciting supervisor: we met in his rooms in New Court in what were really archaeological store rooms: there was no furniture – we sat on crates and handled handaxes. He took us out into the country to see the flint mines at Brandon in Suffolk and the flint-knappers in the Flint Knappers' Arms. On one field visit we were being driven back at breakneck speed by my contemporary, James Stewart, now dead, who worked in Cyprus and was later a Professor in Australia. Louis, who was sitting in the back with me, leaned forward after a while and said, 'When the inevitable accident occurs, as it will do if you go on driving like this, could you see I am not killed? I have a great deal of important work to do in Africa.' We arrived back in Cambridge safely. Years later I talked to the flint-knappers in Brandon and they asked after Leakey. 'He could knap flints better than we could,' they said. 'Wonderful man.' And so he was, brilliant, impulsive, tireless, dedicated.

I was delighted when I got a First in Section A of the Archaeological and Anthropological Tripos, delighted and a little surprised. I was made a Scholar of my College which gave me very great pleasure. In the thirties, travelling scholarships or grants hardly existed and young men like myself with no money had no means of extending their vision of the present and past world. When Charlesworth, Gatty and Boys Smith – all Fellows of St John's – came back from a tour of France in the summer vacation of 1933 they not only introduced Poulet Belle Aurore to the College kitchens and organized the purchase of excellent white wines from north Burgundy, but decided that undergraduates should be encouraged to travel and experience the joys of *outre-mer*. The College offered two scholarships of £30 for undergraduates to travel. To my delight I was awarded one of them and I planned an archaeological tour of Brittany. When I mentioned what I was going to do, de Navarro asked shyly whether he could come with me. He wanted to see the Iron Age pottery in the Breton museums and had never been there. I was alarmed at the prospect of travelling abroad with a very rich man but, sensing my problem, he said, 'We will stay in reasonably cheap hotels and pay our own way except that during our week in Brittany I must be allowed to treat you to three special meals, entirely at my expense.' Relieved, and with the added prospect of those meals, I readily agreed. It turned out a memorable, and for my own future, a very important week.

I set out on my own from South Wales a few days before I was to meet Toty in St-Malo and spent some time in Wiltshire, seeing for the first time Avebury, Stonehenge, the West Kennet Long Barrow, Old Sarum, and the museums in Devizes and Salisbury. It is difficult now to recollect the tremendous excitement which a young man, already slightly affected by megaliths, experienced on his first visit to the prehistoric glories of Salisbury Plain. It was overwhelming, and I retired excited and exhausted to the Red Lion Hotel at Avebury to spend the night within a prehistoric monument. There I met Denys Haynes, a contemporary of mine in Cambridge, who was subsequently to have a distinguished career in the British Museum. We talked and drank well into the night.

With the magic of the megaliths and the glory of Salisbury Cathedral uplifting me I took a bus to Southampton and was in St-Malo the next morning: and at lunchtime was on the terrace of the Hôtel de Bretagne in Dol having made my *puja* in the Cathedral and lit a candle to St Samson. I was sitting behind the discreet box hedge that delimited the café restaurant when, with a screeching of brakes, a car drew up and an old lady jumped out and advanced on me: 'Où se trouve les lavabos? J'ai besoin immédiatement.' My French was not very good; it was a curious question; she looked a very forbidding old harpy, and I didn't know where the lavatories were! I stammered and stuttered. 'Imbécile!' she said, waving a minatory umbrella at me and rushed into the hotel. As she flounced out five minutes later she gave me a disapproving glance.

I met Toty's boat next morning at St-Malo and we took the train to St-Brieuc. He had told A.E. Housman of his proposed trip to France and Housman had looked in that famous little red book that contained, among other entries, the names of the great restaurants which he had visited and approved of. Despite his ascetic appearance Housman was a great gastronome (verging on a gastrobore or gastrosnob). Grant Richards has given a fine account of their gastronomic tours in France and I was to discover later that the Tour d'Argent in Paris had named a dish after him. (This was *Barbue Housman*: the recipe was obtained from J. Hunt, General Secretary of the Housman Society, by Richard Perceval Graves, who prints it in a footnote in Chapter 8 of his fine book, *A.E. Housman: the scholar-poet*, published in 1981.) He would apparently fly from Cambridge to Paris for lunch (Maxim's was his favourite although surely Lucas-Carton with its Edwardian splendours would have been more to his taste?)

79

and dine that evening at High Table in Trinity muttering, no doubt with truth, 'This is not a patch on my lunch in Paris today.'

I tell this story because I have been told it by several Trinity dons over the last fifty years since Housman died. In the *News Chronicle* on 2 May 1936 Philip Jordan wrote: 'In the early days of air transport he was known to fly to Paris and back in order to enjoy the pleasures of a lunch at Laperouse or Marguery's, his two favourite restaurants.' Grant Richards, in his *Housman 1897–1936*, says (p. 43): 'No, he never did that; and these were not among his favourite haunts.' But later in the same paragraph he quotes Jordan as saying that Housman had 'a sweet temper and generosity to which time and old age could do no hurt' and adds, 'Jordan is a good witness'. Grant Richards's memory often failed him: he and Housman had quite different views of when they first met each other.

The little red book said that there was only one restaurant in Brittany worth visiting and must not be missed. It was the Hôtel Moderne at St-Brieuc. So, having clocked in at the Hôtel de la Gare at St-Brieuc and visited the museum, we prepared for our feast in the Hôtel Moderne and were ready to tell the Shropshire lad what a magnificent meal we had had. Armed with a very old *Guide Michelin* which I had bought for a few pence from David's bookstall in Cambridge, I navigated us to the spot marked Hôtel Moderne on the plan. Alas, it had been closed for three years! We retraced our steps and ate very well indeed, by my standards, in the Hôtel de la Gare.

We travelled around Brittany staying at Morlaix and Saint-Guénolé and Quimper. At Morlaix Toty wanted to draw a Celtic decorated pot in the museum. Alas, the case could not be opened without the permission of M. le Maire who had its key and he was away attending a reception at a girls' school. Would we come back in the afternoon? Meanwhile of course we were welcome to inspect the collections safely behind glass. It was after we had been in the gallery for about half an hour that I discovered the cases were not locked. We took out the famous pot and Toty drew it. We replaced it and went off to lunch assuring the elderly concierge that we would return another day. It was the first of my many experiences in the next forty years of the vagaries of small French provincial museums.

At Saint-Guénolé we had the first de Navarro special meal and my first *dégustation de fruits de mer*. I ploughed my way through the lot, from oysters and mussels and clams to crab and lobster. And it was also, as far as I can recollect, my first tasting of Muscadet-sur-lie.

When we got to Carnac we stayed at the Hôtel Tumulus de Saint-Michel which was run by the daughter of the famed Breton archaeologist Zacharie Le Rouzic. We had five delightful days there. I went off seeing megaliths every day in the great heat of the early summer of 1934 and came back footsore and thirsty. I walked the alignments from end to end. I took the bus to Locmariaquer and saw all the preposterous and magnificent megaliths there, and we both took the boat out into the Morbihan to see the wonderfully decorated tomb on the island of Gavrinis: surely one of the seven wonders of the prehistoric European world. I lived in a heaven of megalithic sunshine and good food.

Every night after dinner we walked down through the pine woods to the beach and swam naked in the waters of the Golfe du Morbihan in the dark. On one occasion we were mutually confused about where we had left our clothes on the beach and for several minutes were inconvenienced by struggling mistakenly into each other's garments. Properly dressed, we walked back through the pine trees, the paths edged by glow worms.

Toty's French was excellent and my schoolboy French began to improve under his guidance and the necessity of dealing alone in the countryside looking for dolmens. He was kind in pointing out my mistakes. 'You were surprised last night,' he said, 'when you came back from our walk to the sea and there was a sudden silence when you said, instead of what you had intended to say, namely, "I love the smell of the pines," "I love the smell of penises."'

I went back to South Wales in a haze: I knew that I was going to study megalithic monuments for as long as I could, that I was fascinated by France and its archaeology, and I took home with me the excitement of my first travels in France, the knowledge that I could speak to people, that I was for ever devoted to the Carnac-Locmariaquer area of the Morbihan, the smell of the pines and the taste of my first lobster.

During the year I had realized that I was no longer a human geographer but wished to become an archaeologist. I discovered what was then called Section B of the Archaeological and Anthropological Tripos and decided to take this difficult course. I went home to Wales to prepare for what I thought would be the greatest test of my undergraduate career, and it was.

In my third year I found myself moving, with some difficulty, into real scholarship. That year was the hardest of my student life: the standards of scholarship were so demanding – one was expected to be able to read Old Welsh, Norse, Anglo-Saxon, Latin, French and German. Dorothy Whitelock, who eventually succeeded H.M. Chadwick at two removes – Bruce Dickins was in between – used to tell a story of how when she was being supervised by H.M.C., and coping already with Anglo-Saxon, Old Norse, Latin, German and French, she was recommended by him to read a special book. 'But Professor Chadwick,' she said, 'this book is in Danish.' 'I don't think the Danish language will give you much trouble,' he said kindly.

Chadwick had created what generations of devoted students have always referred to as Section B. It was a brilliant amalgam of prehistoric and protohistoric studies. He himself had come up as a Classic, but late one evening in the Clare College Library had found a copy of Du Chaillu's *The Viking Age*, and on reading it his life was changed. He moved from the study of Greece and Rome to the study of the *barbaroi* and eventually organized the university course which he sometimes called 'the Classics of the North'. He had in front of him a brilliant career as a Classics don: instead he became Elrington and Bosworth Professor of Anglo Saxon. His was a small department which did not teach in university lecture rooms. Chadwick himself taught two mornings a week in his room in Clare College, and then two evenings a week in his house which was the Papermills out, far out, on the Newmarket Road, beyond the Lepers' chapel, behind, and indeed physically attached to a pub, the Globe.

We students caught the bus outside the Pitt Club and trundled out the two miles to The Papermills. There were only three of us – Grace Thornton, myself, and a shy young first-year undergraduate called T.G.E. Powell. After several journeys back and forth in the bus, Grace, with her usual frankness, firmness and ebullience said to the young man, 'You must tell us your name. We cannot go on calling you Powell, or Mr Powell. My name is Grace and this is Glyn.' He blushed and turned away. Obviously his schooldays at Cheltenham had not prepared him for Grace and me. After a while I said: 'Mr Powell is an Irishman, obviously the T stands for Terence, and if he does not deny this we shall call him Terence.' And thus it was that Thomas George Eyre Powell, later to be President of the Prehistoric Society and Professor of Archaeology at Liverpool, author of *The Celts* and

Prehistoric European Art, was christened or re-christened on the top deck of a bus, and was so known from then on by the world and by his family.

To be taught by and to get to know well Hector Munro Chadwick was one of the most wonderful experiences in my life. He was the greatest scholar I have ever met, and one of the most remarkable characters. The stories about him are legion and, surprisingly enough, true. He was to me a scholar-father figure. Several people, including his dear wife, Nora, have told me that I was his favourite pupil. I was certainly not his most brilliant pupil – that accolade must go to J.M. de Navarro, Hugh Hencken or Kenneth Jackson. Somehow we became scholarly friends, how I do not know, except that I was avid to learn and he was anxious to teach. If there is one thing in university life (and Oxbridge often does it to perfection) that is beyond all thinking, planning and money, it is the meeting of minds and particularly the easy meeting of the established scholar and the uncertain questing young non-scholar.

We talk a great deal these days about 'charisma' and apply the term to men with positive outgoing dynamic and dramatic powers of attraction and communication like Winston Churchill, General de Gaulle, Nye Bevan, and I suppose in the field of archaeological scholarship, Mortimer Wheeler. Chadwick's charisma was quiet and intimate, but none the less equally compelling. His study in The Papermills was stacked to the ceiling with books, and piles of books covered the floor. The room was furnished with easy chairs and sofas, most of which had their springs broken long ago – except for two chairs, in one of which the great man sat, and the other and more comfortable in which sat a big black Labrador dog called Grendel.

Chadders was always dressed in a green Norfolk jacket and knickerbockers. His wife, Nora, appeared only when he illustrated his lectures with lantern slides. She worked the lantern and let down a sheet above the fireplace. The lantern was invariably at first on the wrong level and to cries from Chadders of 'Jack it up a little, please,' was brought into a proper position with the help of Icelandic dictionaries.

He taught us Early Britain as he understood it. The Palaeolithic he would have no truck with, dismissing it as unhistoric. He had never visited the Franco-Cantabrian caves and come under the spell of Font-de-Gaume and Altamira: and he disliked and distrusted Miles

Burkitt. Leakey he had never met and never wanted to meet. 'Sounds to me a flashy man,' he once said to me, 'a kind of Mortimer Wheeler.' His archaeology began with the Neolithic and went firmly on through the Celts and Roman Britain to the Anglo-Saxons and the Vikings, ending with the Norman Conquest. And here I found a coherence in my interests in the past. The history I learnt at school had begun with the Normans: my geology at Cardiff ended in the Pleistocene with the first men. Burkitt and Leakey bridged the gap from geology to the Neolithic. Chadders made the bridge from the Neolithic to the Normans. His main teaching was based extensively on non-archaeological sources: we read Tacitus and Bede, Procopius and St-Germanus, the *Mabinogion* and the *Flattyjarbök*. He showed us that we were not just archaeologists but general students of antiquity and ancient history. He himself was primarily a linguist, and an historical and literary scholar; he mildly expected us to read everything from Greek and German and Gothic, from *Beowulf* to Cyndellan. Like another great scholar but in the strict field of archaeology, Vere Gordon Childe, he regarded language as no barrier. Both these great men thought their students ought to have no difficulty in all the main Indo-European languages.

Section B has now been transformed into the Anglo-Saxon, Norse and Celtic Tripos and is still one of the inspired glories of the Cambridge educational system on the side of the humanities.

With such excellent teachers as Chadwick himself, Kenneth Jackson, J.M. de Navarro, Dorothy Hoare, and T.C. Lethbridge I ought to have done well. I had three special and perhaps unfair advantages: I had done Anglo-Saxon at school and knew *Beowulf* virtually by heart; I spoke and read Welsh already and early Welsh was not remarkably different from the language of today; but thirdly I was allowed to submit a dissertation in lieu of one paper and I wrote an account of the Vale of Glamorgan from 2500 BC to the Roman Conquest.

When the results of the examination were published it was a very odd Tripos list. It contained only two names: Grace Thornton had a first and I had a starred first. We both went on to do research but the war found Grace in the Foreign Office and she remained there until her retirement. She was Petty Minister in Iceland during the war, did many years service in Denmark, and ended up as head of the Consular Service in the Foreign Office. She could have been our first female ambassador and Principal of Newnham but time and chance ruled otherwise.

After taking my degree and embarking on megalithic researches, Chadwick said shyly, 'I hope we won't lose contact,' and once a week when I was resident in Cambridge I went out to see him after Hall, and we talked about everything. There would always be an enormous pot of tea. I can see myself, in my mind's eye, sitting with my notebook on my knee in a rather smelly chair with two dogs around me, asking some fairly reasonable question: 'Oh, don't you know? don't you know?' the old man would say, jumping up from his chair and finding a book from his shelves and explaining a passage in some Latin author or Old Norse saga.

The last bus would almost always have gone and I walked back the couple of miles to St John's. Once it was after midnight when I returned to College and had to be reported to my tutor. James Wordie listened to my explanation and when I had left him, wrote a note to the head porter saying I could come in at any time I liked! It was on one of those late-night walks back from The Papermills that I saw the wall of Sidney Sussex College in Jesus Lane sway back and forth and a cold rushing wind blew down the street. But I've only drunk tea, I thought. It was next morning I learnt there had been a slight earthquake in East Anglia.

Chadwick was a man concerned with the antiquity of man in its entirety, or at least in post-Palaeolithic antiquity. He himself never made any break between a past based on literary sources and one based on archaeological sources. His field was the ancient history of northern and north-western Europe. He was not an archaeologist in the sense that he ever practised the main craft of the archaeologist, namely excavation: but he read excavation reports with care and discrimination, and was a very keen field archaeologist in the sense that he liked visiting field monuments from Bryn Celli Ddu in Anglesey to Graine in Aileach in Ulster and Maes Howe in the Orkneys. When the Sutton Hoo ship-burial was discovered in the late summer of 1939 he and Nora and I drove over to Woodbridge and were shown the excavations by Charles Phillips. 'It's the grave of Redwald,' he said on the way home, and wrote to that effect in the special number of *Antiquity* which Crawford devoted in 1940 to this fantastic discovery.

Chadders had a great, if private, sense of humour. When he was setting Tripos papers with Toty de Navarro he suggested they might meet one afternoon halfway between Trinity College and the Papermills. 'Where do you have in mind?' asked de Navarro. 'There is a little house in the middle of Midsummer Common,' said Chadders. 'Let's meet there.' With strange misgivings de Navarro found the only 'house' on Midsummer Common was a public shelter backed by lavatories. He sat there nervously until he saw the green Norfolk jacketed and knickerbockered figure of H.M.C. coming across the Common. 'Ah, there you are,' said the great man, unfolding his file of papers. 'Splendid! I don't expect many Tripos papers have been set in public lavatories before, do you?'

When Nora was not free to ferry him to and fro from Clare to The Papermills he took the bus from Jesus Lane, and at the stop outside the Pitt Club he constantly met a strange person who fascinated him. They sat side by side in the front of the top deck of the bus, and after several days the strange person said to H.M.C. 'I heard the bus conductor call you professor. I'm a professor myself: we ought to get to know each other.' Chadders always had a curious view of his colleagues and was prepared for anything from this co-traveller. 'What's your subject?' he asked. The answer was surprising. 'I'm a professor of palmistry,' he said. 'Anywhere near your line of business?' Chadders was never unkind: 'I told him,' he said to me years after this event, 'that I didn't read hands but what peoples' hands had written hundreds of years ago. He shook me warmly by the hand and said, "Then we are professional colleagues."' It was then he decided to go home by taxi.

In his sixties, as was only natural, his eyesight began to fail and Nora, with great difficulty, got him to an oculist. The appointment had been booked in the name of Mr H.M. Chadwick of The Papermills. Reluctantly he went through all the tests and was relieved when he was told that there was nothing very much the matter with his eyes, but some corrective spectacles were to be prescribed. 'Do you do much reading?' the oculist asked the Elrington and Bosworth Professor of Anglo-Saxon. Chadders decided to play the game. 'Oh yes,' he said, 'I read the evening paper on a Saturday night.'

The most famous Chadwick story, first told me by de Navarro and confirmed by Maureen O'Reilly and Cyril Fox, concerns the false teeth. Before he married and went to live in The Papermills, Chadwick lived with his mother in a house in Station Road with a garden fronting on the street, bounded by a low wall. Late one summer's evening he was holding a class in the garden: the class included Cyril Fox and Maureen O'Reilly, both mature students. Next morning Chadwick went to tidy up the table and chairs in the garden. Underneath one of them was a pair of false teeth probably vomited there by a drunk the night before. Chadwick carefully collected them, packed them in his handkerchief, and took them with him to the Museum in Downing Street. He was sure they belonged to Maureen or Cyril, so both were subjected to visits from H.M.C. who, putting his head shyly round the door of their rooms and making clacking gestures with his hand, asked them if they had lost anything. 'Are you sure you haven't lost anything very valuable and useful?' he said to Fox, and departed, disappointed, leaving behind a more than usually bewildered pupil already aware of his professor's eccentricities.

Chadwick travelled very little abroad but he once related to me a visit he made to France and Switzerland (and then in a curious way to North Italy) with his brother when he was a young man. He had only schoolboy French and no sense of pronunciation: 'The French were not helpful to a nervous foreigner,' he said. 'I went into a Post Office to buy four stamps. "Quatty timbers," I kept saying to the man at the desk but he didn't seem to understand.' Their destination was a *pension* in Lausanne but the very first night at table he moved round sharply and knocked a dish of ice-pudding all over a woman next to him. Embarrassed and humiliated he left the room as he thought in disgrace: packed his bag and caught the train to Milan and booked a room near the station to await the arrival of his brother who would have made all the excuses for him. He went to a small restaurant, and had a meal and said, as he had been told, *vino di casa*. A large flask of red wine appeared: he began to relax and enjoy himself. He went on to La Scala and sat on a wall looking at the opera house. 'I felt a little peculiar,' he said, 'so I began to count the windows of the opera house. I counted and counted and could never get them to the same number. Then, Daniel, I realized I was a foolish young Yorkshireman, alone, in a foreign country, and for the first time in my life, slightly drunk.'

Apart from my tutor, James Wordie, and my College supervisors, Leakey and Bateson, there were two Fellows of the College who, in my undergraduate days, befriended me and many others of my generation, to my eternal benefit and pleasure. They were Martin Charlesworth and Hugo Gatty, and these undergraduate friendships were strengthened when I became a Fellow in 1938. John Boys Smith, then Chaplain and tutor, was another, and I played squash with him regularly.

Martin Charlesworth was born in the Wirral in 1895, went as an undergraduate to Jesus College, then to the Graduate College at Princeton and came to us as a teaching Fellow, largely on the advice of T.R. Glover. He had gained all the classes, prizes and awards that a top scholar was expected to do. I cannot do any better than quote from *The Times* obituary: 'He was the kind of bachelor don that forms the backbone of the college system. Gay and humorous, he carried his learning lightly and was always ready to entertain undergraduates in his rooms or colleagues in the Combination Room with good talk and anecdote. . . . His lectures enthralled his audiences, his presence ensured the success of any party . . . His ready sympathy and help were there for all in need. The help need not be requested. The knowledge that someone needed help was sufficient: Martin took it, offered it, and would not accept defeat.' I know of three contemporaries of mine who would never have achieved the brilliant careers they have done were it not for the faith, the steadying influence and the authority of Charlesworth.

Many a person has found his life reorientated through Martin's influence. I was certainly one. His breakfast parties were a constant delight, and I became a sort of maître d'hôtel of these occasions. In those days of the thirties the food was brought up from the kitchens by porters balancing large green-baize-covered trays on their heads. The standard breakfast fare was scrambled eggs and bacon with sausages, kidneys and mushrooms. Martin introduced kedgeree to the College, but always thought it was too dry as the kitchens made it, and I always had to produce a dish of butter melted over a gas-ring in his gyp room. 'That's better,' he would say as he poured the hot butter over the kedgeree.

Undergraduates, slightly embarrassed but appreciative of his hospitality, used to ask him to their own breakfast parties. 'Not a moment later than 7.45,' he would say, 'when I come out from chapel: we must all be at our desks or lectures by 9 o'clock.' Deryck Williams, now Professor Emeritus of Classics at Reading, arranged a special breakfast party for his 21st birthday. Martin and I and several others were there, and all went well except that the coffee, brought up from the kitchens, was most unusual. No one would have commented but

Martin broke into helpless laughter. 'What can this hell-broth be?' he said, and we all trooped down to the kitchens to discover that a sleepy cook had poured coffee grounds into a saucepanful of mulligatawny soup left over from the previous night's dinner.

His classical interests included Roman Britain: he was devoted to walking along Hadrian's Wall and his Gregynog lectures at Aberystwyth, *The Lost Province*, were a remarkable contribution to Romano-British studies. He was also fascinated by the pre-Roman scene, and we drove together one Easter vacation to Wales and past Avebury, Silbury Hill and Stonehenge to stay with my parents, and to look at the National Museum of Wales and the field antiquities of Glamorgan.

When we were back in Cambridge next term he said, 'James Wordie says you are putting in for a Fellowship. Do all you can. Redouble your efforts. We are always unhappy with people who get their Fellowships at the second or third try. Make a job of it.'

To my surprise Martin took holy orders in 1940. He surprised many who were taken in by his lightness and gaiety of manner, his passion for Gilbert and Sullivan, his brilliant extemporizations of settings for the Bab Ballads or Cautionary Tales. I had long ago discovered his firm beliefs and his devotion to the ideals and practice of the Christian faith but was still taken aback by the ultimate step.

To quote *The Times* obituary again: 'On his College, on the University, and on many other bodies Charlesworth left a clear mark: and many will mourn the untimely death not only of one who might have made further contributions to the cause of classical scholarship but of one whose companionship gave joy to a multitude of friends and pupils.'

He certainly gave great joy to me and many of my friends. The Sunday before our Tripos examination began he and several other dons organized a cavalcade of cars and we drove out into the country for lunch. 'Not too much drink,' he would be heard saying, 'and remember we must all be back, sober, for Evensong.'

When after the war I was made Steward of St John's he said to me, 'Is that really what you want to be? Shouldn't you be a tutor? Let me know when you want to be a tutor. Dear boy, I have high hopes of you and of the College. So many splendid people who could one day run the place: yourself, Ted Miller, Hrothgar Habakkuk, Frank Thistlethwaite, Kenneth Scott, Harry Hinsley. I am so excited.'

Martin died suddenly in 1950 in his fifty-fifth year. I have never forgotten that percipient conversation with him. Hrothgar Habakkuk became Principal of Jesus College, Oxford and Vice-Chancellor of the University; Frank Thistlethwaite created and ran successfully the University of East Anglia, Harry Hinsley became Master of St John's; and Ted Miller Master of Fitzwilliam. Habakkuk and Hinsley have both been knighted.

I was accepted as a Research Student in 1935 and began a survey of the chambered megalithic tombs of England and Wales. Regional surveys of some areas had already been made: Crawford's *Long Barrows of the Cotswolds* was a most notable pioneer effort and so was his *Neolithic Wessex*, and Hugh Hencken's *Archaeology of Cornwall and Scilly*.

I was being adequately financed by scholarships and studentships from St John's College and the State and was surprised when one day Chadwick said to me, 'You ought to put in for an Allen Studentship.' I knew nothing about this but soon discovered it was the top university scholarship. I felt that there was no hope for me but did as I was told and to my astonishment was awarded it. The Master sent for me and congratulated me warmly. 'It is thirty years since I was Allen Scholar,' he said, 'and when I was elected the Master sent for me and said, "You know, young Benians, that an Allen Scholarship is a kind of passport to a College Fellowship." He paused and added, "It was in my case and I hope it will be in yours."'

But it was an immediate passport to what seemed untold wealth, and in those days one was able to hold all awards concurrently without reduction, so that with college, state and university scholarships I was astonishingly well off. I set off on a tour of Western Europe to make a comparative study of the monuments I was listing and describing in southern Britain.

Ireland first, then Iberia, but the Spanish Civil War made a visit to Spain impossible. I set out from Tilbury to Lisbon and spent several weeks in Portugal, based partly in Lisbon and partly in Oporto. In Oporto, Hubert Jennings, the head of the firm of Sandeman, and the British Vice-Consul in the city, had insisted on my staying at his house. He met me at the railway station and said, 'Well, at least you don't smell.' The previous archaeologist he had received was Hubert Savory who had fallen foul of the police in North East Portugal because his *permis de séjour* had run out and he had been clapped in an insanitary prison cell for several days.

The Jennings household was a large and grand one. I got up early and breakfasted with Hubert Jennings. The sideboard in the dining room was filled with dishes of all kinds being kept warm on spirit stoves. There were several decanters nearby. 'A glass of sherry, my dear boy,' he said. 'I always think the day is well started with sherry – not too dry. You can have port or wine if you like but I prefer to wait until mid-morning before I start drinking port.' Every day he put a car and chauffeur at my disposal and we drove out with his daughter Marion and a cousin of hers to see archaeological sites, museums, churches, castles, the countryside. At lunchtime, in the heat of the day, rugs were spread under some trees and the chauffeur unpacked an enormous hamper, and after lunch there was a very generous glass of Directors' Bin Port. We slept quietly for a while, the nightingales singing above our heads, until it was time to resume our antiquarian travels. We were always back in time for a further rest and a bath before dinner.

In Lisbon I found Hubert Savory, who took me to all the right museums and restaurants, and to an extraordinary bar behind the theatre where they served a special aperitif designed by a famous clown. We drank many of these and tottered happily to little bistros and then home to our hotels. I learnt from him a very great deal about the prehistoric archaeology of Spain and Portugal that I could not find out from books and museums. I was delighted that when he left Oxford and joined the Museum staff at Cardiff where he was Assistant Keeper, then Keeper, of archaeology for twenty years, he maintained his interest in Iberian prehistory, and more than ever happy that when I invited him to write a volume in my *Ancient Peoples and Places* series, he readily agreed. *Spain and Portugal* (1968) is one of the best introductions to Iberian archaeology.

The journey out to Lisbon had been rough and I was sick in the Bay of Biscay, stayed in my bunk awhile and visited the practically empty dining saloons with difficulty and no enthusiasm. The menus seemed disgustingly extravagant. The journey back from Lisbon to Bordeaux was a delight, the food provided by the French chefs of the SS *Massilia* beyond reproach. We turned east into the Gironde: a few years later I was to identify on air photographs the same ship as a sunken wreck off the Pointe de Grave at the mouth of the Gironde. But by then we were at war. In 1937 I did not think of war, although many did. I travelled by Sud-Express to Paris and stayed a fortnight in the Hôtel Corneille spending my days in the Bibliothèque Nationale, the Musée de l'Homme, the Institut de Paléontologie Humaine, and, mainly, in the Musée des Antiquités Nationales at Saint-Germain-en-Laye.

The Hôtel Corneille had been recommended to me by Brian Wormald, and I soon found cheap restaurants with *prix fixe* student meals and learned to like yoghurt for the first time. My money was holding out well: I had two gastronomical treats. The first was in the Cochon de Lait next door to the Corneille – it is still there and still does suckling pig with kasha. The second was in Le Tour d'Argent: how curious it is to think now that in 1937 an, admittedly, well-financed research student, with the exchange rate as it was then, could eat in one of the best restaurants in Paris. I was most courteously received, given a table looking out over Nôtre Dame, told the Maître d'Hôtel why I was there and what I did. They suggested, and I agreed, an outstandingly fine meal: I have kept the bill. Towards the end of my meal a distinguished man in an electric-blue lounge suit came to me and, speaking in very good English, said he was interested I came from Cambridge. They had a faithful client from Cambridge, did I know him, 'C'est le Professeur Housman'. Then he said they had created a special dish in Housman's honour. He went away and brought back the recipe which is printed in English in Graves's biography of A.E.H.

I lingered over my coffee: Nôtre Dame was now floodlit. I paid my bill; and when the change came the waiter brought a large glass of brandy. 'With the compliments of M. Terrail,' he said.

I left Paris next day for St-Malo and met my mother in Jersey. We spent a happy week inspecting the antiquities of the Channel Islands, whose megalithic monuments are really part of prehistoric France. We returned to Wales and then I went back to Cambridge to write and complete my dissertation. Two copies in for PhD; two for the Fellowship. What a relief and anticlimax when all was in! Brian Wormald and I had taken our dissertations together to the Master's Lodge of St John's and delivered them to Benians.

A week later Brian called on me and said he had just collected his dissertation from Benians because he had been offered a Fellowship at Peterhouse. Hrothgar Habakkuk had been offered a teaching Fellowship at Pembroke. I began to be dispirited. What should I do if my luck didn't last? I began with little enthusiasm to read the notices of vacant jobs in the papers and was drafting out a curriculum vitae late one afternoon in early May when I heard steps hurrying up my staircase. It was Martin Charlesworth. 'Just to tell you you have been elected. You will dine at High Table tonight. Come to my rooms at seven. There will be champagne': and he was gone.

I collected my change, went down to the 'phone box in the JCR and telephoned my parents, who were delighted, and Miles Burkitt, who was guardedly so. I went round to Nevile's Court: Toty de Navarro was away – I left a note for him. I telephoned The Papermills: Chadders said, 'I have been expecting this news for some while. Come down and see me tonight.'

When I got to Charlesworth's rooms on that memorable evening in May 1938 there was a sallow, somewhat saturnine lantern-jawed young man who was Martin's guest. 'Meet John Enoch Powell,' he said, 'from next door.' 'Congratulations on your election to a Fellowship,' said Enoch. 'It is the real beginning of the climb up the academic ladder.' We talked about Wales and it was established that his family were Birmingham people although perhaps far back obviously Welsh. 'Will your ladder lead back to Wales?' he asked. 'I don't know,' I said. 'Where does yours go?' 'Well, in the first place to Australia: I've been elected to the Chair of Classics in Sydney. I shall enjoy being out of England. Then I shall come back. We may meet again here one day when I am Regius Professor of Greek and you are – he hesitated – "Disney Professor of Archaeology".'

After dinner in Hall, excited, exhausted but exhilarated, I took the bus down the Newmarket Road and was welcomed by H.M.C. and Nora. 'You're my tenth pupil to have been elected to a College Fellowship,' he said, 'now your real career is beginning.' When I got back to College I was congratulated by the porters. I paused as I walked through the Screens from First to Second Court and said to myself 'Good God, I'm a Fellow of the College,' and walked boldly across the grass to my rooms.

Next day Brian Wormald and Hrothgar Habakkuk took me out to lunch at the Bridge Hotel, Clayhithe. We sat before lunch on the lawn by the river drinking a glass of Chablis. 'These glasses must never be used again,' said Brian, and with three elegant gestures we threw them into the Cam. A waiter rushed out from the hotel. 'That will cost you three shillings each,' he said. I turned to him: 'It is worth it,' I said.

CHAPTER FOUR

Baby don and Pilot Officer

THE SUMMER OF 1938 was an immensely happy period. I was a Fellow, had taken my PhD, was planning to turn my dissertation into a book and I seemed to have plenty of money. I went on several visits to France and Ireland, and spent another delightful peaceful fortnight's holiday with my parents in central Wales. I was still living in my old undergraduate rooms but planned with John Cockcroft to turn them into a Fellow's set, which was beautifully done. The shadow of the next war was on many people: but not on me.

I began supervising in October 1938 and my first two pupils in St John's, reading archaeology and anthropology, were J.A. Barnes and P.H. Baldwin. They were most agreeable and diligent pupils and it was the very pleasantest of introductions to teaching: also they did very well, John Barnes getting a first and Philip Baldwin a very good 2.1. When the examinations were over I invited them to a special lunch in my rooms and planned it carefully with the College kitchens: it was a mousse of salmon, chaud-froid of chicken, *crème brûlée* and strawberries. Philip was in the Air Squadron and had been astonished when I told him I had never flown. He decided to take me up on a short flight on the morning of the lunch: it was a two-seater 'plane and I was decked out in a flying suit and strapped in behind him. We made a perfect take-off from Marshalls and were soon over the Fens. 'What would you especially like to see?' he asked on the intercom, and I replied, 'the length of the Devil's Dyke from Reach southwards, and Ely Cathedral.' The view was fascinating. 'Now home,' he said, 'and I'll show you some tricks.' From then on it was hell, we looped the loop, dived, banked, rolled: it was worse than being in the most violent machine on a fairground. 'Are you all right?' he asked. 'No,' I said, 'let's land at once. I am being sick in your flying suit.' I got back to my rooms with difficulty and lay groaning on my sofa looking with repulsion and disgust as they gobbled up my lovely lunch.

They both had very successful careers. John Barnes was elected a Research Fellow of St John's and became a Professor of Anthropology

94

in Australia in 1956 and worked there until he came back to Cambridge as the first Professor of Sociology in 1969. Philip Baldwin had put in for the Foreign Service and the RAF, and in the mounting tension of 1939 told both he would accept whoever offered him a job first. The RAF were quicker off the mark and he had a distinguished flying career ending up as a Group Captain Air Attaché in Spain and Portugal. By the fortune of war, he arrived one day in my office in Delhi, saluted smartly and said, 'Squadron Leader Baldwin presents his compliments to Wing Commander Daniel.'

I had two further adventures in the air with him. He had come back to Cambridge after the war to be CO of the University Air Squadron. He suggested that we should fly to France for a weekend and this we did. He cleared customs at Lydd and as we took off, Ruth, who was sitting by his side in front, saw the sweat pouring down his face. I noticed that we were practically in a belt of trees. 'Thank God we made it,' he said, but as we set out on our return flight from Le Touquet he made Ruth, the lighter parcel, sit in the tail. In addition a great wind had sprung up in Le Touquet and I was instructed by Philip to run along at take-off clutching one wing of the aircraft, after which I was allowed to jump in somewhat exhausted, if not alarmed. A few months later he asked me to go on another flight with him to the Isles of Scilly and said I could chart the route from Cambridge so that I could see from the air anything I wanted, including military sites. It was an irresistible offer and we had a fascinating journey. The landing at St Mary's seemed to bring us very close to the far edge of the airstrip. 'Good,' said Philip, 'we made it. I want to bring the Air Squadron here for an exercise and I wanted to know whether this aircraft could land here!'

When I was elected a Fellow of St John's in 1938 there were 38 of us and it was fairly easy to get to know everyone, if not well, at least on speaking terms. I was warned however that there were one or two difficult Fellows and was briefed about internecine strifes: after their dispute about fish at High Table, Harker did not speak to Briggs, and T.R. Glover did not speak to H.A. Harris, Glover mistakenly thinking that Harry was a foul-mouthed obscene atheist. Martin Charlesworth told me that I should have difficulties with Paul Dirac. 'You may find yourself sitting next to him at dinner in Hall and the evening may pass without any words being exchanged. That doesn't mean he dislikes you. He is thinking of higher things.'

Paul had come up to St John's as a graduate from Bristol in 1921, and was soon revealed as a mathematical genius whose work in theoretical physics was a major contributory factor to the Rutherford-Cockcroft splitting of the atom. Elected to the Lucasian Professorship of Mathematics at the early age of thirty, he was awarded the Nobel Prize in Physics the following year, 1933. After he retired he went to be a Professor at Tallahassee in Florida, was awarded the OM (1973), remained a Fellow and visited us every year until his death in 1984.

I had been a Fellow only a few weeks when I found myself next to Paul: we were the last people in to dinner and there was no one on my left. The soup came and went in silence; halfway through the Sole Véronique I decided the effort must be made – the silence must be broken. But how? Not the weather. Not politics. Not the simple approach, 'My name is Daniel. I study megalithic monuments. Have you any views on Stonehenge?' I turned to Dirac, who was examining the grapes on his sole. 'Have you been to the theatre or the cinema this week?' I asked, innocently. He paused, turned to me with what I supposed was meant to be a kindly smile and said, 'Why do you wish to know?' The rest of our meal was eaten in silence.

There are of course many stories of this kind about Paul. He was once lecturing in America and gave a brilliant discourse, but of great difficulty. The Chairman said that Professor Dirac would be prepared to answer questions. No one spoke. Then, to break the embarrassed silence, a Professor got up and said he had been excited and fascinated by the lecture but had lost his way towards the end and didn't understand how the conclusion had been argued. He sat down and there was further embarrassed silence, Paul gazing blankly into the audience. Eventually the Chairman said that perhaps Professor Dirac would like to answer the question. Paul said, 'But no one has asked a question. One man has made a statement.'

After our initial attempt at conversation we somehow became speaking acquaintances and while I was Steward he consulted me about food and wine for the small lunch parties he gave in his rooms to visiting scholars. I was sitting next to him some time in the sixties when he sang the praises of British Columbia and the beauty of Vancouver. A little devil jumped up in my head and remembering my first encounter I nearly said, 'Why do you think I want to know about Vancouver?' but I pushed the devil down and talked about Captain Vancouver and King's Lynn.

We were 38 in 1938; by 1984 we were 110: it is not so easy to know everybody. Realizing this we installed a book of photographs in the Green Room, where we take a glass of wine before dinner, so that we can see who we are. I do not now dine frequently, but determined a few months ago that I must get to know my colleagues. So before dinner one night I singled out one or two men, studied them in the book, was certain I had got two of them right and arranged to sit next to one of them at dinner. I was determined on no Dirac-ery and plunged immediately into conversation with my victim. 'Edwards,' I said, 'explain to a non-scientist what exactly you do: what is cell-biology?' The young man looked at me with a pitying smile. 'I haven't the faintest idea,' he said, 'I think you have been looking at the wrong photograph.'

Being a member of this large body of Fellows and some 300 colleagues who are not Fellows, is a social and commensal problem. 'Why do you not dine in Hall more frequently?' someone asked Ray Lyttleton, that most distinguished astronomer who came to us from Clare. He replied, 'I don't know half the Fellows, and the other half I do know!'

In that year before the war when I started supervising I was anxious to try my hand at lecturing and discussed this with Dorothy Garrod, then a Research Fellow of Newnham: she also wanted to try out her views on undergraduates. So, together we proposed to Minns, as Disney Professor, that we might give two courses of eight lectures, Dorothy's on the Palaeolithic in the Near East, and mine on Megaliths in Western Europe – and that we would of course do these without any fee. Our offer was turned down, which saddened us, and I mentioned this one evening to Martin Charlesworth who said, 'But why don't you both restart the old system of College lectures?' 'No,' said James Wordie, 'leave it to me.' And in a few days Dorothy and I had lukewarm letters from Minns inviting us to give courses of lectures.

In 1938 we all began to get excited and some of us apprehensive about who would succeed Minns when he retired the following year. It was thought by many inevitable that the Disney Chair ought to and would go to Miles Burkitt: Minns certainly thought this and canvassed widely. Mortimer Wheeler and Tom Lethbridge put in. One morning Dorothy Garrod called on me in St John's and said, 'Come and have a glass of wine in the Blue Boar.' When we were settled she said, 'I want you to know, and I know that this means the

97

world will *not* know, that I have just come from the University Offices where I deposited my application for the Disney Chair. I shan't get it but I thought I'd give the electors a run for their money.'

Months later I received a letter from H.J. Fleure. Could he come to tea with me in College? He had a meeting at 5 p.m. and would present himself at 4 if that was convenient. I had first met him at the Leicester meeting of the British Association and we had corresponded in a desultory way about megaliths and human geography. He was amused that Edgar Jones had insisted that I should go to his department in Aberystwyth and that instead I had ended up in Cambridge disappointed by the Geography Department. 'Nobody any good there except Steers and Darby,' he said. I was and still am a great admirer of the man and of the series *The Corridors of Time* which he and Harold Peake wrote together.

But it was not about megaliths or human geography that he had come to talk to me. 'Women,' he said, 'is it true that they are still not full members of your University?' I said that it was regrettably so. 'But,' he persisted, 'that does not preclude them from holding University teaching jobs, including Chairs?' I said this was so, but that no female professor had yet been appointed in Cambridge. I walked with him to the Front Gate and along Trinity Street to the Senate House. 'I have been thinking a lot recently about Gertrude Caton Thompson and Dorothy Garrod,' he said, and as I went back to my rooms I realized he was here to elect the Disney. My understanding is that the Electors first offered the Chair to Caton Thompson, who had not applied, and that when she declined, appointed Dorothy Garrod. There is, however, no mention of this in Caton Thompson's *Mixed Memoirs*.

The appointment was announced on Dorothy's fiftieth birthday and the Fellows of Newnham took her out on a picnic in the country. Years later she said to me, 'It is credibly rumoured that you told Fleure what to do.' 'Quite untrue,' I said. 'But he did come and see you immediately before the Electors met?' 'True, but we talked about megaliths and human geography and the place of women in society,' I said.

Dorothy's tenure of the Chair was interrupted by the war and with no one to teach, and no enthusiasm for research or writing at such a time, she wrote to me and asked if I could get her into the Air Intelligence branch of the RAF, where I then was. She had been formally refused admission on the grounds of her age. I told this story to someone in the Air Ministry and when I said she had been in the armed forces in the 1914–18 war he explained that this made a great difference: there was a special rule. In 1942 Professor Garrod joined the remarkable collection of people at Medmenham which included at one moment herself as reigning Disney Professor and her successors Grahame Clark and myself. She was immensely good at the job and worked in a special section which included Robin Orr (later Professor of Music in Glasgow and then Cambridge), Sarah Churchill, and Villiers David. Towards the end of the war I visited Medmenham and Section Officer Garrod smartly saluted Wing Commander Daniel. 'Remember, Glyn,' she said firmly and kindly, 'that very soon our roles will be reversed and Assistant Lecturer Daniel will be saluting Professor Garrod!'

She held the Disney Chair for thirteen years and during that time we worked together in the closest friendship: and the new Tripos with its Part II was devised and worked out in detail by herself, Bruce Dickins and me. The creation of a Part II archaeology which started in 1949 was one of the reasons for the growth in importance of the Cambridge school in the post-war years – that, and Dorothy's uncompromising view that students should be taught archaeological facts, get acquainted with artifacts and site reports, and travel. It was fitting that after her death we were able to found a Garrod Memorial Fund, the income from which is expressly used to enable students to travel, and especially to travel to excavations abroad.

Dorothy was not enamoured of university administration and found that lectures and meetings broke her concentration and that she could not get on with her research. She retired early in 1952 and went to live in France: she built herself a house in Charente not far from the family house of the Henri-Martins and worked there and in Paris in very close association with her two great friends, Minne Henri-Martin and Suzanne de Saint-Mathurin, *les trois graces* of French palaeolithic archaeology, as they were called. It was in these years of retirement from Cambridge that she co-operated with Suzanne de Saint-Mathurin in the excavation of the remarkable rock-shelter of Angles-sur-L'Anglin and did several seasons of intensive work at the Adlun site in the South Lebanon.

We saw a lot of her in her retirement in Charente, at Angles, in Paris and on her visits to London and Cambridge. She was a person of great integrity, a skilled excavator and an intrepid field worker. Her later years were clouded by disagreements with the Abbé Breuil, who much resented her critical stance on Rouffignac. There were also French archaeologists who never forgave her for her membership of the Commission of 1927 which declared, rightly, Glozel to be false. The obituary by Gertrude Caton Thompson in the *Proceedings of the British Academy* for 1969 is a sympathetic and perceptive appreciation of her life and work and a clear picture of her as a person.

During my first year as a don my friendships with Martin Charlesworth, Hugo Gatty and John Boys Smith blossomed and flourished. When I told Owen Chadwick that I was writing my memoirs he replied, 'I hope not to write my memoirs but I look forward to yours. Give Martin Charlesworth a good hand – if ever a Don was Glorious, he was it.'

Hugo Gatty came to St John's as an exhibitioner from Harrow in 1925; elected a Fellow in 1931, he became librarian in 1937. He was an exquisite, scholarly bachelor in thought, word and action and the kindest and friendliest of men. I cannot remember how we first became acquainted – perhaps through Martin Charlesworth – but he rapidly improved our acquaintance and for years as an undergraduate and research student I used to lunch once a week with him – he never allowed any form of reciprocal hospitality. We lunched in his elegant rooms *à deux*. The pattern was always the same: a glass of La Ina at 12.45 (although as the years went by I suspected Hugo had had several glasses before I arrived), then the kitchen porter arrived with a large omelette (mushroom, ham or chicken). We drank a bottle of claret, often Mouton d'Armailhacq. Then there was cheese, fruit and coffee and we set out to walk to Grantchester and back in time for tea and our evening work.

Martin Charlesworth in his obituary in *The Eagle* (LIII, 1948–9, 128) brilliantly summed up Hugo. 'No one who conversed with him for long could fail to be impressed by the variety and sincerity of his interests, by the width of his attainments, and above all his sensibility. A visitor to his rooms would note the fine pieces of furniture; his piano and harpsichord with the volumes of Scarlatti and the eighteenth-century composers; the vast bookcases. He would note, too, the tables overflowing with new books, usually the latest poetry and prose; the Chinese figurines and incense-burners; the big bowl of flowers on the centre table. The whole set reflected the mind and character of its occupant, his neatness, his clear-cut notions and his fastidious taste.'

One Sunday morning in late July 1939 when I was laboriously working on the gazetteer of megalithic sites in England and Wales for my book, Hugo Gatty burst into my rooms bearing with him a bottle of champagne and two glasses. 'Stop everything,' he said. 'The world is coming to an end.' When we had our glasses filled he said that he had been listening to the news and was certain that war was imminent. He had already been told that his services would be required in Military Intelligence starting, they thought, in two or three months' time: he did, in fact, spend the war in Bletchley Park with countless others of my friends and colleagues. We had the chance, he thought, of a few days' or a week's holiday in France before the debacle. Would I come with him?

I hesitated because, in my gross ignorance of affairs, I did not think a Second World War inevitable but the prospect of a week motoring in France was more than attractive. I suggested we should have a third person and he agreed on Brian Wormald. Brian accepted our proposal: we met to plan our strategy. We all wanted to see the Prado pictures which were then in Geneva. We were each allowed one private objective. Brian said he wanted to see Strasbourg and Nancy. I said I wanted to see the rock-cut tombs near Epernay. Hugo said he wanted to see the house of his ancestors in Colmar: his forebears were Italians: the Gatti family had moved to Alsace where they were jewellers, and later to England where they made their fortune from manufacturing khaki. As it turned out, though we delightedly saw the Prado pictures, none of our three private ambitions was achieved.

We were to have set out in August, but at the last moment Hugo was delayed by a meeting of the College Council about the security of our most valuable books in time of war. Brian and I drove his car down to Newhaven and he joined us from the last train. It was a pleasant journey: Brian drove as erratically as ever and I navigated a route which went through Ightham and Piltdown; and I thought of Eoliths and *Eoanthropus dawsonii*. I little knew, nor did anyone, that fifteen years later Piltdown man would be exposed as a fake. I paid my respects to him with a pint of beer in The Piltdown Man, an agreeable pub.

We were early at Newhaven, got the car aboard and established three deck chairs on the top deck. All the cabins were booked. It was a peaceful crossing but we didn't sleep well because a tall, darkish, good-looking man spent the night pacing round the deck. It was only in a wakeful moment that I realized it was Mortimer Wheeler. He was just going back to France, where he had been excavating several Early Iron Age hillforts during the summer, from a brief visit to London to arrange the termination of his disastrous second marriage to Mavis, widow of Horace de Vere Cole and former mistress of Augustus John. We bought a copy of *The Times* next day in Chartres and there was a notice saying he was no longer responsible for his wife's debts.

We arrived in Dieppe in lovely sunshine and watched our car being offloaded and the luggage taken ashore. There were two men, identical twins, who were busy offloading the luggage. 'Obviously the Brothers Karryourbagsoff,' said Hugo, and his joke seemed to set the tone for a happy week.

But not so. We lunched expensively and very well in Rouen and clocked in that evening at the Grand Monarque in Chartres and ate very, very well and very expensively. Hugo ordered delicious and rare dishes. Brian and I had stupidly never thought of the finances of the trip and were alarmed. Next day was worse: the car ground to a halt in the outskirts of Chartres. Hugo had not had it looked at before he left. There were serious things to be done. We had another night in the Grand Monarque with expensive lunches and dinners and delicious wine. The Chablis we had seems to me now, as it did then, one of the most perfect white wines I have ever drunk.

We set off with our patched-up car and got to Bourges. Again the best hotel and a very expensive dinner. Brian and I decided we had to make a stand: we said we were poor and couldn't live up to Hugo's standard. He took the point, hardly and unhappily, and we drove, or rather he drove us, with obvious lack of enthusiasm to Geneva. He stayed in a grand hotel and we skulked round the corner to the little Hôtel de la Gare at Annemasse and we dined apart. I began to wonder how our trip would proceed. Next day we saw the Prado pictures and were all enormously excited: the trip had been worth while. And then Hugo invited us to dine with him at his expense. It was a memorable meal with memorable wines: but I felt uneasy and suggested that we all had the next day to ourselves and that he dined with us in our little restaurant and we planned our journey from then on.

This was agreed. I bought a ticket for a coach trip to the Great St Bernard Pass and gratefully got up early and enjoyed the journey alone along the shores of Lake Geneva and up from Martigny to the

Grand St Bernard. I inspected the dogs, found them even larger than I had expected, but was sad that they and their houses smelt so strongly. The monks could improve on this, I thought.

The trip gave us three hours' break and I walked down the south side of the pass, crossed the Italian frontier and went into the first Italian restaurant. It was empty but the patron came and talked to me. I said in French that I had just walked down from the pass, that it was my first time in Italy and could I have lunch. He replied in fluent English welcoming me and from his first sentences I thought there was something about his English that evoked memories. 'If it's your first visit to Italy,' he said, 'you must have a drink on the house: my special cocktail.' Then the penny dropped: he was speaking English with the accent of South Wales. When he brought the drink I said, chancing my arm: 'I'm not English, I'm Welsh.' He shook me by the hand and nearly embraced me. 'So am I,' he said. 'I was born in the Rhondda. My father was an ice-cream merchant who developed restaurants and fish-and-chip shops. When he died I carried on for a long time and then decided to go to Italy.'

We talked about South Wales and then he said: 'Meeting a boyo from South Wales is marvellous. You will have lunch on me: nothing to pay, please. I will give you the best *fettucine* you have ever had, a beefsteak *alla fiorentina*, and the wonderful *zabaglione* which my wife makes. And with it you must drink my favourite Barolo.' It was indeed a wonderful lunch. As I left to walk up the steep road to the pass and my bus, I heard steps behind me and there was the patron: he pushed a thousand lire note into my hand and said, 'When you get back to the old country send me a postcard.' There were tears in his eyes as he turned and went quickly back to his restaurant.

I was late getting back to Geneva and Hugo and Brian were well through their meal when I joined them. Their faces were in the depth of gloom. 'Where have you been?' asked Hugo, tetchily. 'In Italy,' I said. 'Ridiculous,' he said and hesitated. 'Then you haven't heard the news.' I shook my head. 'The Russians and Germans have signed a non-aggression pact. War is now inevitable. We leave for home at crack of dawn.'

As we drove across France and saw soldiers moving to their mobilization depots Hugo's war forebodings became more and more certain and gloomy. 'This is the end,' he said, 'we may never enjoy France again.' We spent the night in the Hôtel Paris et Poste at Sens, two hours south of Paris. I remember our dinner: I had snails for the first time and *Boudin noir aux pommes*. Hugo telephoned Cambridge and came back saying that he must return at once and get all the rare books in the College Library removed away to safety.

We got him to Paris next morning to catch the Flêche d'Or. We were left with his car and a great bundle of francs he hastily gave us as he left. We heaved a sigh of relief as his train left the Gare du Nord and after a few glasses of wine decided that we would not hurry away. What would a day mean anyhow? We parked the car in the Place de l'Odéon and booked a room in the Hôtel Corneille for two nights. The first night we dined in the Cochon de Lait next door and walked up the Rue Vaugirard and down the Boulevard Saint-Michel: there seemed no war fever or alarm. Next day we counted the money Hugo had given us: we were rich! We went and dined in the Tour d'Argent: it was not full. After dinner we took a taxi to La Coupole: it was a beautiful evening and we put down the top (as you could in those days), and drove through Paris sitting on the hood. When we got to La Coupole and walked into the café I heard an elderly woman say to her husband, 'Ce n'est pas la guerre. Les English milords sont encore ici.' We left early next morning and we were back in Cambridge very late that evening. Hugo was away in the country disposing of our College treasures.

I did not see Hugo again until after the war. He spent it all in Bletchley Park, getting more and more depressed: I was in London, Medmenham and India. Someone wrote and told me he was hideously unhappy in his work and at fighting a war against the country which he thought had contributed so much to the development of European civilization in the Middle Ages and later. He was, it was hinted, drinking heavily. I was sent a cutting from the local Cambridge paper saying that on one of his weekend leaves from Bletchley he had a strange accident with his bicycle in Sidney Street, and was charged and convicted of being drunk. When I was back in Cambridge in the spring of 1946 I was warned in confidence that he was drinking more than heavily and I was not to encourage him. Martin Charlesworth said, 'For God's sake help him. You were always close friends.'

Hugo had welcomed me back as an old and long lost friend. 'How boring it has all been,' he said, 'I don't think we shall ever get back to our pre-war days. Something in me has died, or has been killed.' A few days later he said, 'I am going to Paris to enjoy the days I missed in 1939. Come with me.' I demurred. I had much to do and didn't think I had the money. Perhaps I made a mistake. Hugo went alone for a week's trip. He was back in three days. 'A complete failure,' he said. 'No gaiety. No good restaurants. It was a bitter experience. You were wise not to come.'

H.A. Harris told me Hugo was killing himself with alcoholic poisoning. He would come drunk into Hall, be rude to people, and have to be assisted out. Yet in his good moments he continued to be very pleasant company and give elegant and amusing parties. Ruth well remembers some civilized and delightful lunches in his rooms and visits to our little house across the street. He liked giving a large dinner party before our annual May Week Concert and in 1947 in the middle of his party went out to get more wine, fell down his stairs, was concussed and carried off to hospital. And then in 1948 he was discovered unconscious in bed in his rooms. He was taken to Addenbrooke's and died of a cerebral haemorrhage. I think he died of a broken heart, or a broken life.

I was with my parents in Llantwit Major when war broke out and hurried back to Cambridge by train, taking a complicated route through Banbury, Bletchley and Bedford to avoid London, which we all expected to be bombed. Cambridge was bustling with plans for re-organization. I was put in charge of the College fire-engine which was set in a deep trench between the Kitchen Bridge and the Bridge of Sighs. It was a strange responsibility for one so unmechanically minded as myself but the Clerk of Works was my nominal Number Two. When the sirens sounded we manned the engine and I was there when the only stick of bombs to fall on Cambridge occurred, an event which killed Professor D.S. Robertson's wife, on duty as an air-raid warden in Hills Road, and damaged the premises of the Union Society. We had fire drill and practices and pumped water from the Cam to the most distant parts of the College and to parts of Trinity. The door in the wall between St John's and Trinity was opened specially for us: to be firmly locked again when the misfortunes of war were over. I was trained in fire-fighting out at Fulbourn and crawled through smoke-filled rooms dragging heavy sacks simulating human bodies. I also did a first-aid course. Then I was asked to join a special observer group which every night manned a post on top of the University Library and reported and plotted any suspicious lights.

Our group worked in shifts and mine came round every third night: the other man who observed with me was George Stallard, on the library staff, who died a few years ago just after retiring from a lifetime of service to the Library. We became firm friends and in the post-war years he always resolved any problems I had in that great library. The observers' post was organized by H.C. Stanford, a Johnian who was Secretary of the Library. He took me one evening into his office and showed me a key in a drawer in his desk. 'When you want half-an-hour's break during your night shift,' he said, 'this key will open the cupboards with which this room is lined. I think you will find some of the contents interesting.' I did: here was the erotica collection of the Library.

The nights passed more quickly when broken by a brief read in the Secretary's office. At 9 a.m. we walked back into central Cambridge for a large breakfast in the Whim before sleeping until lunchtime. Then Harold Taylor, at that time University Treasurer, asked if I would help him in a special scheme he was running for the University OTC. The numbers in the OTC were so large in 1939–40 that their instruction evenings had to be quadrupled. He had collected together a small group of dons, including Brian Wormald, R.L. Howland, and J.C. Burkill (subsequently Master of Peterhouse). He lectured to us on a Friday evening and gave us lecture notes, diagrams, and training manuals, and on Mondays to Thursdays we repeated these lectures to packed lecture rooms. It now seems fantastic that I should have spent evenings lecturing (sometimes twice in one evening) on the Infantry in Attack, the Artillery in Support, the Organization of the Platoon, but my parrot memory came to my aid. We were made to do a little military training and I remember afternoons firing a revolver at photographs of Hitler. I was not good at it.

This was my first encounter with Harold Taylor, whom I was to know very well after the war: indeed he and I were the executors of Nora Chadwick's will. I have the greatest admiration for his administrative skill and efficiency: he went from being Treasurer of the University to being Secretary-General of the Faculties, then in 1961 Principal of the University College of North Staffordshire and Vice-Chancellor when it became a University (Keele). Through all these years of academic administration he found time to pursue his researches on Anglo Saxon architecture and his books are a model of scholarship and discernment.

Those days of late 1939 and the first half of 1940 were indeed busy ones: I was re-writing my PhD thesis into a book, giving some lectures and supervisions, all interspersed with fire-fighting, sitting on the Library tower and giving lectures to the OTC.

Then came the invasion and fall of France and Operation Dynamo – the evacuation from Dunkirk from 27 May to 3 June. During Dunkirk I was lunching with Clifford Darby in King's. We decided the time had come for some action: after lunch we walked to the recruiting office in the Wesleyan Chapel in Jesus Lane and volunteered as aircraftmen in the RAF. We were politely and firmly told that we were in reserved occupations and must bide our time: we would be called up in due course. Next day I met Margaret Murray in the Market Place. 'Still here?' she said crossly. 'You should be away learning to fight. In the last war we used to send white feathers to people like you.'

When I got back to College there was a letter from the War Office saying that in view of my invaluable service to the Cambridge OTC I was being offered a commission in the Green Howards. I would be required to attend an OCTU for six weeks but could kit myself immediately as a second lieutenant. What a shattering prospect – to become a proper soldier after all these weeks of make-believe soldiering! I went for a walk on the Backs and wrote a letter to the Air Ministry asking if they had any use for a person trained in geography and archaeology with reasonable competence in the interpretation of air photographs. A letter by return of post asked me to attend an interviewing board in the Air Ministry at once. The interview was a pleasant one and I was accompanied into the waiting room by an agreeable squadron-leader. 'How soon can you come?' he said. 'We urgently need air photo interpreters. We'll forget about the medical. Go to one of the big shops round the corner and get yourself a ready-made uniform as a pilot officer. Some time next week? Good.'

I went to Horne's in Regent Street and an hour later emerged with two RAF shirts and the uniform of a pilot officer, and took the train back to Cambridge wondering what was happening to me. Next day came an official letter confirming my commission in the RAF and demanding my attendance in the old office of the Charity Commissioners in Ryder Street, which was then functioning as the HQ of RAF Intelligence Personnel Staff. I had three days to contemplate my translation. I stayed the night with Leslie Illingworth in Bayswater, dressed up in my uniform, and set off wondering to what strange destination I was going. I was alarmed to be saluted by two airmen in Piccadilly and turning down Ryder Street hastily saluted a senior RAF officer covered with gold braid.

I found myself sitting in a room with some twenty other newly commissioned RAF officers, all of us a little self-conscious in our uniforms with their thin light-blue pilot officer braid. We were told that there was no time for training – either in drill or in intelligence methods: we were however given a brief talk on methods of pay and told to report back after lunch for details of our postings. I went down to Fleet Street and Leslie took me for wine and sandwiches in El Vino's.

I returned to Ryder Street: there was a feeling of apprehension in the air. Where would we all be spending the night? Notices were read out posting us, as it seemed to me then, to the ends of the earth – Reykjavik, Singapore, Washington, Colombo, Cairo; and the room emptied as these men set out to be Air Intelligence Officers to squadrons or groups or headquarters in these distant places. Then came the moment when there were only two people left: myself and a man whom I discovered to be Bill Wager, subsequently Professor of Geology at Oxford. Wager's uniform bore one discreet, chaste medal ribbon – all white: the Polar Medal. I wondered whether he was going to be posted to the Faroes or to Greenland. The Polar Medal was an invitation to conversation and I found he knew James Wordie, James Stephenson and Bunny Fuchs.

The officer who had been despatching the contents of the room all round the world seemed to have forgotten us: he gathered together his files and got up to leave with his WAAF clerk. 'But what about us, sir?' I said. 'Dear me, I do beg your pardon. How stupid of me. But I thought, Pilot Officer Wager, that you had already been working in your unit for some while and that today was merely a formal commissioning.' He turned to me. 'Ah yes,' he said. 'You are going to interpret air photographs at Wembley.' His clerk solemnly made out single railway warrants for us to Stonebridge Park. It is the only time in my life that I have been presented with a First Class Travel Voucher for a journey on the underground.

We got to Wembley late that afternoon. Wager, of course, knew the way. We walked along the North Circular Road from Stonebridge Park, under the seven bridges that carry the main line to Scotland, turned up an unsurfaced lane and there in a maze of suburban factories was our destination, PADUOC HOUSE. The name, as I found later, was invented out of the initials of two organizations that worked there – the Aircraft Operating Company, and the Photographic Development Unit. I went into this broken-down looking suburban factory and reported to a Squadron Leader Peter Riddell who was sitting in his shirt-sleeves and braces working out his bank statement. 'Thank God they are sending us some men at last,' he said. 'Good, well you are just in time to join the first training course in the military interpretation of air photographs. Report at 9 a.m. tomorrow.' I saw the adjutant, an Osbert Lancaster caricature with a moustache and great bushy eyebrows. 'Where do I live?' I said. 'Anywhere you like, dear boy.' I bought a ticket back to Paddington and arranged to take up residence in a flat adjoining Leslie Illingworth's. The house in Queensborough Terrace in Bayswater was divided into several flats, all looked after and efficiently run by his lifelong friend Enid Ratcliffe. Breakfast was provided. In the next few months I got to know London well for the first time, although under the alarming conditions of the beginning of the Blitz.

I joined the first interpretation course next morning. It was run by a Flight Lieutenant Douglas Kendall. Two men were present: Claude Wavell and myself. All the others were WAAFs including Leslie Murray-Threipland whom I had known slightly before as an archaeologist. It was a fascinating course and I enjoyed it very much. Claude Wavell was already, in civil life, an expert photo-interpreter and was only attending the course formally as part of his commissioning in the RAF. He was a great help and ally although he was never able to get my non-mathematical mind to understand how to make proper use of a slide-rule. The course over, we were drafted on to shifts, and such was the shortage of people that within three weeks I was in charge of one shift, Bill Wager another. And so I joined the splendid inspired madhouse of civilians and RAF and WAAF officers interpreting air photographs, making photographic mosaics, writing reports, sending out annotated photographs. I was in Wembley for eight strenuous, exciting months.

The heavy days of the Blitz provided many adventures. As we went off duty one evening we discovered that the Stonebridge Park line was out of action: the only way into Central London was to walk along the North Circular Road to Park Royal. This we set out to do: I was with an Australian WAAF in the rear of our little party. She walked very slowly and uncertainly and clutched firmly on to me. The sirens sounded. We could hear the noise of aircraft overhead and flak opening up. Bombs exploded not far from us and some factory off to the right burst into flames. My WAAF collapsed on the ground and lay there moaning: 'I can't bear it,' she said, 'I'm just going to lie here and die.' It took a long time to get her to Park Royal. I delivered her in the dark to where she was living and went on to Bertorelli's in Bayswater for a late dinner. I had become one of its habitués during my London days. The restaurant was, as usual, full: I ordered my meal and was eating my spaghetti bolognese when there was a great whooshing noise and a not very loud bang. The whole building shook, the lights went out, and there were despairing cries from the street. I went quickly outside. A bomb had dropped immediately outside the restaurant: it had knocked down the kitchen walls and out of the kitchen were climbing the cooks, with their clothes in shreds. They seemed cheerful: we shook hands and I said, 'We are all fortunate to be alive. I'll send a bottle of wine down to you.' Half-naked, and in tatters, they returned to the kitchen. I went back to the restaurant. Some bravely imperturbable waiters were lighting candles at the tables but there were strange sights – the blast had thrown things about: there was an old lady wiping a soufflé off her face, and another combing spaghetti bolognese out of her hair.

I went back to my table which I was sharing with a Central European refugee. 'Vot has happened?' he asked. 'There was a bomb,' I said. 'Ah', he said, apparently unmoved, 'I was told that a bomb dropped last night about a quarter of a mile from my house.' 'Tonight,' I said, 'a bomb dropped a few yards from your head. You and I are lucky to be alive.' 'Yes,' he said, 'it is nice to be alive.' I ordered a bottle of wine and shared it with this insensitive character and sent two bottles down to the kitchen. After half an hour I was summoned down to the kitchens and sat drinking with the cooks looking out at the bomb crater that was inches away from our deaths. When I went to go, I asked for my bill. 'No bill tonight, Mr Daniel, we have charged your account to Herr Hitler,' they said, grinning.

Several days later, after a night shift, I was waiting at Willesden Junction for the connecting train to Paddington. My army colleague and I were very tired. Suddenly to my horror I saw him lurch forward and fall on the line. There was nothing I could do except apparently watch a friend being electrocuted. But nothing happened; he picked himself up and climbed back on to the platform in time to hear an announcement that trains were delayed because of electrical failure! We were taken into London by bus. I walked from Paddington to Bayswater and turning into Queensborough Terrace passed the cheerful family who lived five or six doors away from my flat and waved to them as they breakfasted, as I always did on returning from my night shift. They waved back and there was a particularly cheerful wave from the young son whom I had met in the book department of Whiteleys and to whom I had recommended books on archaeology and fossils.

I climbed up to my flat, too tired to undress and have a bath. I had been asleep for half an hour or more when I was awoken by a strange noise and a rushing wind. The mirror on the wall was swinging to and fro and then crashed in pieces on the ground. I got up and went down to the office and enquired what had happened. A delayed action bomb had exploded, I was told, a few doors away. With no conscious purpose I walked out down the street where police were arriving. There was a hideous gap in the buildings where my breakfast party had been. I climbed back to my flat and was sick.

The story of Photo-Intelligence in the war has been well told by Constance Babington Smith in her *Evidence in Camera* (1958) and by Ursula Powys Lybbe in her *The Eye of Intelligence* (1983) and I can only add one or two personal experiences, but at the same time pointing out that the two books I have referred to deal almost exclusively with the war in the West, which was, after all, where photographic intelligence established itself as super-spy and where it assisted enormously in winning the war. They do not tell the story, which should be told one day, of photo-intelligence in the Mediterranean, Near East and India.

I found my first task as a functioning interpreter at Wembley was counting the barges which were being mustered in the ports of northern France, presumably and obviously for the invasion of Britain. Day after night we sat comparing photographs and watching the build up of transports in Dunkirk, Calais and Boulogne. My detailed knowledge of these ports dates from those days, and when I sit nowadays at a dockside café-restaurant, like Les Mouettes in Calais, I see in my mind's eye the harbour filled with barges waiting to be loaded with German soldiers to invade Britain.

I was too busy to think what it all meant or would mean to me personally. I got to know one of my supervising officers, Michael Spender, and yet again his single decoration, the Polar Medal, linked me to old friends and especially to James Wordie. He used to arrive late at night and check through our reports. He was particularly interested in the modifications that were being made to the barges so that tanks and other vehicles could get on and off quickly.

And then one night Spender took me aside and said, 'Haven't you had enough of counting barges? The inevitable invasion of Britain must be tomorrow or the next day. Shouldn't we fold away our stereoscopes and go down to Kent? If we could each kill one German, even if we both were killed in the attempt, it would be a good thing for this country and for history.'

It was late at night: I was tired and disheartened but I agreed to his proposal, remembering how bad a shot I was. 'You are on next the night after tomorrow,' he said. 'I shall have a car ready: we will drive to Dover.' I spent a strange day in London: I walked through Kensington Palace Gardens, fed the ducks in St James's Park, went around the shelves of Hatchards and met Leslie Illingworth in El Vino's. He was with two of his best-informed Fleet Street colleagues. We drank a bottle of Chablis and two or three bottles of Vosne-Romanée. They all agreed that the invasion would come in the next two days: and, with the wisdom and fore-knowledge of Fleet Street, told me what would happen. The landings could not be prevented. We would retreat to a defensive first line from Chatham to Southampton. London would be destroyed. Already the *Daily Mail* and the other newspapers were moving out to the country.

'What are you doing?' someone asked. 'I'm in the RAF and I don't move from London.' They seemed a little nonplussed. I went and had a quiet afternoon in the Jermyn Street Turkish Baths (now, alas, no more). As I was dressing a vaguely familiar face said, 'Don't know whether you remember me. I was two years your senior at St John's: but we met at some of Martin Charlesworth's breakfast parties.' We dressed and he said, 'I need a drink. Will you join me?' We went to one of those curious clubs in the Ryder Street/Jermyn Street area where you could drink all day and I suspect all night. We talked freely: I said what I was doing. He said abruptly, 'I'm in the Cabinet Office.' 'Is the invasion on?' I asked. 'Dear me, no,' he said. 'Most definitely off. Let's have another drink.'

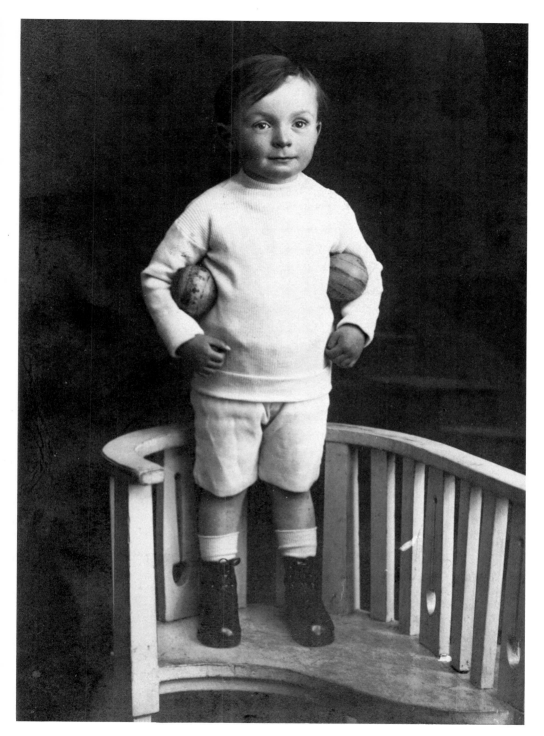

GD aged five

Paternal grandfather William Daniel

Maternal grandmother Marged Edmunds

William Daniel and family, GD top left

Grandmother Edmunds, at the door of her house, Nantymoel

Father, mother and GD, 1923 ▷

The Geneva party 1931: the first three are Gwynfor Evans, GD, and Gwilym Davies; far right, Gwilym Williams

Major Edgar Jones

H. M. Chadwick

*David Williams
unveiling a plaque
commemorating
the Rebecca riots*

M. C. Burkitt

J. M. de Navarro

Squadron Leader Peter Riddell and GD in 'Target for Tonight'

GD broadcasting from New Delhi, 1945

The Central Photographic Interpretation Section, Hyderabad House, New Delhi, 1944. GD centre front

Visit of Lord Louis Mountbatten to Hyderabad House, 1943

A visit from ENSA: Gert and Daisy (Elsie and Doris Waters)

Some of the CPIS staff: Stuart Piggott left of GD, Ian Rutherford
and Terence Powell right. Sgt Keddie bottom left

Wedding photograph of Ruth's father and mother, 1906

Ruth aged four, with hens

Ruth as a WAAF officer in India

Ruth and GD fording a stream on a picnic in India

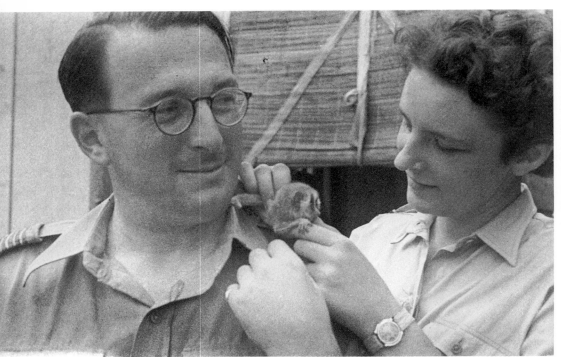

Ruth examining a potto on GD's shoulder, Delhi, 1945

Wedding photograph outside Exeter Cathedral, 12 September 1946.
Left to right: Leslie Illingworth, GD, the Dean (S. C. Carpenter),
Ruth, Ruth's mother and brother, S/L E. J. B. Langhorne

Ruth and GD at Exmouth, 1950

Cheered, I went out to Wembley early that evening and looked at the reports coming in from the constant sorties over the Channel ports. There were certainly no preparations for an invasion and many barges were leaving. When I came on duty that evening I studied the photographs with intense interest. It was indeed true that the barge count was going down and it could mean only one thing. Michael Spender was in at midnight and gave me a hard look. 'So we don't have to go to Dover,' I said. 'No,' he said, 'and just as well. You told me you were a bad shot. Would you now concentrate on the occupied French ports?' And so I did for months and watched with alarm the building of submarine pens in Brest and La Rochelle and briefed bombing raids on them which had little success: the thickness of the concrete roofs was fantastic.

Every night and morning I travelled back to bomb-torn London and was in Bayswater when Whiteleys was badly hit. I began to despair, as many people did, and wondered whether London could survive. On the great evening of 12 September, Leslie Illingworth and I had dined in Bertorelli's with no enthusiasm. 'Boyo' he said, fresh from Fleet Street, 'this is the night London is destroyed: perhaps Britain comes to an end.' We walked out along the Bayswater Road to the Park. The sky was aflame with the redness of the burning city. 'There is nothing we can do,' I said, 'but wait for the end.' 'Oh no,' said Leslie, 'there is. I wonder what is happening to the office cat.' And he got on his bicycle and rode eastwards to the exploding fireworks, the flames and the darkness. I thought I might not see him again, or London, or England as I knew it. But I was wrong.

And that I was wrong was in no small part due to those characters in Bletchley and Medmenham who gradually knew everything that was happening on the other side. Our unit by the Seven Bridges in Wembley was clearly no place to run a Secret Intelligence Unit; we were too close to bombing targets. One evening when I was dictating a report I asked for a document to be brought to us. A corporal whom I had known for some while brought it to me. I went on dictating in our bomb-proof shelter and then there was a whoosh as the door of our shelter slammed shut. Many minutes later it was opened again. We had been bombed and our corporal had been blown to pieces. I wrote to his parents never expecting a reply and had a moving letter from his father. 'These are,' he said, 'the accidents of war. We may, some of us, survive and I hope you will, but for what future?'

While I was enjoying, despite the bombings, my enforced stay in London I was summoned to our adjutant who said that the Air Ministry didn't want any but essential RAF personnel to live in London. 'You must get a billet in the country: I haven't a list. You must find somewhere yourself.' I reported to my colleagues what I had been told and David Bracchi took me aside. David had read geography at St Catharine's, Cambridge, and after the war was a lecturer in geography at Hull. He had gone into Air Surveys and had come into the Air Force when his civilian company was taken over. He was a kind, gentle person with very good technical knowledge and taught me a great deal. 'I live in Berkhamsted,' he said, 'which is only half an hour from here. There are several spare bedrooms in our house: I am sure my mother would be delighted to have you.'

She was, and I spent many happy months in the Bracchi household: papa was a Group Captain in the RAF Education Service and was seen only occasionally; one of the daughters was a nurse nearby, a second lived in Dorset, and David himself came home whenever he could but his visits didn't necessarily coincide with mine. Our first visit did: he drove me from Stonebridge Park to Berkhamsted after a night shift, I was installed, given a marvellous breakfast, slept for a few hours and then David proposed we should lunch in a pub and play a round of golf at the Boxmoor Course. It was when I was teeing up at the third hole I heard a loud aircraft noise and David suddenly said, 'Scram!' I followed him quickly into the bushes and a Dornier doing one of the low-level sorties let loose a burst of machine-gun fire at our golf bags. 'That was a near thing,' said David, and as we came out we heard in the distance a burst of machine-gun fire and some cries. The pilot had on his way back to Germany seen schoolchildren on the platform of Boxmoor station and given them a burst of machine-gun fire, killing five of them. A curious, distasteful, disgusting incident, which I remembered when, comfortably seated in a club in India with a *burra peg* at my hand, I read of the bombing of Dresden.

I had two complaints: one that the pilot had peppered the tee but had not hit my golf bag so that I was never able to point to a burnt hole and say, 'That was where I was shot at by the Germans in the war.' My second complaint was to our adjutant. While I was living in central London, I explained to him, I was free from any direct enemy action. The moment I am sent for safety to the country by you I am shot at by passing German aircraft. He took down my particulars and the details of that bizarre game of golf. 'But how do I come into all this?' he said. 'Danger money,' I said. 'It was you who sent me to the quiet Chiltern hills to be shot at.' He burst out laughing: 'Danger money will be paid in the form of a double gin and French in the pub across the road at noon,' he said. And that was I suppose the only time I was involved in direct contact with the enemy except for the near bombing of my hotel in Algiers a year or so later.

But it became clear that our highly secret and important intelligence unit could not stay in the suburbs of London; we had to find a home in the country and that home turned out to be at Medmenham, between Marlow and Henley. We moved there on 1 April 1941: I was the duty officer in charge and travelled with the last sorties from Wembley to Medmenham. The first shift began working there on April Fools' Day at 9 a.m. and I retired to bed in my new billet, a delightful house just outside Marlow owned by the Hood-Barr family.

It was a grand and splendid house in stock-broker commuter country style. Mr Hood-Barr much resented the fact that he had to put up soldiers and airmen. His house had a very extensive planned garden including a remarkable rockery and aviary reached by a bridge from the main entrance to the house. When I arrived he interviewed me severely. 'I hope you are a gentleman,' he said firmly. 'Your predecessor was the adjutant of your unit. He was no gentleman. A few days ago I found him drunk in my rockery very late at night looking for his bedroom. I said he was no longer to be billeted on me.'

I was accepted and given a large and beautiful room looking down through fields to the Thames. I was looked after by a butler/valet who told me that he was formerly employed by a duke and that this present post was a come-down which he hoped would be temporary. The war did not seem to be anything to do with him. He brought me early morning tea but I fed in the mess. When I came in from day-shifts I used to go in politely to the drawing room and have a brief conversation with the family about this and that. Gradually I sensed a great excitement; it was that Uncle Fred was coming to England from California, where he had been living for a long time. He would be delighted to meet me and they were sure I would be delighted to meet him. I was surprised that in the middle of the war anyone could come to England from California just to see his relatives. They waved an admonitory finger. No, no, they said, he is on a secret mission. Uncle

Fred is in intelligence like yourself. I wondered then how they knew I was in intelligence, but let that pass.

After a few days when I looked in on my way to bed there was a stocky American: Uncle Fred had arrived. He went out of his way to be agreeable. We had a talk next morning and he insisted on driving me up to Medmenham that evening when I went on the night shift. We talked all the way and with the hindsight of the next few days I wondered whether he was subtly trying to pump me as to what exactly went on in RAF Medmenham. He certainly mentioned Bomber Command and the bombing of Germany. I thought no more of it until I was in the Air Ministry in three days' time.

I did not get on very well with our CO, nor did he with me and many of my kind. After all it was a strange outfit for a regular Air Force officer suddenly to find himself in charge of: an ill-assorted collection of dons, artists, ballet designers, newspaper editors, dilettanti, writers (to mention but a few, Humphrey Searle, Robert Rowell, Robin Orr, Freddie Ashton, Julian Phipps, Dirk Bogarde, Lawrence Scott, Pauline Growse, Mary Grierson). I had crossed swords with him only a few days before Uncle Fred's arrival. After a heavy night-shift we went down for breakfast in the Dog and Badger, and after breakfast we were sitting on the churchyard wall, our uniforms open and with no hats on. The CO passed by in his car and next day summoned me and reproved me saying that discipline and proper dress must always be observed. Then a few days later I was summoned to him again and told that I must have been gossiping because I was urgently needed in the Air Ministry to see the Director of Security. I must have leaked some secrets, he said, because I was to be sent up at once in a staff car which was to wait to bring me back. Surprised and alarmed I was quickly driven up to Whitehall and in no time found myself in the Chief of Air Force Security's office. He was a kind man and put me at my ease for a moment and then plunged me into renewed alarm when he spoke into a microphone on his desk and said, 'Please send in Major X and Captain Y.' In came two youngish men in civilian dress to whom I was introduced. 'I am now going to ask you to go with these gentlemen and to co-operate with them in every possible way. And please remember that what you do for them and me is as important as what you are doing looking through your stereoscope.'

Mystified and still alarmed I left his office, and we three were driven to the Oxford and Cambridge Club where we moved into a small private room and three pints of beer were brought. They then revealed that they were interested in Uncle Fred, whom they suspected of being a Japanese agent. Would I listen to his telephone conversations, examine his mail, and tell them anything about his conversations and movements?' I was to go down to the phone box between the house and the centre of Marlow, to dial a number they gave me, and then ask for a code name which they also supplied. I drove to Medmenham wondering whether I was coming or going. The CO summoned me at once. 'Well,' he said, 'what was it all about?' 'I have been forbidden to tell anyone,' I said truthfully, 'but it is nothing to do with my work here. It is concerned with my private life and past.' He seemed mollified. 'All very odd,' he said. 'And the Ministry have instructed me that if you urgently want a car to go anywhere it must be provided.'

I was dazed, but for the next few days I did engage in wary conversations with Uncle Fred, who asked many times about Bomber Command. Naturally I could not hear his telephone conversations but I did observe his incoming and outgoing letters, which were few. I noted the number of his car. These small scraps of information I duly telephoned to London and told them that he was going to lunch with Cecil King. That seemed to excite the recipient of my messages.

Then a few days after my visit to London I came back very tired after a long day's work. I stopped for a drink at the Hare and Hounds and walked up the drive to the house, unexcited by the prospect of an evening chat with Uncle Fred. I let myself in: there was no one about. I went into the drawing room. The family were there looking very solemn. There was no Uncle Fred. I had to make routine conversation for some while before I could get round to asking where he was. 'In Brixton Gaol,' came the answer. 'The police and security men came this morning and took him away. They searched the whole house, including your room.' I made suitable noises and retired gratefully to my room, sighing with relief. My one brief exercise in espionage was over. Next morning when the butler brought my tea he was at his gloomiest. 'They even searched my room,' he said. 'Such a thing would never have happened at the Duke's.'

It was in the Hare and Hounds that my second strange encounter took place. I was having an evening drink when I saw at the other end of the bar Bryan Hopkin, who had been at school with me in Barry and at St John's in Cambridge. I told him I was at Medmenham. 'Ah ha,' he said, 'the photo-interpretation place. Just the man we want.' He then explained he was private secretary to Professor Lindemann (later Lord Cherwell). Churchill would not let Lindemann stay the nights in London and they had taken a house down the road from the pub. Next day I was telephoned and asked to dinner with Lindemann and Hopkin. When I got into their drawing room it was stacked with red despatch boxes. Lindemann waved a hand at them: 'These and my word will protect you,' he said. 'The Prime Minister and I want to know exactly what photo-intelligence is learning about the war.' It appeared that our reports were only getting to the Cabinet in an abbreviated and summary form and that many of the really high-ups were suspicious that intelligence was being withheld from them, especially the right information about the extent of our bombing successes and failures. I did not at that time know that Professor R.V. Jones felt the same and that he had planted in Medmenham Claude Wavell who supplied him direct with the information he needed.

I told them what I knew and that I had recently been specializing in the decoy aerodromes that were deflecting our bombers from their real targets. But I urged them not to take my word and to see my boss, Douglas Kendall. Another dinner party was arranged and Dougie Kendall came shaking like a leaf saying he had been commanded by the Prime Minister's secretary to attend this meeting. As the dinner wore on he relaxed and we stayed for three hours explaining all we thought we knew. From that moment all our reports went direct to the Cabinet Office and Bomber Command were no longer able to over-estimate the success of their effort. It was in its way a small turning point in the war. I did not meet Cherwell again until after the war. I was introduced to him in the Common Room at Christ Church before dinner. 'I don't think you know Daniel,' said my host. 'Indeed I do!' said Cherwell, 'we are old friends from the days of the war.'

The days in Medmenham were heavy and exciting. I made many friends and more acquaintances. One of the WAAF officers on my shift took me under her wing: Barbara Slade lived nearby and I often spent the night in her family house at Twyford, and wandered about the Thames Valley next day. Villiers David lived nearby in Friar Park and I often stayed the night there enjoying delicious dinner parties presided over by his sister Vere. But most of all I enjoyed taking the train to London and lunching with Leslie Illingworth at the Café

Royal after a leisurely drinking session at El Vino's. 'Boyo, this war will never end,' he would say. 'Everybody in Fleet Street knows there is no way we can beat the Germans. They have the stranglehold on us.' And I would catch the afternoon train down to Marlow, report for duty in the evening and gaze sadly at the growing and impenetrable submarine pens in Brest and La Rochelle and wonder if Fleet Street was right.

One day, Major Venner, head of the Army photo-interpreters at Medmenham, asked me whether all my archaeological scholarly colleagues and friends were in the RAF. 'Are there no cronies of yours hidden away in the Army doing worthless jobs?' I immediately thought of Terence Powell and Stuart Piggott who were both privates doing routine army jobs (in the Irish Fusiliers and an Ack-Ack battery respectively). I had first met Stuart Piggott at Avebury, when as a research student I was listing the chambered tombs of Wiltshire: we had discussed Stukeley and he showed me the Stukeley manuscripts which Alexander Keiller had collected in Avebury Manor. That was in 1935, and since then I had kept up a correspondence with him and been to papers he had read to the Society of Antiquaries of London. He had once come to lecture in Cambridge and I put him up in a guest room in College. Our archaeological acquaintanceship was slowly warming into friendship.

I told Venner about Powell and Piggott: Army Records soon found their whereabouts and in less than three weeks the sound of heavy boots announced their arrival at Medmenham. Within three months they were commissioned into the Intelligence Corps and became valued members of the Army Photographic Intelligence team.

My first appearance before film cameras occurred at Medmenham. The Central Office of Information was producing a film explaining how the RAF operated its bombing raids: a film which was released with the title of *Target for Tonight*. There had, of course, to be shots of photographic intelligence and they filmed Peter Riddell, Constance Babington Smith and myself. I had to draw the attention of Riddell to a particular target and was given some unfortunate piece to say such as 'Here's a peach of a target for the boys'. We managed to change the script.

I was seconded for six weeks to Bomber Command: the photographic intelligence section there in the woods high above High Wycombe was a peaceful change after the high pressure of Wembley and Medmenham. No night shifts and mainly interpreting the Medmenham reports to the Air Staff. We walked out after dinner to the Plough Inn at Speen which was kept by Ishbel MacDonald, Ramsay MacDonald's daughter. Basil Megaw, who was in the Operational Research Section at Bomber Command, was billeted agreeably in the pub.

I met Ishbel MacDonald again years later in curious circumstances, when I was a Governor of the Museum of London and the Queen Mother came to lay the foundation stone of the new building. I arrived early, having walked to the Barbican site from Liverpool Street, and sat alone on an empty crate reading a book. I became aware of an elderly woman, dowdily dressed, sitting not far from me and wondered who she could be and what she was doing there. A journalist, perhaps, or some plain-clothes security officer? I didn't catch her name when she was presented to the Queen Mother together with the other Governors: I found myself sitting next to her at lunch: her name was Mrs Peterkin. My neighbour said to me, 'Who on earth is that woman sitting on your left? She has just told me she used to do the catering at 10 Downing Street.' Then the penny dropped: it was Ishbel MacDonald who had 'done the catering' for her father when he was Prime Minister and had been appointed by him to be one of the first Governors of the London Museum but was now retired. We got into conversation and she said she remembered me coming to her pub, and we talked about Basil Megaw. 'I came down from Lossiemouth overnight,' she said, 'and walked to the city: I was led to believe it was very difficult to get a taxi these days in London and that they are most expensive.'

Late one night in Medmenham over spam sandwiches and coffee a fairly new recruit to our personnel staff said to me, to my great surprise, 'Are you looking forward to India?' I replied that I had not heard until that moment I was going to India. 'Oh dear,' he said, very embarrassed, 'I have spoken out of turn.'

Next morning Peter Riddell summoned me to his office and asked me rather diffidently whether I would like to go to India, set up first of all a training school in air photo-interpretation and then create and build up a functioning air photo-intelligence centre which would come into operation when the war in the West was over and the war against Japan began in earnest. He had himself been in India before the war and enjoyed it. 'You will have a chance of seeing the last of the

British Raj,' he said. 'It will interest you. You'll have to travel a great deal and when the Germans are defeated we'll all take over what you have built up and you can go back to being a don in Cambridge. Is it on?' I did not hesitate for a moment. It was one of the important decisions in my life which I was able to make at once and never regretted. 'I might come out and see you,' he said, 'once you've got things going. I rather fancy leaning against the bar of the Imperial Delhi Gymkhana Club and after a few *burra pegs* tottering in to a superb curry. I shall envy you your peaceful departure from the noisy war in the West.'

This is what it was. I left the blackout and austerity and bombs and spent four very happy years in the heat and the sun of the great sub-continent and enjoyed enormously some of the last days of the British Raj. I looked forward to it, though saddened at leaving my friends and colleagues at Medmenham, my father and mother in South Wales, and perhaps most of all St John's College.

My boss in the Air Ministry, Group Captain Stewart, was very unhappy about my posting. He suddenly appeared at Medmenham in the middle of a night shift. He was already considerably the better for drink: he invited me to join him in the bar. 'But it's closed,' I said, 'it's been closed for hours.' 'Ssh, Ssh,' he said, 'Come with me. Always a good thing, d'ye know, to have a set of keys to the bars in the messes you are likely to visit. Prudence and forethought are wise qualities,' he mumbled as we locked ourselves into the bar. He poured himself out a very stiff whisky and gave me a small dose. He lifted his glass, 'Here's to you,' he said. 'I don't like the idea of your leaving us and going out there.' I replied that I was looking forward to it: Delhi, Agra, Mohenjo-daro, Harappa, perhaps Kashmir.

'Wogs,' he said, filling up his glass. 'Natives. It's the journey out that worries me. Shot down over the sea – sharks. Engine failure over the Sahara – death in the desert. Dreadful.' He winked confidentially. 'I have a plan to help you,' he said. 'I am having you issued with a special revolver.' I protested that this was the last thing I wanted remembering my difficulty in shooting the effigies of Hitler on the Cambridge OTC rifle range. 'No, no,' he said. 'It is all fixed. Very difficult to arrange. Special privilege. All fixed. I shall be thinking of you: forced landing in the Sahara. Yes: shoot the damn wogs.' I said, 'But surely, Sir, a flask of iced water might be more helpful in those unlikely circumstances.' He leered at me and gave out a great whisky belch. 'I don't think you are taking this sufficiently seriously,' he said. 'Iced water indeed. And be sure you take a flask of whisky with you.'

Nor was I serious until I read the intelligence summaries next day and appreciated how difficult it was to get from beleaguered Britain to distant outposts of the Empire. The Mediterranean was closed and virtually in German hands. They had been trying high-flying aircraft direct from Cairo to England but apparently our anti-aircraft crews had not been informed of these manoeuvres and their timing, and two aircraft had been shot down as they came down to land at Lyneham. As a result the so-called horseshoe route to the Middle East, India and the Far East had been invented and to my intense delight I learnt I was to go on it. It was, in the event, one of the most exciting and memorable journeys of my life.

The next day a special messenger arrived from the Air Ministry with my revolver and I was driven to RAF Benson to be trained how to use it. When I got back from this ridiculous exercise there was a telephone call from the Cabinet Office. Would I ring a certain number. I did. 'We understand,' said the voice, 'that you are being posted to India. We have valued your co-operation; Professor Lindemann has asked me to say that if you wish to stay in England and in Medmenham this can, of course, be arranged.' 'No,' I said, 'this is very kind and thoughtful. But I want to go to this job in India. It has great possibilities and may one day be more important than staying in Medmenham. Do assure the Prof. that I am not being posted to India in disgrace or against my will.'

I was summoned to the Air Ministry and briefed for my horseshoe trip. We would, of course, be travelling through neutral or para-neutral countries and must be disguised as civilians. A new passport was to be issued to me at once and I was described as an official from the Treasury and told that I was going out to Delhi to advise the Indian Government on income-tax evasion with special relation to British troops stationed there! In the years to come I often wondered where I could obtain that advice I was supposed to be giving others.

It was said that for my new passport I needed a photograph of myself in civilian clothes. Would I go to a certain address in the Strand and bring back my photograph as soon as possible? The photographer's studio was underground. I explained my problem. 'All in the day's work,' he said. 'But you must wear a civilian jacket and a jolly club tie. I can produce a tie but not a jacket to fit you. Go back up to

the street and ask the first chap you see that looks vaguely the same
build as yourself whether he would come down and let you wear his
jacket for a few minutes. It's all part of the war effort, you know.'

I climbed the staircase back on to the Strand and looked at the
passers-by with wonder and an appraising eye. Along came a short
tough chap vaguely like me. 'Excuse me,' I said, and told my
improbable story. Would he come down into a neighbouring
basement and let me be photographed in his jacket? 'Certainly,' he
said, 'with pleasure' – what the bombing had done for the British!

When we got downstairs I realized he was a thinner man than I had
thought and when I put on his jacket and sat facing the camera it was
tight. 'Button it up, please,' said the photographer, and as I did so I felt
the jacket split up the back. I got up and it was only too true: the jacket
was split from top to bottom. To my astonishment both men laughed.
'All in the day's work,' said the photographer. 'Don't mention it,' said
the anonymous man I had dragged in from the street. 'All part of the
war effort?' As a result of this strange manoeuvre in the Strand I
survived the war, and many years afterwards, with two perfectly
genuine passports and I often wondered whether there was the basis
here of a detective murder mystery.

Barbara Slade drove me to Waterloo dressed as a civilian clutching
my new passport, my RAF uniform packed in my suitcase. She was in
WAAF uniform and was severely frowned on and asked to drive away
quickly. A very scholarly looking person seized my luggage and
carried it to the train. 'That was a near mistake,' said the porter in a
very Oxbridge voice, 'there may be more. I hope not. Remember who
you are and forget who you were.'

It was spy stuff and I warmed to it. I was shown to a numbered seat
in one of four specially reserved coaches carefully guarded by plain-
clothes policemen. As I walked along the corridor I said stupidly to the
attendant, 'I haven't got a ticket.' 'Quite so,' he said. We travelled to
Bournemouth in the growing darkness of a winter's evening and, some
sixty to seventy of us, were driven to a hotel. You will be called at two
in the morning we were told, and so we were, most of us weary, many
unshaven, all puzzled.

A customs official went through our luggage. A red-nosed elderly
gentleman, whom I subsequently discovered to be Vice-Admiral
Submarines in the East Mediterranean and who was an amusing
friend on the trip, was furious. 'Customs,' he said. 'But we are at war.'

'Not, sir' I said as kindly as I could, 'with the countries to which we are going.' When they got to my luggage there was a sudden stiffening of the customs official. I was asked to wait behind. There were hurried consultations, furtive glances and eventually there arrived a high ranking customs official with some gold braid. 'Mr Daniel,' he said, and he said the Mister firmly, 'you have a revolver in your luggage which you did not declare.' 'My God,' I said, 'so I have, but I don't want it. Take it away.' 'Have you permission to carry firearms?' 'No,' I said, 'It was given to me by my Group Captain to shoot the natives in the Sahara.' It was two in the morning. 'I beg your pardon,' he said. 'You are not flying to the Sahara. You may be guilty of a very serious offence, smuggling arms out of the country in time of war.' Shocked, I recovered my senses and opened my diary. 'Would you be so good as to ring this number at the Air Ministry?' I said. He came back a quarter of an hour later in a very deferential mood. 'Thank you, sir,' he said. 'Everything is in order. Your luggage is being loaded on the bus. Sorry, sir,' said the gold braid bowing low, 'to have inconvenienced you. All success to your special mission. Have a good journey, sir.' God knows what had been said on the other end of the telephone from the Air Ministry. 'Thank you,' I said, 'we may meet again some time – perhaps in the Sahara?' He did not smile. But I did because I began to think that Group Captain Stuart's revolver would become a minor *histoire* in my life, which might anyway not last very long.

We flew away from Hurn on a Boeing Flying Boat which had just brought Winston Churchill back from his Bermuda conference. I sat next to my Vice-Admiral. After a while he turned to me and said, 'Young man, I have the distinct impression that we are flying west.' 'True, sir,' I said. 'But I'm going to Cairo,' he said crossly. 'And I, sir, am going to Delhi. I think that in an hour or so we shall land on the Shannon in Ireland.' 'Preposterous,' he said.

When we landed in Shannon we queued up in a small room, filled with the smell and smoke of a peat fire, to go through Irish passport control. The Irish knew exactly what was going on, but played the game elegantly but teasingly. I said I was a Treasury official going to advise the Indian Government on income-tax evasion. 'Good luck to you,' said the Passport Controller, and turned to my Admiral friend. 'I work in the Admiralty,' he said. 'Ah, yes,' said the Irishman mischievously. 'And will you be in the fighting or the clerical side of the Admiralty?' I thought the Admiral would explode but he controlled himself with an effort. 'The clerical side, of course, damn you,' he said and stumped away. The Irishman gave me a wink and I winked back. At least there was no revolver trouble!

We stayed the night in the Dunraven Arms Hotel at Adare: the place was overfull of passengers shuttling to and from England and the outer world. I was put to sleep on a very uncomfortable bed on a board set across a bath in a public bathroom. I remember how good the Guinness and the food were and how we went out for a walk: the street lights were on, and after two years of blackout we gathered around a lamp-post and lifted up our glasses to the light.

Next day we were in Lisbon enjoying fresh grilled sardines and a dish of pork and plums in the Palace Hotel at Estoril, and the day after we landed at Freetown, Sierra Leone. Something was wrong with one of our engines: there would be a considerable delay. An RAF transport officer hastily summoned a bus and took us for a trip along the coast to a nice-looking sandy beach. 'We will all now have a swim,' he said. We protested we had no swimming trunks. 'Of no importance,' he said, 'we shall all bathe in the nude.' I was the last to leave the bus. The driver, a young red-haired corporal, engaged me in conversation. 'You don't remember me, do you?' he said, 'I'm the son of the caretaker of your father's school in Llantwit Major. By the way, I would hang back when you go in to bathe: the sea here is infested by sharks.' It was a strange sight: forty to fifty naked gentlemen, many of them elderly and pot-bellied (we were taking the Provisional Greek Government out to Cairo) prancing down to the sea. I had a pleasant swim keeping a cordon of my colleagues between me and the outer sea. When we got to Lagos we were allowed to abandon our civilian clothes and put on our tropical uniforms: there was a great display of gold braid and a sort of formality descended on our erstwhile mufti-camaraderie. I had followed the instructions given me in an Air Ministry booklet and was equipped with a topi of the old Wolseley helmet type. This caused intense amusement and I was persuaded to throw it into the harbour. 'You'll never see anyone wearing a topi of that kind again,' said an Air Vice-Marshal who knew India – but I did see one, on the head of Wingate.

At Lagos we were given a very difficult choice. Our Boeing was returning to England. There were two routes to Cairo: by land plane via Timbuctoo and across the Sahara, or by flying boat up the Congo.

I chose the Congo route and flew over the African rain forest landing at Brazzaville, Coquilhatville, Stanleyville and Leopoldville, where we spent a night, inspected okapi in the local zoo and were shown pygmies shooting the rapids in their canoes. I shared a bedroom with an amusing young Wing Commander and we went to bed in a merry mood. 'Good God, Daniel,' he said, 'look at this' – pointing to the typed list of things one could order stuck up on the back of the door which started with Tea, Coffee, Toast and Oeufs/Bacon and ended surprisingly with Les Girls. He rang the bell and when a boy arrived said, 'Les Girls, s'il vous plaît'. 'Une ou deux?' asked the boy unmoved by what seemed to me a remarkable request. 'Leave me out of this,' I said. 'I'll go for a walk.' A few minutes later the boy appeared bearing a litre bottle of beer with a lewd label depicting two naked girls. I cancelled my walk and ordered a bottle for myself.

We told this story next day to the man whom we now knew to be the Prime Minister designate of the provisional Greek Government. He laughed and told us what had happened to him. He was staying in the house of the Greek Consul and soon after he had retired to his bedroom there was a knock on his door and in came a very attractive young woman who made it clear that she was at his disposal. He said he did not want her services, that he was not that kind of man. Ten minutes went by and there was another knock on his door and he was confronted with a young and attractive boy whom he kindly and firmly sent away. He was just getting into bed when there was another knock at his door. He opened it cautiously, wondering what fresh offerings were being made: it was his host asking if there was anything the matter with him. 'No,' he said, 'you are very kind but I am very tired and sleepy,' and there were no further visitations.

We crossed the great Rift Valley, saw the Victoria Falls, and landed at Kampala; the following day saw us lunching at Wadi Halfa and dining in Khartoum: and early next day we glided down on the waters of the Nile in the middle of Cairo. I got in touch with the Photographic Interpreters out at Heliopolis: Charles McBurney came and gave me dinner and afterwards we drove out in a victoria to see the Giza pyramids by moonlight. I carried away the memory of an enchanting evening as we flew on in another flying boat landing on the Dead Sea, then Lake Habbaniyah and a night stop at Basra. I got into conversation with our pilot and when he learnt I was an archaeologist he made a special detour next day, came down low and circled the

Arch of Ctesiphon, much to the alarm of some of my fellow passengers. We flew on down the Persian Gulf and across the Gulf of Oman to India, and the end of a most fascinating journey – the most exciting, stimulating and memorable journey I have ever made. It was twelve days since I had got on the train at Victoria; I had crossed Darkest Africa from west to east and had landed on great rivers: Shannon, Tagus, Congo, Nile and Tigris-Euphrates; and now landed, if that is the right word, in the harbour of Karachi.

CHAPTER FIVE

Indian interlude

OUR FLYING BOAT came down in Karachi harbour in the early afternoon of a January day in 1942. We were treated politely by the Immigration and Customs officials: but I made a mistake, and it was all due to that pestilential revolver. The form said, 'Had I any firearms?' and, in honesty, I said I had. 'No doubt', said the official, 'for when you go shooting in the hills.' 'No,' I said, and told him the story of why I had firearms at all. He smiled and said, 'That will be all right, please sign here,' which I did. But, alas, when we were all in the bus and about to drive away he came out and asked to see me. 'Sahib', he said, 'I have not got the number of your gun.' 'But I don't know it,' I said. 'We must get out our luggage and find it.' 'That will not be necessary,' he said. 'Please fill in the form, any number will do.' 'But if that is so,' I said, 'why don't you fill in a number yourself?' 'Oh no, Sahib, that would be quite wrong. You must write it in: six figures please.' I did so and he departed happily. It was my first experience of Indian 'babureaucracy'.

We were driven to an hotel and in the foyer, sitting, rather dejectedly, in broken-down cane chairs, were Stuart Piggott and 'Trader' Horne. They had been posted from Medmenham to Singapore, but their onward flights had been cancelled because of the uncertain situation in South East Asia: Singapore actually fell on 12 February of that year, and they were waiting to know what was to happen to them. While they were in Karachi they had naturally improved on the occasion by visiting Mohenjo-daro and Harappa. They were delighted to see me, and surprised, because they had no idea I was being posted to India. We had a pleasant dinner together; and I said that I would hope to see them in Delhi soon.

I left by flying boat early next morning for Gwalior and from there travelled by land plane to Delhi. I reported to the headquarters of the Air Force in India and was greeted by a cheerful and amusing Indian warrant officer who took down all my particulars and found me accommodation. 'Welcome, sir,' he said, 'to the most beautiful country in the world. I hope you will enjoy your stay here and that it will not be a long one.' It was: four years, and I did.

My posting to India was for two reasons. First, I was to organize the training of as many army and RAF officers as possible in the rudiments of air photographic interpretation, and secondly, I was to set up an operational interpretation unit which would work with the squadron taking photographs of the Japanese in Burma and in support of the war in Burma. This unit would eventually take over the main role of photo-interpretation when the war in the West was over.

I was joined in Delhi by Terence Powell and Ian Rutherford, and it was decided to establish a training school as a wing of the Army Intelligence School at Karachi where we installed ourselves in Old Government House and ran three-week courses for several months, each course of about twenty officers. The course also included general intelligence training undertaken by the main school. Powell, Rutherford and I found it stimulating and very interesting to plan these courses: we taught them all we knew and enjoyed doing it. The officers sent to us were always intelligent, critical and perceptive and we learnt a lot ourselves. I think that when we came to give the last two courses they were really good. I found that both Rutherford and Powell, nervous at first, became excellent teachers. Terence Powell and I recognized later, when we became university teachers after the war, that the experience of running the Karachi school had been of the greatest value to us personally.

The Commandant of the school was Colonel Jock Campbell. James Wordie used to classify the world into strange men and good men. Jock Campbell was unquestionably a strange man. The mess was full of stories about him: he was supposed to have spent years in intelligence work in Iran and Iraq in disguise, and improbable stories of long days and nights hidden in Ali Baba-like jars in market places. He neither denied nor confirmed these tales but let an air of mystery gather about his past. He was, I think, slightly mad but a man of principle. I once asked him to dine with me in the Sind Club, to which I was happy to belong, but he refused, saying that as he commanded a unit of Indians and British he could not cross the threshold of an institution which refused entry to Indians.

He used to drop in on our lectures occasionally and once sent for me and said, 'You and your staff teach very well. I want you to give half-an-hour's talk to my main courses on how to teach. I have only one complaint to make. You always enter the lecture room in the same way, stand attentively at your desk in the same position, and leave by the same door. There should be variety in all things: come in by different doors, leave perhaps through the window – keep your audience expectant, on the *qui vive*: surprise them – surprise is the essence of attack.' I thought he was dotty or just teasing me, but decided to play his own game. 'Interesting,' I said. 'Would it be amusing to rig up some machinery so that occasionally I descended from the heavens on to the rostrum?' He smiled indulgently. 'I think that would be extravagant,' he said, 'but you take my point.' And I did, therefore, vary my exits and entrances. Campbell was an eccentric but kindly man and when we packed up and went to Delhi he wrote a warm report on our activities which was full of praise and helped us in establishing ourselves with Army and Air Force Headquarters in Delhi.

Old Government House was in the cantonment and not far from the Sind Club. The short walk from School to Club went past a small shrine occupied by a holy man who had one of those large sheep with enormous fat tails and we became friends – the holy man and the sheep. The Club itself was a haven of peace and cool quiet with its wide balconies. It had a very good library and good food: excellent curries, though perhaps none as good as the prawn curries in the Karachi Yacht Club. The climate of Karachi varied very little: it was 80° F most of the time but always disturbingly humid. There was little to do off duty except occasionally be sailed across the harbour to nearby beaches. I visited the museum on several occasions and once was delightfully surprised when the curator, a Parsee, looking at his watch, said, 'Excuse me, I am due at the Fire Temple.' I travelled around Karachi in open victorias – a very pleasant method of getting about: the slow trotting of the horse and the sea breezes blowing lightly in. There was one great disadvantage in these journeys, and of course it is the disadvantage of all horse-drawn open vehicles. Every cabby in Karachi had a huge pile of greenery beside him – mainly cut from mangrove swamps. This green stuff was fed to the horses with disastrous results. Inevitably, even on a short journey, up would go the horse's tail and the most extensive series of horse farts of great power and pungency, were given off. The victoria filled with a fetid odour of decaying vegetation and rotting fish which remained with one on descending and slightly checked one's appetite.

Which reminds me of the strange affair of Ian Rutherford's constipation. Terence Powell and Ian and I had rooms on the first floor wing of the Old Government House building. There were three or four other staff members in neighbouring rooms including a Captain Sanderson from one of those improbable Indian Army regiments – I think it was Probyn's Horse: anyhow he boasted a bright scarlet forage cap. He was, in the Wordie terminology, a rather strange man. He seemed moody, and often disorientated, and once asked me: 'Do you meditate much?' When I replied that I seldom found time to, he said, 'You should find time', and looking at me with sad eyes recited the lines of W.H. Davies:

> What is this life if, full of care
> We have no time to stand and stare?

There seemed little to say. 'What indeed?' I said, and that is about all the conversation I had with him until the Ian Rutherford episode.

I should explain that we in the south wing shared a bathroom and a separate lavatory and I had noticed, without paying any attention to it, that there had recently appeared on the window shelf of the lavatory a little tree bedded in a pottery bowl.

Ian Rutherford complained that he was feeling unwell and losing his appetite. As the days passed he began to get redder and redder in the face and lacking in energy. In the end he confessed to me that he had been constipated for eight days and had taken all reasonable recipes with no effect whatsoever. 'I'm thoroughly bound up,' he said, 'as I have never been before in my life. You must help me.' He was obstinate and wouldn't see a doctor but begged me to go to the chemist and seek a cure.

This I did: there was an excellent establishment in Karachi, redolent of the nineteenth century. It was almost as good as the famous one in Calcutta which I once visited when I had a nasty outbreak of prickly heat (*Lichen tropicus*). I am a great sweater in normal times and in India in the heat, and particularly moist heat, sweated truly like a pig. When the Chinese Chief of Intelligence was visiting our centre in Delhi I had to change my clothes three times in one morning not to appear like a wet rag when he arrived at eleven-thirty – I expect nervousness added to the condition. Prickly heat is, as any who have lived in tropical countries will know only too well, an inflammatory disorder of the sweat glands characterized by the eruption of small papules or vesicles, accompanied by a sense of pricking or burning. There are curative ointments but the best cure is antiseptic drying powders. Buying anti-prickly-heat powder in Calcutta I idly said, 'I am sure your product is of the highest excellence and efficacy?' and have never forgotten the suave but sober rebuke in the reply: 'We have never had any complaints from the time of Warren Hastings, Clive and Sir William Jones.'

But to return to Ian Rutherford. I asked to see the manager of the Karachi pharmacy and explained my problem to a wise, white-haired old man who told me he had been a chemist and dispenser in India for forty years. 'Black Jack,' he said at once. 'He needs a dose of Black Jack,' and went away leaving me puzzled, thinking of leather bottles and Cornish miners. He came back with a long cylindrical bottle containing half-a-pint of a thick black liquid. 'Your friend must take this,' he said. 'In doses of what size?' I asked. 'Oh no,' he replied. 'He must take the whole of it in one go. And may I say that he should then lie down somewhere fairly close to the lavatory. There should be relief within the hour, perhaps earlier.' He leaned towards me and whispered confidentially: 'It is a form of gunpowder, d'ye know.'

I carried my precious bottle back to Old Government House in a victoria pulled by a horse evidently not suffering from the Rutherford complaint, and explained it all to Ian, who was almost purple in the face and said he was in great pain. He seized the magic black potion and drank it eagerly. I went to my room next door and sat at my desk signing some letters. I had momentarily forgotten about Ian when about half-an-hour later I heard the distant noise of a mild explosion. Curious, I went out into the corridor and saw Ian coming out of the lavatory clutching his trousers. As he tottered towards me I saw he was pale in the face: 'It worked,' he said, 'but it may have killed me. I think I have been split in half.'

By the time the bar opened he was restored to his normal self and, while we were celebrating, Captain Sanderson came up to me. 'May I please have a word with you on a serious matter?' 'Certainly,' I said, 'carry on.' 'No,' he said. 'It is a serious official complaint. May we go to your office?' When we were there he explained that he was in the habit every day of conducting his yogic meditations in our lavatory and had installed there a small sacred *bo*-tree to concentrate his thoughts. He then came to the gravamen of his complaint. 'This evening,' he said, 'when I went for my evening meditation I discovered my *bo*-tree on the ground, its bowl broken. It is clearly a deliberate act of hostility by one living on our floor. As almost everyone is part of your unit I thought I would tell you first before going to see the Commandant.'

I went back to the bar realizing that Black Jack had done evil as well as good. Next morning Jock Campbell summoned me and I told him what I thought had happened. He could hardly suppress a smile. 'It must have been a very considerable explosion,' he said. 'Perhaps we could use Black Jack in intelligence work.' And then I knew he was not as mad as many said but a shrewdly amused observer of life.

We had great problems at first with finances. No one paid us any money but the bank was helpful. I was given no equipment and bought a typewriter out of my own funds. Eventually on the typewriter I wrote an angry letter to the financial officer at Air Headquarters India explaining the position and ending with a sentence I was proud of: 'Is it the deliberate intention of your headquarters that the three officers you especially summoned out from England to run a training school in Air Photographic Intelligence, and soon to create and develop an operational Photo-Interpretation Unit in Delhi, should be left without any payment for three months, surviving on their ever increasing overdrafts?' It had the desired effect.

Back in Delhi I was faced with the job of setting up a small version of Medmenham. This was not difficult to do. There were Terence Powell and Ian Rutherford to assist and advise and we were able to get Stuart Piggott to join us and also David Park, an experienced interpreter, who, like Piggott, had been posted to Singapore. Gradually we collected together the nucleus of a staff and this grew and grew as we trained new staff in India and had reinforcements sent out from England. Our first officers were in hutments near the Secretariat building: one day I looked out through my office window and saw Douglas Keddie who had been one of my NCO friends in Medmenham. I had the highest opinion of his ability and integrity so I rushed round to the personnel office and begged for him. There was no problem and Keddie was astonished on being told to report to a certain room to find it full of his old friends. He became one of my props and stays on the administrative side moving steadily up to warrant officer and ruling the Central Photographic Interpretation Section (CPIS) – as we were called – with firmness and discreet power. Another administrative support of great strength and ingenuity was

Richard Yorke-Radleigh, a teacher, who after the war became an inspector of schools.

As we grew we needed larger quarters with photographic sections and a section to make models for planning and tactical briefing purposes. The model section was very well organized and run by Edward Bulley and Kim Allen. To my delight and surprise we were allotted Hyderabad Palace, the Delhi residence of the Nizam of Hyderabad, and here were able to develop ourselves as we wanted. There were parts of the Palace reserved for the use of the Nizam's family when war came to an end and once or twice I looked at them – bedrooms, a drawing room, a throne room.

One day after I had been in Hyderabad Palace for a year or so I was told that there was a gentleman at the door representing the Nizam and he would like to see me. A neat man in ordinary civilian clothes wearing a turban came in and said he was making his annual routine visit on behalf of the Nizam. He realized that for security reasons he could not see the Nizam's private rooms: he merely wanted my assurance that none of the rooms, particularly the Queen's boudoir and bedroom, had been interfered with in any way and that no Europeans ever visited them. I readily gave him this assurance in all good faith and he bowed himself out. When he had gone I asked Sergeant Keddie, as he then was, where exactly were the Queen's rooms: I thought I might see that they were not mouldering away. Keddie brought back the plan of the palace and showed me that the Queen's apartments were in fact now our main dark rooms and constantly occupied by sweating British airmen. I gave strict instructions that I and I only must interview the Nizam's representative when he next visited us; but he never did, which was a relief.

At first I shared my office with the Wing Commander Photography in India Command, but this didn't work – the technical aspects of photography and intelligence work of interpretation were quite different; then with Stuart Piggott, who was the senior army officer in our combined unit; and then with Tony Wood, Peter Riddell's brother-in-law, who had worked in the library at Westminster Abbey and after the war became archivist for Warwickshire. He was most intelligent and amusing company and his sense of humour sometimes produced situations which made me leave the room in fits of laughter. We had several telephones: one direct outside line was always going wrong. 'Yes,' I would hear Tony Wood say into the machine, 'we are indeed the Imperial Cinema. You must not miss this week's picture. It is a sexual orgy – rape and sodomy every few minutes.' And on another occasion, 'We are indeed the New Delhi Chinese Laundry. Delighted to have your custom. Send us all your clothes and sheets. We will have them torn to shreds and sent to someone else. Goodbye.'

Eventually as the unit grew and I was made a wing commander I had my room to myself. Tony Wood had an office upstairs. One day Keddie came to me with a very puzzled expression. 'Something very peculiar is happening upstairs,' he said. 'There is a small black baby in Squadron Leader Wood's in-tray.' 'What,' I asked, 'is Squadron Leader Wood's explanation of this occurrence?' 'It's his day off,' said Keddie. 'Well,' I asked, 'what do you propose to do? This is an outrageous state of affairs. We can't have babies black or white appearing in these offices.' 'I thought, sir,' said Keddie with his customary caution, 'I would move it to his out-tray and that then it would disappear.' I said, 'This is quite ridiculous. Find out its origins and parentage.'

Half an hour later a rather sad Indian clerk was ushered into my office. 'It is all my fault,' she said sadly, 'I was coming to work this morning and I met my sister who was going shopping and she said to me, "Please look after my baby" and so I brought it with me. Squadron Leader Wood was away so I put it on his desk. It is a very nice baby and doesn't cry.' She seemed on the verge of tears herself. 'I'm meeting my sister outside at 12 o'clock.' She collected the baby and the three of us descended the steps of Hyderabad House conscious of the raised eyebrows of the police at the gate. The sister seemed as nice as my clerk. 'Please remember,' I said firmly, 'there is no parking for babies in this highly secret place.' The police seemed to be with difficulty suppressing smiles when I went back into the Palace. 'Sergeant Rumbelow,' I said fiercely, 'you and your men must take greater care about whom you admit to this office. This morning a baby was brought in without you noticing.' 'But anything,' protested Rumbelow, a very good and loyal Lancashire policeman, 'anything can be concealed in these Indian women's sarees.' By now I could hardly contain my own laughter. 'I leave it to you, Sergeant,' I said, 'to work out the details, but watch out for suspicious bulges. After all, they might be bombs, not babies.' Next morning there was a garland of flowers on my desk.

Sergeant Keddie came into my office shaking his head and

clucking, like the dear maternal hen he was, looking after all his maternal chickens from wing commander downwards. 'More trouble,' he said, 'a cross man from the Secretariat. Says his business is private and most confidential.' 'Stay with me,' I said. In came a crisp, cross, middle-aged Englishman who was vaguely familiar – I must have seen him sometime in the Club.

'Good morning,' he said sharply. 'My business is highly confidential and private. May we please be alone,' giving Keddie a dark glance. 'Why,' I said, 'this is my confidential clerk and he will take down a record of our conversation. There are only two circumstances when his services may be disposed of: a personal allegation against me, or a matter of high security. Does your business fall into these categories?' He swallowed hard. 'Very well,' he said. 'Then what are we concerned about?' I asked mildly.

'Buggery and sodomy,' he said, and I heard Keddie's quick intake of breath. 'One of your officers is billeted in my house. For many nights I have heard noises coming from his room – shrieks and cries and uncanny laughter. Last night I could bear it no longer and burst into his room. The scoundrel was in bed with one of your airmen – a corporal. Monstrous! They must be hounded out of the service and the country. I threw them out of my house at once.' 'In the middle of the night?' I asked. 'Certainly,' he replied. I remembered how deliciously mild the nights in Delhi were at that moment and I thought of my gay colleagues walking through the jacaranda-scented night. 'Please give Sergeant Keddie all the details,' I said, 'and appropriate action will be taken.' 'And I bloody well hope,' he said crossly, 'that it *will* be appropriate.'

By a curious chance, next day we got a signal from our opposite number in Italy asking whether we could make an exchange posting: one of their experienced photographic interpreters due for demobilization wanted to carry on his work overseas. Would I take him? I would indeed, and posted my delinquent officer as an exchange. I forgot about him until at the end of the war someone drew my attention to the fact that he was a town major in southern Italy and had been court-martialled for running a bordello in his headquarters.

It was Sergeant Keddie who had the idea of dealing with the corporal. He drew my attention to a special course being run for training in what to do if ship-wrecked or forced down in the desert or jungle. There was a special part of the course in which one was placed without food and drink on an island in a lake for several days. We posted the corporal on this course, but we were defeated. He made a great success of it, and was very popular with officers and men. When he returned after six weeks he seemed very fit and thanked me for giving him this splendid opportunity. The colonel running the course wrote to me and said what a success he had been, and would I agree that he might join his unit as an instructor. 'One of our more severe experiments,' wrote the Colonel, 'is to send two men out alone into the jungle or on to a deserted island and make them fend for themselves for two or three days. Everyone who went with your man was full of praise for his skill and resourcefulness and his good company.' But he was too good a technician to lose and he stayed with us and prospered in all ways.

I found myself quite soon on a secret planning committee which was working out a scheme to capture the island of Akyab, off the coast of Burma – a worthless objective, but a training for people who would, we suspected, later be trying to capture Rangoon and Singapore. It was a curious body, including Peter Fleming and Orde Wingate: the chairman was Enoch Powell, then BGS Intelligence India Command, who had just come to us from Cairo. I had met Wingate on a flight from the Near East to India: I found him an intelligent, well-read and interesting person. He was not interested in me and had that disturbing incuriosity which makes me always suspicious of people. He didn't want to know my background, or what I was doing, or why: and flying along the coast of Baluchistan he made the strange error of boring me with the story of Napier's *Peccavi* remark. When Sir Charles Napier conquered the Sind territory in 1843 he is supposed to have sent a one-word signal to the Government: *Peccavi* – 'I have sinned'. I refrained from telling Wingate that this was part of the myth of the history of the British in India, and that the pun was composed in 1846 by an anonymous contributor to *Punch* and wrongly attributed to Napier. He would have thought me a dry don: anyway he was wearing a Wolseley helmet and looked fascinatingly out of this world. Indeed I wondered then, as I wondered many times afterwards, whether he was so wrapped up in his own ploys and ideas that he could not project himself to understand other people.

When we met again in Enoch Powell's office in the Delhi secretariat he greeted me warmly and we became for a while acquaintances, at least from the planning office along the corridors to our cars. He always carried a big Irish blackthorn knobkerry. As our meetings went on and we studied the model of Akyab which my unit had made, and talked of our plans, it was obvious that he and Enoch did not get on. One day walking down the dark, cool corridors of the Secretariat building he stopped me and, furious, shook his stick and said, 'Daniel, one day I want to beat the brains out of that stupid man Powell. Will you restrain me? Will you see I don't make a fool of myself?'

Wingate and Powell had one thing in common. They eschewed all close social contacts. I asked Wingate to dine with me in my mess or the Gymkhana Club: he declined without any explanation. I asked Enoch on several occasions for a drink or dinner but he declined with an explanation: he could not waste time on social occasions because he wanted to devote every moment outside his military duties to his work on Donne. It will be remembered that I had met him just before the war in Martin Charlesworth's rooms in St John's and we had dined together at High Table. Martin had then whispered to me that Enoch was without question one of the great classical scholars of all time, and after the war Denys Page said to me, 'I would not be Regius Professor of Greek here if Enoch had stayed in the business.' But once he was a Brigadier Intelligence he had no interest in the classics. He wasn't interested in the Greeks in India, and as far as I know he never visited Taxila; nor could I interest him in Wheeler's discoveries at Arikamedu, which was revealed as a Roman trading post in south India. It was one of my many social failures that I did not get Wheeler and Powell together for a meal. But was it a failure? They were two eccentric and egocentric men who would have been vying with each other and trying to beat each other down. I was spared that occasion.

But when I was about to be demobilized in India, I insisted that Enoch should dine with me and to hell with Donne. He agreed and we had a very good dinner in the Club. I had selected the wines with care and with no attention to cost; the Club still retained the remains of its pre-war cellar. The evening developed well. What will you do, I asked, when the war is over? He said that he would not go back to being a professor of classics. He was faced with two alternatives: to stay in the army or to go into politics. 'Having achieved what I have achieved in this war,' he said, 'I should be the head of all military intelligence in the next.' The thought of the next war appalled me and of the endless drudgery of years in the peacetime army. 'But what will you do in between?' I asked. 'Ah,' he said, 'the next war will not be between America and the West versus Russia. It will be between Russia and Europe versus America. Therefore the key area to understand is Central America. I shall go underground for a year or so and get to know everywhere from Mexico to Peru.' 'And what if not the army?' I asked. 'The Conservative Party,' he said, and added calmly, 'I think I have a good chance of becoming Prime Minister.' That was in December 1945. Six weeks later when I was home and demobbed I met him in the foyer of the United University Club. He had come to begin arrangements for joining the Conservative Central Office. 'So it is to be politics,' I said. He did not reply and looked dreamily beyond me as though India and the Imperial Delhi Gymkhana Club were part of a forgotten past.

But a few years ago, the past with Enoch Powell in Delhi and the memories of his past in Cambridge before the war came vividly back to me.

In reviewing L.W. Fuchser's *Neville Chamberlain and Appeasement* in *The Spectator* on 16 April 1983, Enoch Powell said: 'I am not mistaken in knowing that in 1935 I was convinced there would be another German War and I must expect to be killed in it. I am not mistaken in remembering that in 1937 at a Trinity College Feast when the guest of honour said, "Our Government is doing its best to prevent war," I shouted from the Fellows' table, "But we *want* war". I am not mistaken in remembering that in 1937 driving to Boar's Hill with Gilbert Murray, I said to him, "There's no hope for us unless we go to war with Germany," and he looked me straight in the eyes and replied, "I think so too". Nor have I imagined the immensity of the relief when on 3 September 1939 I thought that appeasement and betrayal were over and that England, if it went down, would go down fighting.'

We now come to one of my most curious memories of my Indian days – the behaviour and mysterious illness of Peter Murray-Threipland, who was posted out to be on the Army staff of CPIS. Peter was a teetotaller with very strong opinions on many subjects, including medicine – he strongly disapproved of doctors: otherwise he was an intelligent man and had twice rowed in the Oxford boat. We did not establish very cordial relations and I gradually learnt that he disapproved of the way I was running the unit and proposed a breakaway unit in Ceylon under his own command.

One morning he came to see me white in the face and trembling with a curious mixture of rage and fear. 'I am afraid, sir,' he said, 'I must deliver this paper to you. It is an adverse report on yourself and the conduct of this important establishment.' I read it with interest – it had one or two good points. I thanked him for it and said I would forward it to the appropriate quarters.

Every week I had a meeting of half to three-quarters of an hour with the Chief Intelligence Officer, RAF, and we discussed our problems and briefed each other. At the time of my adverse report the CIO was Group Captain Jonas, a shrewd, unassuming man with a great sense of humour: he used deliberately to embarrass his staff by asking them what books they were reading or writing at the moment! At the end of the next session I gave him the Murray-Threipland document which he read carefully. 'What did you tell him?' he asked. 'I said I was forwarding the document to the appropriate quarters.' Jonas tore the document into pieces and put them in his wastepaper basket. 'I have now done that,' he said, and paused. 'By the way, I have just asked the C. in C. to mention you in his despatches to the Air Ministry.'

Weeks passed and Murray-Threipland seemed to be avoiding me, or averted his glance whenever I came near him. Eventually he plucked up courage and asked what had been the reaction to his report. 'It went to the appropriate quarter,' I said, 'and I had a constructive and helpful discussion with the CIO.' His face brightened and he became cheerful again.

But then he began to get ill and complained of a sore throat but refused to see our MO. The throat got worse and worse: I thought it might be a streptococcal infection such as I'd had twice while I was in India. There lived a few doors away from me an Air Commodore friend who was a consultant physician to the Air Force in India, and I asked him to call on Peter. He came back to me and demanded a stiff drink. 'Murray-Threipland has diphtheria,' he said. 'He is infectious and dangerously so: I am sending him to hospital.'

I went out to visit him in the military hospital. He got steadily better. One day I went there and there was no Peter. They told me he had discharged himself although he was by no means cured. When I found him back in his quarters he declared that he really was cured but that they wanted him to stay another week and go somewhere else for convalescence, but all this he refused and discharged himself as an officer of field rank was apparently able to do.

Within a few months he began to develop disquieting symptoms.

His hands began to shake and he dropped things. One day when we were breakfasting together in the mess he lifted up a teapot to pour out a cup for me and the teapot crashed on to the table. 'Is it true,' asked Sergeant Keddie later, 'as the story is going round, that Major Murray-Threipland threw a teapot at you?' Then one day he came into my office with some papers and stood in front of my desk. I looked down at my papers and when I looked up he wasn't there. He had fallen on to the ground and couldn't get up. I consulted my Air Commodore friend, and told him how Peter had discharged himself from hospital before the treatment was complete. 'No doubt about it at all,' he said. 'This does happen, he has post-diphtheric paralysis. Tiresome, but not serious. Make him see a doctor who will recommend rest and exercises and give him some drugs.' 'But,' I said, 'he doesn't approve of doctors'. 'Then the fool is likely to suffer horribly, though his condition is not fatal.'

I told Peter this. He refused to see a military doctor, perhaps understandably because they would take him to task for discharging himself before their care of him was over. 'And I don't want to see a black doctor,' he said. I, however, found the name of an Indian consultant physician, made an appointment, enlisted the help of Tony Wood, who was a friend of his, ordered my car and two of our policemen and we got him very reluctantly to the surgery. The doctor was charming and most understanding and recommended various medicaments but mainly rest, change, exercises and, if possible, sea bathing. Sea bathing seemed a difficulty and then Tony Wood had a brilliant idea. 'Goa,' he said; he had always wanted to visit it and see the Baroque architecture. He would accompany Peter and they would bathe in the sea. But Goa was Portuguese and therefore a neutral country. I consulted my superiors and the visit was arranged; the best hotel in Goa was booked and many important documents signed by the Chief of Air Staff and the Adjutant General were obtained and passports were visa'd. We saw them off on the train with sighs of relief. Next day there were agitated telegrams and telephone messages. They had been arrested on the India-Goa frontier and were in gaol, surprisingly in the charge of Irish mercenary soldiers. The trouble was a simple one: there was no document signed by their CO! The great papers from the top were of no avail. I hastily made out a document and sent it as quickly as possible to them and after five days in prison they got to Goa.

Their hotel was a pleasant one giving directly on to the beach and Peter was able to sit in the surf and exercise his legs in the sea water, gaining strength every day. He complained that the hotel was noisy and that there was a great banging of doors and moving around during the night. Tony discovered that it was not only the best hotel in Goa but the best brothel!

It was while they were on this visit that the German surrender took place and the war in the West was over. Wood and Murray-Threipland were in the bar talking to a few acquaintances, including a middle-aged grey-haired man they particularly liked who had never revealed what he did or why he was in Goa. They had talked about many things and the man seemed very well informed about all aspects of the war. 'I think he may be a spy,' said Wood, and how right he was! The news of the end of the war came through on the crackling radio, and they all ordered another round of drinks. Then they noticed the middle-aged grey-haired man was no longer with them. While they were lifting their second glasses a shot rang out from a nearby room. When they were sitting down to their curry the proprietor came and told them that Colonel Kreutzner, as he knew him to be from British Intelligence, had shot himself. 'He was,' he said simply, 'the chief German agent in India.'

I flew back to London in 1943 to renew contact with the Air Ministry and Medmenham and stayed in the United University Club in Suffolk Street as the guest (I only became a member a year later) of my old Cambridge friend, Mervyn Jones, an international lawyer then working in the Foreign Office. He insisted on taking me out to dinner and we stumbled through the dark to the Café Royal. There were few other diners. Mervyn insisted that since I had been out of the country so long we must drink the best claret that was within his budget. A bottle came and he tasted it, and tasted it again, and said, 'Something wrong with this bottle, I am afraid.' The waiter took it away and brought another, and again Mervyn savoured it and tasted it and regretfully said, 'I am afraid this bottle is no better'. The head wine waiter was summoned and he agreed. 'Let me bring you another,' he said, and a third bottle came. By now I was praying that nothing would be wrong with this one. Mervyn smelt and tasted it and shook his head sadly. 'Even worse than the other two,' he said. 'Taste it yourself.' The wine waiter did and made a wry face. 'Would you like to see the maître d'hôtel?' he asked. When the great man came he only briefly tasted the wine and looked dispirited. Mervyn said: 'Has anything happened to your cellar?' and then, 'By God, of course, you had a bomb dropped just at the back. I think some of these wines have been cooked.' The maître d'hôtel nodded his head sadly. 'Only too true, sir,' he said. 'But we don't know which have been affected. You are the first person who has noticed anything'. He hesitated. 'May I bring you a wine which I know to be all right, and it will be on the house?' Then there came two bottles of the most delicious Bonnes-Mares, and they were in perfect condition.

We thanked him and drank some armagnac and weaved our way slowly back to the Club through the darkness and empty streets. Mervyn caught his umbrella in a grating, had great difficulty getting it out, and when he did it was bent in half. We walked into the Club and found Anthony Bevir, Preferment Secretary to the Cabinet, asleep on the settee in the passage leading to the coffee room. 'Drunk again,' said Mervyn agreeably, prodding Bevir with his misshapen umbrella. Bevir opened one bleary eye. 'Maybe,' he said, 'but at least I don't walk round London with an L-shaped umbrella.'

On another occasion Stuart Piggott and I were sent to attend a conference in Algiers between all the American and British photo-interpretation units to discuss aims and methods and forms of co-operation. The conference never happened because of high-level Anglo-American bickerings, but we had set out before this was known and were comfortably ensconced in a seedy hotel in Cairo when I burst out into a streaming cold with great sinus pains. The RAF doctor said I was not fit to fly for several days, that my eardrums would burst if I did. In any case we could not get passages from Cairo to Algiers, our priorities being very low.

We spent a very pleasant few days in Cairo, went out again to the pyramids, and ate and drank surprisingly well. One night after a very good dinner at the St James's Restaurant we were so delighted with the local Egyptian wine bottled by the Société Anonyme Vinicole et Viticole, that we found ourselves unsteadily walking home singing: 'Vinicole et Viticole, let the tide of victory roll' – two putative professors in splendid form! Then one day we went down to Alexandria in the lovely Pullman train and on the way were recommended an hotel with a cellar with pre-war wines at nonsensically cheap prices. We at first mislaid the way and found ourselves in a most insalubrious part of Alex with tall virile men beckoning us and saying, 'This way, sahib, this way. This way to good jig-jig.' We turned tail and eventually got to the hotel. The 1923 hocks were unbelievable and we were allowed to buy bottles to take away with us. The early evening journey back to Cairo through the Delta was memorable, if hazy.

I had been reading a detective story and thought it badly written and badly constructed; I threw it out through the bedroom window with snorts of rage. 'Surely anyone could do better than that?' I said. 'Why not have a try?' said Stuart Piggott, and when I got back to Delhi I did, and that is how *The Cambridge Murders* came into existence. When, next lunchtime in the bar, I met a Brigadier friend also waiting for a plane, he said, 'Damn funny thing happened to me yesterday when I was walking through the courtyard. Something odd descended on my head. Found it was a Penguin detective story. Manna from heaven. Run out of books. Just finished reading it. One of the best and best-written stories I have ever read.' I remained silent.

Eventually we were offered a passage to Malta and told we could get to Algiers that way. My cold was better and we landed in Malta in wonderful sunshine. It was our job to get on to Algiers as quickly as possible, but neither of us wanted to miss this opportunity of seeing the great megalithic temples of the island. I explained to the traffic control officer that we wanted to go on to Algiers but that we had a very low priority and did not expect any special treatment. 'No one has spoken to me like that for weeks,' said the harassed man. 'They are all saying they must be put on the next plane. I shall see that you and Colonel Piggott are in Algiers this evening.' I hastily replied: 'That is most kind, but before we go on we must inspect the camouflage defences on the island.' And so we had two blissful days inspecting the Maltese megalithic monuments. We were surprised to find them spattered with the debris of air battles; I still have on the mantelshelf of my College rooms a piece of Messerschmitt that I picked off the capstone of Mnajdra. We were there in Malta the first day that wine had come into the island since its blockade had been broken; and we spent a good evening with our formerly besieged colleagues. Later that evening Stuart Piggott wrote a poem which is printed in his *Fire among the Ruins* which has this couplet:

> And the bomber found its doom
> In the megalithic tomb.

When, back in Delhi, I told Peter Fleming of our Malta reception and the difficulty of refusing an immediate passage, he said ruefully that the reverse had happened to him. He and Lord Gerald Wellesley were trying to get an air passage in the Mediterranean and were turned down. Fleming said to Wellesley, 'But whom did you tell them you are? You know that from yesterday you are the Duke of Wellington. Go back in and try again.' After a few minutes Wellesley, or rather the Duke, came out crestfallen and said, the man was unsympathetic: he said to him, 'If you have suddenly discovered that you are the Duke of Wellington, I have suddenly discovered that I am the Duke of York. Please, sir, don't waste my time.'

I can attest one comparable incident. In 1936 I was excavating a site in the Vale of Glamorgan on the land of the Mackintosh of Mackintosh, one of the many Scottish aristos who had married into or settled in South Wales. He took an interest in what I was doing and asked me to his house for tea, and told me that this folk story had actually happened to him. He had gone by train to Cardiff and taken a taxi to Cardiff Castle where he was going to see the Marquis of Bute. 'I found,' he said, 'that my man had forgotten to give me any money, and I explained this to the taxi driver saying I was sure the Marquis would provide the fee. He did not appreciate the situation and I drew myself up and said, "But I am a respectable and well-known figure. I am the Mackintosh of Mackintosh." To which the taxi driver angrily replied, "I don't care whether you are a mackintosh or an umbrella, I want my fare."'

The Malta-Algiers trip was full of incident. Although we escaped the worst horrors of the Indian summer, our trip was not without adventures – which included being shipwrecked in Valetta harbour (not through enemy action, merely bad yachtsmanship on the part of our Maltese air-photographic hosts), and being almost bitten to death by bed bugs and other horrors of the night in a staging post in the Western Desert. Not the least exciting part of the journey was being in territory formerly Italian and landing at aerodromes we had studied on air photographs when they were occupied by Axis air forces. At one place we were served by Italian waiters in an RAF mess, while a large bust of Mussolini twice life-size glowered down at us. At another there were twenty Italians cleaning out a hangar: they seemed very cheerful in spite of being guarded by an airman with a tommy gun. At another aerodrome we were surprised to hear heels being clicked very smartly and to be saluted by two German full colonels – prisoners of war on their way to some other destination.

I enjoyed our stay in Algiers, which was largely a holiday since, as I have related, the conference was eventually abandoned. Day after day we reported to Air Headquarters to be told: 'No news – come back tomorrow.' We went off on excursions to the countryside or worked in the university library. An agreeable French-Algerian liaison officer was put in charge of us and a few others waiting for the conference. He was great fun and took us to small and interesting restaurants but his command of idiomatic English was occasionally engagingly odd. We piled into a jeep and before we set out he would turn round with a winning smile and say, 'I hope you are all safely stuffed in the backsides.'

Piggott and I were billeted in a small hotel by the harbour which had a cinema on the ground floor. It specialized in showing war films and we got used to getting to sleep to the constant sound of machine-gun fire and exploding bombs. We shared a double bed and laid in plentiful supplies of wine which we kept cool in the bidet. But one night the gunfire and bombs seemed extraordinarily loud and we had to take a great deal of wine to drug ourselves to sleep. Next morning we discovered that units of the British fleet had anchored in the harbour and had been the target of a severe but unsuccessful bombing attack: many buildings near the harbour had been destroyed including a school directly behind our cinema.

One of the joys of those days in Algiers was to eat French food again and to discover that, though there was rationing, there were a few places where there seemed no difficulty in getting anything one wanted. One such place was a small café called Le Warsovie run by an expatriate Pole. His food was superb and his meals always began with a special and very intoxicating cocktail which he called the Cocktail Winston Churchill. He had no telephone and one day I was sent to book tables for dinner. I discovered the proprietor pouring into a very large jug, and apparently haphazardly, a generous helping from every bottle on the bar shelves in front of him. This was how the special house cocktail was made!

We were introduced by some friendly and discerning American officers to another restaurant. One evening as we were finishing our dinner we noticed that as many of the customers left they leaned over and said something to Madame at the desk who checked their names on a list. When it came to paying our bills we heard the man in front of us say, 'Vendredi soir comme d'habitude'. When it came to our turn I said the same, showed our passports and she wrote down our names on her list. When we left, and during the next few days, we wondered what we had let ourselves in for: was it a brothel or a secret showing of sex films? We half decided not to go and when we got to the restaurant it was firmly closed and shuttered and there was a notice across the door saying *Fermeture hebdomadaire le vendredi*. Perhaps slightly relieved, we walked away, but passed two American officers who went boldly up to the door and knocked twice. We followed them, knocked twice, and were admitted. There was really no great mystery: every Friday when the restaurant was officially closed the management imported two *femmes indigènes* from the countryside who, defying all rationing, cooked us one of the most remarkable dishes of couscous we have ever eaten. Alas, we were on our way back to India before the following Friday.

The Central Photographic Intelligence Section of India Command and later South East Asia Command had begun, if not as two men and a boy, as three men (myself, Ian Rutherford and Terence Powell) and two clerks, to which the redoubtable Douglas Keddie was soon added. At its height in 1945 it consisted of several hundreds, the main part with its modelling section and library being in Hyderabad House, with detachments in Calcutta, and forward units on the Burma front and in Ceylon.

I was always accused of empire building, and to a certain extent this was true of anyone running any specialist intelligence unit anywhere in wartime. I must say I enjoyed the six-monthly session with the establishment boys and got on well with them. On one occasion I had to defend my establishment enlargement proposals before two group captains who were acting as a scrutiny board. One was Hawtrey, a died-in-the-wool pre-war regular of a very testy nature; the other was that amusing eccentric, the Earl of Bandon. Hawtrey pitched into my proposals and I had to fight for every single increase in staff. In the end it was clear that it was not me or CPIS that he disapproved of but the whole idea of using air photography for military intelligence. 'Why don't you use existing photographic archives?' he said. 'People have got collections of postcards, d'ye know. Take my old aunt for example: she travelled everywhere and has a marvellous collection. Bet she has some pretty useful views of Rangoon and Singapore.' 'I wonder,' I said, 'has she or anyone else got detailed views of the beaches around the island of Akyab where, as you know, we are mounting a special operation?' He snorted; Paddy Bandon exploded in mirth. I got my new posts.

Establishment was one thing: keeping one's officers was not difficult because they were in a specialized intelligence category; but keeping one's airmen was difficult. They were in generalized professions classified mainly as 'Photographers' or 'Clerks General Duty'. It was annoying and defeating to have airmen whom we had trained as map clerks, plotters and interpreters suddenly posted away at the whim of some personnel officer. I had to fight continually to retain experienced men on whom we relied a great deal. In the end I thought the only way was to create a special trade in the Air Force, namely Clerks Special Duty (Photo Intelligence). I began what was to be a very long series of letters and minutes. My proposal was approved in India but, of course, as it affected the whole Air Force, the matter was transferred to London. Surprisingly, it was thought a good idea and was about to happen when the war came to an end. It is one of my minor disappointments that I cannot say I introduced a new trade into the RAF.

My life in India during those four years involved constant travel, not only to visit our detachments in Calcutta and Ceylon, but to fulfil lecturing engagements at, and liaison visits with, various schools and special bodies. I was happy to visit Poona and Lahore from time to time and used to go each three months to give a few lectures in the Staff College at Quetta. This was a welcome break from the office in Delhi: a night on the Frontier Mail and then the journey up to Quetta. Sometimes in the hot weather it was almost unbearable. I remember once travelling with an old Indian Army Colonel. We got to Jacobabad, reputedly the hottest place in India: 'Only one thing to do,' said the Colonel, as the train came to a halt, and he summoned a boy who was selling soft drinks on the platform. We loaded into our compartment two cases of assorted drinks: they were of course packed in ice and when the train drew out we took our clothes off and poured these iced drinks over our heated bodies. The cooling result was delicious but of course we were left with a horrid stickiness.

I had many friends in Quetta and between lectures they drove me out in a pony and trap to the quiet hills. The train from Quetta joined the Karachi express and, before the night journey back to Delhi, it stopped long enough at Lahore for a quick dinner in the restaurant.

On one occasion there were two rowdy parties of officers enjoying their dinner with plenty to drink. I finished my meal and was preparing to go to bed in my compartment when the train moved out. By chance I looked out at the station and saw my dining companions storming out of the station restaurant and vainly pursuing the train slowly moving off for the east. I thought this was time for action. I pulled the communication cord: nothing happened. I pulled again: the train trundled on. Not to be defeated I put my feet against the end of the carriage and pulled with two hands. The chain and its handle came off in my hands and I fell back on my bed exhausted: but the train stopped. I looked nervously out of my window: the restaurant party ran panting along and got into the train. I put the communication cord and its handle in my despatch case and got into bed pleased with my day's work: I had never stopped a train before, let alone a major express.

There was a knock on the door: it was the train supervisor. 'I am sorry to disturb you, sahib,' he said. 'There has been some trouble: someone pulled the communication cord.' He looked up above my head, 'Ah, I see it was not you,' he said, 'because you have no cord. We must see to that. Goodnight.'

I treasured that minor relic of my India days and it rests in my College rooms together with the Messerschmitt fragment found on Malta. A curious undergraduate once asked me why I kept a lavatory chain on my notice board. 'Not a lavatory chain, dear boy,' I said coldly, 'it is the communication cord of the Indian Frontier Mail.'

After a while a new Director of Intelligence at Air Headquarters said to me, 'I approve your visits to the Staff College at Quetta but you seem to be away for nearly a week. Next time you go you are to fly: our staff aircraft is at your disposal. Your visit can all be done in two days.' When the next time came I reminded him: all was arranged and I reported with my bag at the military airport at Palam and was flown away in a small two-seater aircraft by an agreeable flight sergeant from Cardiff. I sat behind him but after half an hour the intercom broke down and I was surprised when we landed at Lahore. Something was wrong with the aircraft: it would not take long to mend. It took five hours; we set out in the late afternoon for the flight to Quetta. His radio then broke down and he never received a message saying that the monsoon had spread up into the Punjab, flying was dangerous and we must return to Lahore. He flew on into a tremendous storm with whirling clouds of dust. He flew down to ground level: we picked up the Indus and by great skill he found a landing ground. It was the disused aerodrome of Multan. There was no-one there, but after a while various people arrived, opened up an office and took us under control. Together we tethered the aircraft to the ground with ropes and we were then taken away to a *dak* bungalow. A fire was lit and drinks were produced from nowhere: so was our dinner: chicken soup, an anonymous fish wrapped in batter, chicken curry, crème caramel; and bottles of beer.

Next morning we were awake early and there were crowds of people interested in this strange aircraft which had appeared overnight in their midst. We refuelled the aircraft from cans of petrol: it took a long time. Everyone was most co-operative: they all thought it a splendid adventure and so it was. Eventually to the cheers of the assembled crowds, and my fears and doubts, we took off from Multan for Quetta. But alas, no Quetta – my pilot said there were further technical problems and he was landing at Jacobabad. And at Jacobabad it was said to be not airworthy and its repair would take a week or more. I reported to the District Officer who was a charmer and pleased to receive a strange visitor from the outer world: he himself was leaving for a meeting in Karachi but laid on a delightful dinner party. We would catch the train to Quetta at 2 a.m. After he had left I was installed in a most comfortable bedroom; I remember that by my bedside there were four decanters: brandy, whisky, Grand Marnier and cherry brandy. Despite these allurements I caught the Quetta train, sober, and lectured at 8 a.m. and again at 10, and then did all the normal seminars and discussions that were part of the exercise. I got back to my office in Delhi ten days after having left. My boss made no comment but never offered me special air travel again.

When Mountbatten was appointed Commander-in-Chief, South East Asia Command, he established his headquarters in Ceylon and took over the India Headquarters in Delhi as his Base Headquarters. I was made to go every month from Delhi to Kandy for staff meetings. Mountbatten thought that it was easy for people to work in Delhi for the day, then take the night plane to Colombo, and the train up to Kandy – and he had fixed the Colombo-Kandy train service with a restaurant car serving bacon and eggs from morning to night. But he reckoned without the monsoon: on two of our Delhi-Colombo flights we were brought down at Bangalore and made to stay the night there.

I had few serious administrative and disciplinary problems. One of my airmen died suddenly of a strangulated hernia. It was indicated that I would be the main person at his funeral. I explained to a sympathetic warrant officer that I was a bogus RAF officer and had never been on a parade in my life. He took me through the ceremonial procedure and I did well except for one moment when I nearly stepped forward into the open grave instead of backwards. I stood at the foot of the grave and as the coffin was lowered down it was tip-tilted and out of it there poured a filthy liquid of decomposition and a horrid stench filled the air. I thought I would pass out but I counted twenty; the ceremony was over, and I did in a daze what I was supposed to do and got back to the car. My warrant officer was a few minutes before joining me. 'How did I do?' I said. 'You were marvellous,' he said. 'But we were not. We have been sick in the bushes.'

The heat of the summer and the approach of the monsoon was excessively trying and every year there was an outbreak of what we all called 'monsoon minutes'. Some of Piggott's officers tried to write an adverse report on him. A tiresome army captain called Sowerby (nicknamed Pigprick) insisted on seeing me – I was operationally in charge of everyone in Hyderabad House – and said that Piggott did not carry out his duties and spent his time writing books on archaeology. 'And what do you do on your weekly day off?' I said. 'I spend my day off writing detective stories. I bet you spend your time drinking in the Club.' He retired confused but organized a protest meeting against Stuart Piggott on quite another and amusingly trivial ground.

All army officers who came to work with us were transferred to the Intelligence Corps. Many of them liked to keep their old regimental associations and wore fore and aft caps of scarlet, blue and yellow showing that they were originally in Probyn's Horse or Skinners or whatever.

An order was promulgated saying that officers transferred to the Intelligence Corps could not wear their original regimental colours. Neither Piggott nor I paid the slightest attention to this until Captain Sowerby and his associates demanded an interview with Colonel Piggott to discuss this important issue – it was very hot in Delhi in July. Stuart was marvellous: he said, 'I don't care what you wear on your heads. For all I care you can wear chamber pots.'

His dissenting officers retreated in confusion and thought again about their hot-weather behaviour. They recovered their good temper and humour and when Piggott was leaving for England and giving up his command they planned a very special farewell party for him. 'This is going to be a very special do,' said one of his staff. 'A very special do.' It was. All the assembled company were wearing chamber pots on their heads.

I made many new friends and acquaintances in India: André Bicat, Mervyn Horder as well as Peter Fleming. Mervyn had been a contemporary of mine at Cambridge but we had never met there. I much enjoyed his company in Delhi, and his waspish clinical assessment of our colleagues. He was the Chairman of Duckworths and asked me to write the archaeology volume in his *Hundred Years* Series, which crystallized my interest in the development of archaeology.

Many of my officers became good friends. One such was Harry Boutflower, a Master at Cheltenham. He had a colleague who had been tutor to the sons of the Maharajah of Bundi, a small state between Delhi and Bombay. We were invited to Bundi for a few days; stayed in the state guest house and were driven around regally in one of the Maharajah's limousines. On one occasion, driving through the jungle, the chauffeur brought the car to an abrupt stop. In front of us was a tiger: it stopped in the middle of the road, stared at us, and then walked slowly into the jungle.

I am not very clear how I came to meet Peter Fleming. He was head of deception in the Military Intelligence organization in Delhi, GSI (d) and subsequently Force 256, which carried out operations such as Error and Purple Whales and a version of Operation Mincemeat. I suppose it was through André Bicat who was initially in charge of camouflage, then moved to making all the extraordinary devices to assist deception – Pintails, Parafexes, Aquaskits, Aquatails and Paragons – the last were dummy paratroops. We interpreted air photographs of Bicat's deceptions. One day in Bicat's office Fleming said to me, 'They tell me, Daniel,' in that slightly arrogant way which concealed his shyness and dislike of self-advertisement, so well understood and written about by Duff Hart-Davis in his *Peter Fleming: a Biography* (1974), 'that you are a Cambridge don? Then you must play squash and chess?' I said 'Yes' to all three. 'Then if you have an evening to spare let us play together.'

And so began a long acquaintance, which I think was a real friendship that lasted all the time I was in India. The formula was a simple one: we met for a game of squash in the Gymkhana Club, a swim in the pool, a steak sandwich in the bar, and a game of chess. His chess was not as good as mine: but at first his squash was much better. I knew very well the squash professional in the Imperial Delhi Gymkhana Club and his young nephew with whom I played every morning on my day off. I got them interested in my matches with Fleming and I cheated. 'Study Colonel Fleming's game,' I said. 'Tell me his weak points. I know mine. Tell me how to cope with this man.' In a month I was beating him easily. 'You play a damn good game, Daniel, these days. You seem to be improving.' Then as the first year of our play together crept along into the growing heat of April/May, I said one evening, 'I imagine we shall soon be giving up our games.' He looked coldly at me and said, 'Why?' 'The hot weather,' I said. 'What nonsense!' he replied and I played squash all through the hot weather in Delhi for three years. It was probably good for me.

He was frequently away on trips to China, Burma or England. We nearly coincided on my visit back to England; but he had stopped in Lisbon. 'Friends of mine in the Embassy,' he said, 'took me to a dance and pointed out a very good-looking girl. "That's the number two German spy here," they said. "Please introduce me." They reluctantly did. Later I danced with her and the dance-hall was surprised by her anguished cry. I had bitten her sharply in the ear. You see, I had never before bitten a German spy.'

This curious little story shows the Fleming that Duff Hart Davis captures so well in his book and whom I got to know: detached, amused, debonair, dashing, but deeply concerned with affairs. He went through life successfully acting the part which some have called 'the last English public school boy' – and he did find the day he left Eton one of the saddest in his life: but an astonishingly gifted part in which at Oxford he was President of OUDS, a member of the Bullingdon and took a First in English.

It gave me pleasure to introduce Fleming to Mortimer Wheeler over lunch in the Imperial Hotel. Both were at first disinclined to accept the invitation with warmth and to begin with there was a lot of ice-cold fencing. But as I knew it would, the archaeological work of Sir Aurel Stein in Central Asia provided a common enthusiasm and the lunch was a success. Afterwards Wheeler said to me: 'That was a good occasion. But what a strange fellow. A poseur! Has too good an opinion of himself.' And Peter said to me, 'Much enjoyed that lunch with that Desert and Chelsea Rat. What strange friends you do have. A poseur. Has too good an opinion of himself.'

They were, I suppose, to an extent poseurs in that they were living out successfully parts they had written for themselves and played to crowded houses all over the world for years. They had one curious thing in common, which in Wheeler's case was later completely masked by television: they lacked the common touch. In 1945, when the war was over, I got them both to speak to my airmen and airwomen. Both lectures were voted non-successes. Peter had annoyed them by suggesting that there was nothing peculiar or brave in dangerous travel, that you set out from Peking with sixpence in your pocket and went on walking until you got to Srinagar (these were his words). Wheeler had similarly played down the rôle of the archaeologist who just went walking over the countryside finding the odd sherd or flint implement which revolutionized history. One of my most faithful and trusted warrant officers said to me, 'Funny. They're both famous. But they are both showmen. Wouldn't have them in the house at home. The missus wouldn't feel safe!'

I naturally made many foes and temporary enemies in India. I say naturally because anyone running a large intelligence (or any other) unit in war must have to take decisions that are distasteful to and disagreed with by many people. My greatest misfortune was that my unit contained many of my friends: and to be the commanding officer of your friends and archaeological colleagues was something which I had not thought about, especially in its implications in the heat and monsoon burden of the Indian day.

Terence Powell had come out with me to India and had been selected by me in Medmenham as part of the Daniel-Powell-Rutherford team to build up Indian Photographic Intelligence, and we had run the Karachi Intelligence School successfully and amicably together. When we got to Delhi, and the Photographic Intelligence Unit built up into something very large with its CO constantly involved in conferences in Air Headquarters and visits to Calcutta, Ceylon and elsewhere, I became isolated and the old tripartite relationship began to break down. And then after the collapse of Singapore, India was left with officers with wider experience and seniority than Rutherford and Powell. David Park took over our detachment in Calcutta and was senior to Ian Rutherford – who took the situation well. Stuart Piggott was with us because he had not got to Singapore and as the army side of Air Photo Intelligence developed I found myself in a difficult situation. The army unit wanted to keep its establishment parallel to that of the RAF and as I moved to squadron leader and wing commander they wanted a major and a lieutenant colonel. Who was this to be? I insisted this was the army's concern. They said, 'No, you are in charge, you must tell us what to do.' I demurred, saying that the army staff were not technically under my control. I was summoned to the Director of Military Intelligence, Major General Cawthorn, and it was spelt out what I had to do.

When Stuart Piggott was promoted major and then lieutenant colonel, my relations with Terence Powell moved from coldness to hostility and I realized that his bitterness was such that he was organizing a campaign against me at all levels. He refused to speak to me and I was told that he was mounting an attack against me as an inefficient commanding officer. I was due for a week's leave and went to the Cecil Hotel at Murree. It was an unhappy week and I walked about in the pinewoods thinking: was I really a person suitable to run a complex and important organization of this kind?

When I got back to Delhi there was a note from Peter Fleming saying, 'Why didn't you turn up on Wednesday? See you are in the Club this Wednesday.' After our weekly game of squash and our steak sandwich and chess I poured out my soul to him. He listened carefully, the mask removed, and said, 'Dear boy, I have the same problem. All the people who work with me are friends and I have to deal with their promotions, decorations, postings, and the rest of it. You have to be two persons. Incidentally, I have always been three: myself, my public person, and my official person. I will help you.' Two days later I was telephoned from Military Headquarters saying that London would like Captain Powell seconded to Medmenham immediately for special duties. Did I approve?

Peter was away in China for the next ten days, but when we had another evening in the Club I said, 'Do you remember me telling you about my problem?' 'Oh, yes,' he said, rather quickly, 'the Powell-Piggott problem, wasn't it?' 'The problem is over,' I said, 'Powell has been posted back to England.' 'Really,' he said, 'how interesting. Sometimes things work out for the best. But we are talking too much. It's your move.'

Of course while I was in India there was constant talk of independence and it was obvious to most that these were the last years of the British Raj. I was in Karachi in March 1942 when Stafford Cripps flew in. (I remember the confusion and embarrassment because he had not been properly inoculated.) He came with an invitation to the Congress leaders to join the Viceroy's Council, a promise for independence when the war was over, and a prospect of Pakistan.

Nehru was in favour of accepting the Cripps offer but Mahatma Gandhi said 'No,' declaring it 'a post-dated cheque on a failing bank'. He produced his slogan 'Quit India' and started the biggest wave of civil disobedience the country had known. This was the time when the Japanese were advancing through Burma. Gandhi and the other Congress leaders were interned in the Aga Khan's palace in Poona. Soldiers were used to deal with the civil disorder. Over a thousand people were killed and 60,000 put in prison. And in 1943 famine devastated Bengal: the estimates of those who died from starvation vary from one and a half to three million. I stepped over the dead and dying in the streets of Calcutta.

Lord Wavell succeeded Linlithgow as Viceroy in October 1943. Two years later, when the European war ended, the new British government prepared for Indian independence, which happened two years later. I left India in December of 1945 with the fondest memories of the sub-continent and the saddest memories of the poverty and plight of its people despite years of efficient rule by the Indian Civil Service. On my last visit to the Staff College in Quetta I was staying with one of the assistant commandants. We walked back to his house from dinner in the mess, through the moonlight which showed up groups of people sleeping in courtyards and in the shadows of bungalows. It was a lovely evening and unthinkingly I said, 'I shall take this home with me as one of my memories of India.' 'Yes,' said the Brigadier, half-misunderstanding me. 'But after a few years we shan't be able to blame the British for the poverty and suffering.'

I once met Wavell when he was Commander-in-Chief and a party of us went to sing carols to him at Christmastime. We talked about archaeology and Cambridge and his anthology *Other Men's Flowers*, and he confirmed that he could only remember the order of the senior Indian princes of Hyderabad, Kashmir, Mysore, Gwalior and Baroda by the sentence Hot Kippers Make Good Breakfast!

It was when Piggott and I were in Algiers for the non-existent conference that we went to a high-level party and met Harold Macmillan, C.A. Ralegh Radford, and Mortimer Wheeler who told us that he was to become Director General of Archaeology in India, 'but not,' he said, 'until the present show is over' (meaning the Salerno landings, which he was then helping to plan). This was the first time I had actually met the great man, although I had heard him lecture in Cardiff and London. When the invasion of Italy had taken place and he was back in London I went to see him in the London Museum.

He questioned me very fully about all I could tell him about my years in India. He said he was not going to fly out but travel by sea with a load of books to read. When he arrived he was well informed on the history and antiquities of the sub-continent and had already worked out a plan of action and research.

When I got back to Delhi I met a senior Indian official in the Home Department. 'Will you British never learn?' he said crossly. 'I hear you are sending out some bloody brigadier to be Director of Antiquities.' 'You wait until your brigadier arrives,' I said, 'he is one of the most experienced and dynamic living archaeologists.'

Soon after his arrival in 1943 he took Stuart Piggott and me out to dinner. 'First,' he said sharply, 'what you two are doing is women's work. I want to get you out of the armed forces and into my department.' He then outlined his plans for the next two years: it was a massive campaign of travel, fieldwork and excavation. We protested mildly, saying that for half the year, during the really hot weather, fieldwork and excavation were not possible. He clapped his monocle into his eye, gave a tweak to his moustaches and said, 'I propose to ignore the hot weather!' And he did (see overleaf).

I admired enormously what he achieved in India and went up to Taxila on two occasions. Here he had established a training school and training excavation. It is true that when he assembled his first school it was a mixed bag of creeds and colours. Like the hot weather, he proposed to ignore religious and eating prejudices. There was one dining room: some students complained. He addressed them in the best bloody brigadier manner. 'We are the same people here,' he said. 'I make no distinction between Sikhs, Parsees, Hindus and Moslems. We are all Indian archaeologists and if you don't like it you can go home.' No one left. Gradually he became a semi-divine guru figure to all his devoted and admiring pupils.

'I propose to ignore the hot weathah!' – Stuart Piggott's drawing of Mortimer Wheeler, India, 1944.

Apart from all the difficulties and problems, the joy of running a large unit lay in contact with such a wide variety of interesting people from all walks of life, and when it was proposed that we had a unit magazine we realized what extraordinary talents were temporarily thrown together by the accidents of war. I particularly remember

When I was back on a brief visit to the Air Ministry in London I was told that WAAFs would soon be posted to India. Would I give a talk to the female photographic interpreters at Medmenham who had put their names down to go to India? I spoke to a group of some thirty WAAF officers which included a section officer, Ruth Langhorne, who later became my wife. Her only memory of that occasion was of listening to a slightly bland man playing down the difficulties of life in India. This was certainly true: and I remember answering a question by Anne McKnight Kauffer about scorpions and snakes. I said that she had obviously been reading the RAF India handbook which instructed one to inspect carefully boots and shoes and slippers before putting them on because they were the favourite hiding place of death-dealing scorpions. I had to confess that I had never seen a scorpion and that I had a bearer who always checked my footwear. I said that I constantly saw snakes when I walked from my office to the mess but they were all in jars and came out to the wheedling tunes of their flute-playing masters. Except, I said, on one occasion when I was playing golf and having holed a long putt was astonished when my ball bounced out of the hole followed by a long snake who hissed at me and glided away into the trees, pursued by my outraged caddie who killed it with a mashie-niblick. I have never consulted the rules of golf to see what is the position when a ball successfully holed reappears on the green – by any agency. Snakes cannot be a foreseeable hazard at St Andrews.

Ruth recollects that she was not particularly impressed or depressed by a talk on India by a person to whom she paid little attention. But she did put her name down on the list of volunteers for India because travel at government expense seemed too good to miss; she eventually arrived in Delhi – to my eternal good fortune.

The WAAF other ranks arrived first and naturally caused a great stir among the airmen. Within a week of their arrival one of my sergeant photographers came to see me and asked for permission to marry one of them. She was a very nice girl but I counselled a short delay to which they agreed, and after a month I gave her away in St James's church in Delhi.

Then the WAAF officers arrived and people began going down like ninepins. I posted one WAAF officer, Elspeth Macalister, who had read archaeology at Cambridge, to 'Trader' Horne's office: he had complained for a long time of being overworked. A shy man, he immediately moved his desk out onto a draughty verandah, but in a few weeks they were engaged to be married. I proposed their health after their marriage back in Cambridge after the war.

And then the current affliction spread to me. I became aware that I was increasingly interested in the WAAF officer, Ruth Langhorne; when I went to her birthday party in July 1945 I realized I was in love with her. She reciprocated my affections over the next few weeks when we met for meals in the Club, the Piccadilly Restaurant in Connaught Circus and the Imperial and Cecil Hotels. We took a week's leave together in the Cecil Hotel at Murree, announced our engagement there, and to my eternal happiness and joy were married the following year in England. Those months from July to December were magical ones and we managed to make visits to Agra and Bundi, where we travelled about on elephants and camels and were regally entertained in the Maharajah's guest house.

The war in the East and Pacific was still on and I kept making visits every month to Ceylon: and had conferences in Kandy about the future of air-photographic interpretation. On one train journey from Kandy to Colombo I found myself eating my bacon and eggs at a table with yet another officer wearing the Polar Medal but also the DSO and bar. It was Freddy Spencer Chapman who had been at St John's in the twenties and was, like me, tutorially a pupil of James Wordie. Soldier, explorer, mountaineer and author, after the fall of Singapore and the evacuation of Malaya he went into the jungle as Officer Commanding British Left Behind Parties, and himself spent two years behind the Japanese lines, which story he tells in his book *The Jungle is Neutral*. He was brought back to the safety of Ceylon by submarine in May 1945 and I was talking to him only a few weeks after his return. Alas, after the war he found he could not settle down happily to a life of schoolmastering, and committed suicide in August 1971: he was then Warden of Wantage Hall, University of Reading. I met him once or twice in the postwar years when he came back to St John's to see Wordie. Richard Barker's life of Freddie, *One Man's Jungle* (1975), is a very moving book.

And then I had a horrid shock. In a meeting at Air Headquarters at Kandy I was told that Borneo was to be captured and, from an aerodrome there, an American squadron of reconnaissance planes would fly sorties over Singapore and other targets and the photographs were to be interpreted by Australian intelligence officers. They wanted someone senior and experienced to liaise between Americans and Australians: they would like it to be me. I didn't like the prospect:

not only because at last I was going to be pitchforked into really active service but because I did not think I was ideally equipped to encourage co-operation and hold the peace between American airmen and Australian photo-interpreters. I travelled gloomily down to Colombo and went into the Galle Face Hotel.

There was a curious atmosphere that I could not immediately fathom. Some army officers I did not know gave me broad smiles. Then I saw a group captain I knew carrying a bottle of whisky. 'Come to my room and celebrate', he said. 'Celebrate what?' I asked. 'Don't you know? The Japs have surrendered: the war is over.' It was 10 August. I would now never get to Borneo; I flew back to Delhi, much relieved.

And waiting for me was good news: a letter from Maureen O'Reilly saying that I had been appointed to a Faculty Assistant Lectureship in the Department of Archaeology and Anthropology at Cambridge and that the University hoped I would be back to start teaching in the following January. Ruth and I went and celebrated this with a fine dinner in the Cecil in Old Delhi.

I was to be demobilized in December. Ruth was to stay on for six months and indeed eventually became CO of the unit, which duty she discharged with her customary efficiency and charm. When I was about to make my arrangements to fly home I was asked to see Air Commodore Alan Wheeler whom Ruth and I had got to know well; he was a Trinity man and a friend of Barbara Slade's (and later her second husband). 'SASO [Senior Air Staff Officer] and I think you've done such a good job for us out here that we are offering a top priority open air ticket home. Take as long as you like and stop off as many times as you like.' This was a marvellous offer and it slightly cheered me as I sadly parted from Ruth at the airport and said goodbye to my faithful, kind and cheerful bearer, Aziz, who had looked after me so well for years. I knew I should see Ruth again, but I also knew I would never see Aziz again – I often thought of him during the Muslim-Hindu massacres that followed Independence Day in 1947.

I landed at Basra and went up by connecting plane to Baghdad and stayed with the Seton Lloyds in their delightful house on the banks of the river. Seton was technical adviser to the Directorate-General of Antiquities of the Government of Iraq from 1939 to 1949, when he became Director of the British Institute of Archaeology in Ankara, and subsequently Professor of Western Asiatic Archaeology in the

University of London. Seton and his wife Hydie were kindness itself to a young archaeologist they had never met before: and their friendship and kind hospitality remains in their retirement at Woolstone under the White Horse at Uffington.

The Lloyds drove me out to see various sites and I examined my first ancient mud bricks! One night they gave a dinner party which included Freya Stark and Stewart Perowne. During conversation with Freya Stark she told me how much she disapproved of Gertrude Caton Thompson and how she disliked Stewart Perowne. Later that same evening Perowne told me how he approved and admired Gertrude Caton-Thompson and disliked Freya Stark. That was in late 1945; and I remembered that evening when I read in 1947 that Stewart and Freya had got married!

I flew on to Jerusalem, spent a few days there and a few days in Cairo, and then back to England to a demob centre in the Midlands. It was on the Jerusalem-Cairo trip that I heard one army officer ask another whether many books got pinched from his library. I treasure his adverbial reply: 'Surprisingly infrequently actually.'

Suddenly, in a civilian suit in the Midlands in December 1945, I wondered what to do. What, and how was I to get back to my life before the RAF? I took the train to London, and then on a sudden impulse took the Liverpool Street train to Cambridge. The head porter welcomed me: 'I hope I am not too late to dine in Hall,' I said. 'Oh,' he said, 'this is the Foundation Dinner so the seating plan has been fixed a long time ago. There's no ordinary Fellows' Dinner.' I walked through the College, looked at my rooms, now occupied by another, and crossed the Bridge of Sighs; the moon was full. I hurried back to London and took the night train to Cardiff: and had an enormous breakfast in the Royal Hotel. I telephoned my parents, took the train to Llantwit Major, left my bag in the railway station and walked down to the sea; I stood on the cliffs as the gulls wheeled round me and said to myself, 'Where do we go from here?' I walked back to my home. My mother and father welcomed me with a large Welsh tea. I told them some of my Indian experiences and without expecting any answer I said, 'And now what happens to the rest of my life?' My mother looked at me sharply but kindly: 'You have already got a three-year job at Cambridge,' she said. 'Go straight back there and stay there. That's what you want to do.' And, by the Grace of God, I did.

CHAPTER SIX

Cambridge 1946-77

WHEN I STARTED TEACHING after the war I wondered whether there would be people wanting to read archaeology and anthropology. In January 1946 I went to the first lecture in my course on the prehistory of the Mediterranean and Western Europe with considerable misgivings: there might be nobody there or a large group, including ex-servicemen who had spent their leaves studying the prehistory of Sicily, Malta and France. What sort of an audience would I have? I clutched my gown and my lantern slides and set off to the lecture room. Nobody there. Nobody will ever be there, I thought, and as I shall be lecturing or not lecturing to empty rooms, clearly my academic services will not be required for long. I was arranging my lantern slides when the door opened and an attractive young lady came in with a large notebook. Assuming she had come to the wrong place, I nearly said, 'No, please stay'. But she had come to hear my lecture and for weeks we pursued our way, I on the rostrum, she alone in the middle of the lecture-room, and the assistant working the slides.

I felt I wanted to make closer contact with this young woman who had saved me from speaking to nobody. I suggested that she might like to have lunch, tea, a drink, anything, with me and discuss the lecture. 'You are very kind,' she said, 'but your lectures are so clear I doubt whether it is necessary to accept your kind offer.' Where is that beautiful lady now? The widow of a retired diplomat, I suspect. I hope Lady X has some archaeology in the back of her garden.

In 1947 Martin Charlesworth suggested a course of open lectures on the archaeology and early history of the British Isles. The series was planned by himself, me and Peter Hunter Blair, and we carefully selected the eight lectures. We had no idea what size the audience might be and nervously booked the largest lecture room in Mill Lane which held 250 people. I was to give the first lecture and on the way I met H.M. Adams, then Librarian at Trinity. 'Are you too going to this much publicized course?' he said (the lectures were listed as 'M.P. Charlesworth and others'). 'Yes,' I said, 'I have every intention of doing so: in fact I am giving one this evening.' When we got to the Mill Lane lecture rooms the hall was full to overflowing and the passages were thronged with people. I had to push my way to the door of the lecture room and with great difficulty got in. 'What are you trying to do?' said someone. 'There is no more room.' 'But please excuse me,' I said, 'I am the lecturer.' 'Ha-ha!' said someone else. 'We've heard that one before!' My lecture had to be repeated next morning for those who couldn't get to it and we then transferred our venue to the Large Examination Hall which took 500 people. We maintained our audience throughout. We were worried whether Nora Chadwick would be heard at the back of the hall, and it was arranged that I should stand at the back and wave a white handkerchief when I couldn't hear her. This I did three times during her lecture and it seemed to work. I congratulated her but she said, 'I never saw you wave your handkerchief: I was wearing my reading spectacles and couldn't see to the back of the hall.' Shortened versions of the lectures were given on the BBC's Third Programme and the full lectures were published as a book, *The Heritage of Early Britain*.

During my first six months back in Cambridge after the war, when Ruth was still in India, I had a traumatic experience. James Wordie summoned me and said that the Chair of Geography and Anthropology at Aberystwyth was vacant and I must put in for it. Reluctantly I did so and was well supported by people like O.T. Jones, who really ought to have known better. There were a large number of applicants, including Tom Paterson, the Curator of the Museum of Archaeology and Ethnology in Cambridge. Two people were short-listed for interview, Emrys Bowen and myself. Paterson was furious. 'This is a Welsh plot,' he said. 'I am by far the best candidate. When the truth is known it will be realized that the war was won by my special secret activity in military intelligence.' He was, in Wordie terms, a strange man.

My old headmaster, who was a member of the Court, wrote to me: 'Although I like Emrys Bowen I shall support you through thick and thin and so will many people I have spoken to.' I became depressed and so, I know, did Ruth who, having thought her immediate future was as a young don's wife in Cambridge, was now being threatened with banishment to the west coast of Wales. But I enjoyed the journey on the old Cambrian railway and was greeted by David Williams, given an excellent supper and taken out for a few pints of beer.

The interview was at two o'clock and I spent the morning walking about and wondering, and looking out at the grey sea and saying to myself, 'This is not the place for me'. Apparently I made a reasonably good showing at the interview before the Court (or so at least my friends said), but Emrys Bowen was elected; and has been a firm and close friend ever since. I caught the train to Carmarthen and enjoyed the journey through the countryside of my childhood past Pencader and then home to Llantwit Major. I had telephoned my parents and they were delighted. My father said, 'It was nice to be considered for a Chair at your age but I would prefer you to be in a less exalted position at Cambridge.'

I went to see James Wordie when I got back. 'That was a very worthwhile exercise,' he said. 'It is always a good thing nearly to have had a Chair in a provincial university. I think we shall now have no difficulty in establishing you as a permanent teaching Fellow in Archaeology and Anthropology.'

That strange exercise apart, I was plunged not only into teaching but into endless extra duties. Those who had been in Cambridge during the war now welcomed the warriors back and were only too ready (and why not?) to make them do all the sorts of things they had been doing. I found myself soon Secretary of the Faculty Board of Archaeology and Anthropology and Secretary of the College Council (which I was for twenty years). Then all sorts of minor things were added: I was Senior Treasurer of the University Squash Racquets and Fives Club; then the College asked me to be Steward and after that I began to see that the time had come to say No. I was asked to be Secretary of the Prehistoric Society: that was the first No. Secretary of the Cambridge Folk Museum and the Cambridge Antiquarian Society: that was the second No. Then I was put on the General Board of the Faculties and as my period of duty there came to an end I realized that the powers that were, like that kind man Sir Henry Thirkill, thought, 'Here is a chap we can promote and use'. Would I serve on the Board of Graduate Studies? Would I do this? Would I do that? This was the third No, and Thirkill left me in no doubt that he thought I was making a great mistake.

Ruth came home in the early summer and I joyfully met her at Paddington and we spent a few days in Leslie Illingworth's flat in Knightsbridge. Leslie and Ruth took to each other at once: 'She's too good for you', he said, but agreed to be my best man. Ruth went to her home in Exeter and then came up to Cambridge and stayed with that fierce, forthright, frightening but kind and good woman, Rosamund Rootham, widow of Dr Cyril Rootham, organist and Director of Music at St John's, and mother of Jasper Rootham who wrote *Miss Fire* (1946) and *Demi-Paradise* (1960). Mrs Rootham suffered no fools gladly and many legends grew up about her: one that when she found the Cambridge pavements full of idling and gossiping undergraduates she would brandish her umbrella and charge through them. When we were married Ruth worked a great deal with Rosamund Rootham and Camille Prior in the mounting and performing of the annual pageants which were then a feature of Cambridge, and the operas and oratorios that Boris Ord conducted in the Guildhall. There is a true story that in one pageant, before we were living in Cambridge, there was enacted the visit of Queen Elizabeth I to Cambridge. This was done in the Hall of St John's and Mrs Rootham was Queen Elizabeth. The stage was on the dais and Queen Elizabeth was to stand on a raised section to one side. The performance went well but no one could understand why Mrs Rootham kept moving about and changing from one foot to another. Then it was discovered that her platform was a thin board set over the large hot plate used for keeping dishes warm: and someone had left the hot plate on!

I went down to Exeter with some trepidation to meet Ruth's mother, who fortunately approved of me. Alas, I never met her father, who had been headmaster of the Exeter Cathedral Choristers' School and priest-vicar in the Cathedral: he had died during the war. By all accounts a man of forthright views and a staunch Oxford man, I think he would have enjoyed teasing and arguing with a young Cambridge archaeological don.

It was an exciting new experience, as an only child myself, to be involved in a large family. There had been one son, whom his father, with a slightly pedantic approach to Anglo-Saxon scholarship, had insisted on christening Eadward: and five daughters, Mary, Eleanor, Elisabeth, Ruth and Janet. I never knew Elisabeth who was killed when a German bomb, during a 'Baedeker' raid on Exeter, destroyed the family house which was The Abbot's Lodge in the Cathedral Close – said to be the town house of the Abbots of Buckfast. I know that the destruction of the house and all her personal property, as well as the death of her sister, was quite naturally a great and continuing sadness to Ruth. I never saw The Abbot's Lodge but it must have been a lovely

Sketch of the Langhorne family house, The Abbot's Lodge, made by Ruth's sister Mary from an old drawing.

house. When we came to celebrate Mrs Langhorne's eightieth birthday in 1967, we printed a menu with a pen-and-ink sketch by Mary from an old drawing of the house on the cover and I reproduce it here.

In her little house in the Cathedral Close I found Mrs Langhorne being cosseted by Nurse Harper, faithful nurse to all the children, then matron of the Choristers' School, finally cook-housekeeper: the family was all. When I was introduced to her she looked me over appraisingly, turned to Ruth and delivered her verdict: 'He's going to be a hard man to wash for.'

Ruth went to school at the Maynard in Exeter and was encouraged in her study of geography by Pamela Matthew, later to become Pamela Michelmore, wife of a prominent Exeter solicitor. Pamela took Ruth on trips to London and France and was instrumental in persuading her father to send her up to Oxford.

The Langhornes were close friends of the then Dean, Walter Matthews, subsequently Dean of St Paul's; and of the organist and Master of Music, Dr Thomas Armstrong. Armstrong was translated to Christ Church, Oxford, in the same autumn of 1933 as Ruth was going up as an undergraduate and she went to live with them for her first two years, babysitting and helping with his Latin homework the son, Robert, later Sir Robert Armstrong, Secretary to the Cabinet. Tom Armstrong was knighted in 1958; his son in 1978. It must surely be rare for a father and son both to be knighted.

Eadward Langhorne carved out a distinguished career for himself as a schoolmaster and was headmaster of Dean Close Junior School for many years. His son, Richard, was Dean Matthews's godson. Ruth once took me to see Matthews who had read my two detective stories and said he enjoyed them. 'Write some more,' he said, 'I read a detective novel every night before going to sleep.' Eadward's son, Richard, after going down from St John's, was a lecturer in history in the University of Kent at Canterbury, where he became Master of Rutherford College, and then came back to St John's in 1974 as Fellow, Junior Bursar and Steward. He is Ruth's godson and his son, Daniel, is mine. He is partly named for me, but there was also a famous Daniel Langhorne in the family.

I had been in Exeter once or twice before the war when studying megalithic monuments in Devon and Cornwall: but never appreciated its beauty and charm (despite the wartime bombing) until after the war. We wanted a simple wedding and were married on 12 September 1946 in the small Grandisson chapel built into the thickness of the west front of the Cathedral. It held only ten people and the embroidery of the Dean's festal cope tickled my nose every time he turned round.

We went on our honeymoon to the Isles of Scilly: the aircraft from Penzance to St Mary's was grounded by bad weather. We made a difficult crossing by boat and were both sick. Recovering after a light lunch and a rest we walked down the hill from Star Castle to the harbour: a tremendous gale was raging and I was blown off my feet. I remember being pained that Ruth laughed!

We set up house in Cambridge in late September in the first and second storeys of an old pub called The Merry Boys, across the road from the College chapel (the ground floor was then a tailor's shop, now a baker's shop) and lived there in rather cramped conditions for twenty-one years. The College choir school was housed at that time in another old pub round the corner from us. When it moved to new premises in Grange Road and the headmaster died, we were able to move there – the house to live in and the schoolrooms as an office for *Antiquity*, which I edited from 1958 onwards. We have lived there ever since: it is a haven of tranquillity – we both love living in the centre of a city and 70 Bridge Street is one of the few remaining central houses. We wanted to restore one of the old pub names and discovered it had been variously called Lindum House, the Freemasons' Arms, The Wild Man, The Royal Oak and The Flying Stag. We toyed with the third name but eventually decided that Dr Daniel, The Wild Man, 70 Bridge Street, Cambridge, was possibly open to misinterpretation. So we chose The Flying Stag and in 1973 the Prince of Wales shot for us, at Ruth's request, the stag whose antlers are now over our door. Both The Merry Boys and The Flying Stag belong to the College, as now does all the property in the triangle marked by Bridge Street, St John's Street, and All Saints' Passage – the area that used to be the Jewry of medieval Cambridge.

Those first years of marriage in The Merry Boys were difficult ones in that I had so many official duties. Sometimes the burden seemed intolerable, but we were young and happy and hopeful. I worked from early morning often to well after midnight. I had only slight secretarial help. Looking back on it I wonder how I got through it all when, as well as the increasing burden of teaching and my own research on the megalithic monuments of France, I was writing *A Hundred Years of Archaeology*. The first and main answer was the devoted, loving and understanding help and support of Ruth in those early years, and her understanding of the necessity of being firm about the Nos. She herself had been attending classes in calligraphy at the Tech. and was increasingly occupied in illustrating books for me and others with fine maps.

The fourth No was a more difficult one. I had been Steward of the

College for a few years and things were going reasonably well as described in a later chapter entitled Maupygernons and Mash. Then one lunchtime I was summoned to the Master's Lodge and given a glass of sherry by Benians. Would I become Junior Bursar and take on the full administration of the College including the Stewardship? The Junior Bursar had had a nervous breakdown and I had for several weeks been dealing with his papers, including several files he had thrown out through the window into Second Court, one of them with a substantial refund of income tax!

'You would like to go away and think about it,' he said, 'and consult your wife: perhaps we could have a word tomorrow?' But I knew then what the answer was. 'No,' I said, 'I am enjoying being Steward, but my real job must be teaching, writing and researching. The Junior Bursarship would put an end to that.' 'It did not put an end to the great work of John Cockcroft,' he said challengingly. 'I know,' I said, 'but I am not a Cockcroft. I am an ordinary person whose life must be in the archaeology of Western Europe. I love the College and will serve it for ever if I am asked and allowed so to do, but I must always be away a lot. I think that is the best way I can serve the College by being mainly a teacher and research worker.'

He walked to the window, holding his glass in his hand, and with his back to me he said slowly, 'Daniel, I appreciate what you have said. But some of us believe the best way we can serve the College is by our personal devotion here.' It was not a reproof: it was a statement of faith and when he turned round and looked at me with his clear blue eyes I knew what he meant: that he himself had put aside research and high academic preferment for the detailed and devoted service of the College. 'I shall tell the Council this afternoon,' he said, 'that you will not accept nomination as Junior Bursar. They will be sorry.'

I went away quickly and nearly burst into tears on the short walk from The Lodge to The Merry Boys. But over lunch Ruth confirmed me in the rightness of my immediate decision.

But of course, curiously enough, I was acting Junior Bursar at the time and for some while to come. I had always had the greatest admiration for Benians and believe that he was among the main architects in making St John's in the twentieth century one of the great colleges in Oxford and Cambridge. He didn't bear me any ill-feeling for declining the Junior Bursarship and was grateful to me for standing in until we got a new Bursar. Late one November evening, the candles dimly lighting the Combination Room and the fires roaring away, he asked me about my travel and research plans for the following year. I told him and he listened with interest. 'And you?' I said. He put his hand lightly on my shoulder. 'Daniel', he said, 'my travels are over. You may feel that way when you are seventy and tired.'

He presided over our St John's Dinner on 27 December and next morning went in to be operated on for cancer, and died. John Boys Smith rang me up and said, 'You have to cope with all this – the funeral and the election of the new Master. I am too personally involved and one or two people have already asked me to stand as Master. Please, you must do it all. Indeed as acting J.B. you have to do it all.'

Sylvia Benians asked me to come and see her. She always called him 'My Master'. You know, she said, that My Master gave most specific instructions about his funeral. 'What were they?' I asked. 'It must be a repeat of the funeral of W.H. Rivers Rivers.' I had to discover what that was. Rivers had kept on E Staircase, New Court, and his rooms looked out over the top of the gateway and on to the Backs. He had apparently said that when he died he wished the *Nunc Dimittis* to be sung under the gateway and his coffin taken away from there rather than as was normal custom from the Front Gate, and this was done. We searched through the College files until we found the details of those 1922 arrangements. They were very sketchy and so we had to work it all out for ourselves: the Dean, the Organist, the Head Porter, the Chief Clerk and myself. The real difficulty was getting the coffin on the wheeled hearse all the quarter of a mile through the College from the chapel doorway to the New Court steps. We put down duckboards to deal with the steps from First Court to Second Court and up and over the Bridge of Sighs. And then in the dead of night we had a rehearsal with the undertakers present and a group of undergraduates propelling a suitably weighted coffin. It was a curious and macabre occasion, the procession led by the Head Porter who insisted on being in Full Dress, morning coat and top hat, and bearing the rod with a crêpe flag which Head Porters of St John's had from time immemorial paraded in front of Fellows leaving the College for the last time. It was a successful exercise and the event itself went off well except that the real funeral took longer because the cortège had the full choir and the whole route was lined by undergraduates. It was a most moving occasion, the College bell tolling all the time.

My own father died in 1948. He had retired early from the headmastership of his school and was looking forward to years of pleasant retirement, reading and gardening and making short tours in his car. Gradually we all noticed that he seemed to be getting tired; eventually, after several medical examinations, he had a chest X-ray and was said to be suffering from tuberculosis. He was thin and seemed to be wasting away. He was admitted to the then TB hospital at Sully on the sea-coast between Barry and Cardiff. I went down from Cambridge to see him soon after he was admitted and was taken aside by his doctors. 'Your father is not suffering from tuberculosis,' they said, 'it was a mistaken diagnosis, I'm afraid. He is dying of leukaemia.' And he was dead within a few days.

My mother sold the house in Llantwit Major and went to live in a small house in Porthcawl. Here she spent several happy years in her widowhood – she had many friends in Porthcawl and the region – until she, too, was found to have cancer and died, mercifully after a short illness, in a small hospital in Bridgend, and without that great suffering which is such an agony to the dying and the living in so many cases of terminal cancer. I used to go down and see her from time to time, using the night sleeper from Paddington to Cardiff.

St John's is the only one of the three very rich and large Colleges to elect its own Master. Trinity, Cambridge, and Christ Church, Oxford, are Crown appointments. Harold Wilson, we are now told, asked the Fellows of Trinity whether they would like their statutes changed so that they could elect their Master themselves but they apparently refused: how could a hundred Fellows decide on anyone? We in St John's had to do that when Benians died, within thirty days.

We had many meetings and it was obvious from the beginning that it was a battle between James Wordie, President and Senior Tutor, and John Cockcroft, then head of the Atomic Energy Establishment at Harwell, although a few wanted John Boys Smith at that stage. It was a very close affair and we had a straw vote the day before the election which gave Cockcroft a majority of two or three. Many of us retired to the Blue Boar, the Wordieites to drown their sorrows and the Cockcroftians to celebrate. Some wise man said, 'But it is too early to be certain': I knew, too, that three Fellows who had not been voting that night, and indeed had not been at any of our meetings, were coming down for the election next day. 'Anything may happen,' I said. Anyhow I had prepared two separate menus for dinner on the night of the election: if Wordie was elected there was to be haggis and a wee dram of whisky would be served.

We assembled in the chapel and took a solemn oath and then voted by secret ballot. James Wordie, as President, was in the Chair: the two Junior Fellows were tellers. When they counted the votes there was a dead heat! After what seemed an unusually long pause Wordie said: 'I think, gentlemen, we should adjourn to the ante-chapel for ten minutes.' I remained behind and Wordie walked slowly up the chapel and stood at the altar rails. I walked up and joined the lonely figure: he seemed grateful for someone to talk to. We went back to our seats and voted a second time. The Junior Fellows counted the votes, looked very alarmed, counted them again, and very properly asked the President to count the two piles. James Wordie had been elected by one vote. The Senior Fellow installed him in the Master's stall, I slipped out and opened the chapel doors and signalled to the head porter to break the College flag at masthead: we had elected a new Master. The head porter said there was a 'phone call for me from London. It was one of Winston Churchill's secretaries in the Cabinet Office – Winston had very reluctantly allowed Cockcroft to be a candidate. I told him the result. 'Thank you, thank you,' said the voice. 'The Prime Minister will be pleased.' We had haggis and whisky in the middle of our dinner.

This was all in 1952: Wordie was knighted in 1957 and retired from the Mastership in 1959. Cockcroft, who had been made a KBE in 1948 and a KCB in 1953, and was awarded the Order of Merit in 1957, was the object of another campaign in 1959. I was dining in Christ Church at the height of this campaign and so was John Cockcroft. We sat next to each other. 'It would be absurd,' I said, 'to pretend that your name is not being constantly mentioned at our High Table.' 'I *am* actually returning to Cambridge,' he replied enigmatically. He was made Master-Designate of the new Churchill College in 1959 (the year in which we elected John Boys Smith to the Mastership of St John's) and was its Master from 1960 onwards.

John Boys Smith, who had been a Fellow of the College since 1927, and Senior Bursar from 1944 to 1959, was Master for ten years during which time the Cripps Building was constructed – this is why he is known as the Builder Master, and very appropriately there is a good representation of his head on a corbel in Second Court. He has set down with his characteristic lucidity and impartiality a picture of his life in St John's up to the end of his time as Master, in his *Memories of St John's College, Cambridge, 1919–1969*, which was published by the Oxford University Press in 1983.

He does not tell in that book the story confirmed by James Wordie and not denied by Humphrey Cripps about the early negotiations for the funding of our new building by the Cripps Foundation, the family charitable trust, of which his father (later Sir) Cyril Cripps, was the chairman. Humphrey had been at St John's in the thirties and we overlapped as undergraduates although I did not know him in those days.

In 1958 St John's issued an appeal to some 6,000 members of the College for a sum of £500,000 to finance the repair of Second Court and Third Court and the construction of new College buildings. Shortly after the appeal was sent out Wordie received a letter from Humphrey Cripps saying that the family foundation had decided that our new buildings should be the next task for their fund. Later he called on the Master to explain their purpose and after some talk Humphrey Cripps said, 'What the foundation had in mind was a gift of not more than a million pounds, paid in quarterly instalments of £250,000.' There was a short silence: Wordie showed no emotion, and then he got to his feet and said, 'Have a glass of sherry, Mr Cripps, medium or dry?'

Boys Smith retired early in 1969 and was succeeded by Nicholas Mansergh, who had come to Cambridge in 1953 as Smuts Professor of the History of the British Commonwealth and was immediately made a Fellow of the College. He was a graduate of Pembroke College, Oxford, and the first non-Johnian to be made Master. He was succeeded in 1979 by Harry Hinsley, a contemporary of mine – and so one of Martin Charlesworth's prophecies came true. I have known six Masters in my fifty-four years at St John's – Scott, Benians, Wordie, Boys Smith, Mansergh, and Hinsley, and am full of admiration for the way they have devoted themselves to the running of the College. Scott was only a remote figure to me as an undergraduate: he died in 1933. There was current in my undergraduate days an amusing story about him. The then Dean (later Professor) J.M. Creed had moments of unpopularity, as most College Deans with disciplinary authority must have from time to time. Some rowdy undergraduates decided to remonstrate and fastened up the door of his College rooms with powerful screws. He had no telephone and, discovering his plight, looked out through the window and saw Sir Robert Scott crossing Chapel Court. 'Master,' he cried out, 'help me.' 'What is the matter, Mr Dean?' said Scott. 'I am screwed in my rooms!' said Creed. 'That may well be,' said the Master, 'but there is no need to shout the news of your unfortunate condition all over the College.'

It is often said that the Oxbridge Colleges are breeding grounds of eccentrics, and also that the days of real eccentrics are gone. This latter statement is not true: there were plenty of eccentrics around in my lifetime from F.W. Simpson, the historian, of Trinity, who went around with a pair of secateurs trimming trees and bushes in his own and neighbouring colleges (hence his nickname Snipson), to H.W. Brindley, the zoologist, of my own college who had lost the use of his neck muscles and walked around with his face looking at the ground. Brindley once complained that the University Press had flown its flag upside-down and on being asked how he had observed this said, 'By lying down on the pavement, as I often have to do to observe what is going on.'

Among my most fondly recollected Cambridge characters are H.A. Harris, T.R. Glover and N.B. Jopson of my College, and Paddy Hadley of Caius.

H.A. Harris was a fellow Welshman who came to Cambridge in 1934 from University College and University College Hospital, London, as Professor of Anatomy. He felt out of things for a while. The Cambridge Statutes do not ensure that a professor is automatically a Fellow of a college and Harris was out in the cold for several years until St John's had the good sense to elect him. He became a happy and much-loved member of the society – at least loved by most people. He was loud-mouthed, swore a great deal, spoke his mind freely and openly, told scabrous stories and delighted in shocking his most pious or straight-laced colleagues. He suffered intermittently from coprolalia, the imperative impulse to speak obscenely. Yet he was a good, kind, generous man who always had time for good honest students and acted voluntarily as a kind of unofficial medical consultant and adviser to the Fellows and the college staff: a first-class lecturer, a devoted and diligent teacher, and an excellent raconteur. He delighted in telling the story of a professor of anatomy in Belfast on whom his students played an elaborate joke. They smuggled a goat into the anatomy lecture theatre and tied it to one of the front seats where it bleated from time to time. The professor paid no attention to the goat or his cries of 'Nay, Nay' which punctuated his lecture. At the end he called for the register in which students at that time had to sign their names to certify their attendances. The professor turned over the pages carefully, then looked over his spectacles at the front row, 'But, gentlemen,' he said, 'one of you has omitted to sign his name.'

Another of Harris's stories concerned a Welsh nonconformist minister who was preaching to a crowded chapel in Merthyr Tydfil. 'The Kingdom of Heaven is like a London club,' he declared 'where voting for membership is by placing a white ball or a black ball secretly in a box. Those who are black-balled are not admitted members.' He turned to the gallery full of young men: 'Boys in the gallery,' he thundered, 'when the awful time comes and you stand at the gates of heaven will your balls be black or white?' The same humourless minister on another occasion apparently declared, 'We must respect the wonders of science. If I had two cylinders of hydrogen and one of oxygen here in the pulpit I could make water in front of you all.'

It is these tales that caused some of his colleagues to turn away or to avoid sitting next to him at High Table while others of us sought out the company and conversation of this *enfant terrible*. I got on very well with him and we established a warm and lasting friendship: he even persuaded me to go and give a lecture in his old chapel in Merthyr Tydfil, which I did, but didn't provide much amusement for the no-good boyos in the gallery.

We differed on one issue that Harris felt deeply about. He had been a pupil and colleague of Grafton Elliot Smith, and had the greatest admiration for him; he believed implicitly and whole-heartedly in his doctrine that civilization had begun in Egypt and from there had spread to the rest of the world. He was also devoted to W.J. Perry. He much resented my attack on the Heliolithic Culture and my refusal to countenance the Egyptian origin of, for example, the megalithic monuments of Europe. His devotion to Egypt was such that when he retired from the Cambridge chair he went as a visiting professor to Cairo in 1951 and then in 1952 to Khartoum. He came back more enthusiastic than ever about the Egyptian origins of civilization. 'Your predecessor was a wiser man than you are,' he would declare: and it is true that W.H. Rivers Rivers had fallen for the Egyptian hypothesis which no one now believes.

One of the Fellows with whom Harris could not get on at all was

T.R. Glover, and indeed, as I have related, they avoided speaking to each other, which was sad for me because T.R.G. and I got on very well together. Glover was an ardent Baptist, and when he discovered that I was the nephew of the fine Baptist preacher, Tom Edmunds, whom he much admired, we struck up a firm acquaintanceship although he was disappointed that I was not of his persuasion, and indeed went to the College chapel. I never went to any of his lectures, though all my contemporaries said they were wonderfully lucid and inspiring, but I did read his *The Ancient World* and his *Retrospect* and found them stimulating although, alas, his ancient world was the classic world of Palestine, Greece and Rome and had no use for archaeology. We were once arguing in the Combination Room and he said, 'But you can check what I mean by looking in the Gospel of St Matthew when you get back to your rooms after dinner.' 'Alas,' I said, 'I don't have a Bible in my college rooms.' He looked at me in astonished surprise and next morning when I was breakfasting late he burst into my rooms and presented me with a fine copy of the New Testament which he had just bought at David's Bookstall. 'Here is comfort for you,' he said. 'Read a chapter every day.'

He had a ready wit and was a good versifier. One evening we were talking at High Table about various architectural oddities and someone said that Bury's rooms in Corpus abutted on to St Benet's Church and that when he put the light on in his bathroom it could be seen by the congregation. Without a moment's hesitation Glover said to our surprise, 'That explains the hymn.' 'What hymn?' we asked and Glover recited:

> Sometimes a light surprises,
> The Christians as they sing:
> It is our Bury bathing,
> Praise God the heavenly king.

Norman Jopson was probably the most colourful don in St John's in the fifties. Born in 1890 he had come up in 1910, graduated in 1913, and after distinguished service in the War Office, the Admiralty and the Foreign Office from 1914 to 1923, became an academic in the University of London and then the first holder of the Chair of Comparative Philology at Cambridge from 1937 until his retirement in 1955. During the Second World War he was Head of Uncommon Languages in the Department of Postal and Telegraphic Censorship.

It was a legend that he spoke all European languages, or at least all Indo-European languages, but his appetite for language was certainly voracious. He became an expert in Pidgin English. On one occasion he told me he was taking a boat to Helsinki. 'Doubtless,' I said, 'to start a study of the Finno-Ugrian languages.' 'No, no, dear boy,' he said, 'I know Finnish and Magyar. I just want a few weeks' peace to polish up my Turkish before I go there next term.' He was particularly interested in Romany and the gypsies in general and used to cause any gypsies he met embarrassment by speaking to them in Romany and sadly finding they were not as fluent in their language as he was. He spoke all these languages with an old world pedantry and classic pronunciation: his French was that of the early century and he often, with good reason, corrected my Welsh. I once sent him a young Hungarian archaeological student who was visiting Cambridge. 'Did he speak good Magyar?' I asked. 'Yes,' said Joppy tolerantly, 'but I had to correct his vowels.'

He used to delight in trying to identify where people came from by their accent. One evening at dinner a guest said, 'Professor Jopson, I think we both come from Liverpool.' 'Are you sure?' said Joppy, to the man's surprise. 'Listening to you speak I would have thought you came from south of the river. I should have made you a Birkenhead boy'. And he was right.

The sadness and wonder to me was that he was interested in language only as a vehicle for communication and as something to be mastered and understood. His library was entirely dictionaries and grammars. He was not interested in the history of languages and I could never get him to be interested, as I have always been, in the origin of the Indo-European languages, the correlation of the original Indo-Europeans with any known archaeological group, or such problems as who introduced the Irish language into Ireland. 'All speculation', he would say, 'and really all worthless speculation.' As I grow older I begin to think he was probably right.

He was a dedicated and skilful punter and owned his own racing punt. In the summer, dressed in white trousers, a St John's summer blazer, a boater and smoking a large cigar he would punt up and down the Backs, sometimes with friends, sometimes alone, shaming the usually muddled efforts of undergraduates and visitors. He was also an ardent cyclist, often cycling to London and frequently taking his bike with him to Paris. He found the fact that I had never ridden a bicycle very strange (as I suppose it is) and made plans to teach me. He had a theory that I should start on a tricycle, which I should, as a non-cyclist, be easily able to ride in a straight line, whereas if Ruth (or any other cyclist) tried, they would go round in circles! This exercise was to happen on the Backs, but, perhaps fortunately, it never did, and the theory remained untested.

He travelled extensively and one might find him anywhere: certainly in the Hôtel Terminus opposite the Gare Saint-Lazare in Paris (he always liked the Newhaven-Dieppe crossing), and I once met him *par hasard* in a public lavatory in Lugano. He was friendly and generous and made stray contacts into permanent acquaintances. Once meeting a crippled woman getting into a Brussels restaurant, he developed this chance encounter and for years went to Belgium and gave her meals in the Rôtisserie Ardennes.

I was surprised when he described his undergraduate days to me; apparently his generation always went back after dinner in Hall to someone's rooms and drank, not beer or wine, but spirits or liqueurs. 'I was well off,' he said, modestly, 'and I got through three or four bottles of Benedictine or Grand Marnier a week.' When he was back as a Fellow he liked asking his colleagues to his rooms after dinner and the Joppy post-prandial evenings became a part of College life. 'I wonder if you would like to come to my rooms for a glass or two or three after dinner?' he would say, and six to ten of us would assemble to consume a strange variety of drinks – Commanderie, Marc de Bourgogne, Australian Chablis, Californian Burgundy, Steinwein: he liked touring the Cambridge wine shops and buying strange things. As the evening went on he voiced his disappointment at people wanting to leave – he liked his sessions to go on until midnight. Was he lonely? Was he re-creating the post-dinner days of his youth, or was he just seeking relaxation and quiet after a day of heavy teaching?

Certainly he did a vast amount of teaching, and it is reported that when someone in the central university offices rang up to see whether there was anyone who could teach Latvian and Lithuanian, without hesitation Joppy replied that he would be prepared to do so but 'please give me a fortnight to refresh myself in these languages.' The General Board annually sends out a questionnaire to professors asking – for information only, as they have no statutory obligation to teach – their hours of lecturing during the year. Most people return anything from 0 to 40 but I well remember, during my years on the G.B., Joppy was well away top with 250 to 300 hours a year. He taught in his rooms two hours in the morning and two hours every evening.

He was a neat little man and prided himself on being able to wear, at the end of his life, the clothes he had worn as an undergraduate. One day we were startled to find him standing at the front gate of St John's in morning coat and top hat. You are no doubt off to a wedding, we said. 'Not at all,' came the disconcerting reply, 'but I felt these clothes needed an airing,' and he got on his bicycle and went off down Trinity Street.

My wife and I made several attempts to get him to join us on a small car tour of France but all failed. He was a loner and I think a happy loner until, warned of a heart condition, he sold all his books, moved to a smaller set of rooms nearer the front porter's lodge of the College, gave up his after-dinner parties, and seemed to be waiting quietly for the dissolution of his life, which happened in 1969.

I first met Paddy Hadley in 1938 when I was dining with Mervyn Jones in Caius. We sat talking late into the night and Paddy came into the Combination Room. Mervyn was pouring out some night-caps from the corner cupboard. 'Paddy, what will you have?' He said, 'Whisky, my dear boy!' 'A double?' 'No, a treble please, I can't taste it otherwise.' Later I was told by the head barman on the Liverpool Street to Cambridge and King's Lynn express that Paddy would come into the buffet-bar as he was travelling home from a day's teaching in the Royal College of Music in London: 'We always knew it would be a treble: but we never knew whether it was to be whisky, brandy or gin.' The barmen always referred to him as the 'Music Master'.

On another occasion when I was dining in Caius, Paddy and Robin Orr were dining together and Robin explained that he was driving me up to London next morning: would Paddy join us? Delighted, he said, and we arranged to collect him outside the front gate of Caius at eight-thirty. We were there: no Paddy – he was breakfasting off a bottle of Madeira. Eventually he arrived swaying slightly. 'You're late,' said Robin, and I got out and opened the door for him. He looked at us blankly. 'Excuse me,' he said, 'would you mind not blocking the entrance? I am expecting two kind friends to drive me to London.'

He had studied composition at the Royal College under Vaughan Williams and conducting under Boult and Sargent; and among his own compositions is to be remembered *Fen and Flood* (King's Lynn Festival, 1956). He twice composed the music for the Greek play at

Cambridge, *Antigone* (Sophocles, 1939) and *Agamemnon* (Aeschylus, 1953). Some of his small choral works for cathedral/chapel choirs are quite ravishing, such as 'My song is love unknown,' from *A Lenten Cantata.*

I enjoyed lecturing and enormously enjoyed the personal teaching provided by the supervision system. I became, in the late forties, Director of Studies in Archaeology at St Catharine's and Pembroke as well as at St John's and did this extra chore for five to ten years. For the first few years back from the war I also supervised pupils in geography, and it was during this period that I decided there ought to be a College Geographical and Anthropological Society and formed it. I thought it appropriate that it should be called the Purchas Society. Samuel Purchas (1575?–1626) had been an undergraduate at St John's and wrote *Purchas his Pilgrimage* in 1613, *Purchas his Pilgrim* in 1619 and *Hakluytus Posthumus* in 1625, when he was rector of St Martin's, Ludgate. There already was a Johnian literary Society named after Thomas Nashe (1567–1601) who had been a sizar of St John's. It was Nashe who wrote 'St John's . . . was an Universitie within itself, shining so farre above all other houses . . . in which house I once took up my inne for seven years altogether lacking a quarter, and yet love it still, for it is and ever was, the sweetest nurse of learning in all that University.' And again, in the same vein, in his 1589 *To the Gentlemen Students of Both Universities,* he says of the College, 'no Colledge in the Towne was able to compare with the Tythe of her students; having . . . more candles light in it, everie Winter Morning before foure of the clocke, than the foure of clocke belle gave stroakes.'

The Purchas Society still flourishes; I spoke to it a few years ago – quite predictably, about human geography and archaeology; and, in preparing my talk, thought back to those heady days of 1929 to 1934 when a human geographer in the making was made into an archaeologist. The Nashe Society also flourishes still; I only ever went to one meeting of it. Rhys Thomas, a younger Johnian contemporary of mine, who came from Swansea, knew Dylan Thomas and organized that Dylan should read some of his poems to us. The college room where the meeting was to be held was crowded. Dylan had arrived from London much the worse for wear after a long liquid session in Fleet Street and had been given dinner in the Blue Boar with far too much to drink. He arrived swaying about slightly but got to the desk and began reading: suddenly he stopped and said in a loud voice,

'I am a Dionysiac poet, a Dionysiac poet,' and slumped insensible to the ground, whence he had to be carried away to his bed.

When Hodson retired in 1937 he was succeeded by John Hutton, who reigned as William Wyse Professor of Social Anthropology until his retirement in 1950, when he was succeeded by Meyer Fortes, and in the fullness of time Jack Goody, who held the chair from 1973 to 1984. Fortes and Goody were the first professional anthropologists. Hutton was still in the great tradition of colonial civil servant anthropological administrators. His great work had been the census of India and he had written *Caste in India*. Hodson and Hutton gave a great flavour of India and descriptive ethnography to the Cambridge School. Fortes and Goody were African field-workers and gave a new and theoretical flavour to Cambridge anthropology in the fifties, sixties and seventies.

Hutton was an amusing, outspoken and slightly eccentric character: he had lived for many years alone in India, his wife being installed in a house in mid-Wales near Llandrindod Wells. She never came to Cambridge. I visited her once or twice in Wales: she had no interest in anthropology or Academe. Hutton was an Oxford man whose family had some connections with St John's, Cambridge. We gave him dining privileges until later he was made a Professorial Fellow of St Catharine's. I got to know him well in his Johnian days: he had a maisonette in Portugal Place and on the one night a week when he dined at our High Table he would take me back to his house and talk about India, Wales, anthropology and archaeology. He was a connoisseur of liqueurs and had a very large chest with some twenty to thirty bottles. He introduced me to Blue Curaçao and to Cordial Médoc (which in my thirties and forties I was devoted to), and to the hard ones such as Marc de Bourgogne and Marc de Champagne which I came to appreciate in my sixties when my sweet tooth began to leave me.

Shortly after I came back from the war, Hutton, whose first wife had now died, married Maureen O'Reilly, to the surprise but great pleasure of all her friends. Maureen had been Secretary of the Faculty Board of Archaeology and Anthropology and it was she and her husband who decided that I should take on this job. Hutton was Chairman and before each Board meeting we lunched together, alternately in St John's and St Catharine's, and went through all our business so that under Hutton's Chairmanship the Faculty was very well run and meetings were short. I thought Hutton efficient and sensible but many did not share my view and as he grew older his eccentric anti-establishment oddities became clearer.

When every year we set the paper for the Tripos we had the greatest fun with the essay paper. We wanted this not, of course, to be a literary essay but to test a candidate doing specialist papers by giving him a peg on which to hang a three-hour discourse that would show his worth. The anthropologists set subjects like Rites de Passage, Shamanism, and I set subjects like Diffusion, The Invented Past, and The Dead Landscape. At one meeting Hutton said his proposal was: 'The best thing a man can have is a good working set of bowels.' We were surprised: 'Not my words,' said Hutton, 'Samuel Johnson.' We put it in and had some very good essays.

But at the end of his professional tenure he did something for which I have never been able to forgive him. We had two vacancies for lecturers in anthropology and had advertised them: a small and undistinguished list of candidates was sorted out, referees consulted and all the papers prepared for a meeting of our appointments committee. The only candidate of known repute was Reo Fortune and he was appointed immediately to the retiring age. No one then said he was very very odd, that he had recently chased the curator of the Toronto Museum round his galleries brandishing a tomahawk, or that he could not lecture. It was a disastrous appointment and we suffered as a result for many years. Having read *Sorcerers of Dobu*, undergraduates flocked to Fortune's lectures and then flaked away: the audience was nil by the fourth lecture and Reo, never understanding what it meant, went around looking for the students who had deserted him. He once said to me who was lecturing at the same time, 'I think my students went to your lecture by mistake. What were you lecturing about?' I said: 'The megaliths of Melanesia – and you?' 'The menopause in Melanesia,' he said. 'Same thing really, isn't it?'

But the other appointment was more than disastrous. Having looked through the list of candidates, Hutton suddenly said, 'I know who ought to have this job and hasn't put in for it – Ethel John Lindgren,' and without any reference she was appointed, though only for three years. On reflection I think the Fortune and Lindgren appointments were gestures against the new anthropology. I could do nothing because I was a non-voting secretary at the time.

Meyer Fortes was in despair at being landed with these two

members of his small staff. Fortune we could do nothing about but I told him that he need not keep Lindgren, and read him out the Statutes whereby it was possible not to renew an appointed lecturer. As the next two years went by and his pupils came and told him of their despair at the Fortune-Lindgren lectures, his will hardened to my plan to get rid of Lindgren. He told her, as he had to, that he did not propose to renew her lectureship.

When the appointment committee met to consider the Lindgren re-appointment I was now a voting member of it representing the General Board. We had a long and difficult meeting and it was decided we must adjourn until members had had an opportunity of hearing the candidate lecture. 'I have no intention of doing any such thing,' said Dorothy Garrod, 'and what is more I am leaving for France tomorrow to do research and will not be back for two months. Let us decide the matter now.' We decided by 5 votes to 2 that it should not be decided then.

Dorothy stormed away to France convinced that I was letting the side (which side?) down and was replaced on the committee by Miles Burkitt. Fortes and I attended some of Ethel Lindgren's lectures after asking her permission to do so. They were badly delivered, badly organized and not up to university standard. She was nervous and perhaps not at her best, knowing that her audience contained people vetting her or, as she thought, gunning for her. Yet that sort of challenging situation would in me have produced the best results: I would have said, 'I'll bloody well give them the works,' and pulled out all the stops ending with the *Trompeta Real*.

We met again and reported sadly that she wasn't up to the job. There was a long discussion again because to many it seemed a fundamental university issue of policy, as it indeed was. We were all asked our final views at the end of the meeting. I shall never forget the cold horror which greeted Burkitt's statement, said jovially with a hearty laugh, 'There's so much dead wood in this University that a little more will do no harm.' I caught the Vice-Chancellor's eye and while his face remained unmoved he indicated that the matter was at an end. 'May I now ask,' he said, 'for a proposition duly seconded to prolong Dr Lindgren's lectureship?' Two long silent minutes. 'Thank you gentlemen,' he said, 'for the care and attention you have given to this difficult matter.'

I had thought that the Lindgren case was the first of its kind after the 1926 Statutes came into force, but the present Secretary General of the Faculties, Dr K.J.R. Edwards, tells me that there were at least three cases in the 1930s in which Lecturers were not renewed after the initial three years, and that Dr Lindgren resigned when it became clear that the Committee were not going to re-appoint.

We all used to make fun of Miles Burkitt when he constantly referred to 'my brilliant pupils', and were amused at the map of the world which Grahame Clark kept in his room in the department which was studded with coloured pins indicating the universities, museums and institutes where his pupils were; and now in the last few days with a sense of joyful gratitude and humility I have been contemplating the list of over 250 people whom I taught personally – in supervisions and discussion classes – from 1946 to 1974. They include ten professors, countless lecturers, four directors of British schools abroad, directors and staff of many museums, including the present Director of the British Museum, Sir David Wilson, and half a dozen Fellows of the British Academy.

1962 was the *annus mirabilis* as far as my teaching was concerned. I knew I had been teaching exceptionally able and gifted men when I had sabbatical leave for the summer term and travelled to Hungary, Bulgaria and Istanbul. On the comfortable, quiet journey in a regular Turkish boat from Istanbul to Venice I kept saying to Ruth, 'I wonder how they have done'. I was handed a telegram in my hotel in Venice which said FOUR JOHNIAN FIRSTS. I said to the receptionist at the Luna Hotel, 'Could you make sure that this message is correctly decoded and that the FOUR is right?' When the answer came back confirming the FOUR we went and had celebratory Bellinis at the Gritti Palace but we were not thinking of Ernest Hemingway or Somerset Maugham. We were thinking of those four Johnians, one of whom, Barry Cunliffe, is now Professor of European Archaeology at Oxford, and another, Colin Renfrew, the tenth Disney Professor at Cambridge. I can think of few moments in my long academic career when I felt more happy. As I write I learn that Renfrew has been elected Master of Jesus, Cambridge.

It is a donnish platitude to say that one often learns more from one's pupils than they do from their mentors but sometimes this is true. One of my pupils, Euan McKie, now Archaeological Curator of the Hunterian Museum in Glasgow, took this to an agreeable extreme. He was an unusual and most amiable young man who, at a time when undergraduates were wearing the most tattered and dirty clothes they could find, was always dressed in a dark suit and carried with him a rolled umbrella as though he was walking to the Stock Exchange and not to E 6, Third Court, St John's College. I had set him some standard essay on the origin and distribution of Beakers. He came into my rooms, sat firmly down and said, 'You are not going to have an essay on Beakers. It is high time you learnt more about what you call the lunatic fringes of archaeology. I have prepared you an essay on Velikovsky.' I listen fascinated for thirty-five minutes: it was a clear, concise resumé. We went on discussing long after the supervision hour. When he left he said, 'Well, I had to get that out of my system. You shall have your Beakers next week,' and departed, twirling his tightly rolled umbrella.

I had two failures – or perhaps they were only, in retrospect, one. The first was an undergraduate who, disturbing another supervision, asked for a word with me and said, 'I come to wish you goodbye. I am leaving College and will commit suicide.' All I could think of saying was, 'Good God, no. Have you told your tutor?' 'No,' he said, 'but I am just on the way to see him.' As soon as I had finished with my pupils I rang up James Wordie. 'I know what you are going to say,' he said calmly. 'All will be well. I have given him money for a return ticket to Hunstanton and found him a room in a quiet hotel there for a week. He needs a change.'

I was alarmed and scanned the papers for news of a young man found dead in Hunstanton in unusual circumstances. But no such news, and before the week was up he was back in my rooms. 'Wordie was kind but he didn't understand me,' he said. 'A few days in Hunstanton is not going to cover a lifetime of depression and failure.' I tried to remonstrate. 'No, Glyn,' he said, 'this is the real goodbye.' He looked around and said: 'I shall always remember your untidy rooms as a haven of peace in a world of chaos.' I thought them strange words but he had gone away, off to say goodbye to James, he said.

I let a little time go by and then rang Wordie. 'Ah, yes,' he said, 'I made a mistake: he was away for too short a time. I have given him money for another return ticket to Hunstanton and booked him in a different and more cheerful hotel for a fortnight and I have given him six interesting books to read.' I put the 'phone down and tottered into Hall wondering whether experienced tutors knew what they were at. I read the papers carefully every day. No suicides in Hunstanton. Then

I had a postcard from him saying how lovely everything was. I could not make out whether this was alarming or reassuring. The full fortnight went by and he was back in my rooms radiant and bouncing with energy.

'I have had a wonderful time,' he said, 'and the most extraordinary experience. I went into the parish church and sat down, and suddenly I heard the voice of God and the Holy Ghost descended on my head in the form of a dove, and now all is peace.' He sailed through his Tripos and has become a trusted and scholarly member of society. I decided then and there not to accept any further invitations to be a tutor.

The other was not a success story. He was a good and, as it seemed to me, a sensible hard-working boy but his tutor warned me that he was unstable. 'He has twice tried to commit suicide,' I was told: once he cut his wrists and threw himself into the Cam only to be rescued by some rowing toughs who thought he had fallen in. On the second occasion he was discovered by a don on the roof of the Cripps building saying that he was looking for the best place from which to jump. Watch your step, I was told.

I did. We had agreeable supervisions and they moved on to the ideas of life and death among primitive peoples – the nature of magic, religion and taboo. He was very well read. I set him, deliberately, an essay on how much can we know about the life and thoughts of prehistoric man from the archaeological evidence. We went down to the buttery bar and had a drink together. 'That is a stimulating subject,' he said. I went back to my rooms and wrote a note to his tutor. 'I feel he is getting all right again,' I said. 'I am most hopeful.'

He went back to his rooms, collected some money, took the train to London and the night train to North Wales. He got to Rhyl in the early morning. He had been there often as a child. He went down to the beach and walked slowly and deliberately and purposefully into the sea. When his body was recovered there were in his pocket three sodden sheets of paper on which, since we had been talking the night before, he had outlined headings for his next essay.

Among my most famous and distinguished pupils were the present Queen of Denmark and the Prince of Wales. They were both charming and highly intelligent people to teach and the friendly teacher-pupil relationship which was established during those under-graduate years has happily continued to the present day.

I had known Princess Margrethe, as she then was, for many years before she became an undergraduate in Cambridge. When she was at school at North Foreland Lodge, her lady-in-waiting, Hofdam Kontesse Waby Armfelt, established herself in Cambridge and took the diploma in archaeology. She lived with those delightfully hospitable and kind people, Dr Edward Bevan and his wife, Joan, in Storey's Way, and it was there that Princess Margrethe lived when she was an undergraduate in Girton. We got to know the Kontesse Armfelt well from then onwards: she herself is a very well equipped and practising archaeologist.

I first met Princess Margrethe when she came over to Cambridge from school and I was one of the judges at some summer fair at the Garden House Hotel. She did extremely well and was moving into first place. Waby whispered in my ear – inappropriate to make her the winner, so our judgments were adjusted accordingly. I have often thought of that occasion and especially when Colin Renfrew gave, in the Garden House, a farewell party for Princess Margrethe.

Princess Margrethe was present as a young girl when we made in Copenhagen the *Buried Treasure* programme dealing with Tollund Man. Rik Wheeler was on his best form. The Danish authorities in conjunction with the BBC had laid on a version of the last meal which Tollund Man had eaten. It had been fully described by Hans Helbaek in his paper on the stomach contents of the Tollund Man. The gruel eaten by him before his death in the first century BC included barley, oats and linseed, but also seeds of sixteen wild species which no doubt provided him with starch and fat. We tasted this gruel in front of the cameras; it was dreadful, and then Wheeler made his oft quoted remark: 'No wonder the poor chap committed suicide if that was the sort of cooking he got at home.'

I have no doubt that Princess Margrethe enjoyed the year 1960–61 when she was in Cambridge as an undergraduate enormously. Ruth and I took her and Waby Armfelt out to meals in the countryside and she came to our annual fieldclass in Wessex when we stayed in the King's Arms in Salisbury. I had instructed them that no special arrangements of any kind were to be made but when we arrived it was too much for the landlord's wife who curtseyed deeply and fell on the floor. We all assisted her to her feet and from then on all was well.

Towards the end of her visit, when the examination results were published, I met her on her bicycle outside Woolworths. She dismounted and said, 'Glad I've met you. Can you come to the

Bevanry at twelve-thirty this morning?' I became suspicious. 'Is it a party?' I asked. 'Not really. Any clothes will do but your gardening clothes.' When I got there at twelve-thirty there were assembled half a dozen others who had taught her, and by the instruction and authority of her father, King Frederick VIII, we were all invested with orders of the Dannebrog. I treasure the fact that I am a Knight (First Class) of the Dannebrog: I am allowed to wear my decoration only on private occasions (like our 6 May Feast) or when Danish royalty is present. I wore it with pride at the Banquet given by the Queen at Windsor for the royal Danish couple in 1974, and at the splendid soirée at Buckingham Palace before the marriage of Prince Charles to Princess Diana, when Queen Margrethe was, of course, present.

Queen Margrethe retains the keenest interest in archaeology, as did notably her ancestor, Frederick VII, in the 1850s and 60s, who encouraged J.J.A. Worsaae, 'the first professional archaeologist,' as Brønsted has called him. Heredity may mean nothing in these matters but her grandfather was King Gustav Adolphus VI of Sweden who was a devoted, competent and practising archaeologist, and as Princess Margrethe she travelled with him in Italy and dug Etruscan tombs.

The Prince of Wales developed his interest in archaeology and anthropology without any family tradition of interest in these matters. It was his own decision to read Archaeology and Anthropology Part I when he came up to Cambridge as an undergraduate in 1966. His director of studies at Trinity was John Coles and I was one of his supervisors. Coles and I thought it would be a good thing if we took him for a short trip to France to see the palaeolithic cave-art of Dordogne and the megaliths of the Carnac area in the Easter vacation and a plan was worked out in conjunction with Squadron Leader (now Sir) David Checketts who was his equerry. There was to be no publicity until we landed in France and to ensure this the bookings in the hotels at Les Eyzies and La Trinité-sur-Mer were to be done by me and in my name. Les Glycines in Les Eyzies now proudly bears a plaque saying 'The Prince of England [*sic*] slept here'.

Prince Philip said he would fly us to Bordeaux and we set off from Heathrow in an aircraft of the Queen's Flight, lunching on the way out of hampers provided by Buckingham Palace: we were a party of five, Prince Philip, Prince Charles, David Checketts, John Coles and myself. It was a pleasant and memorable journey. When we arrived at

Bordeaux-Mérignac it was raining: there was an official party waiting to receive us, mainly mayors and prefects, but also a secretary from the British Embassy in Paris who was attached to us and Monsieur B, General de Gaulle's special adviser on social affairs to visiting VIPs. I was the last to leave the aircraft and said to Prince Philip: 'Aren't you getting out, sir?' 'No, no,' he said. 'I'm only the driver today and am due back to a cocktail party in London. It's his day – and yours. Enjoy yourselves.'

I joined the tail end of the reception to hear one mayor say to another that he thought he was rather drearily dressed and the reply that as it was pouring with rain he decided not to put on his number-one kit. The official reception over, we drove off in a cavalcade of five cars – the first car being French police and the last car the Special Security Service. But, as I soon learnt, the police in the front car could not communicate directly with the security boys in the last car and all messages from car one to car five had to go via their separate headquarters in Paris; this seemed, then and now, odd.

We drove off in good order but after ten minutes to my astonishment we were all signalled down to a lay-by. The security police came to David Checketts and myself and said they were very worried: we were being followed in a sixth car by a suspicious American wearing a wideawake hat and a string tie. Alarmed, I walked back with them to discover that this was Professor François Bordes, the distinguished palaeolithic archaeologist, who had been attached to us for our Dordogne visit. Bordes was devoted to western America: he stayed with us and was most helpful, but he bored us all, night after night, telling us how he had won the war by his *maquis* activities.

When we got to Les Eyzies the whole world knew what was happening and every free room in Les Glycines was booked by the French press. I don't think I could have managed the whole affair differently: the management said mildly, 'We were surprised by your letter. Normally you ask for a double room for your wife and yourself: this time you asked for eight rooms and accommodation for five cars. We thought you had gone up in the world.' 'I have,' I said, 'temporarily.'

I was particularly furious that *Paris Match* had offered untold sums to have the room opposite Prince Charles, and was even more furious when I discovered the occupant of the room was a bright flashy blonde who immediately took me aside and asked for a private interview of my views of Prince Charles, and mentioned a very large sum of money.

We were pursued by reporters all the time, and it certainly spoiled our chances of having a quiet look at towns and villages in the countryside; but the caves of course were different. I had planned that after a morning of palaeolithic archaeology we should drive up to the lovely walled hilltop town of Domme. The pursuing photographers and reporters were with us all the time. 'Why,' I said to Prince Charles, 'do they photograph your back view?' He laughed, 'My father says they want an overall view of royalty.'

Monsieur B. took me aside. 'Your programme has made no provision for lunch,' he said. 'No', I said, 'I have left that to you.' 'Bien merci,' and he disappeared. We drove away from Domme and fetched up at that delightful Hôtel Bonnet at the enchantingly sited place, Beynac-et-Cazenac on the banks of the Dordogne. 'What a splendid choice,' I said to Monsieur B., 'but where are the press and the photographers?' 'Ah,' he said, 'you will know there are only two entrances to Domme. By a curious chance one of my cars broke down in each entrance: an amusing coincidence, n'est-ce-pas, Monsieur?'

So we got to the Hôtel Bonnet unescorted by the press and were ushered into a private room. A most wonderful lunch had been laid on with the best display of hors d'oeuvres I have ever seen, including snails and foie gras. They were the first snails Prince Charles had ever tasted: 'I find them rather like little bits of rubber in a delicious garlic sauce,' I said. He agreed. We told him how the geese were force-fed so that their livers were enlarged and showed him postcards of Le Gavage. He pronounced it disgusting and cruel and said he would see that foie gras was no longer served at Buckingham Palace. By then the press had managed to get out of Domme, had consulted their *Guide Michelin* and guessed correctly that we had gone to the nearest starred restaurant. Prince Charles went out to greet them on the terrace and made a delightful speech in very good French ending by wishing they would have as excellent a lunch as he was having.

When we went back to the hotel I said I was going for a walk through the village. 'I wish I could come with you,' he said, 'and sit quietly in a café, but' (waving a hand at the crowds of reporters) 'it's quite impossible.' I came back with a copy of the local paper which had pictures of the visit and an account saying that the Prince of Wales was accompanied by his governess, Mademoiselle Danielle.

The journey from Dordogne to Brittany went past Fontévrault where we inspected the tombs of Henry II, Eleanor of Aquitaine and Richard Coeur de Lion in the abbey, and the great megalithic tomb on the outskirts of Saumur. My careful calculations were based on my own rate of driving through France with an allowance for large chauffeur-driven limousines. I had made no allowance for General de Gaulle who had insisted that nothing untoward was to happen on this trip and there were police at every crossroad and we sped across France unimpeded by any traffic.

After inspecting the megaliths, we drove from Carnac to Saint-Malo and boarded a civilian aircraft for Jersey and London. Prince Charles was spending a few days digging at Charles McBurney's site, La Côte de Sainte-Brelade in Jersey, and we said goodbye at the airport. John Coles and I went into the cafeteria for a cup of tea and suddenly realized that our luggage, thought to be part of the royal baggage, had been swept off to Government House. We explained the situation to the airport authorities and they provided a car for us. When we got to Government House the party were all gathered together at the head of the stairs. 'What's the matter?' said David Checketts. 'We thought we had got rid of you.' I explained the situation and had a word with the Governor's ADC, asking him if he could perhaps get us seats on the next aircraft. Our own was leaving in five minutes. He went away to arrange this: we took our second farewell and, our baggage safely stored in the car, drove quickly back to the airport. Our aircraft would, we thought, have departed half an hour before but as we got out of the departure entrance we heard a voice on the tannoy asking passengers to board the aircraft – our original aircraft 'which has been delayed by circumstances beyond our control'.

The Prince of Wales often came to lunch in The Flying Stag and kept up his friendship with Ruth and me all through his three years as an undergraduate. He has retained his keen interest in matters archaeological and anthropological and it was his speech when he was admitted a Royal Fellow of the Society of Antiquaries of London on 11 November 1982 and spoke of his special interest in the antiquities of the Duchy of Cornwall, and of the Rillaton Gold Cup, that prompted Professor Christopher Hawkes to write a fresh account of this remarkable prehistoric find which was used by King George V for keeping collar studs in (*Antiquity*, 1983). A few years ago he created an

Advisory Group on Archaeology to the Duchy of Cornwall and asked me to be its chairman, which pleasant task involves field meetings in the West Country.

The Disney Chair of Archaeology is the oldest chair of archaeology in the British Isles. It was founded in 1851, but only just! There was a division of the Regent House about the advisability of accepting the bequest of Mr Disney and having a Chair of Archaeology: there were 7 *non-placets* but fortunately 8 *placets*.

John Disney was a gentleman of Ingatestone in Essex who came up to Peterhouse in 1796. He was a collector and a dilettante: he delighted in the arts while practising the law – he was called to the bar in 1803, the same year in which Lord Elgin, passing through Paris, was arrested under Napoleon's decree. The first case of Elgin's antiquities had arrived in London the previous year. Disney was much affected by his contacts with Edward Daniel Clarke, travelled to Greece in his footsteps, and also presented his collection to the University of Cambridge. He even went one better than Clarke and founded the Chair of Archaeology. 'It shall be the duty of the Professor,' said the terms of his agreement with the University, 'to deliver in the course of each academic year . . . six lectures at least on the subject of Classical, Medieval and other Antiquities, the Fine Arts and all matters and things connected therewith.'

Hugo Gatty told me he was once staying in Norfolk and was introduced to a gloomy man called Major Disney. He said to Hugo, 'You're from Cambridge, I hear. I bear that University a grudge. My ancestor founded a professorship there many years ago. That's why I'm so poor.'

The first holder of the Chair was John Howard Marsden, a Fellow of St John's, and he was succeeded in 1865 by Churchill Babbington, also a Fellow of St John's. In 1880 Percy Gardner of Christ's became the third holder, and when he migrated to Oxford in 1887 was succeeded by George Forrest Browne, a Fellow of St Catharine's who subsequently became Bishop of Bristol.

If there were some mechanism whereby we could meet and talk to people long ago dead and gone – and why not? Radio, television, space travel have been achieved, why not travel to the past? – the one departed Disney Professor I should like to meet would be George Browne. Yes, his successor from 1892, William Ridgeway, would be fun – noisy, Irish, cantankerous; but Browne fills me with admiration.

He was a successful master at Trinity College, Glenalmond, a university administrator of great distinction – he was one of the secretaries of the 1877 Commission on Universities and had been Secretary of the Local Examinations Syndicate since 1871. He was Disney Professor from 1887 to 1892; Bishop of Stepney from 1895 to 1897; and Bishop of Bristol from 1897 to 1914. He wrote his autobiography called *Recollections of a Bishop* (1915) which makes very good reading, particularly for his successor four times removed, who is doing the same thing but without benefit of clergy.

G.F. Browne wrote in his memoirs (p. 190):

> In the late autumn of 1887 Mr Percy Gardner resigned the Disney Professorship of Art and Archaeology on his appointment to a corresponding professorship in Oxford. My companions in Rome and the leading archaeologists in Cambridge surprised me by urging me to become a candidate for the vacant professorship. I had already more to do than I had properly time to do, and any extra work in term time must be done after ten oclock at night. . . . I had far too high an idea of professional work to regard myself as fitted to undertake it.

Browne was appointed: the runner-up was J.W. Clark whom Browne thought would have done the job much better than himself. The salary was still £112 a year and the duties just to give six lectures. His own special interests were in pre-Norman sculptured stones and these he recorded and interpreted with scholarly skill and imagination. His interpretations were often criticized and he wrote of his critics:

> Not being either scholars or historians, or not being able to give life and actuality to scholarship or history, they had no sympathy with the calculated guesses of those who were most adequately equipped. I well remember the remarks which proceeded from some of them when I interpreted the panels on the great cross now in the parish church at Leeds. They were offended by the use of the imagination in a case which cried out for imaginative or creative treatment. It was always the imaginative side of archaeology that attracted me: not dry-as-dust but fresh as life.

A lovable man, perhaps forgotten by modern archaeologists.

The last Disney Professor under the original statutes, the redoubtable William Ridgeway, was a Peterhouse man who became a Fellow of Caius and held the Chair from 1892 to 1927. In 1927 the University, after long deliberation, decided to make the Disney Chair a full one and to assign it to the Faculty of Archaeology and Anthropology. E.H. Minns held the Chair under its new terms from 1927 to 1938, Dorothy Garrod from 1938 to 1952, and Grahame Clark from 1952 to 1974. I was elected the ninth holder in 1974, and when I retired in 1981, was succeeded by my former pupil Colin Renfrew. It is amusing and pleasant to reflect that four out of the ten Disney Professors to date have been Johnians.

I was enthusiastic about taking students away from Cambridge to see sites and monuments and visit museums, and gradually made the annual departmental field classes a standard and essential part of the Cambridge archaeological training. Though Garrod and Clark were interested they were not wildly enthusiastic – they were more anxious that students should have extensive field training in excavation. Our plan was to go to Salisbury Plain once every three years so that once in his undergraduate career a student saw Stonehenge, Woodhenge, Avebury, Wor Barrow and Maiden Castle – the classic sites of British prehistory. In other years we made trips to Wales, S.E. England and the North Country.

Dorothy Garrod had been easy to get on with: she was a generous, lovable, outgoing person who was interested in people. Grahame Clark, great scholar though he was and a man who brought great distinction to Cambridge during his two decades as Professor, was not interested in people and did not get on easily with colleagues or pupils. In his heart of hearts I think he sometimes doubted whether there were any really good archaeologists other than himself, but as he mellowed he was prepared grudgingly to recognize the good work of Mortimer Wheeler, Christopher Hawkes, Stuart Piggott and some of his pupils like Desmond Clark and Charles McBurney. Charles Phillips shared his prejudices. Clark and Phillips were driving Terence Powell and me to a meeting of the Prehistoric Society in London in the mid-thirties: they spent their time denigrating every archaeologist we had ever heard of until Terence, with undergraduate innocence asked, 'Are there then no good archaeologists?' There was a silence. Then Phillips said, 'You don't have to look very far.'

Those years in the Department of Archaeology in Cambridge with Grahame Clark as Professor were not entirely happy. He genuinely thought that many, if not most of us, were second rate. I was written off as someone who did little excavation, spent his time travelling in France (indeed had even written a book called *The Hungry Archaeologist in France!*), and wasted his energies appearing on television programmes. We were all of us aware of an alarming and chilling self-centredness. It was so difficult to conduct any reasonable conversation or get the business one had come to see him about properly discussed. Clark would immediately talk about what he was doing, what was in his mind, the progress of his researches: all often very interesting but not what one had come to see him about. Armed with a brief agenda – the problems of a particular research student, the need to organize the details of a visit by a professor from Germany, my ideas for the next field class – one was overwhelmed by his stimulating ideas about the relation of the mesolithic hunter-fishers to the megalith builders in Sweden!

His inability to understand the problems of other people was sadly shown on one occasion when he tried to persuade a former pupil of ours to go in for a lectureship in our department. The young man already had a better paid appointment in London and said that moving to Cambridge would mean a loss of salary. 'Salary, yes,' said Grahame, 'but there's always your private income.' The young man said coldly, 'My private income is nil.'

In 1955 I reviewed Sigfried de Laet's *L'Archéologie et ses problèmes* and praised it saying, 'An enterprising English publisher should issue an English edition of it as soon as he can' (*Antiquity*, 1955). This immediately happened and the English edition, translated by Ruth, was a great success everywhere except in the study of Grahame Clark. He thought it plagiarized his own *Archaeology and Society* and for a while he and his publisher, Peter Wait of Methuen, were planning some legal action; on the London-Cambridge trains we studiously avoided speaking to each other. It was a form of mild paranoia: what of course had happened is that De Laet had written his book from his lecture notes, and that in preparing his lectures over the years he had noted down some ideas from Clark's excellent *Archaeology and Society*.

One day at the annual London party of the Cambridge University Press I said to S.C. Roberts that what was now wanted, after all the *Cambridge Histories*, was a *Cambridge Prehistory*. Excellent idea, he said, and wrote to me next day asking for details: I set out a scheme for a three-volume work. He replied asking if I would edit it. I said no, but would be happy to be a member of a team and suggested Grahame Clark, Geoffrey Bushnell, Curator of the Museum of Archaeology and Ethnology, and myself. This idea was taken up and both Grahame and Geoffrey agreed. With the approval of the Press it seemed the *Cambridge Prehistory* was on its way. It seemed too good to be true.

We heard nothing for a while and then we all three had a brief meeting at which Grahame Clark told us that the Syndics of the Press had changed their minds and instead of a three-volume work of chapters by a wide selection of authors they now wanted a single volume written by the three of us. We went away to think. Nothing happened. We were all busy with other ploys: I was getting involved with the *Ancient Peoples and Places* series and from time to time saw Geoffrey Bushnell whose book on *Peru* was to be its first title. We asked each other what was going on, but had nothing to say. Then we were both surprised to receive inscribed copies of a book called *World Prehistory* by Grahame Clark.

Our project had been transformed into this – but at no stage were we told by the Syndics or by Clark what was happening; Geoffrey Bushnell asked me to dine with him in Corpus, and we decided there was nothing we could do. Although Geoffrey is dead, I still hope that the idea of a *Cambridge Prehistory* will be revived by a new body of Syndics and will come to fruition in some post Clark-Daniel era.

One of the joys of being on the academic staff at Cambridge in the thirty-one years embraced by this chapter was the generous interpretation of sabbatical leave. After six terms' teaching one was allowed one term off and these could be accumulated until a whole year might be taken off, and on full pay. The University Statutes contain a remarkable phrase about sabbatical leave which, they say, 'may not unreasonably be refused'. And so I had off from June 1955 to October 1956 – a wonderful break in one's early forties.

The generous system of sabbatical leave enabled me to give lectures and be Visiting Professor at other universities. I gave the Munro Lectures in Edinburgh in 1954, the Josiah Mason Lectures in Birmingham in 1956, the Ballard-Matthews Lectures at Bangor in 1968 and the Gregynog Lectures at the University College of Wales, Aberystwyth, in the same year. I was Visiting Professor at Aarhus in 1968 and in Hull in 1969 but the most delightful extra-Cambridge appointment was to be George Grant MacCurdy Lecturer at Harvard which meant that we spent the semester from September

1971 to February 1972 in that lovely place, the American Cambridge, second only in my affections to the English Cambridge.

Ruth and I celebrated our twenty-fifth wedding anniversary by travelling in 1971 from Southampton to New York on the SS *France*, a memorable experience. Our friend, Edyth Dial from Pasadena, who travelled regularly to Europe each year on the *France*, accompanied by her white Jaguar, in which she had driven from California, had written to the purser and the chief steward and we got extraordinary preferential treatment. The first-class restaurant menu of the *France* was naturally outstanding: the steward waved a hand at it disparagingly and said, 'This is only a general guide: you say what dishes you would like from anywhere in the world. Our chef would be delighted to make them for you.' We took him at his word and one night ordered caviare, Sole Colbert, Tournedos Périgourdin, and Crêpes Suzettes. No wonder the French government had to subsidize the *France* so heavily and eventually give her up. But it was nice just once to cross the Atlantic in the lap of luxury.

I had been in North America on several occasions before, notably on a lecture tour of schools and colleges in California, and I gave a lecture in Harvard on the history of archaeology as part of the centenary celebration of the Peabody Museum: it was published in J.O. Brew (ed.), *One hundred years of Anthropology* (1968). To return to Harvard and to teach there for four months was a great pleasure: the lectureship founded in memory of MacCurdy was in European prehistory and had been previously held by Christopher Hawkes, Grahame Clark and Stuart Piggott. The teaching load was not heavy and there was plenty of time to work in libraries – the library of the Peabody Museum is remarkably good – and to give lectures in Montreal, Yale, Philadelphia and New York, and to make visits to places like Colonial Williamsburg, where Ivor Noël Hume has been doing such remarkable archaeological work.

We lived in a top-floor apartment in Leverett House with a marvellous view over the Charles River and enjoyed the close friendship and warm hospitality of Ken Andrews, the then Master, and his wife Carolyn, who between them ran Leverett House admirably. We made many new friends, the Lamberg-Karlovskys, the Sabloffs, and the Stephen Williamses, but the great delight was to improve and cultivate our old friendship with the Gorden Willeys, the Movius family, and the Henckens, as well as with Jo Brew, then presiding over the Peabody with his usual ebullience and enthusiasm.

Nancy Movius had been a contemporary of mine as an undergraduate in Cambridge: and we had seen something of her husband Hal and herself on visits to Les Eyzies where he was excavating, with great care and distinction, the rock shelter of Abri Pataud. Hugh Hencken, now alas no more, had been a friend for many years. He was a Johnian and the story goes that when he was a student at Princeton he went to some lectures by Martin Charlesworth, was impressed by them, and was even more impressed when late one evening he found Martin singing songs, playing the piano and dancing on the dining table. He determined to follow him back to St John's where he became a devoted pupil and friend of H.M. Chadwick and J.M. de Navarro. His PhD dissertation on the Stone and Bronze Ages of Cornwall and Devon was masterly and should have earned him a prize fellowship at St John's were it not for the fact that O.G.S. Crawford, when asked to referee the work, instead of sending in a detailed, closely argued report, replied on a postcard that if the Fellows of St John's did not immediately elect Hencken it would only confirm his view of the stupidity of most Oxbridge dons. The Fellows were unsympathetic to such crisp comment and Hugh missed his Fellowship: but years later, and very properly, he was made an Honorary Fellow, in the same year as was Louis Leakey.

Thalassa, his wife, I hardly knew before our Harvard days, but knew her distinction as an archaeologist – I had heard nothing but praise of her from such a hard judge as Mortimer Wheeler – and that she had become a television star through her gardening programmes.

The Henckens went out of their way to be friendly and helpful (indeed, who didn't in Harvard?) and I well remember a special trip with Hugh to see the Newport Tower, claimed by some to be Viking but in fact proved to be a colonial mill by one of Hugh's pupils.

Ruth and I became devoted to New England and the beauty of the trees in the fall there is of an unbelievable loveliness. Our Harvard days of 1971–2 are a very happy memory and we have been back on several occasions, renewing with pleasure the walk across the Yard I so often made from Leverett House to the Peabody, the trees changing to russet and red and the squirrels scampering across the paths. I am grateful that while I have spent most of my adult life in Cambridge (England) on the Cam, I have also experienced Cambridge (Massachusetts) on the Charles River.

CHAPTER SEVEN

Writing and editing

MY FIRST ARCHAEOLOGICAL PAPER was written in anger. I was in the middle of my PhD researches and the undergraduates had asked Miles Burkitt to give their Society a talk. To my surprise he chose megaliths as his subject. To my horror he propounded an old-fashioned doctrine based on the Montelian classification of dolmens, passage-graves and long stone cists. Even in 1936 it was ludicrously *vieux jeux*. I hurried back to my rooms in College and began setting down my own views. I wrote far into the night and by lunchtime next day had finished a short paper entitled 'The "dolmens" of Southern Britain', which I typed out and sent with considerable misgivings to Crawford. By return came a postcard accepting it, and it was published in *Antiquity* in 1937. A few days after it was published I got a card from Gordon Childe which just said, 'I liked your *Antiquity* paper and am glad to know this is the beginning of what I hope will one day be a book.'

My first book was not about megaliths. It too was written in anger. I was not only furious that the word 'dolmen' was being used indiscriminately for a wide variety of structures, but that the three-age system of Thomsen and Worsaae was being used to describe time and economic change – at that time I saw no future in speaking of Bronze Age times and the Neolithic Revolution: and so I wrote a long essay on this subject which the Cambridge University Press published in 1943 when I was away in the RAF in India: it was called *The Three Ages: an essay on archaeological method*. Both my first paper and my first book were protests against what I then thought, and rightly, was the complacency of establishment archaeology.

I finished the typescript of *The Three Ages* before I joined RAF Photographic Intelligence in 1940. I did not think I would be doing much writing for the next few years but I found myself impelled to write. I turned to short stories and one was published in an anthology of stories by Welsh writers.

I have already described how in a hotel in Cairo I threw a Penguin detective story out of my bedroom window and that Stuart Piggott

216

suggested I should try my hand at writing one myself. I began to think of taking up Piggott's challenge. I remembered that a few years before, late one night in College, I had propounded to Deryck Williams and Bob Marchant an idea for a detective story in which the key point was to be someone murdered in College right at the end of term, the body put in one of the many large trunks that were carted away, and only discovered when some unfortunate undergraduate opened his luggage miles away from the scene of the crime. 'But could you get a body into a trunk?' they said. We tried. You could.

Back in Delhi from the Algiers Conference that never happened, I began to work out a story based on the body in the end of term trunk and in the evenings after work and on my weekly days off and visits around India I wrote *The Cambridge Murders*. When it was finished I read it through and thought that it was not bad, not good – an average 2.2 story. I packed it off and sent it to Gollancz. In a very short time back came a letter provisionally accepting my book but making many helpful suggestions, all but one of which I accepted. They immensely improved the book. Off went the revised MS: back came a telegram of acceptance. I sent back at once my agreement.

I had become a different kind of author. Perhaps if I couldn't make my way professionally as an archaeologist after the war I might earn a living as a creative writer. I told Martin Charlesworth what was happening and asked whether I should publish under a pseudonym. He replied, 'Yes. If the book is unsuccessful no one in College except you and me need know who wrote it. If it is successful, as I am sure it will be, you can gracefully reveal the identity of the author.' I took his advice and the first edition of *The Cambridge Murders* in 1945 appeared to have been written by a certain Dilwyn Rees.

To my intense relief it was well reviewed except for a pedantic piece by Gardner-Smith, then Dean of Jesus College, Cambridge, who said: 'This book is obviously not written by anyone who knows Cambridge. The author puts the post office in Regent Street, and makes deans of colleges responsible for discipline' – as indeed they are in most colleges. Years later I met Gardner-Smith, introduced myself and referred to his review. 'I don't know what you are talking about', he said, 'I have never read your book.' Perhaps he hadn't.

Encouraged, the pseudonym was dropped, and now with an itching pen I wrote another detective story. *Welcome Death* was published by Gollancz in 1954 under my own name. It was a story about a man (a thinly disguised version of myself) who returns from the war to his native village in the Vale of Glamorgan. I thought it was better than *The Cambridge Murders* but both Agatha Christie and J.B. Priestley told me in conversation that while they both liked it, it was disappointing after the promise of my first novel. 'Try again,' they said. I did, and wrote a novel set in India which I called *The Mysterious Barricades*. I put it away in a drawer determined to let it rest for a while. It has now rested in that drawer for thirty years. I read it the other day and thought poorly of it.

For *The Cambridge Murders* I invented, as I had to do, a fictional college: 'In the older and more beautiful of the two ancient universities' I wrote, tongue in cheek, and went on: 'Fisher College lies between Trinity and St John's and stretches from Trinity Street down to the Cam.' My amateur detective, Sir Richard Cherrington, was an archaeologist and many have thought him a portrait of Mortimer Wheeler, or that even more improbable fantasy, Wheeler and Daniel combined. Jessica Mann, herself a distinguished writer of detective fiction, wrote in her article 'Dons and Detection' in *Antiquity and Man* (1981) edited by Evans, Cunliffe and Renfrew: 'With hindsight we may recognize a certain proleptic, or even prophetic, self-portrayal in this worldly, learned bon-viveur, unable to make up his mind whether scholarship was just another animal pleasure, like a squirrel's in collecting nuts, or whether in it could be found "something transcending brute nature, something of the spirit – the eternal, unsatisfied quest for truth".'

The two stories sold well and eventually went into green Penguins and for a while I was half-amused and half-bored by visitors who asked me to show them where Fisher College was. 'I can't find it in the standard guide books,' said one cross American. But I turned away from fiction writing to devote myself to archaeological teaching and research and to college and university administration.

In the years following my return to Cambridge after the war I was engaged in preparing for the publication of my PhD thesis: it was eventually published in 1950 by the Cambridge University Press under the title of *The Prehistoric Chamber Tombs of England and Wales*. Its value was that it contained a near complete inventory of all the known and vanished megalithic tombs in southern Britain – it provided a basis for future workers and an overall distribution pattern which has not been materially changed since.

This over, I turned to a book on the French megaliths and this took ten years to do. On the whole I have found writing easy and have often discussed this with Stuart Piggott, who is an exemplarily quick and efficient writer. He thinks that the training we had as staff officers in the war made a tremendous difference to our attitude to writing and I think he is right. Samuel Johnson may well have been right too in saying that 'when a man knows he is to be hanged in a fortnight, it concentrates his mind wonderfully.' In my case, when I was told late one afternoon that I had to produce a paper for the Chiefs of Intelligence of South East Asia Command on some topic or other by two the following afternoon I found it did concentrate the mind wonderfully.

In 1955 my former pupil, Simon Young, alas now dead at the early age of 50, who had joined the staff of Thames and Hudson on going down from Cambridge, wrote to me asking what I thought of Christian Zervos's *Les Antiquités de la Sardaigne*; Walter Neurath, the managing director and inspiring genius of the new firm, wanted to know whether it should be published in English – was it good, would it sell, was it the only book of its kind? I did not have to think long in answering these questions. Yes, it was the only book of its kind but anyone interested in the subject would read the book in the original French, probably in the library. What we need, I wrote, is a small book based on Zervos and others dealing with the antiquities and ancient history of Sardinia in a brief and authoritative way, and well illustrated.

Next day the telephone rang; Simon Young asked whether I could come to London in the next few days and lunch with Walter and Eva Neurath and himself. Over that ever to be remembered lunch, the *Ancient Peoples and Places* series was born and I found myself its sole editor. The first volume in the new series, *Peru* by Geoffrey Bushnell, was published in 1956. The hundred-and-first volume, *Cyprus from the Stone Age to the Romans* by Vassos Karageorghis, was published in 1982. During that quarter of a century the editing of that series took up a great deal of time: letters, interviews, meetings in London, reading of texts and proofs. But it was all immensely worthwhile and out of the hundred volumes published in the series I would rate two-thirds as standard reading for anyone interested in man's past and at least twenty as classics of archaeological exposition which will go on being revised and brought up to date for many years to come.

It would be invidious to mention any books or authors by name just as it is impossible to record any of the authors on my blacklist – that list of authors who eagerly asked for and signed contracts and have never produced the goods. Editing the series has been an education in patience and in the vagaries and self-deception of potential authors. Once when I was in Copenhagen I crossed to Malmö and visited Holgar Arbman in Lund. He had readily agreed to write a book for us, *The Vikings*. Before he took me out to lunch we went into his office in the University and he pointed to a pile of paper. 'Here is the manuscript of my book,' he said, and handed me the first three pages. I was delighted, but when I recounted this occurrence to David Wilson, he said, 'But you should have looked further down the pile. All the other pages were blank.' That may have been so: it was two years before we received Arbman's *The Vikings* but an excellent book it was.

Professor X was quite a different story. He had readily accepted an invitation to do a book. A year went by: he assured me he was busily engaged in writing the book for me and was enjoying it. I met him one day on King's Parade in Cambridge: he was carrying a large despatch case. This he tapped and said, 'Here are the illustrations for my book. Just off to London to show them to Thames and Hudson.' Two days later I asked T. and H. what they thought of Professor X's illustrations: he had not been to see them. I telephoned X. 'There must be some misunderstanding,' he said, and put down the telephone.

The excuses began to multiply: his parents were ill and dying, he had had a nervous breakdown, his university work was too onerous, he would have to have a sabbatical year and travel abroad before he could finish the book. Thames and Hudson were justifiably impatient and wanted to cancel the contract. I happened to be going to Professor X's university to give a lecture and told him it would be pleasant to have a conversation together. He readily agreed and a time was fixed. I went to his room in the university: he wasn't there – 'Alas,' said his secretary, 'he has unfortunately had to go to London on urgent personal business'. When I told this to my hosts that evening they laughed outright. 'He was in the Coach and Horses at lunchtime,' they said, 'and gave a seminar at 3 p.m.' Even my patience was at last exhausted. I rang him up and told him I was advising T. and H. to cancel his contract. 'Oh dear,' he said, 'I shall have to look around for another publisher.' Needless to say the book, if it ever existed, has never appeared.

That was a strange case. Another was of Professor Y who told us that he had completed his book but on re-reading it found it so unsatisfactory that he had thrown the whole typescript on to the fire in his study. 'But the carbon copy,' I said, 'could we not have that and see whether we find your own judgment too severe?' 'Of course,' he said, 'I'll send it off tomorrow.' Days passed and no manuscript appeared either in St John's College or in 30 Bloomsbury Street. 'How sad,' said Professor Y, 'it must have been lost in the post.'

But the baddies were far outnumbered by the goodies and how pleasant it has been dealing with responsible and good authors. Our American authors have been particularly helpful and I am just looking at a note from Professor Michael Coe of Yale which says: 'Do you want this book written in English or American? I can speak and write both languages.'

Our aim in the series was simple: to summarize in an authoritative but readable way all that was known about an ancient people such as the Scythians, the Etruscans, the Phoenicians or the Maya, or an ancient place such as Babylon, Constantinople, Mexico, New Grange, or Brittany. We wanted the books to meet the needs of the student or the general reader who looked for an up-to-date summary of what was known of a people, a place, or a topic in antiquity: but also to enable a serious specialist to go further by providing careful bibliographical notes and lists of books for further reading. And it was always our intention to save archaeology from falling back into its own dust, by reproducing the artistic achievements of ancient peoples in the form of as many illustrations as possible. We set a limit of 40,000 words – a very long essay – and were horrified when one author told us proudly that he had managed to keep to our limits and produced a text of 100,000 words!

I think we succeeded from time to time. Cyril Connolly once, very generously, described the series as 'the ideal bridge between highbrow and lowbrow'. And Professor Brian Fagan wrote in *Antiquity* (1982):

Geoffrey Bushnell's *Peru* appeared in 1956 to enthusiastic reviews. Everyone admired the striking design and magnificent photographs, the clear exposition of an archaeological topic little known outside the confines of Americanists. But few people realised they were witnessing a revolution in archaeological publishing. . . . A whole generation of archaeologists has been nurtured on the series, and cannot remember the pre-A.P. and P. days when a long library journey was the fate of anyone interested in anything but the broadest sweep of world prehistory. . . . Anyone fortunate enough to possess an entire set of A.P. and P. has a veritable archaeological world at their finger tips. . . . [the volumes] navigate through a mass of undigested data about world prehistory and provide, through their clarity and superb illustrations, a unique perspective of humanity that has influenced not only thousands of students, but an enormous general audience as well. They are *haute vulgarisation* at its very best.

How much Walter Neurath would have liked to read those words. But, alas, to the great loss of publishing and of course even more to his family and friends, he died in 1967. The idea of such books may have been sown in his mind by my letter about the translation of Zervos, but it was his brainchild and that of his wife, Eva, who was responsible for the design of the books which made them so attractive and immediately interesting in bookshops. But it was the editorial archaeological staff at Thames and Hudson – first Simon Young, then Eric Peters, and now Colin Ridler – who have maintained the high standards of clear writing and good illustration which we all wanted. I worked with Eric Peters for nearly a quarter of a century: he was painstaking and rigorous in his editing, meticulous and efficient in all administrative matters: nothing foolish or slipshod passed by him. He was affectionately known in and outside the firm as 'schoolmaster Peters'. He worked on until a day or two before his death. When he died in 1982 at the age of eighty, I felt that at last I had left school. He was certainly one of my most valued and respected mentors.

Walter Neurath was one of the great figures of post-war British publishing and I paid a warm and sincere tribute to him when I spoke at his funeral in Highgate. He was a man of vision and enterprise: the *World of Art* must be one of the most successful, if not *the* most successful, series in modern publishing, and the publishing house he founded, still independently owned, the envy of many. His flair, infectious enthusiasm and faculty for hard work and punishing travel to German, Austrian, Italian and American publishers have been inherited by his son, Thomas, who in his first year as an undergraduate in Cambridge reading the Archaeological and Anthropological Tripos, told me that he was trying to persuade his father to let him leave Cambridge at the end of the year. 'I don't think a Cambridge degree will help me to be a publisher,' he said, 'I want to get into the business as quickly as possible.'

In the years 1955–1967 I had endless dealings with Walter, mainly in his office in London. Our editorial conferences were invariably punctuated by long distance telephone calls. 'Excuse me,' he would say, picking up the receiver. 'Munich' – or 'Milan' – or 'New York, on the line'. We had only one quarrel and it didn't last very long. I was pressing for some changes in bibliography, in the notes to illustrations and one or two other matters. He seemed intransigent: his face darkened and he said sharply: 'Are you trying to teach me my job?' It seemed no time for compromise, tense though the atmosphere was. 'Yes,' I said. He looked up, startled, and burst out laughing. 'Good for you,' he said. 'Let's go to the White Tower for lunch.' It was an excellent idea to found in conjunction with Birkbeck College the series of Walter Neurath Memorial Lectures and I was happy to give the fourth one published in 1972 as *Megaliths in History*.

Eva is now chairman of Thames and Hudson with Thomas, Walter's son by his first marriage, as managing director. She sometimes attends our monthly or bi-monthly editorial conferences and her discerning charm and clear views are always most welcome and helpful. One day she declared that what we needed was a second archaeological series which could include larger books than the 40,000-word essays of the *Ancient Peoples and Places* series: and so *The World of Archaeology* series was born and I found myself editor of that too. It has already produced some excellent and important books such as the Willey/Sabloff *History of American Archaeology* and Ole Klindt-Jensen's *History of Scandinavian Archaeology*.

We had a party to celebrate the publication of the 25th volume of the *Ancient Peoples and Places* series, and another when the 50th volume was published. 'I wonder,' said Walter, 'whether we shall both be alive and working when the 100th volume comes out.' I was, but alas he was not. Eva and Thomas demanded that I should write the 100th volume and I suggested it should be called *Ancient Peoples and Places*: they demurred and commissioned me to write *A Short History of Archaeology*, which I did, protesting that I had already said what I had to say on the subject in several books. But I found it a good exercise to concentrate my ideas into a long essay, emphasizing matters that seemed important to me, not only in the history of archaeological discovery, but also in the history of man's ideas about his ancient past.

I met Allen Lane at a party in London in the late fifties and we immediately discovered we had a great deal in common. We were both Welshmen – he was born Allen Lane Williams but changed his name by deed poll when he joined his kinsman, John Lane, in the publishing house of the Bodley Head. He had a keen interest in archaeology and in travel and we shared an enthusiasm for and serious interest in good food and wine. I told him of my excitement as a third-year undergraduate going into Woolworths in Bridgend and buying in July 1935 the first ten Penguins. We had meals together in London and I got him, and Tony Godwin, then his blue-eyed boy, down to a feast at St John's. I said how sad I was that the first archaeological Penguins were those unworthy books, Winbolt's *Britain B.C.* and W.J. Perry's *Growth of Civilisation*. He told me how there had been such an outcry about Winbolt that he had had to commission Christopher and Jacquetta Hawkes to write their *Prehistoric Britain*. He said that he had invited Max Mallowan to be his archaeological adviser but that Max would only plan books on Near Eastern Archaeology and he wanted wider and more far-reaching books dealing with all parts of the world. Would I become archaeological adviser to Penguin Books? I agreed. He sacked Max and my dealings with Max were a little strained for several years: Allen Lane liked behaving quickly and dramatically and his notorious dismissal of Tony Godwin is part of English publishing history.

I accepted his challenge and a carte blanche to produce archaeological Penguins which would be good and would sell all over the world. The titles I commissioned included Buchanan's *Industrial Archaeology*, Leslie Alcock's *Arthur's Britain*, Nora Chadwick's *The Celts*, John Coles and Eric Higgs's *The Archaeology of Early Man*, Pat Phillips's *The Prehistory of Europe*, David Trump's *The Prehistory of the Mediterranean*, and the best-selling book by Warwick Bray and David Trump, *A Dictionary of Archaeology*.

My friendship with Allen Lane burgeoned anew when Nikolaus Pevsner entered my life: it was Stephen Glanville who introduced me to him. He became Slade Professor of Fine Art in Cambridge in 1949 and held that appointment – normally for one year – until 1955.

Nikki was a truly remarkable man and a very good friend. Born in Leipzig in 1902 he had come to England in 1934 as a refugee from Nazi Germany: it was not for fifteen years that he became an eminence in the world of scholarship and a household name. In 1955 there appeared the first volume of what was to be a 47-volume series, *The Buildings of England*; the last volume came out in 1970. I well remember buying the first volume dedicated to his wife, Karola: 'To Lola, who drove the car.' I learnt later that it was the enthusiasm and confidence of Allen Lane that got this remarkable enterprise launched.

Nikki was a brilliant, enthusiastic, inspiring lecturer and part of his lecture performance consisted of exquisite lantern slides properly keyed to his words: the experience of Leipzig and Dresden was improved on in Cambridge. His lectures were so popular and good that he had to repeat them: the first time was 5 p.m. on Fridays and then that curious but intensely popular time for general Cambridge lectures, 12 noon on Saturdays. The Examination School was always full to overflowing and justly so.

I found him such an interesting and worthwhile person that I set about getting him made a Fellow of St John's, not always an easy task with an oligarchic Council of thirteen. This was in 1950, and in 1967 he was made an Honorary Fellow. He said to me, 'If I am made a Fellow of St John's it must be on one condition, namely that I have rooms in that most exquisite of buildings, your New Court.' This was arranged and he lived on E Staircase looking out over the Rickman doorway on to the Backs – that view which Rivers Rivers had so much enjoyed.

Allen Lane and Walter Neurath admired and envied each other, and there was a slight unhappiness that I was editor of the Thames and Hudson *Ancient Peoples and Places* series and also archaeological adviser to Penguin Books. There was a moment when it was thought that the two series should come together, and indeed many of the Thames and Hudson books were Penguinized. But it never happened, and for several years I was in the extremely happy and powerful position of being able to work with both Thames and Hudson and Penguins, and thus to see that the books I wanted written and published did happen.

Allen Lane died in July 1970. In a great farewell party in April 1969 which he gave in the City – we all knew he was dying of cancer – he told me to press on with my Penguin archaeological plans, but he said, 'You may not find my successor as interested as I am'. This was only partly true, but I began to feel a lessening of interest and what was more disturbing, a critical examination of every proposal I made. I began to be bored and cross with the necessity of having to spell out the case for a new book which I knew would be a great success and the people I had to deal with at Penguins kept changing.

Sally Green was an archaeological student of Colin Renfrew's at Sheffield and as her dissertation for her MA she wrote a very good essay on the life and works of Gordon Childe. She elaborated and improved on this for a PhD and I examined her thesis. It was obviously made for a book and I told Penguins they must snap it up. They demurred. I told them that it was their moral duty to publish this book as they had made so much money out of Gordon Childe's *What Happened in History*. I put the case for Sally Green's book as convincingly and clearly as I could and it eventually went up to the new American boss of Penguins who was not persuaded. I decided to make this an issue of principle. 'If you don't accept my advice about the book,' I said, 'you will cease to have me as your archaeological adviser.' My blackmail (it was really whitemail) didn't work. I ceased to be their archaeological editor: I was paid £400 as a golden handshake. Sally Green's excellent book was published elsewhere and is a redoubtable success.

Peggy Piggott, who remarried and became Peggy Guido and lived for several years with her second husband in Sicily, had already written for my *Ancient Peoples and Places* series a very successful volume on *Sardinia*. She suggested to me that she would like to write an archaeological guide to Sicily. Faber and Faber were immediately interested in a series of archaeological guides and I found myself midwife to yet another clutch of books. I think some of the volumes of this Faber series were most successful: the first volume by Peggy Guido certainly was, and so were David Trump's *Malta*, Euan Mackie's *Scotland*, Christopher Houlder's *Wales*, Elizabeth Munksgaard's *Denmark*, and James Dyer's *Southern England*. There were to be many more but Faber and Faber lost interest. I had many other titles in mind but this series, curiously, died on me; yet the existing volumes are much in demand.

The year 1957 saw a holocaust of great men who had founded and practised present-day archaeology – Stephen Glanville, Sean Ó Ríordáin, J.F.S. Stone, Paul Jacobsthal, Charles Seltman, Georg Leisner, A.J.B. Wace, and Gordon Childe. As he sent the December 1957 *Antiquity* to press its editor, O.G.S. Crawford, had just heard of the death of Gordon Childe and wrote: 'He will be mourned by archaeologists all over the world, and not least by the writer of these words, who had known him for over thirty years.' In the same week as those words were being published the writer of them was himself buried in Nursling churchyard.

Crawford died in his sleep during the night of Thursday/Friday, 28/29 November. That evening he had returned home from giving evidence at a public enquiry held by the Minister of Town and Country Planning in Southampton about Southampton Corporation's proposals for the re-planning of the city. He was there as president of the Friends of Old Southampton and had handed to the Ministry Inspector his own plan of medieval Southampton.

On Friday, 29 November, I received a telegram from H.W. Edwards, the publisher of *Antiquity*, telling me that Crawford was dead. I wondered why I had been sent this news so quickly and in the next few days all was made clear. Crawford left no mandate as to who was to succeed him in the very considerable and worthwhile task of editing the journal *Antiquity* which he had started in 1927 at the age of forty-one. It was made clear to me by Edwards and Mortimer Wheeler that I was to succeed Crawford as editor of *Antiquity*. There were many anxious meetings in London in December 1957: Edwards, Mrs Edwards, Wheeler, Stuart Piggott, myself and Ruth. I had misgivings and for days wanted Stuart Piggott to take on the editorship with my assistance, but he would not do so.

In *The Times* for 31 December 1957 there appeared this letter from Edwards:

In the obituary of O.G.S. Crawford in your columns on 30 November it is recalled how he had founded *Antiquity* as a quarterly review of archaeology in 1927 and had edited it for thirty years. In that time it achieved an international status as a vehicle for archaeological studies and interests, and, as its publisher, I have received many inquiries as to the future.

While appreciating the essentially personal character of Crawford's editorship, a number of leading archaeologists have agreed that its continuance is highly desirable and Dr Glyn Daniel, of St John's College, Cambridge, has consented to become its new editor. He will be assisted, as advisory editors, by Professor Gerhard Bersu, Dr G.H.S Bushnell, Professor M.E.L. Mallowan, Professor Stuart Piggott and Sir Mortimer Wheeler, and publication will continue without a break.

That was so, and Ruth and I saw that the March 1958 number appeared on time: it was a major effort and I had to write an editorial. I said: 'This, the 125th number of *Antiquity*, is the first issue which does not contain from the pen of O.G.S. Crawford some of those Editorial Notes which, for the last thirty years, have enlivened our reading at the beginning of each quarter and endeared the late editor to us all.'

Crawford had drafted some notes for the March 1958 issue. One began as follows: 'The editing of a journal like *Antiquity* is a pleasant task, but there are times when the editor wishes that he did not have to cope with book reviews. There is, of course, no escape from this; it is necessary to keep our readers informed about the best books on archaeology that are published, and some others.' I quoted this in my first *Antiquity* editorial and ended by saying:

> We hope that experience proves the truth of the first few words: the pleasantness of editing *Antiquity* must depend on the ready cooperation of its contributors in writing articles, notes and reviews, of its readers in criticizing what is written and saying what they want to read, and on everyone seeing that the editor and advisory editors (whose immediate agreement to advise and whose ready advice in the difficult changeover period the editor and publisher of *Antiquity* gratefully acknowledge), are kept informed of all relevant developments in the world of archaeological learning. We commend to all the words of Charles Lamb in a letter to B.W. Proctor dated 22 January 1829: 'When my sonnet was rejected, I exclaimed – Damn the age: I will write for Antiquity.'

I got Mortimer Wheeler to write a short piece for that March number entitled 'Crawford and *Antiquity*' and it is worth re-reading.

> The author of *Microcosmographia Academica* would slyly have approved of Crawford: 'The Principle of Sound Learning is that the noise of vulgar fame should never trouble the cloistered calm of academic existence. Hence, learning is called sound when no one else has ever heard of it: and "sound scholar" is a term of praise, applied to one another by learned men who have no reputation outside the University, and a rather queer one inside.'
>
> That [went on Wheeler] was written by a Cambridge man in 1908. Today another Cambridge man takes over the honourable burden of *Antiquity* and will promptly turn F.M. Cornford's definition inside out. No one else is so liberally qualified to do this,

and those of us who were Crawford's familiars like to think how warmly he would have welcomed the succession!

These were heartening words. Others had different views and believed that *Antiquity* would die with Crawford. I determined to see whether this was an unduly pessimistic view and in the first few months of taking over was enormously encouraged and supported by Wheeler, Stuart Piggott and most of all by my wife. The support of those three people continued and increased during the years. Wheeler lunched with Ruth and me once a month; we discussed all sorts of matters and everything to do with *Antiquity*. One month it would be in the Athenaeum, next month in the United University Club in Suffolk Street, as it then was until it amalgamated with the Oxford and Cambridge Club and moved to Pall Mall. ('I cannot understand,' said Wheeler, 'why the food and wine is so much better in your club than in mine.') We certainly did not always agree and on one occasion our disagreement became so profound and bitter that I sacked him from being an advisory editor!

I have spoken to Stuart Piggott on matters relating to *Antiquity* almost every week from 1957 until the present day. To his friendship with Ruth and me he has added wise advice and good counsel. If *Antiquity* has succeeded since Crawford's death (and it certainly has as a viable journal) it has been due in no small measure to the constant help from advisory editors. Once, Stuart Piggott, Ruth and I were in Venice, and there were many *Antiquity* matters to discuss. We went into St Mark's. Wandering about waiting for the Treasury to open, Ruth and Stuart discovered me in a quiet corner checking proofs at a prie-dieu. They joined me for a brief conference and Stuart did a quick sketch entitled 'The opening of the *Antiquity* branch office in Venice'.

But of course *Antiquity* would not have survived and prospered under my editorship were it not for the devotion, skill, expertise and hard work of my wife. Ruth was written in as production editor in 1967. She has coped with block-makers, printers and advertisers, and made paste-ups from galley-proofs which have kept the journal clean, clear and elegant, and typographically distinguished.

In his autobiography *Said and Done* (1955) Crawford set out how *Antiquity* came into being. 'At the end of 1925, I conceived the idea of starting a quarterly journal which would serve as an organ of the very live and active group of archaeologists then working in England. We needed such a journal, and as appeared later, the public wanted it too.' He decided not to have a publisher but to edit it and run it himself: with John Bellows as printer and Roland Austin as assistant editor. Up to Austin's retirement in 1948 the journal was Crawford's private property: then he turned it into a private company with H.W. and Mrs Edwards as directors and himself as chairman. He had met Edwards, who was a bookseller in Newbury, on the boat on which he was travelling from London to Leningrad in 1932.

When Crawford died and I was appointed editor I became a director of the company. The relations of my wife and myself with Harold and Mrs Edwards were never cordial. It was clear that they thought of the journal as a commercial profit-making undertaking and that their new editor with his television notoriety would boost the sales: they saw a future with a colour-cover journal on sale at all railway bookstalls. They misunderstood my parergon activities and were disappointed. I was determined to keep *Antiquity* as it had been in Crawford's time, a scholarly journal suitable for reading by the general public. Relations deteriorated in 1959 when it was clear I was not mainly interested in the journal making a commercial profit and disliked any editorial advice and interference by Edwards. During 1960, Edwards, who had for some months indicated his readiness to sell the journal, informed me on 6 December that he did not intend to publish *Antiquity* after the December number and wished to sever his long association with it as from 31 December 1960.

What to do? We and the advisory editors took counsel and decided that this was the moment to see that a journal which over the previous thirty years or so had meant so much in British archaeology and in the appreciation of British archaeology overseas, should be owned by an independent archaeological body and not by an individual or publisher. We needed £5,000 to buy the journal from the Edwardses. Where was this money to come from? Ruth and I retired to the Dol-y-coed Hotel at Llanwrtyd Wells in central Wales and set about writing and telephoning, inviting subscriptions from individuals and trusts interested in archaeology.

We were immediately heartened and enormously encouraged when two friends and well-wishers, I.D. Margary and Professor Richard Atkinson, each separately offered to underwrite the whole sum required. Full of hope we pressed on with our letters and telephone calls: the response was immediate and generous and with the money subscribed it was possible to purchase *Antiquity* and vest its ownership in a charitable trust. In the June 1961 issue we were able to thank 78 subscribers (and there were five who wished to remain anonymous): the list is a very impressive one.

The first trustees were Professor Atkinson, Mrs M. Aylwin Cotton, Professor Max Mallowan, Mr I.D. Margary, Professor S. Piggott and Sir Mortimer Wheeler. The primary purpose of the fund subscribed to by individuals, institutions, and trusts was to acquire the whole of the issued share capital of the company and thereafter to publish *Antiquity* as a non-profit-making periodical.

Antiquity was saved and Ruth and I have gone on editing it until now. When the trust was established we decided to make a change and have the journal printed and published by Heffers of Cambridge, on the express advice of Sir Basil Blackwell. They have served us well and faithfully for over a quarter of a century: Ruth and I owe them a very special debt of gratitude and a personal one to Frank Collieson whose careful, cheerful and scholarly editorial help has meant so much lightening of the burden of editor and production editor.

The fiftieth volume of *Antiquity* was published in 1976 and curiously enough coincided with the centenary of Heffers. Stuart Piggott wrote in that year a short personal memoir of the founding Editor. In that same issue we recorded the death of Sir Mortimer Wheeler, who had done so much during those fifty years to support and encourage Crawford and the Daniels. The trustees meet once a year and, after a morning's business, lunch together. Mortimer Wheeler looked forward to those occasions and despite failing health and his age – he was 86 – he was with us on 12 May 1976 and made a warm and generous speech about how well *Antiquity* was being edited. It was the last time many of his friends and colleagues saw him. Ruth and I were most touched at the great effort he had made. In a brief private conversation with me he referred to the time I had sacked him from being an advisory editor. 'No one else has ever sacked me, d'ye know,' he said. 'But we buried the hatchet soon enough, didn't we?' 'There was no hatchet to bury,' I said and he turned away, a tear in his eye.

Why did *Antiquity* succeed in the twenties? It was partly, as Wheeler has often said, that Crawford was 'a journalist, with all that ingenious capacity for proclaiming one's own or the next man's achievement that is native to the art.' Crawford once said to Wheeler, 'I am a journalist. What I want is simple, clear-minded stuff that any intelligent fool can understand.' But Crawford had a Messianic desire to get archaeology and its message across to the people of the world: he had spelt this out in his *Man and his Past* (1921). And he was a bold, brave man who was delighted to express his own views even if they meant crossing swords with many others.

Professor E.A. Hooton, the distinguished Harvard professor, whose book of essays *Apes, Men and Morons* is still a delight to dip into, dug the Wexcombe long barrow, or partially dug it, with Crawford on the outbreak of war in 1914. When Piggott met him in Harvard forty years later, Hooton asked after Crawford, and said he hadn't seen him since 1914. 'What's he like now?' asked Hooton. 'He was a red-haired opinionated Scotsman then, and I reckon he'll be a white-haired opinionated Scotsman now.'

But an additional reason for the success of *Antiquity* from the twenties onwards was that we now had a public interested in the subject. The discovery of Tutankhamun's tomb and of the Royal Tombs at Ur had excited everyone, but the public interest had been growing steadily since Schliemann's discoveries at Troy and Mycenae, Flinders Petrie's work in Egypt, and Arthur Evans's work at Knossos. No one underestimates the part played by *The Illustrated London News* in interesting the public in archaeology.

There were moments during the 1939–45 war when the circulation of *Antiquity* dropped sickeningly but Crawford persevered; and was delighted, as we all were, when after the war it picked up. The new interest in archaeology, stimulated in the fifties by sound and television broadcasting, brought new subscribers to *Antiquity* and encouragement to others to start new journals: we now have in England *Current Archaeology, Popular Archaeology, World Archaeology*, and more recently, *The Oxford Journal of Archaeology*; in France, *Archéologia* and *Préhistoire*, and in America, *Archaeology* and *Popular Archaeology*. Archaeology is now, certainly, as Charles Picard said, 'à la môde'. There is no doubt that Crawford was a most important factor in this development.

Crawford's great interest in air photography and the discoveries that were made by his friend Major Allen enabled him to fill the pages of *Antiquity* with excellent and informative air photographs. Allen was, alas, killed in 1941. In 1948 Dr Kenneth St Joseph was made Curator and subsequently Director of Aerial Photography in the University of Cambridge, until his retirement in 1980. He once complained to me of the difficulty of getting the new discoveries made by the Cambridge department published. I placed at his disposal a plate and 500 words of text in each issue of *Antiquity* and the series 'Air Reconnaissance: recent results' went on from 1964 until it reached its fiftieth number in 1980.

Crawford had been openly and wisely in favour of young writers and of encouraging new names. I began this chapter by saying how surprised I was that he immediately took my first article. I have followed his policy and a good interesting article by a young archaeologist anywhere in the world has a high place in the long list of possible articles and notes.

In 1970 I set up a competition for young archaeologists to write an essay entitled 'Whither Archaeology?' There were many admirable entries and the prize was shared between Evzen Neustupný of the Archaeological Institute of the Czech Academy of Sciences, and Glynn Isaac, then Professor in Berkeley now, alas, dead. I had known Neustupný as a young man: his father, Dr Jiri Neustupný, who has since died, wrote the excellent volume on *Czechoslovakia* in my *Ancient Peoples and Places* series. Evzen's article was published in the 1971 volume of *Antiquity* and contained two surprising sentences: 'Almost all that is of importance in archaeology has been known since the beginning of this century. This applies not only to the methods and theory . . . but also to the results.' As I quote these words a decade or so later I wonder how the self-styled New Archaeologists of America and those in Britain who organize conferences on the Theory of Archaeology, view these pronouncements.

When later in life Crawford began to write general books, he revealed his ignorance of many important developments in archaeology. Stuart Piggott reviewed very sharply his *Archaeology in the Field*. I was alarmed by his book *The Eye Goddess* which, if it had been an undergraduate essay, I would have criticized very severely. It had extraordinary errors of date and even provenance and in the end I wrote to him and said how much I enjoyed the book and its spirit, but how could he have made so many mistakes? – and I listed ten of them.

By return of post there was a Crawford card saying 'just P.B.I.'. I was mystified and said so: back came the famous postcard which I immensely treasure saying 'Pure Bloody Ignorance. O.G.S.C.'

The *Antiquity* editorials from 1958 to 1979 amounted to well over 250,000 words. The hundred volumes of the *Ancient Peoples and Places*

233

series come to more than 4 million words. Such a programme has involved endless correspondence and if our secretaries, Mrs Eva Cousins and Mrs Evelyn Ward, had not been in charge of me, could not have happened. All this, added to normal research correspondence and heavy administrative duties, made for the despatch of hundreds of letters every week.

When these things were building up I had a conversation with Liza Hill, now Dame Elizabeth Hill, Emeritus Professor of Slavonic Languages in the University of Cambridge. 'One piece of advice to you, dear boy' she said. 'Do not write more than five thousand letters a year.' 'But,' I said, 'what about Edward Lear who wrote thirty-five letters a day mainly before breakfast?' 'He must have breakfasted late,' she said coldly. 'But what should I do with letters that don't come into the five thousand?' 'Buy a larger waste-paper basket', she said, 'and steel your heart.' I acted on her advice, almost certainly to the dismay of endless correspondents.

I have always wanted to write non-archaeology. The detective novels were, I suppose, part of that desire. My next literary topic was gastronomy. When I had the year (1955–6) off as sabbatical leave to write my *Prehistoric Chamber Tombs of France* I spent a lot of time in Paris in the Hôtel Paris-Dinard, 29 rue Cassette. It was a hotel Ruth and I had stayed in for many years and the bells of the Carmelite school across the road are still remembered music in our ears. I was fascinated one day to see a notice at the restaurant Royal St-Germain – no longer there, it has become the St-Germain pub – which said that their great *plat du jour* on Fridays was *Chicken Pie comme à Oxford*. I went there on a Friday with Suzanne de Saint-Mathurin and ate the Oxford Chicken Pie. It was excellent. Why, we asked, 'comme à Oxford'. The waiter was nonplussed and eventually produced the maître d'hôtel. 'It is,' he said, 'a great and very well-known speciality of Oxford,' and suggested that as an Englishman, I ought to have known about this. 'Oxford,' I said to him, 'but what about Cambridge where I come from?' His reply was firm: there were no gastronomic specialities anyone had ever heard of coming from le Cambridge.

I wrote something about all this in *The Spectator* at the time but from then till now I have never been able to find anyone, in or out of Oxford, and in or out of our most comprehensive cookery books, who has ever heard of Oxford Chicken Pie, and it does not appear in Lady Quinton's *Don's Dinner*. But this made me think about what dishes were or are associated with the universities or the constituent colleges of Oxford and Cambridge.

My first problem was *crème brûlée*. There is a widespread belief that this is a Cambridge dish and one of the glories of Cambridge cookery – a dish some colleges claim was invented in Jesus or Trinity, or Trinity Hall or Clare. I have always denied the undergraduate claims that it was a great Johnian dish – it is wonderfully well done by our Johnian pâtissiers but they did not invent it.

Even so discerning a writer as Theodora Fitzgibbon regarded *crème brûlée* as a Cambridge dish. In her *The Art of British Cookery* (1965) she says: 'This is an extremely old dish and is a speciality of Trinity College, Cambridge, and on account of this is sometimes known as "Cambridge Cream".' She then goes on to say that: 'It used to be browned on top by a "salamander" which was a flatiron made hot and passed over the top of puddings. However as these are now quite forgotten, the grill must be used.'

Theodora Fitzgibbon is wrong on two counts: first, salamanders are still used to good account in Cambridge college kitchens; and secondly Cambridge is not the place of origin of *crème brûlée*.

Eleanor Jenkinson gives another version in her remarkable book *The Ocklye Cookery Book: A book of recipes by a Lady and her Cook*, published by H. Wilkins in Crowborough in 1909. The lady, by the way, was Eleanor Jenkinson herself and the cook was her cook Annie Hobden. She writes of *crème brûlée*: 'It is amusing to remember that this recipe, which came from a country house in Aberdeenshire in the sixties, was offered to the kitchens of Trinity College by an undergraduate and rejected with contempt as an undergraduate folly. When this undergraduate became a Fellow of Trinity he presented his order again and this time it was accepted and soon became one of the favourite dishes of May Week.' From Mrs Jenkinson's work we can now date the introduction to Cambridge of this delectable sweet to 1879. Lady Quinton, in her delightful *Don's Dinner* (1984), seems to suggest it is an Oxford dish, part of Trinity College and Trinity Term. Recently in Norwich I was interested to read an advertisement by Lloyds of London Street that among their take-away dishes was *crème brûlée*, described as 'a traditional 18th-century English dish.'

I ought to have worked harder and written to all the stewards of all the colleges in Oxford and Cambridge and begged for their special recipes: but time was short and so I just put together a collection of a few recipes and published it privately as *Oxford Chicken Pie* (1965) as a birthday present for Ruth. It has some very good things in it and three recipes deserve not to be forgotten. Here they are:

NEW COLLEGE PUDDING

Mix together a quarter of a pound of shredded beef suet and a quarter of a pound of grated breadcrumbs, or, if preferred, biscuit crumbs. Add a quarter of a pound of currants, a pinch of salt, two tablespoons of sugar, half a grated nutmeg, one ounce of shredded candied peel, three well beaten eggs and sufficient milk to make a thick creamy consistency. Fry the mixture in spoonfuls in a little hot butter browned on both sides, shaking the pan frequently so that they do not burn. Serve on a very hot dish dusted with castor sugar.

That was an Oxford recipe, and so is the next from Trinity, Oxford.

TRINITY SALAD

Ingredients: cos lettuce (washed and drained very dry), spring onions shredded and washed in water, cheddar cheese grated, olive oil, Orleans vinegar, garlic vinegar, tarragon vinegar, salt and pepper. *The method*: blend the grated cheese with the oils, vinegar and condiments as if for a mayonnaise; then mix with the lettuce and onions when ready to serve.

My third recipe that I wish to have wider publicity than it has had hitherto is Mr Whibley's *soufflé*. Charles Whibley was a distinguished Fellow of Pembroke College, Cambridge. He once travelled to America on the *Mauretania* and fell in love with the cold *soufflé* which was served: he persuaded the chef to give him the recipe, and here it is, often now referred to as Pembroke cold *soufflé* but no more Cambridge in origin than *crème brûlée*:

MR WHIBLEY'S SOUFFLÉ

Line half-an-inch thick the bottom of a glass *soufflé* dish with apricot jam. Mix fifty per cent cream with fifty per cent *crème brûlée* mixture; flavour well with maraschino and sufficient gelatine to set lightly. Pass through fine sieve into dish. Allow to set, and when set pipe cream round the dish and heap on roughly grated chocolate in the centre.

Noël Small, a dear friend who died long before her time, was steward of Gonville and Caius College – perhaps the first woman steward of a men's college, and a brilliant exemplar of how these things could and should be done, told me that there was a Caius variant of Mr Whibley's *soufflé*. It was confectioned with alternate layers of chocolate cream and maraschino cream and had a tablespoonful of brandy in each helping. It never came my way although I often dined in Caius: it sounds devastatingly good.

Oxford Chicken Pie was privately printed by the Carters at the Rampant Lions Press in 1965. This was not my first book or booklet published by the Rampant Lions Press. Will and Barbara Carter and their son, Sebastian, have been among our closest, kindest and warmest friends for over thirty years and have often advised us on typographical matters relating to *Antiquity*. I was delighted when Will found time to design the jacket and titlepage calligraphy of my *Festschrift*; and he has repeated his kindness for this book.

My first little book published by the Rampant Lions Press had been *The Pen of my Aunt* in 1961: I described it as 'a fugitive essay . . . first published, in part, in *The Cambridge Review* soon after I had my first startling acquaintance with Pedro Carolino's *New Guide to the Conversation in Portuguese and English*, published in Paris in 1869 by Peking and to the house of all booksellers in Paris.' Stephen Leacock in his *Humour: its Theory and Technique* (1935) introduced Pedro Carolino to us all, and I still find him unbelievably funny and cannot refrain from a few quotations. He orders his meal: 'some rings, a chitterling sausage, . . . some marchpanes, an omelet, vegetables boiled to a pap, some succony and purslains'. And his comments on his hotel room: 'This room is filled of bugs. . . . This spy-glass is good for nothing. . . . Never I have you rumbled. . . . Is there what is beautiful? – I am pricking me with a pin'.

Perhaps this is what I have been doing in this chapter: but as I look through the pages of *The Pen of my Aunt* I am still astonished at the phrases I collected: 'The thunderbolt is falling down. Go quickly but don't shake the palanquin. . . . I fear you are not kind to my baby: flap the mosquitos away instantly. . . . Shorten Mr Fulcher's trousers. . . . Take that boy and whip him too much?' Some time I must produce a revised and extended edition of *The Pen of my Aunt*, and perhaps also of *Oxford Chicken Pie*.

CHAPTER EIGHT

The spoken word

IT IS A CURIOSITY of the academic profession that while allegedly the main duty of dons is to teach, very little instruction is given in most universities on how to teach. This results in some extremely bad lecturers. George Macaulay Trevelyan was such a one and sadly knew it. As freshmen, my generation flocked to hear this great historian whose books we had read at school. He began his course in the largest lecture room in the Arts School and started with a strange announcement. Next week I shall be lecturing in Room B, he said, and from the division of term in Room G. We assumed that his audiences would be swelling. On the contrary after the first lecture, when we soon realized that he was doing no more than reading out passages from his own writings, the audience dropped rapidly and the audience in Room G at the end of term was a mere handful. Is it not strange that a great writer could not communicate directly by a spoken lecture? It is, in truth, only rarely that one finds a scholar who writes well, talks well, lectures well, and can also perform well on sound radio and on television: Noel Annan is such a one.

We also all flocked to hear Sir Arthur Quiller-Couch. He did not disappoint. He gave few lectures, which were specially written and never repeated, but were published. He always arrived by taxi to give his lectures, impeccably dressed in morning coat and striped trousers. He studiously refused to recognize the presence of women at his lectures. There were always many women reading English. Arranging his script on the lectern he would look round the crowded lecture room and begin firmly: 'Gentlemen'.

I have often fallen asleep in lectures, particularly at five o'clock – that dead hour for any intellectual activity, as S.C. Roberts used to call it – especially at lectures when the blinds are drawn, the light dimmed, and the slides shown. It is indeed a recipe for a late siesta. Many people have fallen asleep in my lectures but no one with such devastating effect as Dr Rose Graham. I had been warned that she would fall asleep the moment I began speaking and snore loudly, but I had not been warned that she uttered words during her sleep. My first ten minutes were punctuated by strangled cries of 'No, No'. It was off-putting to the lecturer and the audience, and David Wilson and Gale Sieveking kindly, but mistakenly, decided that it was too much and she should be woken up. As they advanced on her, seated in the front row she cried out, 'No, never'; they persisted and as she came awake she looked at me and said loudly, 'Nonsense, nonsense,' and was asleep again in a few minutes.

I have never fallen asleep while lecturing and I think this is a rare occurrence for any lecturer. It did happen in a small class to which Sir Harold Jeffreys, Plumian Professor of Astronomy and Experimental Philosophy at Cambridge, 1948–58, was lecturing. He was seated at a table reading from his notes when his voice got slower and quieter and then ceased. I heard this from one of the students present; they discussed what to do. Wake him up? Tiptoe quietly away? Or just wait? They decided to wait and five minutes later Harold woke up and went on as if nothing had happened.

I often sleep during boring parts of board and committee meetings and so do many people. Clémenceau used to be furious with Lloyd George who, at the Versailles Conference, always managed to take cat naps of five to ten minutes during the dull speeches of his colleagues. Paddy Hadley, when he was Professor of Music at Cambridge, much disliked the Monday afternoon Faculty Board meetings he was required to attend. He had always lunched very well and invariably fell asleep during a lot of boring business. A succession of enraged and unsympathetic chairmen used to get him woken and try to interest the professor in their doings. 'What are the professor's views on the matter under discussion?' they would craftily ask. But Paddy was not to be put out. He had organized three answers: 'Hadley agrees with the previous speaker,' he would say briskly (he usually spoke of himself publicly in the third person), or 'Professor Hadley must confess that for the moment he is sitting on the fence.' Those were good answers, but his third was such that no chairman dared to try him again. 'Mr Chairman,' he would say, 'I have listened to the discussion with great interest but I must admit that towards the end I slightly lost the thread. Would you be so good as to summarize the arguments to refresh me? You do these things so well.'

There are many stories of lost or misplaced lectures. Benians told me that he was terrified when asked to lecture but prepared his first

The spoken word

lecture with the greatest care, had a sleepless night and set off in the bus from Barton Road to the centre of Cambridge. So upset and nervous was he that he left the bus without his lecture notes. Halfway across the market place he realized with horror that he did not have them. 'What did you do?' I asked. 'I immediately took a taxi,' he said, 'and told the driver what had happened. We pursued the bus and caught it up at the terminus, rescued my notes, and I was back in the lecture room with five minutes to spare. Curiously enough the adventure had a traumatic effect on me. All my nervousness had gone.'

When I was secretary of Section H of the Cambridge meeting of the British Association in 1958 Professor J.T. Wilson telephoned me from the Anatomy School asking if he could come and see me and discuss the length of Dr Broom's paper which he was going to read: he thought it too long for the twenty minutes allowed. He set off, called in at the Museum of Archaeology and Ethnology and arrived at the porter's lodge at St John's. The head porter telephoned me to say that he had in his office Professor Wilson, in a state of absolute panic. I hurried to the front lodge. Wilson was almost in tears. 'I have lost Broom's lecture,' he said. The problem was when and where. I telephoned the Museum: Wilson had left the Museum with his file of papers under his arm. 'Let us retrace your steps,' I said. We went back to the Anatomy School and then to the Museum and I made him walk the way he went. 'Did you visit a bookshop?' No. 'Or anywhere else?' No. We walked down the dullest of all Cambridge streets, Corn Exchange Street. In the corner near the Guildhall there was at that time a small urinal. 'You didn't by any chance go in there?' I asked. 'No, no certainly not,' said a very agitated Wilson. Something in the violence of his voice or some unexplained inspiration made me go in to the urinal. There on the top of the marble stalls was the lecture on *Australopithecus africanus*. 'Fantastic', he said. 'How could it have got there?'

There are many essentials to good lecturing, but the first two are obviously audibility and timing. It has always astonished me when lecturers mount their rostrum and address their audience in their normal drawing-room talking voice. Lecturing is a performance, but even experienced lecturers can get lazy: so I now make a note that twenty minutes past the start and twenty minutes before the end, I should check my voice level and start again in a loud lecturing tone.

Timing is an easier problem but so few lecturers seem to be aware that the average talking rate for a BBC talk is 120 words a minute. For a public lecture, which is not given at a consistent BBC talk rate, fifty minutes means a maximum of 6,000 words, and if one makes asides and impromptu remarks the full text must be less than that. Double spacing on 10″ × 8″ paper gives 200 to 220 words a page and a lecture is thus 25 to 30 pages: A4 paper gives 250 to 300 words double-spaced and a normal lecture is thus 20 A4 pages. But A4 pages are bad for lecturing, they are invariably too large for most lecterns or reading desks. The old 10″ × 8″ is still for me the best format; and when will people, including those preaching sermons, learn that you must never have your notes clipped in a file and turn them over? They must be loose and moved sideways: this is another lesson which sound broadcasting has taught us all.

I have spelt out these simple points because when I first explained them to Terence Powell he was flabbergasted and said he had no idea there were such simple mechanical guides to what he described as the mystery of public speaking.

Often, wanting to make a lecture a success, I have tried it out to myself in my college rooms, remembering that without an audience one gets through the text more quickly and should allow an extra time-factor of at least 5 to 10 per cent. From time to time I have recorded a lecture and listening to it have been able to improve and shorten it.

The first time I had to give a lecture in French in France I had it written into good idiomatic French by Camille Prior and recorded by her. The conference was at Tournon and Ruth and Stuart Piggott and I drove across France. They went down to the bar for aperitifs while I lay on my bed and listened to my lecture in Camille's clear tones. When I left my bedroom to join the others I met a *femme de chambre* who gave me a wink and raised eyebrows. She too had heard Camille's dulcet tones and thought the worst (or the best) of me as I went down to join my wife.

But timing still bedevils people. Christopher Hawkes, that very distinguished scholar who has so much to say to people and wants to say it with all his infectious enthusiasm, has sometimes gone on for nearly two hours when scheduled for an hour's lecture. When I was Disney Professor I asked him over from Oxford to give a lecture to my students. I carefully fixed it for twelve noon and explained that it must stop at five minutes to one so that students could get to their lunch, but to no avail. At one thirty-five he eventually stopped, having given a brilliant lecture.

Others find a different trouble, and I recollect two tales involving Fellows of St John's. R.L. Howland – Olympic weight-putter – had carefully prepared his first university lecture. He told me how dismayed he was when it was over after 25 minutes. What to do? With his usual imperturbability he said to his audience: 'I wonder if you have managed to get down all my points. May I repeat them?' And gave his lecture all over again bringing him to the proper closing time.

Hugo Gatty's adventure was much sadder. He had been a Fellow of St John's for many years but had not taught in the university. He was then asked to give a course of eight lectures and was honoured but frightened. He spent the whole summer writing his lectures but as the date for the first lecture came in October he was terrified. We dined together in Hall and afterwards he said, 'Come up to my rooms. I cannot bear to be alone.' We went up to the roof of the tower in his set and drank a bottle of hock. 'All will be well,' I said. 'Remember they are coming to hear *you*. All luck.'

Late the next morning the telephone rang and an agitated Hugo said, 'Come to my rooms at once, please. Drop whatever you are doing. A terrible thing has happened.' I went round as quickly as I could, fearing the worst, and wondering.

There was a bottle of champagne in an ice bucket and two glasses were poured out. Hugo's hands were shaking. 'How did it go?' I asked. 'Absolute disaster,' he said. 'I took with me the text of all my eight lectures. The first one was over in the first ten minutes, so I read the second; my whole course was over by ten minutes to the hour. I'm a failure. I've said all I have to say in my first lecture. What am I to do?'

'As you gave eight lectures in one hour,' I said cruelly, 'you now have to write fifty-six more to fill up the next seven sessions.' 'But it took me six months to write the first eight (or rather one),' he cried. I couldn't help him; nobody could. His lectures were suspended at half term and he was never asked to lecture again.

There seem to me three main ways of preparing a lecture. The first is to have it written out completely to the proper length and deliver it from the text: but the text should be a text for speaking and should have breaks where the lecturer can if he so wishes and is so inspired, give impromptu asides. The second way is to have a collection of

factual notes and give your talk around them. The third is to lecture
entirely without notes but this takes courage and experience. I like
trying all three techniques but always take with me a few cards on
which relevant quotations or bibliographical references are written.
Some lecturers have an amazingly accurate time sense. Professor
Emrys Bowen of Aberystwyth used to pride himself and astonish his
audience by beginning on the hour and finishing exactly five minutes
before the hour without benefit of reference to clock or watch.

Undoubtedly the worst lectures are those when people read out
from their books, as G.M. Trevelyan did. The story is told that the late
Sir John Rhŷs used to take the galleys of his unpublished books or
articles and read them out to his lecture classes and that on one
occasion he stopped, absentmindedly, took out a pen, made a few
corrections, and said in a loud whisper, 'That must be put right in
page proof.'

Writing on a blackboard is essential in most university lectures,
spelling out clearly the names of people, places and things that may be
new or unfamiliar to one's audience. Visual aids are essential to
lectures in archaeology and art history, and the mastery of the lantern
slide is an additional craft the archaeological lecturer has to learn. I
have never learnt the very special craft of using two lanterns for
comparative purposes which art historians do with such skill and
aplomb. The old days of clicking a frog-like device in one's hand, or
stamping on the ground with a pointer, or shouting 'next please' are
virtually gone and the lecturer can now happily control his slides and
focus them and go back to a previous slide by pressing buttons on his
desk, or in his hand.

There remain timing and arrangement difficulties with slides. One
can talk with slides all through the allotted time but it is important to
arrange that an illustration which becomes irrelevant is not fixed on
the screen for minutes on end while the lecturer is talking about
something else. Blank slides should be inserted so that the screen is
clear. But the best way is to break up a lecture into periods of
unillustrated talk and slides, with the house lights on in between,
which gives plenty of time and opportunity for note taking. In a large
hall with a microphone one either needs a light pin-pointer on the desk
or if one wants to walk about pointing to parts of a picture, a neck
microphone.

Indeed giving an illustrated lecture to a large audience with microphones is a complicated technical affair, as is giving a television talk, and demands considerable expertise on the part of the performer. But even before these added hazards the problems of the lantern lecture are legion: apart from major disasters such as the lantern sticking, the power failing, the heat causing slides to melt, there is the overall problem of the arrangement of slides. We all know that they have to be put in the lantern upside-down and back-to-front and arrange them accordingly in long or circular containers. It is when writing appears that the greatest care has to be taken. I am now so cross and humiliated when things go wrong with my slides in a lecture that I run them through with my wife on our lantern at home.

Stuart Piggott and I have long had an imaginary competition for the lecturer who suddenly finds on his screen a rogue slide, say that of a bearded naked lady upside-down. How does he cope? The nervous young lecturer hastily presses his button or says quickly, 'Next please'. The moderately experienced lecturer will not panic, go on with his lecture, and then call without comment for the next slide. But the really experienced lecturer who realizes that someone is playing a trick on him will take control of the situation. We think he should look carefully at the screen, turn his head upside-down and then say coldly to the lanternist: 'I think this is upside-down. May we see it the right way up?' The naked bearded lady then appears again and the lecturer says quickly: 'Ah yes. I am afraid this has been misplaced in my slide carrier. It comes from another course of lectures I am giving.' That would be game and set to the lecturer and an enlarged audience for his next performance.

When all is said and done and the lecturer has mastered all the techniques of his craft it is still difficult to keep one's audience for a course of eight or sixteen lectures, however good you are. Some can do it. Nikolaus Pevsner was such a person, who filled the largest lecture room in Cambridge week after week and ended up with the largest audience of all, triumphantly cheering and clapping.

There was once a discussion at Magdalene High Table about whether there was anything one could do at half-term to keep, or even interest one's audience. One classics don took a bet that in the fifth week of term he could give a lecture which would make the sixth week's audience noticeably larger. The bet was taken but it was insisted that his ploys must not include scurrilous jokes, gross abuse of other dons, or pornography.

In the middle of a fairly staid lecture on Greek poetry he suddenly said, 'I can best illustrate this point by singing you part of a Victorian ballad.' His class had observed that an old piano had been brought in to the lecture room. The lecturer sat down and played and sang the strange ballad of a woman who had married a man with a wooden leg but did not discover this until her wedding night and cried out, 'I have married half a man, and half a bloody tree.'

Next week his lecture room was packed – there were no gimmicks: his last two lectures were back to normal. But he had made a good point. The element of surprise is one to be exploited even by the best lecturers, particularly at five p.m. in a darkened room.

From lecturing to a seen audience to speaking to an unseen audience was a natural and interesting transition. I first came face to face with a microphone right at the end of the war when I did a talk on the Indian radio about air photography: it was entitled *The Eyes of the RAF*. Soon after I was demobilized and back in Cambridge I was telephoned by Gilbert Phelps who had been at St John's before the war; he had just taken over Geoffrey Grigson's job as a features producer in the BBC at Bristol. Would I do a talk on air photographs and archaeology? I said I would: the talk was approved of, and out of it grew the successful sound series *The Archaeologist* which went on for years and was usually printed in *The Listener*. It was the beginning of archaeological broadcasting, although Stanley Casson had done one or two talks before the war.

Gilbert Phelps was a sympathetic and enthusiastic producer and it was a delight to renew my friendship with him. We planned *The Archaeologist* series together and cast the speakers: Stuart Piggott was one of them, Mortimer Wheeler another. They were both natural broadcasters and I early learnt in my Phelps Bristol days what made a good broadcaster: knowledge of the subject goes without saying, but a desire to communicate, an ability to talk to an unseen audience rather than lecture to a seen audience, the facility of writing a script which did not sound like a written script (and a readiness to ad lib.) and the projection of a personality which was confident, persuasive and sincere. To be natural and sincere are the really difficult crafts in broadcasting. It is no good saying that one must forget the microphone and cameras. Often it is highly important that one should be speaking to the right camera!

By a curious chance it was O.G.S. Crawford who was responsible for that first broadcast of mine in England. Phelps had asked him, as the pioneer and doyen of archaeological air photography, to do the talk he wanted but O.G.S. had declined on the grounds that he disapproved of broadcasting and that scholars should not waste their time in such meretricious activities. He then asked me, who had no such scruples, and was only too anxious to earn what was then a reasonable fee of £20. Crawford's view was a fairly common one at the time but it changed slowly and performing on the media is by now not only highly respectable but a much sought-after activity. Curiously enough, one of Crawford's last acts was to broadcast on the language of cats. He was, as I am, devoted to cats and firmly believed that he could understand what they said, and they what he said.

Perhaps because of my air photography broadcast, or maybe because I knew from Medmenham days Tristram Weatherhead, who had become on demobilization a senior official in Hunting Air Surveys, I received a letter from that firm offering me £100 to do a special job of air photographic interpretation for them. This seemed money for jam, but when the project was explained to me my hopes were dashed. A Mrs Maltwood, a wealthy lady living in Somerset, was fascinated, as many have been before and since, by Glastonbury. She was not concerned so much about Arthur and Joseph of Aramathea but with Glastonbury Tor itself; and again not with the ridges which surround the hill and which many believe to represent an ancient maze; Mrs Maltwood's view was that the signs of the zodiac were set out around Glastonbury Tor and could be traced in the modern landscape of fields, hedgerows, tracks, rivers and houses. This seemed palpable nonsense and when I studied the air photographs that had been taken, it was quite clear that this was observer-imposed fantasy. I sent the photographs back saying I could not undertake the task. This was a mistake: I needed that £100. I would not be so scrupulous today. I should write a report explaining that I could not see that the air photographs supported Mrs Maltwood's views. But I was young.

Five years after my initiation into sound broadcasting in Bristol my telephone rang. BBC Television were starting an archaeological quiz programme: would I come to London and take part in a dry-run? I did so with misgivings and faced a battery of TV cameras for the first time, and very nervously. This was my first meeting with Paul Johnstone, David Attenborough and Nancy Thomas and my first experience of filming for television which has now gone on for over thirty years in studios and in the field. The idea of the series was based on an American programme invented and developed by Fro Rainey, then Director of the Museum of the University of Pennsylvania at Philadelphia.

Fro had conceived a programme called *What in the World?* in which a panel of three experts were confronted by archaeological and ethnographical objects and asked to identify them. The formula had seemed an unlikely one for success, but it did become a great success and the programme ran in America for nearly forty years. Mary Adams, that kind, endearing and very shrewd person who was then a high executive in BBC Television, thought that a version of *What in the World?* could be put on the English screen and, out of her idea, *Animal, Vegetable, Mineral?* was born, with Paul Johnstone as its first producer. The Mary Adams idea was that each programme should be a specific challenge by a museum and this device was of great value to museums.

We met, a motley collection of archaeologists and ethnographers, in the Lime Grove Studios one dark, cold evening in 1952. I found myself sitting next to Rik Wheeler and Adrian Digby, then Keeper of Ethnography in the British Museum; we were all bewildered by the cables and lights, the camera crews and the seemingly crowds of people involved in this enterprise. We went through the routine of being shown objects and talking about them. Wheeler was fluent and amusing. I was faltering and dull. As the hours wore on we got bored. We broke off for sandwiches, dry martinis and wine. Wheeler became more fluent and very funny. I ceased to falter, forgot the cameras and the occasion and said something which made everyone laugh.

Eventually released from what had at first seemed a nightmarish and wasted exercise, Wheeler and I travelled back on the Underground. 'Well, my boy,' he said as he got off at Sloane Square, 'that's the last we or anyone else will see of that. But keep in touch. Come and have lunch one day in the Athenaeum.' I travelled on to Liverpool Street and gloomily read supervision essays in the train back to Cambridge.

Ten days later we were summoned to Lime Grove again for the first live performance of *Animal, Vegetable, Mineral?* Lionel Hale was in the chair and clearly ill at ease in dealing with specialized archaeological objects. Wheeler showed the brilliance and panache which he was to display to a delighted British public for many years to come. I fumbled along and managed to identify two objects. The third member of the panel was Julian Huxley and he was not good. I went home realizing that this sort of programme was not my *métier* and I was confirmed in this view when I did not appear in the next two programmes. I watched them with interest and one had a startling incident. Some object – I think it was a pot from Central Europe – was correctly identified, and then dated by Gordon Childe, then the greatest living authority on these matters. 'No,' said Lionel Hale, 'I am afraid you have the date wrong.' 'Nonsense!' said Gordon. Nonplussed, Hale said, 'But this is what the museum have put on my card.' 'Ha! Ha!' said Gordon chuckling, 'they're out of date. They clearly haven't read the latest edition of my books.'

Lionel Hale said he couldn't cope with such situations and to my surprise and slight dismay I found myself made the chairman and managed to hold that often hot seat for seven years. The drill was a simple one: once a museum had been selected they produced a list of possible objects and the producer and I chose ten out of them and discussed the most suitable panellists. Then on the day I would travel up to London in the afternoon and sit in the library of the United University Club (as it then was) in Suffolk Street, going through the cards prepared by the museum and checking in reference books. Then a car would take me to Lime Grove, where we had a rehearsal, naturally without the real performers. Then off to meet the panellists, dine with them, and back to Lime Grove for the performance. They were exhausting days but exhilarating, and often rewarding and amusing.

Apart from Rik Wheeler, Stuart Piggott, Gordon Childe, Geoffrey Bushnell and Sean Ó Ríordáin, they brought one into close and frequent contact with a very large number of people who subsequently became friends and acquaintances, such as Adrian Digby, Julian Huxley, Tommy Bodkin and Hugh Shortt. Hugh Shortt, who was curator of the Salisbury and South Wiltshire Museum and who died at an early age in 1975, contrived more cleverly than most to give the impression of not being an expert and yet being a very nice and knowledgeable person. 'I'm not an expert you know,' he would say, 'but I think this is possibly, just possibly, a so-and-so . . .' and he was usually right. Wheeler knew practically everything and I was only able to fault him two or three times in over a hundred performances. He made many memorable quips which passed into the private language of *AVM?* and the general language as a whole. Of a small strange bottle he would say: 'This, Glyn, is the sort of thing filled with hot water which my aunt would put in her muff when on rare occasions she went to church.' And one of his famous and most memorable quips, which became a by-word with many viewers, was when, given an object to identify, he said, with a wicked twinkle in his eye, 'Actually, Glyn, I was there when this thing was dug up.'

Gordon Childe was not a success on the programme; he could not enliven his great learning with a little wit and insisted on smoking a pipe so that clouds of smoke blew across the screen. Margaret Murray appeared only once, wearing a large beehive shaped straw hat covered with brightly coloured flowers. The producer asked me to tell her we didn't wear hats on the programme. 'Why not?' she said sharply. The producer or Mary Adams tried to persuade her to remove it but she firmly refused. 'It is a very nice hat,' she said, 'and will look well on television.' Which indeed it did.

I was a little terrified of Ma Murray, who was born in 1863 and seemed to me a ghostly survival from a remote archaeological past. I persuaded her to write me something for *Antiquity* when she was 95 and she then, encouraged by the reception of her piece, sat down to write her autobiography. She sent me a letter asking for suggestions for a title: Ruth and I thought up several and she chose our first title. This is how *My First Hundred Years* came into existence. Alas, this formidable lady lasted only one year after her hundred.

Women were somehow not a great success on *AVM?*; even Jacquetta Hawkes's astringent humour and delighted awareness of people and things eluded a complete success on the screen. It was perhaps her shyness and essential reserve that was responsible. Wheeler, Paul Johnstone and I thought she would captivate the millions of viewers and storm to stardom as Julia Childs and Thalassa Cruso did on American TV, but it was not to be. The TV screen needs a degree of extroversion, showmanship, extravagance and flamboyance, such as Gilbert Harding and Rik Wheeler brilliantly displayed. Jacquetta for all her many virtues of scholarship and lucid exposition and honest thinking, all of which I have admired since I first met her in 1934, hadn't this flair for the semi-sincere semi-insincere projection of a charismatic personality which is the essence of successful television. This she shared with many men whom we tried out on *AVM?* over the seven years it ran. We realized only too well that it didn't exist in many archaeologists and anthropologists whom we therefore never tried to drag to Lime Grove.

It existed only too splendidly in Thomas Bodkin, that ebullient, joyous, noisy Irishman who began life as a Dublin lawyer and ended up as Sir Thomas, Director of the Barber Institute of Fine Art in Birmingham. His account of his childhood, *My Uncle Frank* (1941), is one of the most delightful books of its kind and it sits on my shelves alongside that other gem, Margaret Phillips's *Without the City Wall*, describing her upbringing in York, and Simona Pakenham's *Pigtails and Pernod*. Tommy was never tired of declaring that he was the only real expert on the programme: all the rest are dabblers, he would say. 'I am an expert on Poussin – a real expert. Otherwise I know nothing' – and this was often true, although he was a brilliant guesser.

Our paths crossed many times in Dublin and he gave me dinner in the University Club and we lunched together on several occasions in Jammets, that great restaurant in Nassau Street whose passing we all regret. Bodkin had a special table reserved for him at Jammets. 'When in any difficulty,' he once said to me, 'ask for Tommy Bodkin's table.' One day I went unbooked to lunch in Jammets. It was full to overflowing. I said how disappointed I was and added, half in jest, 'Even Dr Thomas Bodkin's table?' The head waiter became immediately friendly and deferential. 'This way, sir,' he said and whisked me away to the little table behind the entrance door. A large burly man detached himself from the small crowd waiting to lunch. 'And how can Glyn Daniel get a table at once,' he said agreeably, 'when Eamonn Andrews has to queue up?' I told him it was the Bodkin magic and invited him to join me. He did, and told me of the plans and teething troubles of Irish television.

I last saw Tommy in Pall Mall, near the point where I imagine the Augustus John-Rik Wheeler brief dialogue took place ('Hullo Rikki, still digging?' 'Hullo Augustus, still sketching?' Wheeler subsequently called his autobiography *Still Digging*). 'You haven't been with us in *AVM?* recently', I said to Tommy. 'Hope you haven't been ill?' 'I have indeed, me boy,' he said, 'I'm dying.' I saw he wanted no sympathy or expression of regrets. 'So are we all,' I said. 'Ah, yes,' he said, 'but I'll be through the Golden Gates before you.' He put his hand on my shoulder, turned and walked away into the distance.

As *Animal, Vegetable, Mineral?* developed over the years we tried to vary it by moving from artifacts to paintings and natural history, and even to racial types. I was extremely nervous about the natural history programme and redoubled my homework, the more so because Julian Huxley was on the panel. All went well until there appeared a very large and softish white egg. Julian and the two other panellists produced answer after answer which I said were wrong. Infuriated, Julian produced a £1 note from his wallet. 'You know very well, Glyn,' he said, 'you are not a naturalist: I am, and we have gone through all the possibilities. If I'm wrong, here is a pound.' Nervously I looked at my card again and said: 'I am advised that it is the egg of the giant South American land snail.' 'Oh, my God,' said Julian throwing the note at me and clutching his head. 'My God, how could I have been so stupid!' The checking in the Club library had paid off!

Discussing this episode recently with David Attenborough, who had been directing the programme at the time, and has probably become as well-known a naturalist as Julian Huxley, I was told he believes that the egg was, in fact, the 'catch' undergraduate exam specimen *achatina achatina* or the Giant West African Snail: a well-known freak that J.H. should have recognized but didn't. Be that as it may I tell the story as I noted it in my journal at the time, and the detail is of no great import. David also told me that he was hard put, as director, to decide whether to cut to Julian looking apoplectic, me looking marvellously pleased, or the next object – and tried to do all three in quick succession.

It made good television. What did not make good television – although entertaining to viewers – were the strange incidents of Sir Leigh Ashton and Professor Margaret Mead. It was the custom of the BBC to give dinner before the performances, which always went out live, and we always met in Beoty's in Wright's Lane, then a delightful Cypriot restaurant run by Theodore. That restaurant in Kensington no longer exists but its sister in St Martin's Lane still flourishes. I got to know the potentialities and specialities of Beoty's very well over the years. They made an excellent moussaka and their taramasalata and dolmades were most satisfactory. Theodore had one very special dish which I must have eaten many times, namely *crevettes Theodore*. I am very fond of *canapés Diane* as a savoury: chicken livers wrapped in bacon. I thought this dish could be improved by flaming the *canapés* in brandy and Theodore readily agreed to do this. I do not know who the original *Diane* was but I have christened this dish *canapés Diane de Poitiers* and it makes an excellent savoury to end an English-style dinner or an excellent *warmspeise* as an opening to any meal.

The drill of an *AVM?* evening was that I went to Lime Grove for a rehearsal and briefing and then with the producer and a representative of the museum joined the three panellists at Beoty's: then after dinner we all drove back to the studios, did one non-broadcast beginning and dealt with one object which naturally did not appear later; and then plunged straight away into the main exercise.

One evening the challenging museum was the Fitzwilliam Museum, Cambridge, and among the three panellists was Sir Leigh Ashton, then Director of the Victoria and Albert. He was late for dinner: 'I hope he's all right,' said Paul Johnstone darkly. 'There have been rumours you know.' Jack Goodison, the Assistant Director of the Fitzwilliam Museum, said coldly, 'Facts as well as rumours.' Paul Johnstone was summoned to the telephone and came back looking very worried. 'He's not coming to dinner,' he said. 'He's delayed at a reception in the Belgian Embassy.' 'How did he sound?' asked Goodison. Paul shrugged his shoulders. 'Rather thick and muzzy,' he said. 'Oh, my God,' said Goodison.

When we got to the studios there was no Ashton. He arrived ten minutes before we were due on the air obviously much the worse for drink. He waved aside my handshake and slumped down in the chair. His tipple had obviously been brandy. We began, and I saw to it that the first object was given to the other panellists first. When it got to him he said loudly and aggressively, 'It's a fake. A bloody fake,' and handed it back to me. We moved to the second object and I deliberately gave it to him first. 'Another fake,' he said, 'palpably a fake. Ridiculous that any museum could think otherwise.' The air of the large studio began to tense. Up came the third object and this came to Ashton last. 'Another obvious fake,' he said, thickly. 'The Fitzwilliam is full of fakes. Disgraceful.' A card from the producer was put in front of me. 'Don't ask the old fool any more questions,' it said. The rest of the programme proceeded with the other panellists manfully playing the game. Leigh Ashton fell asleep in his chair: the cameras politely kept off him though the sound recorded his drunken snores. Afterwards Goodison, who was hurt and shamed, told us he thought it all dated back to a time when Louis Clark, then Director of the Fitzwilliam, had once proved that two objects in the V. and A. *were* fakes. This was Ashton's way of revenge but it was inelegant and unhappy. He did not appear on *AVM?* again.

The affair of Margaret Mead was even more bizarre. I had never met her before but knew well two of her husbands, Reo Fortune and Gregory Bateson. It was my idea that we might have an *AVM?* in which the objects were live people of different racial types (this idea might be a dangerous one these days, when even Robertson's marmalade golliwogs are thought to be racist) so that the panel could argue as to whether the subject was a Sudanese negro or an Ainu or an Amerindian. Christoph von Fürer-Haimendorf thought this an excellent idea and agreed to produce the material we wanted from among his own students in the School of Oriental and African Studies. He assured us that none of them would feel self-conscious and we all agreed that their normal tribal or national clothes would be an additional clue to their identity; so that it was a racial-cum-ethnic competition.

Margaret Mead arrived in London and some gracious polite lady from the BBC (it might have been Mary Adams or Grace Wyndham-Goldie or Nancy Thomas) called on her in her hotel to welcome her. Apparently La Mead felt very strongly about the treatment of women in public places and public life and expected a senior male from the BBC to call on her with a bottle of champagne and a bouquet of flowers. So her relations with the BBC got off on the wrong foot. She arrived at Beoty's in a bad temper and appeared to have been drinking. When asked what she would like as an aperitif she looked round at our dry martinis and camparis and said firmly 'Champagne'. I introduced myself, refraining from saying I knew two of her husbands, and said jocularly as the champagne cork popped: 'We are glad you have honoured us by taking part in this circus.' She looked at me as though I were some BBC floor-attendant: 'I took some persuading,' she said, 'but you sure spoke true when you call it a circus.'

She then turned it into a circus, drinking the better part of a bottle of champagne during dinner and talking extravagantly about the downtrodden position of women in England, the horrors of English food, and how much nicer life was in New Guinea than in New or Old England. As she got more garrulous and bibulous the producer passed me a note: 'Watch your step. Remember Leigh Ashton.'

The programme began and the first subject was a beautiful Indian girl from the Madras region. I turned first to Margaret Mead. 'Where,' I said, 'do you think this charming lady comes from?' She hesitated, and then said with calculated rudeness, 'I've got to take your word that she's charming'. A pause, and then the shattering reply. 'She's the sort of person you could meet any day in Grand Central Station, New York.' Astounded I persisted and said: 'But where would her home be?' 'I don't know and I don't care,' she said, 'I've given my answer.' A hasty note from the producer, 'Ask her third next time.'

We moved to the next subject who was a young south Chinese man. The other panellists successfully placed him and I turned to Margaret Mead. 'Do you agree?' I said. 'They may be right,' she said, 'but you could find him any day in Grand Central Station, New York.' There was ill-suppressed laughter in the studio. I determined to take issue with this formidable anthropologist. 'I am sure,' I said, 'you could find almost any racial or ethnic type on the platforms of Grand Central, except perhaps Eskimos, Bushmen and Ainus. But where did this man come from before entering the great melting pot on 47th Street?' Stung, she said, 'I expect he came from one of the Chinese restaurants on 47th Street. And by the way, young man, I'd have you know I've seen two Eskimos at Grand Central.'

A quick note from the producer. 'Don't ask her anything, please.' And the rest of the programme proceeded without incident and no participation by La Mead. But when we came to the last subject, who was one of Fürer-Haimendorf's students from the Himalayan foothills, who had been correctly identified by the two other panellists, I turned to the slightly somnolent Mead and said, 'I would be surprised, wouldn't you, to find such a person as this at Grand Central Station?' She smiled, 'Sure, sure,' she said, 'you've got more brains than I first credited you with.' What an extraordinary woman! Fortunately the BBC were now fully alerted to her idiosyncratic needs and expectations. There was waiting for her a bouquet of flowers and more champagne. Few people could have less earned their fees than Margaret Mead and Leigh Ashton.

Most of our programmes were shot in the Lime Grove Studios and many curious incidents took place there. Once, when I summoned a lift and opened the door, I found an agreeable little donkey inside obviously destined for some Passion play or children's programme. We travelled up together and it got out with me, but clearly was not expected there since there was soon pandemonium as it cantered about the studio tripping over cables and knocking down lights. 'This is a madhouse,' said a camera assistant to me. 'Two days ago I found a baby elephant in the loo.' It was a madhouse, but a most agreeable madhouse with everyone co-operating and helping; and having fun and enjoying themselves. On one occasion I was left alone in the make-up room and gave myself villainous eyebrows, a red nose and a diabolic moustache. No one paid the slightest attention as I picked my way to my chairman's seat until a few minutes later Paul Johnstone's quavering voice was heard on the intercom protesting mildly, 'I think something has gone slightly wrong with Glyn's make-up.'

But from time to time instead of the specimens coming from museums to London, we went to the museum, which was more fun if more time-consuming. We went to Cardiff, Aberdeen, the British Museum itself (which was then not allowed to permit objects to leave its premises without Act of Parliament), York, Copenhagen, Brussels, Turin and twice to Paris. The first visit to Paris was to the Louvre and was a great success except that when, after the performance, we were ushered into a neighbouring gallery for a restoring glass of wine, we found that the French camera crews had drunk it all. The second visit which was intended to be to the Musée des Antiquités Nationales at Saint-Germain-en-Laye was a near disaster.

It was at a time when I had associated myself with Dorothy Garrod and Suzanne de Saint-Mathurin in questioning the authenticity of the paintings and engravings discovered at Rouffignac in Dordogne (see Chapter 11). I published my doubts in *Antiquity* and an article by Dorothy Garrod in the same vein. The Abbé Breuil, then the doyen of French prehistory, and who had himself authenticated Rouffignac in one hurried visit, was furious. When he heard of the plans for an *AVM?* programme at Saint-Germain he pulled every string – and he had access to many strings and pulled well – to prevent the programme. He was successful. The programme was transferred to the Musée de l'Homme and here again the evil machinations of the Abbé pursued us. Somehow he learnt of the list of objects to be used: one was a fine Acheulian axe which had come from his collection and he insisted that it should not be used. The producer was in despair. 'What shall we do?' he cried, for all the camera captions had been printed and detailed instructions issued to the staff. I had a flash of inspiration and remembered that among its collection of replicas the museum had a plaster cast of the fine hand-axe. I hastily bought one and when the time came produced it from my pocket to the fury of the Abbé and his associates.

That second Paris programme was marred by another unpleasant incident. The BBC liked to change the producer of *AVM?* each year, which annoyed us old hands. Wheeler once said to a new producer – and it did not endear him – 'No, no, dear boy. That isn't how we run this show.' The same producer had a fit of nerves in the Musée, partly no doubt brought on by the affair of the Acheulian axe and the Abbé Breuil. He was anxious to make a success of the programme and made the outrageous mistake of taking Wheeler aside and asking if he would like to see the list of objects to be guessed. It was a hideous blunder. Wheeler was justifiably furious. I have never seen him look so angry: with beetling brows and twitching moustache he stormed over to Ruth, explained what had happened, and said he was not going to appear. We took him out to a café and eventually calmed him down over several Pernods. But that was a nasty evening. Afterwards he declined to join in the BBC party and took us to a late supper in Montmartre to a restaurant he had often frequented when he and Alfred Clapham made their little visits to Paris. I have seldom enjoyed a better *gratin de langoustines* or deserved it and the excellent Muscadet-sur-lie more.

AVM? was a success because it lived up to the Reith formula of what broadcasting should do, namely 'instruct, inform and entertain'. It was a success because Paul Johnstone had unerringly picked people who were natural broadcasters. It was a success because it demonstrated experts at work showing that they were indeed experts: it is the same reason that makes *Face the Music* such compelling viewing – and just as I am flabbergasted and excited by the knowledge and expertise of people like Robin Ray, David Attenborough, Richard Baker, and the, alas, now dead Joyce Grenfell, so were the five million viewers of *AVM?* flabbergasted and excited by the knowledge and expertise of the archaeologists. But there was a fourth reason for its success and that is one which many professional archaeologists are often not prepared to admit. Archaeology and ethnology are not concerned with dull objects: they are concerned with the artistic achievements of man in past time and the objects shewn and discussed on *AVM?* were often things of beauty and delight.

Every broadcast programme apparently has to have a signature tune. Paul Johnstone selected for *Animal, Vegetable, Mineral?* the beginning of the Prelude in E Major from Bach's Violin Sonata No 6 played by the Boston Symphony Orchestra, conducted by Sergei

Koussevitsky (recorded by HMV DB6 456): and I can never hear this without a sense of apprehension that I am on the air again. When I appeared on Roy Plomley's *Desert Island Discs*, I chose this as one of my eight records.

I am often asked why *AVM?* – that English television institution of the 1950s – came to an end. There are many reasons. First, there was a feeling in the BBC that such a programme should not go on and on; if it did it might never stop. There should be change and new ideas. Yet some BBC programmes did go on and on, such as *What's My Line?* and *Any Questions?* This first reason was not a powerful one. The second reason was that we – chairman and performers – were getting fed up with the annual change of producer and very dissatisfied with our last season, and particularly with the events in the Musée de l'Homme. Looking back on it I think that Wheeler and I, as the central characters in this affair for so long, would not have wanted to go on and on.

But there were two more powerful and political reasons, and these were the personalities of two high-placed people in the BBC Television hierarchy: Grace Wyndham-Goldie and Leonard Miall. Wheeler proposed to do a special programme on Greek archaeology and fixed it in conjunction with a Swan's Hellenic Cruise of which firm he was a director. The producer was to be Stephen Hearst and he and Wheeler got on very well, and indeed made an excellent programme. But Mrs Wyndham-Goldie decided to accompany the camera team and have an Aegean holiday. This annoyed Wheeler; his annoyance grew to rage when she accompanied them on location and even interfered with the producer. He took her firmly aside and said: 'You are a bitch, and if you follow me about again I shall cancel my participation in this programme and fly back to London tomorrow.' This made for very frigid relations and she was no longer an *AVM?* or Wheeler enthusiast.

One day in May 1958 the telephone rang in my house: would I lunch in the University Arms with Lord Townshend and three of his colleagues to discuss developments in television? I looked up Lord Townshend in the College library. He was waiting for me and introduced me to John Woolf, Aubrey Buxton, and Laurence Scott who had been at Medmenham and whom I knew slightly. Over lunch it was explained that they were forming a consortium to apply for the East Anglian regional franchise of the new Independent Television Authority. They wanted representatives of the University of Cambridge: would I be one? They had already got the agreement of Dr Audrey Richards, at that time Vice-Principal of Newnham, later Smuts Reader in Anthropology. After correspondence and discussion I agreed and in due course all members of the consortium appeared before the Authority, to argue our case. I was asked by the chairman what contribution I thought we could make to television and on the spur of the moment said I wanted to show the people of East Anglia their homeland from the air, and paraphrasing the motto of the National Museum of Wales, declared that one of our purposes should be to teach the people of East Anglia about themselves and the world about East Anglia.

We gained the franchise, Anglia Television was formed, and I was a director from 1959 until I retired in 1981, believing that younger people should take over. I enjoyed my twenty-one years as a director of Anglia Television: I was not, of course, an executive director and the duties were not onerous: a monthly meeting alternately in London and Norwich. I found the whole affair of the birth and growth of a television company interesting and at times exciting and was happy to be involved in it. I watched with pleasure and pride Anglia establish itself as one of the most respected and efficient of the regional TV companies. It soon became very well known because of its prowess and performance in two fields: drama and natural history. I was allowed and encouraged to initiate and take part in archaeological and historical programmes. We began with a series called *Once a Kingdom* which portrayed East Anglia from its geological beginnings to the present day. The next two series were *Who were the British?* and *The Lost Centuries*. Both these successful series were directed and produced by Forbes Taylor and used Brian Hope-Taylor very extensively as adviser and performer. When the new A11 bypass for Newmarket cut through the Devil's Dyke, rescue excavations were directed by Hope-Taylor, and Forbes Taylor made a film of the whole operation.

Paul Johnstone and some others did not feel that a director of an Independent Television company was precluded from working for the BBC. But Grace Wyndham-Goldie and Leonard Miall did not accept such a position with pleasure. Grace gave me tea (yes, tea!) in Brown's Hotel to discuss the problem and made clear her disapproval of my association with Anglia. She also said that she thought Wheeler had served his purpose and was losing his touch. Leonard Miall had, as I have said earlier, been a junior contemporary of mine at St John's when he was a Cambridge undergraduate. I always thought of him as suave and kind to the point of weakness. In a talk at Lime Grove he indicated that joining Anglia was near-treachery to the BBC: and that he was not recommending the continuance of *Animal, Vegetable, Mineral?* I am told that at a programme meeting shortly afterwards he announced the end of the programme and said: 'Gentlemen, please think up another comparable programme. The formula is simple: a group of people talking amusingly about objects in the round.' *AVM?* really died because of a few powerful opinionated personalities in the BBC.

When *AVM?* was at its height of popularity and had an enormous viewing audience, I began to think with Paul Johnstone of introducing a new series of archaeological programmes that would deal with a single topic and give them full television treatment. The new series we created together was called *Buried Treasure* and ran from 1955 to early 1959, so that for nearly four years *AVM?* and *Buried Treasure* were transmitted more or less concurrently.

Paul Jordan, who worked for years with Paul Johnstone in the BBC and is now in charge of archaeological and historical programmes with Anglia Television, wrote in a volume called *Antiquity and Man*, edited by Evans, Cunliffe and Renfrew:

> Especially for those of us who were in our fifth and sixth forms at the time, this was really the Golden Age of archaeology on television: archaeology was attracting the public in general, exercising museums and libraries, but with their television programmes it was also engaging the interests of the next generation of diggers and archaeology students, making for itself a much broader academic and professional constituency than it had ever enjoyed before. It is not too much to say that these programmes created the classes of '59, '60 and '61 that have gone on to include some of our leading academic archaeologists and excavators – and even television producers, and through them, the interest has continued and grown with succeeding years.

In our *Buried Treasure* programmes we covered all sorts of topics: Tollund Man, the Piltdown Fraud, the Etruscans, Jericho, Pompeii, Mohenjo-daro, Maiden Castle, the Mammoth Hunters, Skara Brae, and Zimbabwe for example. For the Skara Brae programme I appeared as a Neolithic man dressed up in a cowhide and with a beard which made me look very much like my Carmarthen grandfather.

Paul Johnstone wrote a book about the first few *Buried Treasure* programmes. I was asked to write a preface for a hefty fee. Two good friends counselled me against doing this: 'You must begin to extricate yourself from the media,' they said, 'if you are going to exist as a respectable archaeologist.' Paul was pained when I declined to do a preface: we spent the greater part of a day in a hotel in Vannes going through his book and arguing the pros and cons of my preface.

The powers that then were in the BBC in the sixties, with what Paul Jordan has called 'a relish for all things new and current as against the past and the reflective', turned away from archaeology for a while as they seem to be doing again at this present moment. *Buried Treasure* came to an end and Paul Johnstone and Nancy Thomas found themselves in further education; but while there they asked me to do five half-hour television programmes on the history of archaeology in their further education series, and these I did in my rooms in St John's in five strenuous and rewarding days in December 1965.

We decided not to broadcast from scripts and not to use jumbo pini-prompters. I spoke throughout without notes – after all I had been lecturing on this subject to university audiences for twenty years. The technique of recording was interesting. I tried out what I intended to say in the first ten minutes, discussed it with Paul and Nancy, took a short walk in the Backs, returned to my rooms and we made a recording of that ten minutes, and, if it was not up to scratch, another. I enjoyed the challenge. The monitored texts of these unscripted talks were published later by Duckworth's in London and Crowell in New York as *Man Discovers his Past* (1966).

One of the private rewards of that December week of recording was that while on Monday and Tuesday the BBC technicians coping with the cameras and the light and sound equipment in my rooms spent every spare moment reading the magazines they had brought with them dealing with mini-cars and bees and bungalows, at the end of the week they were reading avidly every and any archaeological book they could find on my shelves. Perhaps I delude myself, and it was just that the next editions of their magazines had not yet come out.

1966 saw the revival of the BBC's interest in archaeology. Paul Johnstone attracted a large audience with his story of the 1939 discovery at Sutton Hoo. But the good news was the elevation of David Attenborough, whom I first met as a minor cog in the *AVM?*

wheel of 1952, to be Controller of BBC 2. This wise, clever, cultivated human being (who would unquestionably be Director General of the BBC if he had not preferred the swamps of Borneo to the sofas of Langham Place), now himself a household name after his brilliant programmes, notably *Life on Earth*, formed a new Archaeology and History Unit with Paul Johnstone as executive producer and me as adviser. The title *Chronicle* was coined for the regular programmes which Paul produced until his untimely death in 1976. *Chronicle* and the BBC broke new ground in sponsoring the Silbury Hill excavations directed by Richard Atkinson in the late sixties, although the excavators and the BBC were disappointed that there was no spectacular climax: no discovery of a Bronze Age chieftain with rich gold ornaments in the centre of the mound. Silbury Hill keeps its ultimate secrets still but the *Chronicle* exercise showed the public very clearly the nature of archaeological work.

Chronicle fathered offspring in the form of special series on Ancient Egypt, the archaeology of Bible lands, and the Vikings. The last programme I did with Paul was on Colonial Williamsburg: he was in failing health and left the filming and editing to Antonia Benedek, who didn't like me and of whom I had no high opinion. I had to rescue her on several occasions when she was making a mess of things. She took her revenge and when editing the programme all my commentary on site was taken away. My doctor watched the programme and said, 'Did the BBC really fly you to America just to say 'Yes' on three occasions? No wonder our licence money is so high.'

Paul had already had one heart attack when he was at the production desk at Lime Grove. A second killed him in 1976. He was a very great friend and a good and great man. He was in a way a don *manqué* and could well have spent his life teaching history at New College where he had taken a First. He took another path to present the past to the present, and to the great benefit of us all. To quote Paul Jordan again: 'He had a sure instinct for what was reputable in a scholarly way, however ingenious he might be in popularizing it.'

Paul Johnstone had been made a Fellow of the Society of Antiquaries and very appropriately a memorial service was held in St James's, Piccadilly. I read one of the lessons, and David Attenborough gave the address, which he has kindly allowed me to reprint as Appendix I.

Chronicle was taken over by Bruce Norman after Paul Johnstone's death and he asked me to stay on as adviser. But I thought it was time for change, and in any case I was now firmly entrenched in Anglia Television and knew that several people in the BBC had expressed their disapproval to Paul that his adviser on archaeology was a director of an independent company already making rival archaeological programmes. I was glad to bow out.

When Forbes Taylor left Anglia to advise on TV production in the Gulf States he was replaced by Paul Jordan from the BBC as archaeological and historical producer. Paul had been a pupil of mine at St John's in the early sixties and worked for thirteen years in the BBC in the *Chronicle* unit. Paul Johnstone had a very high opinion of his work and over the years he produced some outstandingly good programmes. He fell in love with Egypt and wrote *Egypt: the black land* in 1976. After coming to Anglia he made many programmes. *North Sea Saga* showed the relations between East Anglia and the continent of Europe from prehistoric times onwards and I much enjoyed visiting Schleswig-Holstein and Denmark with him and planning the series. We visited Sylt, travelling in our car in the train that goes along the Hindenberg embankment.

The next year saw work on a film on *Stonehenge* and in 1983 we worked together on *Myth America*. I took the title from an article by Denis Brogan originally published in the *Spectator* in 1967 and reprinted by me in *Antiquity* in 1968. The theme of our programme was to discuss in broad outline some of the theories put forward for the discovery of America in pre-Columbian times by people from Europe, North Africa, Egypt and China. It took us to Minnesota to see the Kensington Stone in the runestone museum at Alexandria, and the astonishing replica of the stone five times its size set up at the outskirts of the town. The city fathers of Alexandria are loud in professing their belief that this stone, discovered in 1898 (and regarded by most competent scholars as a forgery) is authentic, and outside the museum they have built a statue of a Viking twenty-five feet high (locally called 'Big Ole') bearing on his shield the legend 'Birthplace of America.' *Myth America* was first transmitted on Channel 4 on 2 September, 1983.

Forbes Taylor had planned a programme about my life and work and while I was a little dubious about it the Anglia authorities decided it should be done. After Forbes Taylor had left Anglia the film was taken over by Paul Jordan, completed and shown in 1981.

The temporary fame (or notoriety) that came my way in the fifties during *Animal, Vegetable, Mineral?* brought in endless invitations to appear on other BBC programmes, to lecture, to open bazaars and new schools, and even in those early days to advertise. I was offered a lucrative contract by a major firm of Scottish distillers to advertise their whisky. I knew that my constant appearances on the TV were arousing criticism and disapproval (and perhaps a little envy) among my academic colleagues. Advertising whisky would have, at that time, been the end. Not, I think, now. Magnus Magnusson, though not a professional academic, has been Rector of Edinburgh University (and, everyone tells me, a devoted, hard-working and most useful occupant of that job); he is now chairman of *Mastermind*, and often appears in advertisements. But this is thirty years later and our society is more permissive in every way.

It would have been unthinkable, unwise and unfortunate in the mid-fifties for a young don to appear advertising whisky and I wrote saying so. Back came a polite and firm letter saying that I was mistaken, that in a few years all public personalities would be only too happy to advertise, and that the time was not far distant when the Queen would appear recommending various products! Well, at least the first part of their forecast was right although I do not myself buy products because David Niven and Robert Morley told me to do so.

I put my name down with various lecture agencies like Foyles and for several years spent a few days each year lecturing all over England and Wales. I eventually managed to concentrate the engagements into a lecturing week in the Easter vacation, performing at luncheon clubs and evening lectures every day. It was entertaining and rewarding and the questions taught me what ordinary people wanted to know about archaeology and prehistory. There were many strange incidents. I was sitting quietly in the lounge of a hotel in Grantham recovering from a Ladies' Lunch when I heard a woman pass by talking loudly to her companions. 'I was disappointed,' she said, 'I knew it was called Archaeology and the Public, but it was all about archaeology. As a member of the public I feel cheated. Do you think I could ask for my money back?' In Wolverhampton I lectured in a very large hall to a tremendous audience: it was part of a season of celebrity concerts and lectures. The great hall was in darkness, illustrations were appearing on the screen and I was in a kind of pulpit. Halfway through I heard footsteps and became aware of someone climbing slowly up the circular stairs to where I was. What was to happen? Would he attack me? Would he seize my microphone and say that I was talking nonsense and preach fundamentalism or some fringe lunacy? He did seize the microphone: I was alarmed and intrigued but relieved when all he said was, 'If Dr Featherstone is in the audience will he please go to the Maternity Hospital at once'.

I went on lecture tours in America, including one delightful week in California when I fell in love, as surely everyone must, with San Francisco. I well remember my visit to Sacramento for two reasons: I was giving an illustrated lecture on Early European Art and had put together my fifty best slides from the Venus of Brassempouy to the Alfred Jewel. When I pressed the button for the first slide some devilish mania seized the carousel and it rushed all my slides through in two minutes and there was nothing we could do to halt its mad progress. 'You have had,' I told the large astonished audience, 'and not by my design, a rapid preview of my lecture. Let us now look at my illustrations at greater leisure.' The second reason was that at the end there was the predictable mad questioner: a fierce middle-aged woman who fired question after question about Egyptians in America, the Lost Tribes, Atlantis, Mu, Vikings in Minnesota, men from outer space – the lot. The chairman was getting nervous. 'This is getting out of hand,' he said as she got up to ask another question. 'Shall I tell her to shut up?' 'No,' I said, 'let her have one more chance.' 'I've been surprised at your answers to my questions,' she said. 'Can't we believe all we read in books?' I had been polite and courteous in my earlier answers. This seemed the moment for the hatchet. 'No, madam,' I said, and the audience laughed and cheered.

There were naturally invitations to appear in other programmes like *What's My Line?*, *Any Questions?* and *Desert Island Discs* but I declined except that in 1981 I relented and enjoyed doing a *Desert Island Disc* programme with Roy Plomley. When Noel Annan and I were asked to appear in a revamped TV version of the famous *Brains Trust* programme with Julian Huxley and Jacob Bronowski we thought hard about it but after a lot of hesitation agreed. We drove up to London and had an excellent lunch in Scott's, then still in Leicester Square. Julian I knew from Ad Eundem dinners but I gradually took a dislike to Bronowski: his views on prehistory and archaeology seemed to me ill-informed and confused – a view which was confirmed by the early programmes in his broadcast series *The Ascent of Man*.

We were driven to the studios and had a brief rehearsal. No one told us where to sit: I took any chair and was surprised to receive very black looks from Bronowski. When we stopped for the break before the real programme the studio manager took me aside and said, 'Oh, my God, I forgot to tell you. You sat in Bruno's chair. He is terribly conscious that he is a very small man and the chair where you sat has a special blown up cushion so that he can look the same size as the other participants. He will now be in a furious temper throughout the programme.'

When we sat down for the programme Bruno was poised on his cushion in his special chair and I watched him bouncing up and down. It was not a wildly successful programme: I thought Julian and Bruno were not on their best form. Noel was his usual scintillating, amusing, teasing self; I was dull but made a few jokes. After the programme Julian reprimanded Noel and myself. 'You are not taking the programme seriously,' he said. 'You both made jokes and laughed too much. This is a serious information programme. The public want to know what the brains of the nation think on important issues.'

Chastened, Noel drove me back to Cambridge. 'Whether we were good or bad on the programme,' he said, 'we are probably doing ourselves no good by appearing on the tele. You may already have destroyed yourself by *Animal, Vegetable, Mineral?* We shall get nowhere: we shall be called the young Cambridge dons who became showmen because they were no good at their jobs. Will you survive the meretricious image of being a telly star?'

That was in 1955. The following year he was elected Provost of King's at the early age of forty, and ten years later, to the great sadness of his Cambridge friends and colleagues, he became Provost of University College, London, and later Vice-Chancellor of the University of London. He was made a life peer in 1965. *He* had got somewhere. When I was elected to the Disney Chair of Archaeology in Cambridge he wrote to me a characteristically generous and delightful note recollecting our TV discussions of 1955.

Dear Glyn,

My grapevine gave a melodious twang last week when David Wilson told me that you had been pre-elected into the Disney Chair. Can it be true? Can dear, dreary, stuffy, beloved Cambridge have had the sense to make the only appointment which is just, sensible, appropriate and in every sense right? Can it be true that they can have forgiven the scholar who did more than anyone else in the nineteen fifties to awaken England to her marvellous archaeological heritage and the miracles of discovery abroad? I swell with pride that I know you! I bombinate no longer in a vacuum when I contemplate – not without relief – the departure of staider spirits. I am so very glad, and so deeply pleased for you – for Ruth – for all the thousands who admire you and are grateful to you for introducing them to new worlds – and for your pupils to whom you have always been devoted and a wonderful inspiration.

Yet even as I write this I realise how selfish my pleasure is! I'm just so delighted that an old and dear friend (of how many encounters on the croquet lawn) – and such a good and generous friend, always the first to rejoice at any luck that came my way, should be so honoured. You are ex officio at the head of your profession.

And so deserved. Of course none of us can forget the great days of *AVM?* and the enchanting way you ran that programme, always so ready to let those prima donnas take the limelight. But even I, who really know nothing in a *real* sense about the triumphs of modern archaeology, know at least how greatly you have contributed to its advancement – even if we only catch a glimpse through a glass darkly by reading good popular reviews and articles. (I've just finished reading a book by a lecturer at U.C., John Morris, called *The Age of Arthur*, and I never knew how *much* archaeology, grave goods, hoards, the lot, had transformed history and were as important, if not more so, than the chronicles.)

There's yet another reason why I rejoice: even though it is a reproach to myself. At one time when we sported on the General Board together, I thought that you might be tempted to go the way that I have gone into University administration. How wise you were not to do so! Of course I could never have got within light years to where you have now got, but it must have been a temptation to fall for that most beguiling snare of Cambridge life, the life of the good College man who sits on all committees and is noted for his wisdom on syndicates, and subtly neglects his true calling as a scholar. You could have followed such a role with great aplomb. But you went on in your incomparable debonair way, never trimming your sails – and now you have reached port (while not denying yourself the opportunity to reach for *the* port.) Mes felicitations vieux copain de ma jeunesse!

Gaby joins me in ecstatic rejoicings. Your putative pupil, Juliet*, sends respectful greetings – alas, all too putative: she came down with a temperature of 102 last week in the middle of A Levels, has taken 3 papers in her nightdress and is very woe-begone. So whether she will make it next autumn is doubtful.

Love from us both to you and Ruth,

Yours ever,

Noel

* His daughter: she made it.

To return to the *Brains Trust*. Unlike Noel Annan, Bronowski thought it was a successful programme, and said he hoped he would meet me on forthcoming programmes. He never did, but, most curiously, thought he did: and this confusion has been most amusingly described by Gwyn Thomas in his *A few selected exits* (1968) from which I am allowed to quote. I should say that Gwyn Thomas, alas, now dead, and I were of the same general physical type, had the same voices, and the same sense of fun.

Gwyn Thomas writes of Bronowski after his first appearances on the *Brains Trust*:

After he had met me several times, he had no clear idea who I was. Twice we shook hands in the private reception room at Scott's in Piccadilly, . . . and he said 'Ah, Dr Glyn Daniel. Delighted to meet you.' Dr Daniel is an eminent Cambridge archaeologist, a native of Wales, whose face is as nationally well-known as any in Britain. His eyes and eyebrows and mine have a vaguely similar Celtic cut, but, apart from that, we are as clearly distinguishable as Vernon Brody and the Venerable Bede (Brody was a wrestler and not venerable).

When the Doctor made this mistake of identity for the second time, I still stood in such awe of his infallibility, my will caved in, and I told myself he must be right and that I must be Glyn Daniel. In any case, in that strange ambience, I felt like a change of image. I prepared a short statement on my latest dig in the burial chambers of north Brittany . . . Then my mind went into its usual perverse double shuffle and I said firmly that I was not Dr Glyn Daniel and had never probed the burial secrets of the Ancient Celts. No, I was

Harry Secombe, the well-known Welsh comedian and tenor. The sage turned away from me without a word and I heard him tell one of the other panellists that he thought it a devastating error on the part of the producer to invite people like professional fun-stars on to a programme that was supposed to have a serious aim.

The fifties in television were strange and heady days. Rik Wheeler was elected Television Personality of the Year in 1954 and, to my surprise, I was elected Television Personality of 1955 and received my award at the hands of Edith Evans at a dinner in the Savoy. I have enjoyed television but have been irked by the constant public recognition it gives you and on the whole disappointed with its educative impact on the general public.

In the hey-day of *AVM?*, when admittedly I appeared on the box nearly every week, it was impossible to go anywhere without being recognized. I am shortish, 5 ft $7\frac{1}{2}$ (the average height of the human species) but I always appeared seated behind a desk, and so no one had any idea of what I really looked like. I once summoned a taxi outside Chelsea Cloisters where we shared a flat during three busy London years, and before I got in the taxi driver stared at me in amazement and said, 'Good God, I had no idea you were a short-arsed bastard!' Dick Joice, that admirable, honest and cheerful Norfolk farmer who has been so successful on Anglia Television and is my classic example of the common unpatronizing touch in broadcasting, tells how he once drove into King's Lynn from his farm near Castle Rising to get some supplies. He was in his farm clothes and wearing mud-covered wellingtons. 'Look,' said someone, 'that's Dick Joice.' 'No,' said the other, 'not that filthy farmer. Mr Joice is a very proper and well-dressed man.'

But my strangest recognition – or non-recognition – incident occurred on the Harwich-Esbjerg boat. I went to the bar and there was an elegant woman lowering her second or third vodka-martini. She turned to me with a winning smile and said: 'How nice to meet you. I so much enjoyed your television programme last night.' I knew I had not been on a live programme the previous evening: perhaps there had been a repeat. The purser had a copy of the *Radio Times*: the previous evening Richard Atkinson had been appearing in one of his Silbury Hill programmes. I avoided the lady as much as I could but met her on the moving pavement that takes you from the boat to the dockside at Esbjerg. 'Good morning, Sir Mortimer,' she said. 'Sorry not to have had a longer talk with you.'

And yet I no longer despair of the real educational and informational aspect of sound and visual broadcasting. It is now more than respectable for an academic to be a success on radio and TV. Tony Quinton appears as chairman of quizzes in between his appearances in the House of Lords, his duties as President of Trinity College, Oxford, and his serious and scholarly writing. We have seen a complete change in thirty years and I am delighted to have taken part in this change. It seems to me still surprising that the visual image remains so compelling. Only a few days ago I met a man who said, 'It's Glyn Daniel, isn't it? You don't know me. How d'ye do? When are you and Sir Mortimer coming back on the box? Used to like your programme. Nothing like it these days.'

Television fame once brought me the best meal I have ever had on British Rail. I was travelling north to give a lecture in York and went into the restaurant car to be greeted with smiles and the warmest of welcomes. The food was excellent, the portions generous – a delicious fillet steak cooked exactly as I wanted, pink inside and burnt outside. When I had finished I was brought a large brandy 'with the compliments of the staff'. Puzzled, I protested mildly, but was told that it was the least they could do for me after all I had done for them in the discussions about catering wages and restaurant-car staffs. They had mistaken me for Woodrow Wyatt: we were about the same build and age, wore bow ties and spectacles, and were constantly appearing on the box in the fifties.

Hamilton Kerr, then MP for Cambridge and a member of St John's, thought that my television notoriety and my academic status made me eminently suitable to be an MP, and without asking what my politics were brought me an informal invitation from the Conservative Central Office to stand for Cardiff North, then a safe Tory seat. I did not hesitate before turning down this invitation. 'Quite incompatible with the things I do,' I said, but Hamilton disagreed: 'Other people manage', he said, and mentioned Christopher Mayhew and Kenneth Pickthorn.

Ham was a very entertaining and colourful man, an excellent linguist, no mean painter and a generous benefactor to the University of Cambridge through his bequests to the Fitzwilliam Museum. He was also an amusing raconteur: I remember one of his favourite stories of travels with friends in France. The party included a lady with little French and a bad back. He was horrified, but much amused, to hear her trying to explain politely to the receptionist of their hotel that she would like *deux matelots* on her bed, and the controlled surprise of the receptionist who merely said, '*Deux*, madame?'

It is now twenty-eight years since the box marked *Animal, Vegetable, Mineral?* spun round for the last time to the music of Bach's Prelude in E Major from the Violin Sonata No. 6.

Mortimer Wheeler and the author: a cartoon view of their relationship by Jewell, in the days of 'Animal, Vegetable, Mineral?'

CHAPTER NINE

Maupygernons and mash

A FEW WEEKS after my return to Cambridge in 1946 I was asked by the Master to be Steward of the College. It had been offered to Hugo Gatty but he had turned it down: a man who enjoyed food and wine, he knew he would not be happy dealing with the problems of staff, finance, equipment, rebuilding: and in any case he came back from the war a disillusioned, depressed man. I, too, liked eating and drinking, and then, as now, am sorry for people who regard food and drink as matters of necessary ingestion rather than delights to be cultivated; but I had no qualifications for taking on the job. The Master brushed my doubts aside. 'No one is born or trained into college duties,' he said. 'You will have to learn as you go along, and fortunately in your kitchen manager, Mr Sadler, and your head gardener, Mr Thoday, you have two mentors to whose service before and during the war the College is much indebted.' He went on to say that there were two things for the new Steward to do: the total re-equipment and reconstruction of the kitchens, and the gradual restoration of feeding and drinking in St John's to something approaching pre-war standards. My heart sank. Then, with that kindly twinkle in his eye, which made all who dealt with Benians love him, he opened Walter Scott's *The Antiquary* and read to me the passage which in 1950 *The Cambridge Review* used as a Valentine to me: 'If you want an affair of consequence properly managed, put it in the hands of an antiquary, for as they are eternally exercising their genius and research upon trifles, it is impossible that they can be baffled in affairs of importance.'

It was a compliment and a challenge and I accepted both. I felt that the successful performance of a college office might be the beginning of a permanent career as a don, and my ideas about my own future began to crystallize. When my appointment was confirmed, Ruth took me to Lear's bookshop in Cardiff and bought me a copy of André Simon's Wines and Spirits volume of his *A Concise Encyclopaedia of Gastronomy*.

That I survived for nearly ten years as Steward without appearing (at least outwardly) to be baffled by affairs, was due to the fact that I had three supporters: A.J. Sadler, the kitchen manager; R.E. Thoday, the head gardener; and Ruth Daniel, the Steward's wife. Without these three I would have had a very hard time; with them I was able to achieve all I wanted to do and my ten years as Steward are among my most often and most happily recollected years of my dondom.

My kitchen manager, Alfred Sadler, was a most admirable example of the sort of person who ran college kitchens in the second quarter of the twentieth century. Born in 1895 he spent two years in the kitchens of Emmanuel College and came to St John's as an apprentice cook in 1912. The kitchen manager and head chef at that time was a well known Cambridge figure, a Mr Parsley: Sadler regarded him as a very good teacher and a very good cook. When in 1912 Sadler joined the College, the kitchen staff consisted of seven cooks, five apprentices and twelve kitchen porters.

He became kitchen manager in 1932 and held that onerous position with tact, charm, distinction, and an imperturbability rare in his profession, for twenty-eight years, to the great benefit of the College and especially myself as Steward during 1946–55. He saw enormous changes in College life and catering between 1912 and 1960 when he retired. He saw, for example, the number of undergraduates he had to feed go up from 250 in 1912 to 750 in 1960. When he began work, undergraduates and Fellows could walk directly into the kitchens up to 1.30 p.m. and select dishes from an *à la carte* tariff which were then delivered to their rooms by the kitchen porters. When I was an undergraduate and a Fellow, just before the war, it was a naturally expected and readily given kitchen service that all meals could be sent to one's rooms.

Breakfast parties were a joy to give and the day seemed already made when the door of one's keeping room would open and in would come on the head of a kitchen porter a tray covered in green baize cloth, the tray put down skilfully in front of a brightly burning coal fire, the baize cloth removed, and dishes of sausages and scrambled eggs, of kidneys and bacon, put in the hearth with the coffee and toast to await the guests. My favourite breakfast dish was *Croustades à la Saint-Jean*, which I allowed to be eaten in that neighbouring house, Fisher College, in my detective story *The Cambridge Murders*. It consists of an hour-glass shaped piece of fried bread through which a central hole has been cut vertically: this central hollow is filled with minced creamed chicken, and a poached egg is balanced on top. Difficult to eat without demolishing the structure, but delicious to demolish.

In the years before the 1939–45 war the sight of college porters with trays on their heads, walking, with the elegance and assurance of Lisbon fisherwomen, from the kitchens to college rooms or lodgings outside, was one of the standard features of Cambridge life – and a great surprise to visitors from America or the continent. The war killed this elegant and luxurious service; all college kitchens now have relatively smaller staffs (hardly any kitchen porters) even though they have to feed larger numbers of undergraduates and dons. I was most anxious after the war to get back to some service of meals to rooms and Sadler did all he could to help me in this aim. What we soon realized was that if the kitchens prepared and cooked the meals, undergraduates, and even Fellows, were quite ready to collect them from the kitchen themselves and carry the food to their rooms. One of the difficulties of providing meals from the kitchens to rooms was the distance involved. It is a College legend, but true, that it is a quarter of a mile from the main porter's lodge of St John's to, say, the late Professor Jopson's set on I Staircase, New Court, and that many rooms in the Great Court of Trinity were much nearer the St John's kitchens than sets in New Court and the Cripps Building.

It seems to us nowadays almost unthinkable that the college kitchens should be open all day and that it was possible to walk in, or telephone, and order china tea, anchovy toast, crumpets or muffins, and that it should arrive in one's rooms within fifteen minutes. The late Professor Sir Percy Winfield used almost every day to order tea and buttered toast to be sent to his rooms. One day his order arrived without a jug of hot water: Sadler recollected that on every single occasion for the next twenty years, when Winfield ordered his tea, he always said fiercely, 'And don't forget the bloody hot water this time'. Of such stuff are learned eccentric dons made, and what stories Stewards and kitchen managers could tell if only they did not value continuing good relationships with their colleagues.

Percy Winfield was an enchanting old man when I knew him, but as he got more and more deaf he became slightly embarrassing. He was careful to cultivate the company of new Fellows but would confuse them at High Table by saying loudly, 'Don't let them overwork you' – he himself as a young man had been a coach teaching fifty to sixty hours a week – or, most embarrassingly, 'What have you got on the stocks at the moment? How is your book getting on?' The nervous young Fellow would quietly reply that he was not writing a book and become further embarrassed when Percy boomed out: 'Bad show. You must get something between hard covers soon or they'll throw you out.'

I, as Steward, had to deal with him at feasts, and at the last May Feast he attended we had arranged that he should go home early. Grace after food was being said antiphonally between President and choir, and during a pause Winfield's voice rang out clearly, 'Master, I must leave you now. Glyn has a taxi waiting for me.'

Freshly back from India I was shocked at the curried dishes which the kitchen was happy to serve: it was, of course, a simple way of using up left-over dishes concealing their lack of taste by quantities of curry powder. I banned them: curry must be made, I said, with fresh ingredients and freshly ground condiments. No curry dishes were served during my Stewardship.

I appreciated the skill and experience of Sadler, Dring (head chef) and their staff and (apart from curries) let them have their heads – except for feasts and Wednesday nights. I devised the High Table menu every Wednesday and tried not to repeat any dish during my ten years and I served a different wine every Wednesday – which was a great education for the Fellows of St John's and for their Steward.

Wine, yes, here was the problem. It had been traditional for a very long time to serve a pint of beer free to each Fellow or guest dining at High Table. I produced good arguments to show that one large glass of wine was no more expensive than a pint of beer. Wine was allowed and nowadays it is more widely drunk than beer and I am fascinated that now Fellows are allowed two glasses of wine, which costs little more than a pint of beer.

My Wednesday dinners became well known. One Fellow wrote to a guest inviting him with these words: 'You never know what you are going to get to eat – sometimes not enough – and the wine will be something you've never heard of.' There certainly were disasters, because in my enthusiasm I did not brief the kitchens and waiters sufficiently. I once put on a cassoulet but forgot to explain that there should be a generous serving per person. Kitchens and servers thought it a curious little bean stew and gave each Fellow a small spoonful. I wasn't dining in that evening; enraged and angry, the Fellows revolted and were each served with a supplementary dish of cold ham and salad.

Nothing went wrong with the wines. The late forties and early fifties was a time when, through travel and war experience, people were becoming interested in the wide variety of wines and wanting to buy and drink French country wines and experience changes from the standard menus of the twenties or thirties which inevitably had sherry, Chablis (what has happened to this once much-loved wine?), Burgundy, Claret, and Port. So I bought in all kinds of local wines: Muscadet, Saumur, Coteaux de Layon, Bourgueil, Chinon and Vouvray from the Loire Valley, Pouilly-Fumé, Pouilly-Fuissé, Quincy, Reuilly, Sancerre and Saint-Pourçain from the middle Loire, all the Beaujolais marks (my own favourites being Morgon, Chenas and Chiroubles), Rully, Mercurey and Saint-Véran from Burgundy, Gigondas, Tavel, Cassis, Corbières and Minervois from southern France, Cahors, Bergerac, Montbazillac, Gaillac, Jurançon and Irouléguy from the south-west.

I also tried to reintroduce into our repertoire some old English dishes, such as Sussex partridge pie, Cornish leek tart, Derbyshire pie, fidget pie, and boiled beef and dumplings, as well as encouraging treacle pudding, summer pudding and brown Betty pudding. I then began to collect recipes from Oxford and Cambridge Colleges, some of which I published in my *Oxford Chicken Pie*, which I have already referred to: dishes such as Oxford John, New College pudding, Trinity College salad, Grassy Corner pudding and Marigold pudding.

I was once teased by Dr Palmer and Professor Walker that, while I sought for strange dishes from foreign countries, it was noticeable that I never put on a dinner displaying the food of my own country. I waited, and on St David's Day 1955 the menu was Cawl (the Welsh soup), the Welsh Hermit's Favourite Chicken and Leek Pie, and Caws Pobi (i.e. Welsh Rabbit). The recipe for the Welsh Hermit's Pie appeared in Lady Hall's *Good Cookery* (1867) and is reproduced by I.K. Fletcher in *Wine and Food* (1935); it has become a steady favourite in the College kitchens.

There was no bar in the College in 1946 and it seemed to me that returning warriors would find this strange. I proposed a bar for junior members. Martin Charlesworth said, 'This will be very controversial. You have all your facts, of course?' Steward's business was always the last item on the agenda of the College Council: and, after several weeks, my proposal had still not come up. I became disheartened: was this a clever ploy to stop the matter being discussed? After two months I spoke to the President and he said, 'Just go ahead, dear boy. After a while the Council will have forgotten that they never gave permission for this revolutionary change.' And that was how the now very successful Buttery Bar in St John's (a much larger and grander version of my small beginning) came into existence.

One of my immediate post-war difficulties lay not in establishing a bar but in stocking it. Beer and wine were in short supply for some while, and I could get no cider. Looking through our accounts I saw that we had for a very long time dealt with Gaymers of Attleborough in Norfolk. I wrote to them asking if they could help. They replied saying they had been going through their books and found that St John's College, Cambridge, was their first customer outside Attleborough when they founded their business. They would be happy to help in any way they could; and they did, to my pleasure and to that of thirsty students.

One of the pleasures of being Steward was buying and learning about wine, and making friendships with wine merchants, shippers and growers. At that time we in St John's dealt mainly with Dolamore's (Sherlock Holmes's wine merchant in Baker Street), Harveys and Avery, and I count among my close acquaintances in those days Tom Gummer and Colin McIver from Dolamore's, Harry Waugh from Harveys, and Ronald Avery himself. We once stayed in Ronald's flat in Bristol: it was filled with sample bottles of wine – in the kitchen, the living room, the bedroom, the bathroom, and there were a dozen small bottles on the windowsill of the lavatory. Ronald kept urging us to sail with him to Brittany; he would provide the boat and the booze, I was to show him the megaliths. It would have been a marvellous and vinous occasion but, alas, it never happened.

Tom Gummer and Colin McIver were our main advisers and there have been more occasions than I care to remember when I have tottered away from a Baker Street Dolamore lunch. Colin McIver had kept wicket for Essex in his earlier years and he was deeply attached to Ruth, not only for herself but because she had been Captain of the Oxford University Women's Cricket Eleven. This he found tremendously exciting – a highly intelligent attractive woman who was also a cricketer! On his visits each term to Cambridge he always reserved one day to lunch with us. On one occasion I served blind a Mouton d'Armailacq '47 which I had got from Matthews the grocers in Trinity Street. 'What's this, my boy?' he said. 'It's marvellous.' I told him what it was, that Matthews had twenty dozen, and the price they were offering it to me. 'Buy the lot,' he said, 'and if you don't like it in a year's time, Dolamore's will take it from you.' I went nervously to the telephone and bought the lot: a wine that was most appreciated in the College over the next three years.

Dolamore's endeared themselves to generations of Oxford and Cambridge dons by organizing a box at Lords during the Oxford v. Cambridge match, and my memory of summers in the forties and fifties is enriched by those long, lovely, languid days at Lords where so many amusing and entertaining characters from both universities met under such agreeable conditions. Wine flowed from the start of play to well after closing time and a delicious buffet lunch was served. Cricket was watched by most, but by no means all. Enid Starkie, always in bright scarlet from beret to shoes, arranged herself with her back to the pitch. With a cigarette in a long holder, looking like a substantial ghost from the twenties, she would say, clutching a glass of champagne, 'I'm here for the booze, dear boy, and the company'. Ruth, and Denys Page, Regius Professor of Greek at Cambridge and in his day no mean bowler, steadfastly enjoyed both forms of entertainment.

The Gummers and Colin McIver presided gently over these fine occasions and all their friends looked forward to the next Lord's match. When in Oxford Colin always stayed with his old friend J.C. Masterman and it was here, resting before dinner on a sofa in the President's Lodgings at Worcester, that he died; my second detective story, *Welcome Death*, had slipped out of his hands.

It was the Lord's cricket lunches that introduced us to so many new friends: such as Michael McLagan, who subsequently wrote for me a book on *Constantinople*, and Denys and Katie Page, whom we were to get to know very well. I was at a Royal Academy banquet and Denys, then Master of Jesus, was there and offered me a place in his car home. I think I was Rik Wheeler's guest; eventually we found Denys knocking back large glasses of whisky. 'There is only one way of leaving a Royal Academy banquet,' he said. 'Drunk.' We tottered down the stairs to our waiting car and I thought, agreeably, a long sleep, and the next thing I shall know is being shovelled out of the car at my front door. Nothing of the kind. 'I am at my best,' said Denys, 'on these occasions,' and talked brilliantly all the two hours back to Cambridge about every subject under the sun from Homer and Troy to truffles and wine. He stopped the driver halfway home so that, he said, we could have a pee. He produced a flask of whisky and two containers from his pocket. 'I thought we needed a little topping up, my boy,' he said. We got back into the car. Then he turned to me, 'Now let me tell you my view of Blegen's work at Troy'.

I remember most our wine contacts with the Heidsiecks in Rheims, the Hennessys and Martells in Cognac, Louis Latour in Burgundy, and many in the Bordeaux area such as the Cruse, Kressmann, and Calvet families; and that tremendous day when we tasted first-growth clarets in the morning, lunched at Langon off lampreys, tasted Château d'Yquem in the afternoon, drank pink St Emilion champenoise and ate macaroons on the terrace above St Emilion at six and dined at Les Eyzies. We were young in those days.

One day we were summoned to lunch by the Hennessy family in Cognac and it was excellent. The boss of the firm had been an undergraduate at Clare and we had much to talk about. We retired to our hotel beds at three-thirty, promising ourselves a *croque monsieur* and a glass of Perrier later. The telephone rang at four. It was the Hennessys. An aircraft-load of whisky merchants from Scotland had just arrived. The brandy merchants were giving them dinner: it was essential we should be there to help entertain them. It was all part of a great financial deal of exchanging whisky and brandy. The car would be at the door of our hotel at seven o'clock.

It was a magnificent occasion and by the strangest chance, one of the Scottish delegation had been an undergraduate in St John's. We tottered uncertainly to our beds well after midnight. As we left the hotel the following morning the hall porter said, 'Don't forget this case,' and he put in the boot of my car a dozen bottles of Napoleon brandy with a note on it saying, 'Come again. Business is brisk'.

I greatly enjoyed the special duty of planning and organizing feasts although the most difficult job which I did in consultation with the President and Master was the seating plans for these occasions of 150 to 250, remembering who did not speak to whom, and who was completely deaf on one side; and then later on the problem when Fellows' wives were invited to special dinners – some wives would only come if they were sitting next to their husbands, others only if they were placed as far as possible away from them.

I append here the menu for the 6 May 1952 dinner which I regard as one of my more successful efforts.

Gjëtost
Smoked Cod's Roe
Château de Nozet, 1948

***

Terrine St Jean
Tavel Rosé, 1947

*

Boiled Tay Salmon
Prawn Butter
Meursault, 1947

*

Le Saupiquet Montbardois

*

Roast Duckling
New potatoes   Green peas
Orange and watercress salad
Pommard, 1947

*

Asperges Mousseline

*

Fraises au Porto
Hot Apple Pie
Irroy, 1945

*

Mrs Raffald's Whet

***

Dessert   Café
Cockburn, 1927
Château Lafite, 1934

Ruth's nephew and godson, Richard Langhorne, who was Steward of St John's from 1974 to 1979, and a most successful one, unearthed College feast menus for a quarter and a half century before mine of

1952, and I print them here as a matter of general interest. Alas, no wines were printed on the menu or given in a Feast Book. It will be seen that the great difference between the 1877/1927 menus and the menus of the period 1939 to the present day is that there were alternatives to all the main courses: indeed the main course in the 1877 Feast had five dishes to choose from: and what I find interesting is that *after* one of these dishes one was offered Roast Duckling or Cold Lobster. Incidentally the cost of the 1877 Feast was ten shillings a head, including wine!

1 8 7 7

Potage Jardinière aux quenelles
Potage à la Reine

*

Saumon sauces persil et tartare
Blanchailles

*

Croquettes de turbot à la crême
Blanquette de volaille aux truffes
Cotelettes de Mouton sautés à la Financière

*

Quartier de devant d'agneau
Poulets nouveaux à la Béchamel
Jambon sauce madère
Hanche de Mouton
Aloyau de boeuf rôti

*

Canetons rôtis sauce aux Pommes
Aspic d'homard sauce mayonnaise

*

Pouding Victoria
Crême Diplomate à la d'Orléans
Gêlée de fraises au Marasquin
Glace panaché

*

Dessert

1 9 2 7

Pamplemousses au kirsch

*

Consommé hongrois
Potage Romeo

*

Darne de saumon, sauce matelote blanche
Mayonnaise d'homard

*

Perdreau blanc aux olives
Petits-pois

*

Selle de mouton
Chapon à la piémontaise
Haricots verts   Choux de mer
Pommes nouvelles   Pommes rôties

*

Croûtes Maréchal
Pâté de groseilles vertes

*

Crême glacée aux mille fruits

*

Croustades à la Roquefort

*

Dessert

I was, as I have already said, exceptionally fortunate in the main
members of my staff: Sadler the kitchen manager with Dring his head
chef; Ken North the accountant; Ward the butler and head waiter,
whom many took for the original of the famous Kensitas advertisement; and Ralph Thoday, the head gardener. During the war and the
rigours of rationing and black-outs the imperturbable Sadler maintained the College kitchens at a high standard, serving not only the
Fellows and the few graduates and undergraduates who were up, but
the airmen of part of an RAF training wing which was billeted on us.

Ralph Thoday was one of the most remarkable and interesting men I have ever had to deal with. Had his education been different he would have made a fascinating don, a professor of horticulture somewhere as, indeed, his son Peter is on the way to being.

In my time as Steward he not only looked after the College grounds and ornamental gardens which were the responsibility of the Junior Bursar but also seventeen acres of kitchen gardens which came under me. They comprised the gardener's house, extensive outbuildings and greenhouses, a vinery, a large fruit store, orchards, vegetable and fruit gardens and a piggery. These the College has now given up.

Mr Thoday began exhibiting on behalf of the College at the Royal Horticultural Society's show in 1932, and in that very first trial of strength was awarded first prize for Allington Pippin, second prize for Bramley's Seedling, and two third prizes – one for Brussels sprouts and one for Cox's Orange Pippin. The record of prizes from then on is a most remarkable one. In 1935 he won first prize for Brussels sprouts at the Royal Horticultural Society's show and on this occasion the *Daily Telegraph* published this agreeable and amusing verse:

> We Johnians love our Tudor rose;
> and now with gladsome shouts
> Though Oxford rear its verdant greens
> We hail our Brussels sprouts.

Mr Thoday still vividly remembers his own apprentice days. 'I gained my first experience,' he has written, 'by sweat, blood and tears; in those days sweat was considered necessary; blood came from scratches, cuts and chilblains. My first job was weeding a frozen path with a pocket knife. Tears came readily when mistakes were found out. The fear of the sack was always a cloud through which the hot sun pierced. The dread of dismissal without a "character" was the goad to improvement. In those days heavy premiums were demanded by head gardeners for apprentices; consequently to get into good establishments was difficult for any youth without means.' He regretted the circumstances which have caused the eclipse of the large country houses of England, which, in his opinion, were better training places for rural and domestic economy than the centres we have today.

What manner of man was he, this head gardener? Here is his own picture of himself, characteristically terse and frank: 'Of a morbid nature, meeting trouble half-way, though obtaining some results, his garden is very untidy, and badly managed; could have achieved nothing without the constant help and advice of his wife.' And here is mine: a man of the greatest integrity and charm, hard-working and resourceful, who suffers fools with difficulty – and incompetent bunglers not at all – and whose bark is sometimes so loud that you are deafened to the fact that the bite which follows is either non-existent or well-deserved.

My predecessors in the office of Steward have included some very distinguished men: Bateson, Blackman, Brindley, Cunningham, Briggs – three of them Fellows of the Royal Society.

When I was made Steward in 1946, Mr F.F. Blackman wrote to me wishing me well, and expressing the hope that I would have an easier time at the hands of the Fellows than he had had. Blackman was Steward for six years from 1908 to 1914: he succeeded William Bateson when the latter was elected Professor of Biology in 1908, and was succeeded by H.H. Brindley. Recently Mrs Blackman found some interesting letters and papers belonging to her late husband's days as Steward, and has very kindly allowed their publication. The first letter is from T.G. Bonney the geologist, and is splendidly characteristic of his forthrightness.

26.iii.09
9 Scroope Terrace
Cambridge

Dear Steward,

I wish you would impress upon the College cook that unless he brings the standard of cookery for the Fellows' table to the level of a household where they give a female from five and twenty to thirty pounds a year, there will be 'reactions' – if I can get any to back me. To take yesterday's dinner for an example. It began with what he calls Scotch Broth – a coarsely flavoured compound full of little bits of insipid meat – I wish my cook, who is a Scotch woman, could give him a lesson. With the meat, the grated potatoes were 'sopped', as they have been for some days past – and in the next course the 'Sherry Jelly' was tasteless – just the stuff which would be bought from a grocer in a glass bottle. I am sure, so far away was any vinous flavour, a Rechabite might have eaten it.

I do not want a more luxurious dinner than we have, quite the reverse; but I do object to getting bad dishes for good money in consequence of a servant's sloth, negligence or rapacity.

Yours very truly,
T.G. Bonney

Blackman was away when this letter was penned by Bonney and did not receive it until he returned to London. He sat down in the Royal Societies Club to answer Bonney's complaints, and kept a draft of his reply. Here it is:

Royal Societies Club,
St James's Street, S.W.
19 Ap. 09

Dear Bonney,

Returning from a trip to the other end of the continent during which I have eaten meals in some ten countries of Europe with my digestion unimpeded by pursuant letters, I find your complaint awaiting me.

I know that the dinners run downhill in vacation time and I hope to find the explanation and prevent it. Something must be allowed for differences of palate. I and many others think 'Scotch broth' is an uncommonly good soup. Jellies I never take but will look into the matter and transfer some of your protest to the person of the cook when I come up.

Yours very truly,
F. Blackman

All Stewards, past and present, will appreciate the delightful restraint and firmness of the phrase 'my digestion unimpeded by pursuant letters'. But this did not stop the letters which continued to pursue Blackman. On Sunday, 13 June 1909 the following dinner was served to the Fellows:

Potage à la reine

*

Salmon Mayonnaise

*

Roast lamb

Cold chicken and tongue

French salad

Potatoes   Spinach

*

Cold Leeds pudding

Hot and cold cherry pie

This did not satisfy Bonney who pleads not for luxury but for 'careful performance'. He sent the menu with the following covering letter:

June 14th, 1909
9, Scroope Terrace,
Cambridge

Dear Steward,

Would it not be possible to get the cook to pay a little more attention to the Sunday dinner than to that of weekdays, because that is the day on which 'weekenders' are present and one wishes a good impression of the College to be produced – not of luxury but of careful performance. I enclose that of yesterday as an example of what I mean. I presume it was planned on Saturday, but it has, except for the kind of soup, a dominant note of 'coldness'; though the thermometer then was abnormally low. White soups should be barred on Sundays, for those made in our kitchen are about on the level of what you would get at a second or third class hotel. I gave up taking them some time ago, because they were so bad. Then the green vegetable was spinach. When this is sent, there should be an alternative, for so many actually dislike it – just as some like it very much.

These are small matters, but they produce the impression of negligence; and the result of a year's observation after I returned, was that a kind of 'slouch' had notably pervaded the domestic as contrasted with the educational departments of the College.

Yours sincerely,
T.G. Bonney

There was obviously a friendly exchange of letters, but Bonney is writing again at the end of the month, pressing for special attention to be paid to the Sunday evening dinner. The postscript explains why no menu was included this time.

30.VI.09
9 Scroope Terrace
Cambridge

My dear Steward,

I am sorry again to trouble you, after your friendly answers to my complaint, but I enclose the menu of last Sunday's dinner. Again a white soup which I took care to taste and found of the usual second class hotel type, though I must admit some grated cheese was served, which, for those who like that condiment, served to disguise its defects. Then he sends up his worst and most tasteless entrée, a chicken omlette [*sic*]. *Omlette au jambon* is good, and so is that *aux herbes*, but that which our cook delights in is the flavourless seasoned by the insipid. Fortunately there were no guests. Had I brought one I should have been ashamed. It is, I believe, really important that special care should be given to the Sunday dinner, so that it may become a habit to bring a few guests. Neglect of such matters has, I know, done much to pull down the College and attention to them in small matters will help to pull it up. Nil mihi reseritas attamen ipse 'rebuke'.

yours very truly
T.G. Bonney

P.S. The confusion of private papers due to press of examination work, which has delayed the writing of this, has made the menu vanish.

No further letters from Bonney were kept by Blackman. The only other thing he preserved with these letters was a menu from 1914. Here it is with four annotations: the annotations were by T.R. Glover and are reprinted here without comment.

Brunoise Soup

*

Fried Sole[1]   Lemon Sauce

Saddle of Mutton[4]
Roast Fillet of Veal[2]   Bacon
Potatoes   Cauliflower

*

Black Cap Pudding[3]
Stewed Pears and Cream[4]

Friday, May 22

1 No flavour
2 Generally refused
3 Served tepid
4 Supply ran out

Brindley was succeeded by Ebenezer Cunningham who took on the office only on condition he did not have to deal with a Fellows' committee. When Briggs succeeded Cunningham he, too, did the Stewardship without the doubtful benefit of a committee, and I inherited the office, committee free, and, perhaps it was the war, but by the forties and fifties there was far less passing of sharp letters. George Briggs was fond of telling the story of how one night at dinner in Hall he received a note from Harker, eminent geologist, saying, 'Why has the Steward the effrontery to serve plaice described as sole?' Briggs got a sheet of paper and made two anatomical drawings, one labelled sole, the other plaice, and sent them along the table to Harker with a note saying he was surprised than an eminent geologist did not know the difference between sole and plaice. Harker was furious and never spoke to the Steward again.

While I was spared a committee of Fellows I had to deal with a committee of undergraduates and this kitchen committee met every Saturday morning at ten. In the immediately post-war years this committee was full of young men who had been majors and colonels running army messes. They expressed themselves forcibly, many of their suggestions were good and many of their complaints were helpful. There was one occasion when they thought they had really caught us out and I too was horrified – I thought they had. I received a furious note from the senior undergraduate member of the committee asking me to explain why I had been deceiving them and serving rooks as chicken. He enclosed a label marked 'Frozen Rooks' which he said he had found on a case in the Kitchen Lane. I carried the label down to

287

the kitchen manager and said, 'Mr Sadler, what is the meaning of this?' To my great relief, he burst out laughing and explained that Pettits of Reedham, from whom we bought our chickens and game, had had so many cases of these stolen that they had decided to label them 'Frozen Rooks' and 'Frozen Badgers' – to the discomfiture of thieves, and also my kitchen committee!

Then there was the curious affair of the cockroaches. Agitated and incensed undergraduates declared they had seen large cockroaches scuttling about under the stoves in the kitchens, and then one black beetle appeared on an undergraduate's plate at dinner. I thought this was an easy problem to deal with: I knew nothing about cockroaches but my works of reference said they were harmless, but infested kitchens. I determined they should not infest my kitchens, but when I mentioned my plan to my predecessor, George Briggs, he said, 'Good God, you can't do that. Consult Clifford Evans and Brindley.' Clifford was a botanist contemporary of mine as a Fellow and Brindley was a zoologist as well as former Steward. 'Ah,' they said, 'let me assure you this is not the American *Periplaneta*; it is *Blatta* and is harmless, but what is important is that we appear to have in the college kitchens a special variant of *Blatta* and every year we collect them for undergraduates to study. It would be in the worst interests of scientific teaching to destroy our Johnian kitchen cockroaches!'

I cancelled the visit of a pesticide man and braced myself to tell my undergraduate kitchen committee that they were the proud owners of very special *Blatta*. They took it well; after the Frozen Rooks and the cockroaches I seemed to have with me an understanding kitchen committee.

The kitchen gardens, as we have seen, included a small farm where pigs were kept. When I took over the Stewardship in 1946 I asked how many of the pigs were used for food in College: I was told none – they were all sold for the general good. Then I remembered that most RAF and other service messes in the war had pig clubs. Could I, I wondered, turn our pig farm into a pig club for the benefit of the College? There was a long correspondence with the local pig controller at Ware and St John's College was registered as a pig club, and for years until the end of rationing we were able to enjoy our own pork – but only half of it: the rest went to the state, and when I signed forms for killing pigs they always said two half-pigs.

But we got good pork every so often and the complaining

undergraduates were surprised and nonplussed when it said on their menus 'Roast Pork by courtesy of the College Pig Club'. 'What is this?' they said, at a Saturday morning kitchen committee. I explained to them and said, 'Do you know who the adviser to the Pig Club is? A frozen rook.'

The St John's College Pig Club was founded on 4 September 1946 under the auspices of the Small Pig Keepers Council (Incorporated): it had to have members who were allegedly involved in the care of the pigs. The original membership was Martin Charlesworth as chairman, myself as secretary, Ken North, the kitchen accountant, as treasurer, and ten Fellows and members of the College staff. We met once a year, we inspected our pigs frequently, I as Steward every fortnight; and we all remember the astonishing pig telegram of 7 May 1954 at 5.45 p.m., just as we were settling down to an undergraduate feast: 'Casualty Pig Condemned Dropsical and Unfit. Bacchus, Slaughterhouse Manager.' We had already arranged a pork dish in the undergraduate feast. 'What shall we do?' said Mr Sadler. 'Nothing,' I said. 'But tell me at noon tomorrow how many undergraduates complain of being dropsical and unfit. I suggest,' I said, 'that the *Sauce Robert* is very generous.'

When meat rationing ended in 1954 the Pig Club ceased to have any necessary existence, but at its meeting on 14 November 1953 it gave 'some consideration to retaining the Pig Club as a club although the purpose for which it came into existence would have ceased.'

I cannot now remember whether it was I, or H.A. Harris, or Norman Jopson who said, 'Let's keep on the Pig Club as a splendid anomaly'. It think it was probably me in an extravagant moment, but ably supported by Harris and Jopson and by John Crook. An extraordinary general meeting was summoned for 11 June 1954 and I quote the account of that meeting from *The Eagle*: a good example of non-pedantic donnery.

The business before the meeting was 'arrangements for winding up the Club necessitated by the end of meat rationing', and the notice of the meeting went on to say: 'It is hoped that the meeting will not take more than a quarter of an hour, and at 12.15 the President and Chairman has kindly invited all members of the Club to a farewell reception at which products of the pig will be served. . . . At 12.30 Professor H.A. Harris will make a short speech on "The Place of the

8. THE PIG CLUB ANTHEM

Set to the tune of 'Goshen', or 'Summer Suns are Glowing',
by Robin Orr, *Keeper of the Pig's Music*,
1955

The Pig Club Anthem, by Robin Orr.

Pig in Human History" and propose the health of the Club.' But before the meeting of the Club the following was received signed by Mr Farmer and Mr Crook, two faithful and energetic members of the Club: 'It being customary in matters of University business to circulate a fly-sheet when changes are under consideration, we consider it appropriate to circulate a pig-sheet. . . . We think it desirable that the Club, far from being wound up, should continue its existence as a society for convivial purposes (there being in our view abundant precedent in the University for bodies – such as Colleges – which continue in existence although the original purpose of their foundation has been lost sight of). It would indeed be a valuable historical exercise for posterity to illuminate the origins of a Club with so peculiar a title.' For these reasons Mr Farmer and Mr Crook gave notice that they would *non-placet* the winding up of the Club.

The meeting endorsed their view, and, by a joint resolution of the President, Secretary and the two Pig-sheeters, decided that the Club, 'should continue in existence for social and unspecified purposes as a glorious anomaly'. Professor Harris then gave his address and spoke eloquently and with characteristic charm and directness about pigs, the origin of agriculture, Vergil, sausages, salami, King's College Chapel, Egypt, cosmetics, cowrie shells, missionaries, and civilization. Professor Jopson then pronounced the word 'pig' in all known (and several unknown) European languages and it was resolved that this should be done at all meetings of the Club. Maupygernons and wine were then served.

And so the Pig Club still exists and will continue, so long as the University of Cambridge does, as an association of Fellows and college servants: it meets three times a year and the summer meeting in the Wilderness is a very good occasion with ladies and guests.

Robin Orr wrote the Pig Club Anthem which we reproduce. In 1963 we had a splendid letter in verse from Sir Joseph Hutchinson regretting that he could not be with us: it was written from the Sudan Hotel, Khartoum.

> Dear Mr Secretary,
> Alas! That I have to decline
> The fruits of the pig and the vine;
> For no man's a glutton
> On Nubian mutton.
> And Muslims don't offer you wine.

And then curiously the accidental nature of the Pig Club made many of us think about the discrepancy between dons and servants. I was made to have a long talk with H.A. Harris as a result of which he set up a fund 'for the relief of poverty among present and past members of the College assistant staff and their families', and he prescribed that 'the persons who are for the time being respectively Master and Senior Bursar of the College, together with whoever happens to be secretary of the College Pig Club, should have complete and unfettered discretion in the application of the capital and income of the Fund'.

The 1939–45 war was a great testing time for College Stewards and kitchen managers: my predecessor, George Briggs, and the kitchen manager we shared came out of it all with flying colours. There were three reasons for Mr Sadler's trials and worries. The first and most obvious one was rationing; undergraduates who during and after the war realized the restrictions and exigencies of rationing at home and in hotels, seemed often curiously unaware that the same problems existed in college life. The second difficulty in St John's was that part of an RAF initial training wing occupied New Court and had to be fed in Hall – at first without any cooking staff from the service. Over a quarter of a million meals were prepared by the college kitchens for the RAF during the war by a staff that was constantly being depleted. Mr Sadler did everything: he was cook, stoker, boilerman, bottle-washer; he kept the kitchens going and preserved the traditions of College cooking and service. The third reason was, of course, the black-out.

The buildings to the south of the Kitchen Lane had been built as an annexe to the main kitchens (dating from the sixteenth century) in the 1890s, and at the same time the height of the kitchens had been increased for purposes of ventilation by taking in a set of rooms formerly occupied by William Wordsworth and approached by E Staircase, First Court.

When Mr Sadler and I, together with our architects, came to discuss in detail the modernization of the kitchens it became clear that Kitchen Lane would have to be closed and that, in the fifties, it was no longer necessary to have a high kitchen for ventilation – this could be done by extractor plants. The College Council approved our schemes and in 1952 Kitchen Lane was closed, a single unit kitchen built from the screens to the wall between ourselves and Trinity and the roof of the kitchen brought down to its old original level. As a result of this, Wordsworth's old set appeared again as a physical entity; but was extended and refurbished as a Wordsworth Room for private dinner parties and entertainments, with direct access by lift and stairs to the kitchens below: no longer a nook obscure.

More interesting than the reconstruction of the kitchen fabric and equipment in the post-war years was the reconstruction of the kitchen traditions of cooking and eating: although at first a kitchen manager and Steward were cabined and confined by rationing and had to improvise with soya-like sausages and whale-meat. The Pig Club, of course, helped and gradually we came back to some semblance of pre-war days, but at normal High Table we never went back to the traditional five-course dinner. As rationing ended, the controlling factor in planning food for undergraduates was money. It must always be difficult to plan varied and interesting food on an institutional basis when large numbers have to be served in a short period of time, and the cost of the meal kept down as low as possible. It is inevitable that a low-price lunch should frequently feature meat-loaf, rissoles and sausage and mash.

It was forecast by some that after the war we would see the disappearance of formal dinner in Hall. After my time my successors introduced a self-service cafeteria which serves inexpensive meals quickly and cheaply but this has not killed the custom of dining in Hall: there is now agreeably the choice of two worlds to everyone's benefit.

The planning of feasts, private dinners and special entertainments was the really enjoyable part of being a Steward and brought me in close, profitable and most agreeable association with Mr Sadler, although to the end of our professional life together he could not bring himself to approve of my refusal to print menus entirely in menu French when there were no native French words for English dishes. He also regarded the footnotes which I began to append to feast menus as a rather dubious eccentricity – as indeed did many of my colleagues. Menu French is, of course, one of the bugbears of English catering: few people go so far as the *Pouding à la Yorkshire* of many a story, but Welsh Rabbit, which suffers so often with the false name of Welsh Rarebit (an unhappy solecism), was found by me on the menu of the French restaurant of the Midland Hotel in Manchester as *Croûte Galloise*.

In my view dishes should be listed on menus in the language of their country of origin and I regard it as right, proper and honest to have a menu which says *Gaspacho, Baked Cromer Crab, Wiener Schnitzel, Stilton Cheese, Zabaglione.*

George Briggs tells a good story about the time when some dons of the College were so infuriated by bogus menu French that they asked that menus should always be in English. This, of course, is equally as stupid as writing menus always in French, but Briggs knew this, he bided his time, solemnly putting everything into English until one night when *fonds d'artichauts farcis* appeared on the High Table menu as *stuffed artichoke bottoms*, even the most rabid anti-menu-French don was compelled to recognize that some things are better in their language of origin. Which brings me to think that I have, perhaps, been irrational in continuing to call that delectable dish, of disputed origin, *crème brûlée*: it is not, as we have seen, a French dish; perhaps we should rename it burnt stone cream.

I heard so often about the St John's Christmas feasts of olden days and one day Edward Rapson gave me a personal account of what happened: he remembered them well. Rapson was born in 1861 and became a Fellow of St John's in 1887, nearly a hundred years ago. He went as a boy to Hereford Cathedral School and had a wide and lifelong interest in music. He knew well Samuel Butler, author of *Erewhon* and *The Way of all Flesh*, who was up at St John's 1854–58. Rapson told me the story of how Butler said to him that he could not stand modern music and when asked what he particularly had in mind, he said 'Beethoven'. I was proud and happy to know Rapson, if only slightly; he had written *Ancient India from the Earliest Times to the First Century A.D.*, published in 1914, the year of my birth; and had edited the first volume of the *Cambridge History of India*, which appeared in 1922. He died *felix opportunitate* (as his obituary in *The Eagle* says) suddenly and painlessly on Sunday, 3 October 1937; he collapsed while dining at High Table and was assisted out by H.A. Harris and another Fellow and died in the ante-room. I was sitting at the BAs' table and as Harris and his burden passed we all stood up.

Rapson had explained to me that the old Christmas feast went on for twelve days and was a way of bringing friends and co-authors up to Cambridge for a few days of cooperation and discussion of books and articles they were writing together. Every day began with breakfast in the Combination Room from 9 a.m. onwards: it was a very large and varied affair. Then Fellows and their guests separated to write, read and talk; they came together for dinner at 5 p.m. and dinner was over by 7 to 7.30 p.m. Then there was conversation, cards (mainly whist), chess, until at 10 p.m. there was brought in a cold collation of boar's head, turkey, foie gras and other delicacies with a special cold punch.

Those were leisurely but stimulating days. The twelve-day feast at St John's has now become just one day for Fellows – only on 27 December, St John's Night.

Towards the end of my stewardship there was a discussion in the House of Commons about food, about catering in the House and about the decay of English traditions of cooking. Someone commented on the fact that nowadays no one ate lovely things like maupygernons. 'What,' Mr Sadler asked me on reading the reports of this discussion, 'are maupygernons? They sound like some of the funny things you make us cook on Wednesday nights.' I had no idea but did a little research and found several good recipes for this medieval and Tudor dish which is nothing more than spiced balls made of fresh pork. The word, by the way, is an old English one, *Maupygyrcheons*, or urchins, or pig's belly urchins: my authority is that excellent historian of food, Dorothy Hartley, in her *Food in England* (1954). Apparently maupygernons were last served at the Coronation Banquet of Charles II: the King refused to eat them.

I got the kitchens to make me maupygernons, colouring some of the balls gold and others red, as was the old custom, and a dish of these gaily coloured meat balls was served at the next meeting of the Pig Club. They were delicious and afterwards we served them once or twice at dinner in Hall. Discussing all this afterwards Mr Sadler burst out laughing and said, 'For all their high-falutin' name and the mystery about them, there's nothing mysterious really – they are just very good sausages without skins.' I, too, laughed and said, 'Do you think we should have less complaints from undergraduates if occasionally instead of sausages and mash we put maupygernons and mash on the menu, and instead of meat pie we put Mr Pickwick's pie?' 'I don't think so,' was his wise answer looking back on long years of dealing with undergraduates and dons. 'The undergraduate likes standard things when he is lunching or dining in Hall, and will only try out new and interesting things in his private dinners.' 'And the dons?' I asked. He smiled, 'They don't have any choice, do they?' he said. 'You give them what you think they should have. All they can do is sack their Steward.'

It is most important that from time to time there should be a change in the stewardship of a College. If a Steward is a good one he will make his contribution in five to ten years: if he is a bad one, he ought to be got rid of in under five years. I was happy to give up my Stewardship after nearly ten years knowing that it had been part hard and unrewarding work, such as dealing with undergraduate complaints and staff wages, and part easy and rewarding work like planning feasts and buying wine. But that is what a College Steward's job is – sausages and mash, maupygernons and Muscadet.

When I made my last annual report to the governing body of the College and my successor was appointed, I was astonished and so were my colleagues, when Claude Guillebaud got up and made a speech thanking me for my stewardship and adding: 'The College will well remember your Wednesday evenings.' And I was delighted when *The Eagle*, the College magazine, in an amusing feature called 'Who's Who in St John's' printed this entry:

> Glyn, Duc de Camembert, Marquis of Alexandra Palace, Earl of Lyonesse, Vicomte de Veau Rôti, Baron Stonehenge, Chevalier of the Légion de Bonheur (deuxième classe), Steward of the Stilton Hundreds, Gentleman of the Chamber Tomb, Companion of the Most Distinguished Order of the Scholars' Buttery (and Bar).

And a colleague wrote to me saying, 'Here is your epitaph as Steward: he created the Wordsworth Room, the College Bar, the Pig Club and revived maupygernons – and enjoyed doing so.'

CHAPTER TEN

Travelling antiquary

I TRAVELLED ALL ROUND England and Wales when I was making the survey for my PhD thesis that eventually became *The Prehistoric Chamber Tombs of England and Wales*. Then in the years 1937–9 I travelled quite extensively in France. The war years gave me remarkable opportunities for travel in Africa and in India. When I settled down after the war as a don in Cambridge I thought that perhaps my major travelling days were over. Not at all.

I enjoyed the opportunity of visiting many countries through British Council and other tours. My first was to Finland in February 1958. The aircraft to Helsinki had been deflected to north Germany because Copenhagen airport was out of action: we arrived in Helsinki at 3 a.m. It was bitterly cold; I drove in a taxi to the Palace Hotel along roads three or four feet deep with packed frozen snow. The road along the harbour was so covered with hummocky snow and ice that the taxi could not get to the front door of the hotel. I had to walk the last two hundred yards lugging my suitcase and my lantern slides and slithered uncertainly to the front door. My bedroom was warm but I couldn't see out of the windows: they were completely blocked by drifts of snow.

Francis King, novelist and short-story writer, was the assistant British Council representative in Finland at the time and he took me in hand next morning, as did Dennis Arundell, the actor, composer and producer, who had been a Fellow of my College 1923–9, and was producing an opera in Helsinki. I was equipped with a fur hat, pads for my ears, and pills to keep me awake in the late afternoon and early evening. These were necessary as I found when I began to tour the country: the usual routine was a large meal with drinks about 5 p.m. and I was expected to lecture and engage in discussions until 9 o'clock when there were more potions and food.

I travelled around extensively by train, car and plane – my first experience of flying in an aircraft with skis rather than wheels. I went up to the Russian frontier and looked across. Each day I was asked, 'Have you yet tried our sauna?' I found myself with a spare morning in the amusingly named town of Lappenranta where the nomadic Lapps had traded with the settled villagers, and fixed a sauna session. I went nervously down to the basement and was met by an old crone who pointed to a cubicle and gave me a towel. I undressed and emerged with a towel neatly wound around me. She led me into the sauna chamber, snatched my towel away with a high cackle and indicated I was to lie down on one of the slatted shelves. I thought it was too hot and that I would emerge marked like a grilled steak, but I had to grin and bear it. After a few minutes she came back, told me to stand in the corner and turned an ice-cold shower on me. This process of boiling and freezing was repeated four times and in between she beat me lightly with a bunch of twigs. I retired to my bedroom exhausted but in half an hour felt amazingly refreshed. The next time I was asked, I was able to reply, 'Yes, I have had sauna'. I have had sauna baths many times since and in the last thirty years they have certainly become a common feature of English life, but that first experience with the old lady in Lappenranta was memorable.

I lectured in English, of course, and found the Finns spoke and understood English well. Sometimes there were curious turns of phrase; when I was leaving the country I was asked, 'Are there many families in England eagerly awaiting your return?'

I have two vivid memories of Helsinki: the Academic Bookstore with its huge department of English books, and going to see the Olympic ski-jumping. We were warned not to take off our pyjamas when we got up but to use them as a warm undergarment and then put on everything we could find. It was bitterly cold at the site of the ski-jump and the crowds looked like stuffed owls except for the gaily dressed Lapps. As the day wore on the circulation in our feet needed attention and slowly we all began to stamp until in the late afternoon the surrounding hills reverberated with the noise of the stamping thousands. The beauty of the event helped us to forget the cold; the diminutive Japanese came in for special applause.

Afterwards we went to President Kekkonen's farm and were revived with food and drink. I was shown the farm and only then realized that the livestock was indoors for three-quarters of the year and out in the snow-free fields for only a few months. The large byres were filled with horses, sheep, cows and pigs and the sweet smell of the cattle pervaded everything. As a result of their long months indoors the animals were all very tame and the cows licked my hands.

Of the Finnish food I remember reindeer tongues and the Arctic air-berries. I remember, too, that the state-licensed drink shops were called *Alcoholilikki* and that people, other than foreigners, were allowed to buy liquor only on Fridays. I was told that every Friday drinking parties of men were organized but that one man had each Friday to practise total abstinence in order to deliver his intoxicated colleagues back to their houses and flats. On one occasion, unable to get an answer, a driver had propped his friend up against the front door. Next morning there was no trace of him. It was thought that he had slumped down and disappeared under five feet of snow. 'I am afraid this happens from time to time,' said my informant. 'There is nothing that can be done but wait for the thaw. Then the police will have to decide what to do. Leaving someone out in the freezing cold with sub-zero temperatures is a serious offence – manslaughter.'

I went back to England via Sweden, Norway and Denmark, and it was my first experience of Stockholm and Copenhagen and Oslo. I have often been in those countries since, particularly in Denmark. On one visit to Stockholm I lectured to the Anglo-Swedish Friendship Society and the then king, Gustav Adolphus, was present, as well as Princess Margrethe of Denmark, his granddaughter. The king was a very keen archaeologist and we talked about all sorts of archaeological matters, especially Carbon-14 dating. Emboldened, I told him that J.M. de Navarro always recounted the story of how, as a young man, the king was excavating with the great Swedish archaeologist, Oskar Montelius, and one day Montelius said to him, 'Young man, you would make a very good archaeologist if you didn't have another job to go to'. Was this tale true, I asked, as I was now repeating it in my lectures? He paused for a while and said, 'I must confess, Daniel, I do not remember the occasion, but then I am an old man. If I were you I would keep it in your lectures.' He was a very kind and generous man; he paid for the first C-14 laboratory in Stockholm out of his private purse and created and endowed the museum of eastern and Indian arts. Ruth and I said we were disappointed this museum was closed during our visit. 'I will see that it is specially open for you tomorrow morning,' he said; and it was.

Shortly after the war, the British Council had the good sense and imagination to invite to England twenty continental archaeologists who had naturally no chance to visit us during the war years. The meeting took place mainly in Salisbury and was organized by Stuart

Piggott and Richard Atkinson. (There is a photograph of the group in Stuart Piggott's Retrospect article in *Antiquity*, 1983.) The group included four Danish archaeologists, two Belgians and three Dutch. Among the Dutch was that enchanting character van Giffen, head of the Biological-Archaeological Institut at Groningen, who himself did so much remarkable work in Dutch prehistory. He spoke good English but had many amusing mis-remembered phrases: he referred to the megalithic tomb called Kits Coty House in Kent as Cats Kitty Hole and entertained us by describing how he had had a car accident and been thrown out of the car and over a hedge. 'How do you describe it in English?' he asked, 'I was salt-a-somerset and into a field.' It ranks in my mind as an amusing example of off-English with the statement of Professor Pia Laviosa-Zambotti who appeared at the breakfast table at a conference in Spain, clutching her throat and declaring, 'I am having trouble with my tomkins'.

The four Danish archaeologists at the British Council Salisbury Conference stayed as my guests in St John's College on their way across England and I have cultivated their friendship over the years, particularly that of Carl-Johan Becker. On my first return to Denmark, Becker was still in the first division of the Danish National Museum: the director of the Museum was then Johannes Brønsted, that elegant and kindly gentleman. Brønsted once insisted that I came on the annual summer expedition of the Société Royale des Antiquaires du Nord. Among other places we stopped at the Academy at Søro. He took me for a little private walk: 'I was at school here,' he said, 'and over there I learnt to play cricket.'

When Brønsted retired his place was taken by that colourful figure, Peter Glob, excellent distiller of *schnapps*, generous host at his farm in Jutland, and writer of engaging works of *haute vulgarisation* translated into English under the titles of *The Bog People* and *The Mound Builders*. Becker became Professor of Archaeology in the University of Copenhagen: my wife and I almost every year have enjoyed the generous hospitality of himself and his wife, Birgit, at dinner in their home.

Ole Klindt-Jensen was not one of the four Salisbury Danes but I soon got to know him when he was working in the Nationalmuseet and invited him to write the volume on *Denmark* in the *Ancient Peoples and Places* series. When he set up the Institute of Prehistory at Moesgaard, outside Aarhus in Jutland, and became Professor of

Archaeology in the university there, we became close friends. Just before the Hamburg Conference of Prehistoric and Protohistoric Sciences in 1958 we went on a week's trip in his car across Germany ending up at Kramer's excavations in Manching. 'I'll do the driving,' he said. 'You read the maps and guide-books and find out where we lunch and dine.' In 1968 I found myself for six weeks a Visiting Professor of Archaeology in Aarhus and successfully commuted each week between Cambridge and Aarhus. I was driven each Sunday afternoon to Harwich to catch the DFDS boat to Esbjerg – and what happy memories I have over the years of that excellent service, arriving in Aarhus on Monday evening in time to play table tennis with the Klindt-Jensen sons and dine together with him and his wife, Tøve. I lectured next morning at ten, went out to the Institute at Moesgaard, ate the fine *aeggekagge* made at the Skovmulle Kro nearby, held a seminar in the afternoon, took the comfortable night boat to Copenhagen (alas, now no more), lectured in the university there in the morning, and was back in Cambridge to lecture there on Friday and supervise on Saturday. It was not, as many have suggested, an exhausting and punishing programme: and I found it stimulating every week talking to students in Aarhus, Copenhagen and Cambridge on the same themes.

My subject was a development of ideas first set out in my Josiah Mason lectures in Birmingham, published as *The Idea of Prehistory* (1962); namely the development of ideas about the nature of cultural change in prehistory. It was suggested that they should be published as a book, but other ploys intervened and they were condensed into an article entitled 'From Worsaae to Childe: the models of prehistory', published in the *Proceedings of the Prehistoric Society* in 1971 and were probably the better for that condensation.

Together Klindt-Jensen and I planned a conference on megaliths and their origins. This was held in Moesgaard in 1969 and the papers (edited by Poul Kjaerum and myself) were published in 1973 as a volume of the Jutland Archaeological Society entitled *Megalithic graves and ritual*. Encouraged by the success of this we planned a conference on the history of archaeology and this was held at Moesgaard as one of the many small conferences arranged to celebrate the fiftieth anniversary of the University of Aarhus in 1978. We were to have edited these proceedings together, but to the great sadness of his friends and colleagues he died suddenly in 1980. He was driving home on Friday evening from his Institute at Moesgaard to his home in Aarhus when he had a heart attack and crashed into one of the trees forming the fine avenue leading from the house to the main road. He was only sixty-two.

Sadly I carried on the job of editing the papers, ably assisted by Eric Peters of Thames and Hudson. They were published under the title of *Towards a History of Archaeology* in 1981 and we sorrowfully dedicated the book to his memory. I think the conference was more his brainchild than mine, although our many years of talk together no doubt stimulated his interest in the history of archaeology, and it was I who persuaded him to write for *The World of Archaeology* series his *A History of Scandinavian Archaeology* (1975).

He had succeeded Sigfried De Laet as Secretary-General of the International Congress of Prehistoric and Protohistoric Sciences and at the Nice Conference in 1976 he proposed a special section on the history of archaeology, of which I became chairman and Gordon Willey vice-chairman.

Ole was a man of great charm and infectious enthusiasm who combined wide-ranging scholarship with administrative flair and drive. I admired his love of life, his gifts of friendship and the unflagging energy that took him on visits to China, Mexico, Russia and the United States. When he died I wrote to the Rector of Aarhus University suggesting that a lectureship be founded in his memory: this idea was taken up by many, including my old friend Olaf Olsen, then Professor of Medieval Archaeology in Aarhus, and now Glob's successor as Director of the Danish National Museum and Riksantik-variet.

This idea blossomed, and in March 1983 I was back in Aarhus giving the first Klindt-Jensen Memorial Lecture in the presence of the Queen of Denmark and the then British Ambassador, Dame Anne Warburton. We had a fine dinner afterwards and I silently drank to his memory and to the way he had, over the years, taught me to love Denmark and understand the development of Danish archaeology.

I have devoted some pages to my Finnish and Scandinavian travels because I so much admire the development of Northern European archaeology from the time of C.J. Thomsen in the nineteenth century – if not Olaus Wormius in the seventeenth – onwards and so much admire the Danish way of life: *smorgasbord*, *schnapps*, Carlsberg and Tuborg beer, Tivoli, Danish humour, all of it. The Danes often speak the most excellent English. In 1957 the Danish National Museum celebrated its 150th anniversary and I was invited to the celebrations in Copenhagen which began with a royal reception and speeches at 10 a.m. and went on all day – we were in white tie and tails from morning to night. The special performance in the opera house in the evening found me sitting next to a person whose face was vaguely familiar. We got into conversation. I thought that even for a cultivated Dane he spoke English astonishingly well. After a while he said to me, 'I hope you will not think me rude. I know how good your countrymen are at speaking foreign languages but I have never heard a Dane speak such idiomatic and fluent English. I must congratulate you, sir.' I explained who I was and he then revealed he was Dr Richard Barnett, of the Near East Department, representing the British Museum at the celebrations. Collapse of both parties.

France has been a most powerful influence in my life, and I count myself very fortunate that my archaeological researches in the years immediately before the war and again in the twenty-odd years after the war, took me to every part, or almost every part, of that great and large country. I was the first non-Frenchman, or for that matter Frenchman, to have studied in the field a representative selection of the megalithic monuments all over France. When I published my *The Prehistoric Chamber Tombs of France* in 1960 it had one merit – perhaps only one: that I had travelled the length and breadth of France and seen at least two thousand dolmens.

My French travels in the decade 1945–55 coincided, as I have related, with my stewardship of St John's and enabled me to visit vineyards and taste the regional foods of France. I have told how my wife and I enjoyed the hospitality and welcome of the Heidsieck family in Rheims, the Louis Latour family in Beaune, the Calvets in Bordeaux and many smaller growers and merchants in the Rhône valley and the Loire. It was a liberal, necessary and important education and we gradually, on our own, visited and sampled the white wines of the middle Loire; became aficionados of the named Beaujolais growths; and, travelling in the hills south-west of Macon and north-west of Lyon, we visited Vaux (the original of Clochemerle) and of course Solutré, famous for its Palaeolithic associations, and learnt that the wine now known as Pouilly-Fuissé was nearly given the appellation Pouilly-Solutré. We began to make detours to taste unusual and little known wines like the soft lovely wine of Château-

Grillet in the Rhône valley made from the Viognier grape; the raspberry-tasting Bourgueil of the Loire; the wines of Quincy and Rully; and one of the strangest discoveries, a white wine from near Poitiers called La Pissotière de l'Impératrice. Josephine, on her way south-west, was supposed to have pee-ed in the corner of this little vineyard; the tale is told on the label. Curious memories crowd in on one from those years – visiting the *caves* of Chateau d'Yquem and tasting half-a-dozen exquisite vintages; sitting on the terrace above the remarkable village of St-Emilion with its monolithic church hewn out of the rock and, in the late afternoon, drinking sparkling wine from its own vineyards and eating macaroons; or going to Dijon during the annual Fête Gastronomique. I stayed at Dijon in the Hôtel de la Gare near the station where the proprietor was running a special stunt: there were two taps in the bathroom in addition to the ordinary hot and cold water – they supplied red and white wine *à volonté*. I asked him in the morning how he coped with this apparent munificence; what if someone came with a suitcase (or two) full of empty bottles and departed in the morning with them full? Quite easy, he said, we monitor the consumption in every room and if such a thing happened that client would find there was no room free when he next tried to come here. But monitoring or not, I noticed that this experiment of free wine in the bathroom was discontinued after a short while.

We also became *amateurs de fromage* – how could one not be when cheese is served in every main meal in France and very properly between the main course and dessert, not after dessert as is the less satisfactory English custom? We learnt to eat our Munster sprinkled with caraway seeds and to enjoy the variety of goat cheeses particularly the *chabichou* of Poitiers, la Motte-Saint-Heray, and the pyramidal Valençay. We made a special study of the cheeses of the Central Massif – Saint-Nectaire, Cantal, Roquefort, Fourme d'Ambert, and the *bleus* of Auvergne and the Causses. Cantal is hardly ever found in England: it is the first cheese we buy when we get to France. It was, apparently, very popular with the British troops in the 1914–18 war – perhaps because it bears a resemblance to Caerphilly; it makes excellent Welsh rabbit.

We wanted to visit Roquefort-sur-Soulzon in the Aveyron to see where and how that remarkable cheese of sheep's milk is made, and after a long and tiring drive got to the Grand Hôtel in the small village. I had not telephoned and was told the hotel was full: it was the annual meeting of the directors of the production of Roquefort. I walked despondently back to the car and then, talking to Ruth, I had an idea. 'I shall tell them I have come all the way from England to study their methods and that I buy cheese for the King of England and all the colleges of Oxford and Cambridge.' It worked: a special suite was found to be free and we had the same excellent dinner as the directors: I remember it started with a mouth-watering *feuilleté de roquefort*.

In the early years of our married life we returned from a short spring holiday in France saying sadly to each other that it would be another year before we could again afford to cross the Channel. A few days later I found in a Cambridge bookshop the notice of a competition run by *Les Guides Nagel*: the first prize was a week's de luxe holiday in France: no expense spared. There were questions to be answered, comments to be made on the Nagel *Guide de France*, and a short essay to be written. The essay was on French hotels and restaurants and I remember saying that except in the very best places good hot French food was so often served on cold plates. I went through all the motions and thought nothing of it until, a month later, I was rung up from London and told I was the winner. Alas, the holiday was for one, and I set out alone, while Ruth was busy helping to mount and produce a pageant with Camille Prior and Rosamund Rootham.

I was flown first class to Paris, met by a director of Nagel at the airport, driven in a limousine into Paris, shown to a splendid suite in the Grand Hôtel du Louvre, taken to the restaurant and left there alone, the *maitre d'hotel* and the *sommelier* carefully instructed that I was to be served any food or wine I ordered. I had a splendid lunch.

So far so good. Then the de luxe treatment disappeared. I had chosen the French Alps for my five days outside Paris. My train ticket was not first class and I shared a six-berth couchette with two French families and screaming children. The small middle-class hotel at Pralognan-la-Vanoise was not pleased to see me; and I was told that I was on *demi-pension*. I had to pay for my other meals and the wine at dinner. And I had to pay for my bus to the next stage of my free holiday which was to Annecy. The Hôtel Splendide knew nothing of my booking: and it had no restaurant. I had to eat out and my money was getting short.

I asked to see the manager, told him my story and showed him all my documents: his English was better than my French. 'I am the head of the Chamber of Commerce,' he said, 'and of the Tourist Board for the department. Leave it to me.' He shook his head: 'Ce n'est pas bon pour la France,' he muttered.

In two hours he summoned me to his office. 'All is arranged,' he said, 'and I am authorized to give you this sum of money for your incidental expenses. You will dine tonight and tomorrow night at the Auberge de Savoie: a seat is booked on the lake steamer for you and you will lunch at the world famous Auberge du Père Bise at Talloires. Nothing to pay.' Lunch at Talloires on the lawn under the trees looking out at the lake was one of my most memorable meals: I still remember the *Terrine chaude de brochet* and the *Turban de soles aux pommes* and the Seyssel wine.

I was driven to the night train for Paris and travelled alone in a first-class wagon-lit. A car met me at the Gare de Lyon and drove me to the airport. The chauffeur handed me a letter from the Nagel firm regretting any inconvenience I may have suffered, and explaining that it had been due to administrative difficulties that were not of their making. I got home that evening to find my wife still rehearsing the pageant. 'Did you have a good time?' she asked. 'Yes,' I said, 'on the whole.'

I used to receive many letters in the late forties and early fifties from people travelling to France wanting to know how to get to the painted and engraved caves of Dordogne and the megalithic monuments of Brittany and looking for advice on where to stay. It seemed simpler after a while to put my thoughts and knowledge into a small book. The result was *Lascaux and Carnac*, published in 1955. This informal gossiping guide to archaeological travel and gastronomy in parts of France was widely welcomed. Elizabeth Nicholas wrote generously of it in *The Sunday Times*: 'Can best be described as belonging to the Long-felt Want Department . . . a most delightful and valuable book.' It was soon out of print and out of date. Eight years later I revised it, including a special chapter on Rouffignac, the controversial site whose 'discovery' was announced at the Congrès préhistorique de France in Poitiers in July 1956. It was now called *The Hungry Archaeologist in France: a Travelling Guide to Caves, Graves and Good Living in Dordogne and Brittany*, and was published by Faber and Faber in 1963. It is now again in need of revision and re-writing.

These books express my love of France and what it has meant to me. I quote two brief passages. I wrote of my first visit to Carnac when I stayed in the Hôtel Tumulus de St-Michel:

I remember after dinner walking to the great Carnac alignments and in the soft moonlight wandering along those miles of serried large stones, their dark shadows a reminder of their darker past, and our ignorance of their makers and builders. For me that was a great and personal moment, and I knew then what I know even better now: that these megalithic monuments of Western Europe would exercise an irresistible fascination for me for ever.

Later I made my south Breton centre La-Trinité-sur-Mer, a small village which is half fishing port and half the home of yachtsmen who come there from as far afield as Paris and Lille; and in that village my headquarters, the Hôtel des Voyageurs, on the quayside, run by the Le Rouzic family. I wrote of it:

> I know that when I drive over the bridge and see the harbour and the boats before me it will only be a few minutes before I bring my car to a halt outside the Hôtel des Voyageurs, and walk into the bar and order a glass of Muscadet. Will Madame Le Rouzic still be there playing *belotte* in the corner? She is, and all is well with the world. I can walk next door to buy the papers from the newspaper boy with the limp, and walk on down the street past the butcher, and the charcuterie, the shop selling everything for ships, and the *épicerie*, and two cafés, and down to the end of the harbour and look out into the Atlantic. I find, and I know it is subjective and emotional, a peace passing all understanding on occasions like this.

I think those two books were worth doing but I know that some of my colleagues thought they were a waste of my time that should be spent on more serious matters. They disapproved of my joking use of the word gastro-archaeology and one annoyed reviewer of my 1960 *Prehistoric Chamber Tombs of France* said that 'the author knows his French gastronomy better than his French megaliths'.

After the war Sean Ó Ríordáin wrote to me from Dublin, where he had succeeded R.A.S. Macalister in the chair of archaeology at University College, asking me to come and lecture to his students. Remembering my earlier visit, I went to Ireland with alacrity. I was then appointed external examiner in archaeology and when the tenure of that agreeable duty came to an end I continued to visit Ireland each year to see Ó Ríordáin's excavations. Sometimes I stayed with him and his dear wife, Gabriel, the well-known sculptress, sometimes in the Conyngham Arms at Slane, but most times in the large and comfortable guest rooms in Trinity College, which fine institution has brotherly relations with St John's College.

There was one well-remembered and potentially alarming occasion when I went across to examine two PhD candidates, Máire McDermott (later Máire De Paor) and Ruadhri De Valera. Their dissertations and my notes were packed in my suitcase. As I waited for the luggage delivery machine at Collinstown airport to produce my suitcase it became painfully clear that it was not on my aircraft. I insisted on seeing the airport supervisor and explained that my suitcase contained the PhD dissertation of the Irish President's son and, exaggerating, said it was a matter of life and death that it should be retrieved. I began to think it had been stolen or sent to Amsterdam, Paris or New York. I was going to bed in the Trinity College guest room late that evening when there was a knock at my door and an Aer Lingus official was there with my bag. I did not tell Ó Ríordáin or the two candidates this story until, their examinations satisfactorily concluded the following morning, I took them all to lunch at Jammet's.

During every visit I would spend a day or half a day with Sean in Newgrange. He was employing his students to make an inventory of the decorated stones in the tomb and they had already found much new material unnoticed by George Coffey. He suggested that he and I should co-operate in writing this up as a volume in the *Ancient Peoples and Places* series. 'I can't do it alone,' he said, 'I'm beginning to feel very tired.' I reluctantly agreed and we worked at Newgrange for several seasons, cosseted by the inimitable Mrs Macken at the Conyngham Arms. But gradually I saw that he was listless and often falling asleep. His doctor came to see us one day and told me that Sean had a cancer and did not have long to live. His wife Gabriel took me out into the garden and said, tearfully, 'Is there nothing the great medical men in London and Cambridge can do to save this fine man?'

I went sadly back to England and a few months later heard that he had been hospitalized. Ruth and I went over to see him and were delighted when his doctors said he was much better and would like to be driven out into the country by us. 'I am afraid,' said one doctor, 'it is only a remission but let him enjoy it; he is so fond of you and Ruth and has been looking forward to this day.' I told Sean I had never seen the megalith in Phoenix Park and we drove there. It was a stiff climb up a hillside. 'You go on,' he said and we did. He seemed a long time joining us and I went to the edge of the hill. He had taken off his boots and was slowly climbing up on his hands and knees. We went back to tea with Gabriel and delivered him back to the hospital. That was the last time we saw him.

I was in the East Mediterranean when I learnt the news of his death. I could not get back to his funeral but Terence Powell was there and wrote to me, 'As I stood in that cemetery today, I felt part of my own life had died'. Which is how I, too, felt.

I was left to finish our book together: *New Grange and the bend of the Boyne* was published in 1964. But already the surveys and excavations of Brian O'Kelly at Newgrange and George Eogan at Knowth were beginning to change completely our knowledge of the great Boyne monuments. Eogan published an excellent series of interim reports on his Knowth excavations and O'Kelly's account of his excavations were published in late 1983, shortly after he himself had died. Now Ó Ríordáin, Brian O'Kelly, Ruadhri De Valera, and Terence Powell are all dead – to the great loss of archaeology and of myself.

I made one extensive British Council tour in Spain and Portugal, setting out on the Barcelona Express from the Gare d'Austerlitz at 20.57 and waking up as the train was leaving Toulouse for Narbonne. I love travelling on the great European expresses and was glad to add the Barcelona Express to my list, which already included the Sud Express from Paris to Madrid; the Nord Express which I have often travelled on to and from Paris and Copenhagen; the Direct-Orient from Paris to Belgrade and Istanbul; and the old Orient Express from Paris to Budapest. Cook's *International Railway Timetable* and the *Horaires Mayeux des Grandes Relations SNCF* are by my bedside and when I cannot sleep I plan long trans-European journeys.

I lectured in Barcelona, then in Madrid and in Coimbra, Oporto and Lisbon, enjoying myself everywhere. In Barcelona there was dear Luis Pericot y Garcia, Professor of Archaeology, with whom I had corresponded about megaliths for years. Pericot had taken charge and drove me around the countryside to see megaliths and Ampurias. He looked at my Madrid schedule: 'I see you are free for lunch on Thursday,' he said, 'I have to be in Madrid for a meeting that afternoon. Meet me in El Hoggar Gallego at one o'clock and we can enjoy the Galician fish which comes overnight to Madrid daily.'

I presented myself promptly at one o'clock and Pericot was there beaming. 'Splendid,' he said. 'Every time I come here, young friend, I feel young myself again and am reminded of those far-off days when I held my first academic appointment, professor in Santiago de Compostella: sometimes I wish I had never left there.'

It was a most memorable lunch and began with the largest and most varied *dégustation de fruits de mer* that I have ever seen – and I have degusted seafood in many restaurants in Brittany and the Pas-de-Calais. I tried everything, but one rather repulsive item I avoided. 'Oh,' said Pericot, 'you must not miss those. They are percebes.' Pulling myself together I tried them and enjoyed them.

Percebes are what we call goose barnacles in English. Christopher Driver recently described them in the *Guardian* more vividly than I can: 'A central core of suction,' he wrote, 'from whose perimeter wave mud-brown earthworms four inches long, pimpled like the skin of ox tongue and bloated, each terminating in a neat set of ladies' toenails painted scarlet at the tips.'

The lunch went on in triumph to a whole lobster each, grilled and flamed in brandy, with an exquisite sauce of langoustines and lobster coral. It was half past four when I said, 'What about your meeting?' Pericot smiled. 'There wasn't any meeting,' he said, 'I came to Madrid to give myself the pleasure of giving you lunch and talking about megaliths and shell-fish.' The distance from Barcelona to Madrid is the distance from London to Penzance or Newcastle upon Tyne. This was indeed a major conspiracy for pleasure, and that lunch in El Hoggar Gallego is one of my definitions of real friendship.

My invitation to visit Bulgaria in 1962 came from the Bulgarian government to my wife and myself because of their appreciation of our publishing articles about Bulgarian archaeology in *Antiquity*. When we told the British Council of our invitation they asked us to go to Romania and Hungary as well but we had no time for this extended East European trip, so in the end it was a fortnight in Hungary and a fortnight in Bulgaria. We took the Orient Express from the Gare de L'Est to Budapest arriving at about eight o'clock in the evening. There was no one to meet us and we had not been told where we were staying. We took a taxi to one of the two main hotels: they had not heard of us but telephoned and we drove off to the delightfully situated hotel on Margaret Island. Next morning I was astonished when Ruth emerged from the bathroom: her bottom was coloured blue! We discovered that the healthy waters from the nearby thermal lake deposited blue crystals on the bottom of the bath.

We were allotted by the Hungarian government a charming middle-aged lady as our guide and interpreter and she came with us everywhere – or nearly everywhere: she politely declined to enter the premises of the British Council with me, and declared she had been expressly forbidden to attend my lecture. We lunched one day with the Italian Ambassador to Hungary, the father of the geographer and Johnian friend Claudio Vita-Finzi, and she promised to deliver us to his residence, but the moment we turned a corner and saw the soldiers guarding the gate, she gave us a hasty goodbye and disappeared.

We very much enjoyed our days in Budapest, saw all the sights, worked in the National Museum, went out to see the famous Roman organ at Acquincum, and wished we had time to take one of the steamers that plied up and down the Danube. The food in the restaurants and our hotel was very good: I particularly remember one evening when we were taken out to dinner by the archaeologist, Madame Bognar-Kutzian (whom I was trying to persuade, unsuccessfully as it turned out, to write a volume on Hungary in the *Ancient Peoples and Places* series) and her economist-politician husband, who was a minister in the government. We were taken to a restaurant high on a hill overlooking the Danube and the twin cities of Buda and Pest.

We were specially befriended by Mademoiselle Mosoliczs of the Archaeology Department of the National Museum and she joined us and our guide-interpreter on the four-day tour we made through the Hungarian countryside. We visited Hviz and bathed in the allegedly radio-active and beneficial waters of the lake. We had no bathing costumes and were issued with wonderfully old-fashioned garments which made us look like the people on postcards of the early bathers in Brighton. So garbed we walked out into the lake on underwater plankways and stood up to our necks in the health-giving water – we were told it was medically dangerous to swim! I must confess to being tremendously invigorated by this experience and ready for my next glass of Tokay.

Mademoiselle Mosoliczs was a most entertaining person and an excellent raconteur. She told us of how Gordon Childe was given an honorary degree by the University of Debrecen; the only professor there who could speak English carefully prepared a speech; Childe himself carefully prepared a speech in Magyar. The speeches were delivered and were incomprehensible to all: a neighbour of Mosoliczs turned to her and said, 'I wonder why both speakers decided to give their addresses in bad German?'

I was sorry to leave Hungary: and our misgivings about Bulgaria increased when, as we drew into Sofia railway station, all of us who were looking out of the windows were showered with sand and gravel from a cement mixer. Dirty, and shaking sand from our hair and clothes, we were met by Mark Heath, then a Secretary in the British Embassy, now Sir Mark and Ambassador to the Holy See. He took us to the Grand Hotel, explained our programme, told us that we were invited to a dinner party in the Embassy and to the garden party on the Queen's Birthday. 'We are delivering the official invitation to you at the hotel tomorrow,' he said.

Before we set out from England we had been given a special briefing for travellers behind the Iron Curtain. A dry Foreign Office official told us laconically: 'Remember your bedroom will be bugged, usually through the lights above your bed. Always leave your suitcases unlocked. They will want to go through them and if you lock them they will have to break them open. This will put them in a dilemma as the only explanation, when you complain, is that it was the work of common thieves and it will be sad for them to have to admit that there are such people in a Communist republic.' We left our suitcases open and noticed how carefully they had been gone through.

After Hungary the food in the best hotel in Bulgaria was very poor; when we asked for special dishes they were off. One evening, after a particularly bad meal, Ruth stood on the bed and spoke clearly and slowly into the light fitting above our bed saying how disappointed we were with Bulgarian cuisine. I do not think it was an illusion that the next night there was a marked improvement and all the dishes we asked for seemed to be on.

Day after day we asked if there was a letter for us from the British Embassy and were told there was not. The day of the Queen's Birthday party arrived: still no invitation. Mark Heath said 'Typical, but never mind. Come all the same.' On our return from the party we were handed the invitation! The Bulgarian authorities gave us very generous sums of money for our out-of-pocket expenses. We made a few purchases in the few unattractive shops. These included an additional suitcase to contain all the pamphlets, photographs and books we were collecting. It was a miserable affair which turned out to be made of compressed cardboard and later fell to bits on the boat.

There had been organized for us a five-day tour of Bulgaria, which was fascinating and took us to Panaguriste (for the treasure), Kazanluk, Stara Zagora, Plovdiv, Tarnovo and Varna, where we had a night at Sunny Beach. Resting on our beds we heard an unmistakable sound on the beach outside, last heard in Egypt. Looking out we saw the camel, there was only one, walking to and fro on the beach. We visited museums and archaeological sites and went up the Shipka Pass where we had the most wonderful yoghourt I have ever tasted, topped with a thick creamy crust. Our driver and our guide-interpreter were both young men but had obviously been told never to let us out of their sight. They dined and lunched at tables nearby. Eventually we insisted that they sat at the same table, and one evening succeeded in persuading them to go off to the cinema on their own.

When we were in the middle of the wine-growing area we had the greatest difficulty in getting them to take us to a taverna and sample the local wines. Not the place for us, they said, and certainly not for a lady. But we insisted, and were immediately welcomed by a splendid old man who had come back to retire in his native country after thirty years in Chicago. When we returned to Sofia from our delightful tour we were summoned to see Madame Abramowicz, who was Deputy Prime Minister and Minister for Culture. The summons was for nine o'clock in the morning and we were served with plum brandy and cakes. We partook of these sparingly, which displeased this rather fierce and forceful woman. 'Eat and drink,' she commanded. 'You do not like them,' accusingly; 'these are our country's great specialities.' She, herself, did not partake. Several months later we were summoned to a reception in the Bulgarian Embassy in London and duly presented to Madame Abramowicz. Through her interpreter we said what a pleasure it had been to be entertained by her in Sofia. She muttered some sharp words and the interpreter told us that she had no recollection of ever having seen us before. We moved on.

After the weeks of travelling, lectures and receptions it was a joy to catch the train from Sofia to Istanbul, an allegedly *rapide* which became slower and slower, stopping often for us to buy food from itinerant vendors and wayside cooks. After enjoying the beauties and delights of that remarkable city, we returned to the west by a most comfortable Turkish boat that called at Smyrna, the Piraeus and Brindisi before making that most exciting of landfalls, Venice –

perhaps equalled in wonder and beauty only by the landfall of New York.

The Hungarian-Bulgarian sortie of 1962 was not my first adventure in Eastern European Communist countries. At the International Congress of Prehistoric and Protohistoric Societies in Hamburg in 1958 it was decided to have smaller meetings in between the large Congresses and a small conference on the origins of the Neolithic in Europe was organized to take place in Czechoslovakia in 1959: it was to spend a few days in a Conference Centre at Lidice and then a few days in Brno. Stuart Piggott and I were the British representatives and we set off from Heathrow in a two-engined Ilyushin together with six Czechs and a mysterious man in black who was hurried into the aircraft just as we were leaving. We had been served with lunch and paid for some drinks, when over the English Channel the starboard engine ceased; I felt sure we would ditch in the English Channel or make an emergency landing at Calais-Marck. We were told to fasten our seat belts and our lunch and drinks were taken away from us. We flew on and prepared to land at Brussels. Flames then came out of the port engine but as we circled to land the starboard engine came to life again. The propeller of the port engine stopped: the pilot made a fine landing, but his braking power was impaired and we careered along the airfield stopping a very short distance from the perimeter bank. I learnt later that the airfield was on full alert and that fire engines and ambulances were screaming along behind us. 'I think I shall never fly again,' said Stuart Piggott, 'at least not in crates like this Ilyushin.' 'Why didn't we make an emergency landing in the English Channel?' I asked. 'Becàuse we had no gummy-rings,' was the answer: and I suppose it was unreasonable to suppose that aircraft flying primarily across the land face of Europe should carry lifebelts.

Exhausted and shocked, we were driven into a small hotel in the centre of Brussels and told the flight would continue to Czechoslovakia the next day in a different aircraft. (I decided not to alarm Ruth by telephoning her, but I sent her a postcard saying we had made a stop in Belgium to pick up more passengers.) 'We need a stiff drink and a good dinner,' I said to Piggott, and we did our best to enjoy our dinner in the Rôtisserie d'Ardennes. We didn't sleep well and there was an air of forced cheerfulness as we drove out to the aircraft. 'We didn't see you at dinner in the hotel,' said one of the Czechs. 'No,' I said, unthinkingly, 'we went out and had a jolly good dinner in a brasserie.'

'We would have liked to join you,' said the Czech, 'but we had no foreign money.'

The flight to Czechoslovakia was uneventful. Piggott and I were hustled off the aircraft, passport examinations and customs brushed aside, greeted by a dark and suspicious looking man and bundled into a large car which immediately drove off at high speed. We discovered the driver spoke no English or German. It was getting dark. 'Do you realize,' said Piggott, 'that we are being driven rather recklessly, possibly to an unknown destination?' 'I hope', I replied, 'that we will eventually find ourselves in the Conference Centre.' Outside in the countryside there was a strange noise: the baying of wolves?

After what seemed an endless and perilous drive the car turned into an avenue leading to a large château. We had arrived at the Conference Centre. Just outside the front door was a broken-down basket chair. 'No doubt,' said Piggott, his good humour restored, 'where the Archduke was sitting when he was shot.' We went into the dining room where the other delegates were preparing to sit down. Our Czech host came forward to greet us. 'We have had an adventure,' we said. 'We are lucky to be alive. Our aircraft virtually crashed in Belgium.' He frowned and cut across what we were saying, turned to the others and said, 'We are glad to welcome Piggott and Daniel who were delayed by business in London.' Obviously Russian aircraft were not allowed to misbehave!

Next morning our Czech host found me writing a letter. 'Ah,' he said, 'letters take a long while to get through to England. Postcards are better.' I wrote several postcards to my wife in the next few days; the only card she received from that trip was from Brussels.

The conference was interesting, valuable and well run, and its proceedings have been published. One morning, when we had transferred to Brno, we discovered that one whole session was to be devoted to papers by the two Russian delegates. We already had the text of their papers in French and English and went to the conference lecture room prepared for an interesting discussion. We then were told that for reasons of prestige the Russians insisted on reading their papers to the assembled company in Russian. 'I am not going to sit here for three hours listening to papers in Russian,' I said. 'It might be thought rude to leave,' said Stuart. 'Excuse me,' I said, 'I have been taken short. I must go to the lavatory,' and I escaped before the session had got going. I met our Czech chairman on the steps. 'I feel a little unwell,' I lied, 'I am going to take a little fresh air. See you later.' I was halfway down the street from the university when I heard footsteps. It was Stuart. 'I, too, had to go to the loo,' he said.

We spent a lovely morning exploring Brno and visiting its many fine churches. They were all full to overflowing and masses were being celebrated everywhere. It was 8 October, St Bridget's Day. As it got to midday we agreed that we would not go back to our hotel but lunch in a restaurant in the town. It was the only opportunity we had of being away from our colleagues and the fixed meals. We went down a side street and came across a modest-looking restaurant which advertised that its proprietors spoke German, Russian, Italian, French, Spanish and English. We went in and immediately discovered this to be a wildly extravagant claim. No one spoke anything but Czech and the menu, unrelentingly in Czech, had one French word by a dish set in a square frame: 'Specialité'.

We agreed that as we didn't understand the menu the safe thing was to have the speciality of the house. The waiter seemed perturbed and was obviously trying to dissuade us: we insisted and he went away shrugging his shoulders. He came back and could not understand that we also wanted wine. We made gestures and a welcome carafe of water appeared. We made more gestures and two pints of beer appeared. I followed the waiter into the kitchens, opened a large refrigerator and took out a bottle of white wine. Everyone smiled. We sat sampling a very good wine when with a flourish the speciality of the house appeared: it was an enormous jam omelette flaming in a very strong spirit. We ate it with surprise and pleasure and drank to St Bridget who gave birth to eight children in a château in Sweden, wrote eight volumes of her *Revelations* and founded the Order of St Saviour.

Later that day Marija Gimbutas, now Professor of Archaeology at the University of California at Los Angeles, said to us: 'I gather you two had a happy morning and you visited six churches and one café-restaurant.' 'How did you know?' we asked. 'When you left the university,' she said, 'you were followed. I heard a security man reporting this to our chairman. They seemed unaware that I understood Czech. At first I disbelieved the report; it seemed to me so out of character. Now if they had told me you had visited six cafés and one church I would have believed it at once!'

One of my most unusual and amusing travels abroad came about because of my friendship with Bernabò Brea, the Superintendent of

Antiquities in Eastern Sicily, and his with Stuart Piggott. One day in 1959, out of the blue there arrived an invitation from him on behalf of the government of Sicily to bring twenty students from the Universities of Edinburgh and Cambridge with Piggott and myself for a ten-day field and museum class in Sicily. Our own Universities were to pay the costs of travel to and from Sicily. All costs once we got there would be met by the Sicilian government and it was said then, and many times afterwards, that this was nothing to do with the *Italian* government. It was too good an opportunity to miss and we organized the travel costs and set out to Rome with our assorted bag of students. Aboard the night train down to Messina there was some confusion: through some linguistic misunderstanding it was thought by a group of lecherous Italian soldiers that one of our female students had been sold to them by our male students. We travelled from Messina to Milazzo on the north coast and took the boat to the Lipari Islands. I had been to these delightful Aeolian islands before and watched with amusement the discomfort of our students as they approached the island of Vulcano. As the evil sulphurous smells from the *fumaroles* began to envelop us, there were nervous lookings-around and rapid movings-away. Of no avail – these filthy non-human stinks remain with you until you sail away to Lipari, the main island which was our headquarters. We had trips to the other islands and the highlight was Stromboli, where after dinner it was scheduled that we should climb up to the summit of the volcano. Piggott and I opted out of this exercise and sat quietly in a belvedere looking up at the sky reflecting the red interior of the active mountain. Two or three of the maids and waiters from the hotel in which we were all staying joined us and after a while asked us to teach them a useful English phrase. Stuart was helpful and went through a routine of Good Morning, Good Evening, Good Night, Thank you. When it came to me I suddenly felt mischievous and light-headed, and taught them all a mad phrase which came into my head, 'The white mouse is in the lighthouse.'

Much later that evening when we were all together in the hotel eating our dinner, Nicholas David, now Professor of Archaeology at Calgary, said to me: 'Is this a mad-house? I have just been trying to explain to one of the girls that my shirt and pants were burnt when I went too near the edge of the crater, and all she said was: 'The white mouse is in the lighthouse.' I could hardly resist bursting out laughing. 'But that, my dear Nicholas,' I said, '*is* where the white mouse is.'

317

There were invitations to be guest-lecturer on cruises to the Mediterranean and Egypt. One from Fairways and Swinford which was most attractive, was for Stuart Piggott, John Evans and myself to organize a special personal Mediterranean cruise that was to be different from the normal Greece or Greek islands Hellenic cruises and visit sites not normally included in those cruises. We planned it with excitement and it was a great success, visiting the Balearics, Corsica, Sardinia, the Etruscan tombs, Pompeii and Herculaneum, Sicily, Tripoli and Malta, as well as Crete and Greece.

Ruth, Stuart and I had driven across France to Marseilles to join the cruise ship. When we stopped halfway down the Rhône Valley we realized it was *mi-carême* and the shops were full of carnival ploys. Remembering that the last night of the cruise was a 'gala' evening, we bought masks and false noses and moustaches with which we were able to surprise our fellow cruise companions. On the last day we sailed up the Adriatic on our last lap from Dubrovnik, where we had all bought bottles of the locally brewed *slivovic* in quayside cafés.

We all arrived happily in Venice; the captain took a group of us off to lunch in the Graspa da Ua, and we then went to the railway station to wish the party goodbye. Ruth and I were taking another train across Italy to Marseilles to collect the car. As the train left Venice, Stuart, who was sharing a cabin with John Evans, said with a sigh of relief: 'Now we must celebrate the end of this most successful cruise with a glass of my *slivovic*.' He opened his suitcase and discovered to his dismay that the cork had come out of the bottle, there was nothing to drink, and all his clothes were soaked in this powerful liqueur.

When he got back to London he discovered that our club was closed and that a bed had been reserved for him in the Senior. He dumped his suitcase with the porter and went into the bar. When he came out his suitcase was gone. 'The valet has taken your bag upstairs,' he was told. When he got to his room he found that his bag had been unpacked. The drawers of the dressing table were filled with his neatly folded *slivovic*-drenched underwear and on the top was set out carefully with his toilet requisites a false nose and moustache. 'It was not surprising,' he wrote to us later, 'that I was given some odd looks by the waiters when I went into the dining room.'

I was delighted when George Bales of Bales Tours asked me to act as guide-lecturer on a Nile cruise. Ever since I had read Amelia Edwards's *A thousand miles up the Nile* I had wanted to go south of Cairo, which I knew. I enormously enjoyed the two cruise journeys we made to Egypt. There is something entirely special about sailing slowly up and down the Nile: the peace and quiet, the view of villages and villagers on the banks and the great antiquities to be visited. Karnak and the Valley of the Kings is one of the highlights of my archaeological tourism, and suddenly getting up one morning, walking on deck, and discovering that we were moored in front of Abu Simbel, was one of the most moving experiences of a travelling antiquary. A few days later I was in Jordan descending the Petra Valley with Crystal Bennett, then Director of Archaeology in Jerusalem, and entering that rose-red city, half as old as time, capital of the Nabataeans.

My most recent British Council visit was to Cyprus where I felt that one was, both at the present and in the past, halfway between the East and the Mediterranean, between Egypt and Mycenae, between Syria and Sicily, between the Turks and Europe. Has anywhere suffered so many invasions and changes in prehistory and history? Cyprus still suffers from her most recent invasion and the sad dismemberment of 1974, which the dis-united nations approved for their private and secret politics. I gave lectures in Nicosia and Paphos, in the Republic of Cyprus, but did not cross into the Turkish-held part. Dr Vassos Karageorghis and his staff have made the National Museum in Nicosia a remarkable place and the service of antiquities unobtrusively efficient and competent. I took away most of all the memory of the originality, inventiveness and skill of the early bronze-age Cyprus potters. We visited the monastery of Stavrovouni, founded by the Empress St Helena *c.* 327, who not only brought the relic of the True Cross from Jerusalem but introduced cats to combat the reptile population and as companions for the monks, in preference to catamites. We made a special expedition to the Forest Station of Stavros tis Psokas, the natural habitat of *ovis ophion*, the Cyprus moufflon, only just saved from extinction. A herd is kept in a large enclosure but these wild sheep are very shy creatures and would not come on view during our visit.

How lovely it was in Cyprus after a day of visiting museums and sites in the hot sun to drive down to a taverna in a quiet seaside village and eat the delightful local *mezedhes* such as *houmous*, *tahini*, and *haloumi* and drink the good local wine while waiting for some grilled red mullet, swordfish or *kolokassi*, as the sun sank into the Mediterranean.

319

The pleasures of archaeology are many but none more rewarding than travelling to ancient places from Finland to Abu Simbel, from Middle America to Middle India. I count myself fortunate that I have seen so much and enjoyed so much in the fifty odd years since, with my college travelling scholarship, I set out to see Avebury and Stonehenge and crossed to Brittany. I shall count myself even more fortunate when I have seen Macchu Pichu, Santiago de Compostella, Angkor Wat, the Great Wall of China, and the Hermitage Museum. The travels of an antiquary are never over until, alone, he makes that last journey to a country which has no antiquities, no cafés and restaurants, and from which there is no return.

*Painting of GD
by Villiers David,
1954*

*GD's rooms in
St John's,
overlooking the
Kitchen Bridge:
top floor under
round window
(Cambridge
University
Almanack, 1840)*

French children at Carnac telling GD 'the legend of the menhirs'

Excavations at Barclodiad y Gawres, 1953, by GD and Terence Powell (cross-legged, centre). David, now Sir David, Wilson (top left, fuzzy hair, Manx sweater)

GD being made up at Skara Brae for
BBC 'Chronicle'

A break in filming at Stonehenge
for BBC 'Chronicle'. Left to right:
Paul Johnstone, Richard Atkinson,
GD, Stuart Piggott: a joker has
daubed the van

GD puts archaeological finds to practical use, while Sir Mortimer Wheeler holds the mirror: a facetious view of 'Buried Treasure' by Emmwood, published in Punch, 1954

Dame Edith Evans presenting the TV Personality of the Year trophy to GD, 1955

GD being filmed in his college rooms for Anglia TV

*Walter Neurath, with Eva Neurath on his right, introduces GD
(far left) to a meeting of booksellers in London, 1962*

*A display of book-jackets to celebrate the 50th volume
of the 'Ancient Peoples and Places' series, 1966*

*Walter Neurath, Gabriel Ó Ríordáin and GD on the
publication of 'New Grange', 1964*

*Elsie Clifford's 80th birthday party: GD, Elsie Clifford and
Sir Mortimer Wheeler*

Degree Day conversation with Lord Adrian, then Vice-Chancellor

Outside Buckingham Palace after Stuart Piggott's CBE investiture, 1972

Grahame Clarke and Stuart Piggott speaking to students on a field class at Stonehenge

V. Gordon Childe

Ole Klindt-Jensen

Rik in a BBC film

Colin Renfrew examining an artifact in Brittany

Seán Ó Ríordáin and Máire de Paor

HRH the Prince of Wales and GD at Stationers' Hall, 1981

Before a lecture at Moesgaard, Denmark. Ruth, GD and Queen Margrethe

Air view of Zouafques.
The house, La Marnière,
left foreground

In the garden, La Marnière

About to set out for home from Zouafques

GD scrambling eggs at Zouafques

GD gathering winter fuel for La Marnière

Megaliths and men

MY FIRST SERIOUS INTEREST in archaeology was megalithic monuments and that interest has remained with me all my life. Estyn Evans once described me as the only person he knew who had studied and written about megaliths all his life and remained sane: but that was in 1962! I am now, forty-five years after I first wrote on this subject, writing a book which is just called *Megaliths*, and will be, I hope, the last word I have to say on this fascinating and important subject which has intrigued and interested archaeologists and antiquaries for so long.

It would be nice to say that when I visited the Tinkinswood and St Lythan's megalithic chambers near my home in the Vale of Glamorgan, as I frequently did in my childhood, that I there and then decided to dedicate myself to their study – but this would not be true. But I did write a thesis on the archaeology of South Glamorgan for my third year Tripos examination: it included an account of the megalithic monuments of south-east Wales; gradually out of this grew my plan to extend the survey to the whole of England and Wales and I proposed this as a PhD subject. As I have said earlier, Miles Burkitt tried hard to dissuade me. 'It's all been said,' he declared. 'There's nothing new to work on. Read the papers of Wilfred Hemp and you will see he has said the last word on the subject.' This hardened my resolve. I consulted Chadders and he was, as always, helpful and encouraging. 'You know my view of Burkitt,' he said, 'and in any case no one has said the last word on anything.'

O.G.S. Crawford had produced his *Long Barrows of the Cotswolds* in 1925 and was embarking on a more general cartographical survey. This work inspired me to do a general survey of England and Wales.

There were three people who were responsible for my growing interest in megaliths in the thirties and I owe a great deal to their inspiration and encouragement. The first was Zacharie Le Rouzic, whom I met on my first visit to the Carnac region of southern Brittany in 1934, and again three years later. James Miln was an eccentric Scotsman who took up residence in Carnac and excavated various sites. He lived in the Hôtel de Commerce in Carnac and it is said that when he died, all the finds from his excavations were found in boxes underneath his bed. One day a small boy visited him when he was out in the countryside doing a watercolour of some antiquity. That boy was Zacharie Le Rouzic and Miln took him on as an unpaid assistant and helper. After Miln's death Le Rouzic continued his archaeological survey and excavation work in the Morbihan. A museum was created to house the finds from the Miln and Le Rouzic excavations and is appropriately called the Musée Miln-Le Rouzic. The old museum I have sometimes cruelly described as a charnel house, has now been re-organized and modernized: the material it has is of very great interest and value. The Musée of the Societé Polymathique du Morbihan in Vannes was also years ago a charnel house, but has also been modernized. I visited Le Rouzic's excavations and discussed with him his scheme for the development of the Morbihan megaliths which he had set out in a paper to the International Congress of Prehistoric and Protohistoric Sciences in London in 1932. I was particularly interested in monuments like Klud-er-Yer and Keriaval which seemed in plan like Cotswold monuments and Parc-le-Breos Cwm in South Wales. It was in these discussions that I developed the idea that what I was later to call the Severn-Cotswold tombs of the South West Midlands and South Wales were derived from prototypes in southern Brittany, and this I still think to be true. But it was Le Rouzic's general and genuine enthusiasm for megaliths that rubbed off on me and stimulated me to think of British-French connections in Neolithic times.

I found in Terence Powell an aficionado of megaliths as devoted and enthusiastic as myself, and over our undergraduate years in Cambridge we discovered together the literature of the subject and eagerly read and discussed Thurnam, Borlase's three-volume *Dolmens of Ireland*, Bonstetten's *Essai sur les Dolmens*, Fergusson's *Rude Stone Monuments*, T.E. Peet's *Rough Stone Monuments*, Montelius's *Der Orient und Europa*, the writings of Crawford, Kendrick, Hencken, Macalister, Childe, Daryll Forde, Peake and Fleure, and most of all George Coffey's *New Grange*.

Terence lived in Dublin and invited me over in 1935 to visit some of the Irish monuments. We went to see the great monuments in the Bend of the Boyne, Newgrange, Dowth and Knowth, spent a day at Loughcrew and trudged the countryside visiting every one of the forty or so tombs on those widespread hills. At Tibradden we both made one of our first major mistakes in comparative archaeology. We thought it a classic passage grave, like those of Alcalá in south Portugal, and later in his pioneer paper on 'The Passage Graves of Ireland' Powell made it the first in his developing series. Only later did we find that it was a nineteenth-century construction so that an excavated stone cist could be visited!

We drove down to Cork; it was my first meeting with men whose friendship I was going to value and cultivate for many years – Sean O Ríordáin, Brian O'Kelly and Paddy Hartnett – the excavator of Four Knocks and now, alas, no longer with us. Sean, Terence and I went on to explore many sites and to visit among other places a splendid Irish pub where poteen was made and drunk. Driving along an extraordinary road over the Sheehy mountains Terence, at the wheel, got more and more alarmed and finally refused to drive any further when we came round a steep bend at the end of a shocking single track mountain road and found ourselves confronted by a stream some six feet wide. 'I'm not going on, and I'm not going to reverse,' he said. Sean Ó Ríordáin said, 'We can't spend the rest of our lives in the wilds of these mountains'. 'Someone else must bloody well drive,' said Terence who had a violent temper. I suggested we abandon the car and walk. I went out, put on a pair of gumboots and walked through the stream. I thought it possible to drive through it. Terence said, 'Be it on your head,' and pulled his hat down over his eyes. Nervously and slowly I drove through the stream and on along a hideously narrow, excruciatingly bad road until we got to a village. We stopped at a pub. When we told them where we had come from they said, 'But this is impossible. No one has driven over the Sheehy mountain for years. Look at the notice.' We did: it said 'Road impassable for cars.' 'How bloody true,' said Terence and took another Paddy.

Terence, several years later when I was a research student, came on a great megalithic tour of north-western France with me. This was when Eleanor Hardy and her mother accompanied us for the first few days of our trip. When we had all seen the great monuments at Carnac and Locmariaquer, the Hardys returned to Cambridge and we went on down to St-Nazaire and Nantes, saw the Pornic tombs, and went across from Fromentine to Ile d'Yeu where Pétain was eventually to spend his exile. It was a very rough crossing and we were both horribly sick. I recover from such episodes very quickly and ate a large and delicious lunch when we landed. Not so Terence, who was ill for the rest of the day. He watched me demolish a *plâteau de fruits de mer*, a sole meunière, a steak, cheese and *tarte aux pommes*, and said, coldly, 'This is one of the most disgusting and deplorable exhibitions I have ever seen'. But his appetite returned; we went to Paris and at Saint-Germain pledged ourselves to the study of megaliths and the Celts. I never did anything about the Celts except lecture about them; he produced his *The Celts* in 1958: one of the best introductions to the subject ever written, re-issued with extra illustrations under the guidance of Stuart Piggott in 1980.

We went and worked in the Bibliothèque Nationale on old French periodicals. The charming lady who negotiated our passes said, 'To which of the three English universities do you belong? Oxford, Cambridge, London?' We went on her recommendation to a small restaurant nearby, Le Gratin Dauphinois, which specialized in a delicious *tarte aux pommes* which was browned under a salamander.

My third megalithic inspiration was Elsie Clifford. Mrs E.M. Clifford was a local Gloucestershire archaeologist who had, among other things, discovered the first Palaeolith in the county. She was encouraged by Miles Burkitt to come and spend a year in Cambridge attending all the lectures she wished to but not taking any examinations. She resided for a year in the Garden House Hotel, and when her year was over came back every term for what became a state visit. She always wore a leopard-skin coat and drove, very slowly, a Chrysler coupé – the first car with automatic transmission that I had ever travelled in. She always gave a series of dinner parties: I was invited to one of these in 1934 and it was then suggested I should join Clare Fell and Eleanor Hardy at her excavations at Notgrove. We all stayed in her house at the foot of Birdlip Hill, a charming old Cotswold farmhouse beautifully transformed into a modern house. Here Elsie and her husband, Harold, who ran a number of garages, dispensed lavish hospitality. I have never been given so much to eat. The Notgrove excavations of 1934/5 were my first introduction to the excavation of a chambered tomb. We then went on to excavate Nympsfield, then Rodmarton. Rodmarton was a joint excavation of hers and mine and I was proud of this association. It had been excavated by Lysons in the nineteenth century. It had a false entrance and two side chambers. In the south chamber Lysons had found a broken leaf-shaped arrowhead. Our excavation revealed the details of the north side chamber with its porthole entrance still with its original blocking, and in the chamber I found the tip of a leaf-shaped arrowhead. It fitted perfectly with the find Lysons had made years ago. Clearly the arrowhead had been ritually broken and one part put in the south chamber, the other in the north. It was the most exciting and intriguing archaeological discovery that I had hitherto made. We published the excavations together in an article in the *Proceedings of the Prehistoric Society* for 1940 and I added to this article a long essay on portholes in megaliths. These Gloucestershire excavations were my first proper introduction to the digging of megaliths and were most enjoyable and instructive.

I have already described how I wrote my first paper, and how happy I was when Crawford accepted it. Encouraged by this, Terence Powell wrote his excellent pioneer paper 'The Passage Graves of Ireland', and sent it off to Crawford, who rejected it by return of post. Grahame Clark had better judgment and published it in *PPS*. He also published my first effort in comparative archaeology which was a study of what I called transepted gallery graves in North West France and the Severn-Cotswold region of the South West Midlands and South East Wales.

My friendship with Elsie Clifford grew and prospered after the war and she immediately took to Ruth, whom she often described as one of the most lovely persons she knew. 'Too good for you, my boy,' she would say, and she may well have been right. I was gradually over the years adopted as a sort of son. When she was very ill (largely due to being given too many pills) and we thought she was going to die Ruth took over the report of her excavations at Bagendon and saw it through the press. I was her literary executor but she had so organized her affairs that there was little to do. We celebrated her eightieth birthday and many came to pay her homage. It was at that lunch that Seiriol Evans, that wise and benign man, then Dean of Gloucester, hatched a plot with me to get her work recognized. She was delighted when she was awarded the OBE. There was no kinder or more generous person and I owe a very great deal to her friendship, encouragement and enthusiasm. We visited every megalithic monument in the Cotswolds together and when I published my *The Megalith Builders of Western Europe* in 1958 I was happy to dedicate it to her. The dedication reads: 'For Elsie Clifford: Notgrove, Nympsfield, Rodmarton'.

Miles Burkitt was devoted to Wilfred Hemp who was Secretary of the Royal Commission on Ancient Monuments (Wales and Monmouthshire). Hemp had excavated two very important megalithic sites in North Wales – the Capel Garmon long barrow and the passage grave of Bryn Celli Ddu. He had also written interesting papers about the *navetas* of the Balearics, and the rock-cut tombs of the Arles region and Champagne. In 1936 he was excavating the site of Bryn Yr Hen Bobl in Lord Anglesey's park and Burkitt arranged that I should join the dig for a week. It was the most boring week I have ever spent on an excavation; I was not allowed to do anything: all was done by Hemp's foreman and his excellent staff. I took an instant dislike to Hemp and he to me. He was hardly ever at his excavations which were admirably run by the foreman. He was a snob: my humble origins and my simple upbringing were only just redeemed by the fact that I was a scholar of a very distinguished Cambridge College, and that Miles Burkitt and Cyril Fox spoke well of me. But he much resented what I was doing for a PhD, believing himself to be the megalithic king-pin, and he reported very adversely on my PhD thesis and my Fellowship dissertation and was furious (so Mortimer Wheeler subsequently told me) that St John's and the University paid no attention to his recommendations. He never wrote to congratulate me on my election to a Research Fellowship; this may, of course, have been an honest appraisal of what he regarded as the folly of the College Council. We tried to discuss megalithic problems together but it was the same as talking to Burkitt; there were no problems, everything was done. There was no more to be said. Hemp was a curious character to evaluate. He did some good work, but was a lazy dilettante and to a certain degree bogus. These views were shared by people like Laurence Munro, Gerald Dunning and Stuart Piggott, who worked with him. He was in many ways a nasty man and was aware that I thought so. When Terence Powell and I were excavating Barclodiad y Gawres in Anglesey in 1952 and invited him to visit our dig, he said he would only do so on a day when I was not present. When my *The Prehistoric Chamber Tombs of England and Wales* was published, the Society of Antiquaries of London asked him to review it. When Mortimer Wheeler (who, curiously enough, liked Hemp and went on fishing holidays with him), then Director of the Society, read the review he, as he told me later, tore it into pieces and threw it into the fire. Yet Hemp was responsible for at least one good thing in the world of archaeology, albeit unintentional: in 1934 Piggott was excavating the Thickthorn Down Barrow with Alexander Keiller during his leave from the Welsh Commission. The dig was not finished when Piggott's leave was over. He telegraphed Hemp asking for a week's extension without pay. The reply came, 'No'. Keiller asked Piggott what he was paid by the Commission and when told said, 'Would you become my archaeological secretary for twice that salary?' From that moment Piggott began a career which was to culminate in his Professorship of Archaeology at Edinburgh. So we must not judge Hemp too harshly: some good came out of evil! And it is true that he did introduce many of us to the *navetas* of Menorca and rock-cut tombs of Arles-Fontvielle.

When I joined my mother in 1936 in the Channel Islands and saw their fine megalithic monuments, including the statue menhirs of Le Câtel and St Martins and the figure on the underside of the capstone of Le Déhus, I went through the Lukis and Dryden MSS in the Guernsey Museum and was startled and excited to find two drawings of megalithic monuments near the village of Salles-la-Source near Rodez in the Aveyron. My geography of France was not what it is now and I had hardly heard of Rodez, the ancient Ruthenia. I found Aveyron on the map and realized that here in southern France were chambered long barrows. Now there is no mention of long barrows in Déchelette's *Manuel*. Southern Britain was full of Neolithic long barrows, chambered and unchambered. They must have been introduced by the Neolithic settlers who colonized Britain from France. Ergo, despite the silence of books, there must be chambered long barrows in France, as at that time all our eyes turned from North West Europe back to our surely certain Neolithic origins in the early Mediterranean. The Rodez long barrows seemed a discovery of major importance and as soon as possible I took the train from Paris to Rodez and went out to Salles-la-Source. I had no idea where these sites might be and discussed them in a café. After a while someone propping up the bar said, 'Ah, Monsieur. Vous cherchez les tombeaux des Anglais!' I was flabbergasted by this reply because I was indeed looking for the origins of the long barrows in southern England, but of course he was talking about the English of the Hundred Years' War. The English had left Rodez in the mid-fifteenth century, but it was nice to know that they had already become folk heroes and that prehistoric monuments were being attributed to them.

I was directed to my sites and there they were: monuments that

343

could equally well be found in Wessex or the Cotswolds. I returned to Rodez and had talks with Louis Balsan, the Director of the Museum. He seemed surprised that we in Britain did not know about these chambered long barrows of southern France. I went back and published a note in *The Antiquaries Journal* on the subject. It seemed we had a fixed point in our British-Irish megalithic studies: the passage grave had come from Brittany and Iberia, the chambered long barrows from France and perhaps ultimately the islands of the West Mediterranean.

My PhD dissertation was approved in 1938 and the Cambridge University Press agreed to publish it: *The Prehistoric Chamber Tombs of England and Wales* eventually came out in 1950. Meanwhile, as the shades of war darkened, Grahame Clark asked me to write a general paper giving my overall views on megalithic problems and origins. 'After all,' he said agreeably, 'if you don't write it now you may not be here after the war to do so.' It was a pleasure to meet this challenge and 'The Dual Nature of the Megalithic Colonization of Prehistoric Europe' appeared in the *Proceedings of the Prehistoric Society* in 1941, by which time I had left academe and was poised over a stereoscope.

Ruadhri De Valera regarded it as his bible: 'the best thing ever written about megaliths,' he wrote to me, and he regarded my changes of view and my U-turn from 1960 onwards as a foolish mistake. The Dual Nature was, I suppose, all right for its time – a pre-C14 pre-thermoluminescence dating time. It was a development of Childe's ideas in his famous paper to the Glasgow Archaeological Society and argued for a passage-grave origin in Spain and ultimately in the East Mediterranean and a gallery-grave origin in the surface and rock-cut tombs of the West Mediterranean.

The four years of my war service were a welcome and intriguing break from megalithic studies, although while in India I took a special interest in the Deccan megaliths and was fascinated when Wheeler was able to date them accurately to the Roman Iron Age. Back in England after the war I was surprised to get an invitation from Christopher Hawkes to write a volume in the Hutchinson series of which he was archaeological editor. This was the origin of *The Megalith Builders of Western Europe* which was Penguinized and translated into many languages. Richard Atkinson kindly wrote that it was a milestone in the study of megalithic monuments. What neither he nor I realized was that it was the last milestone on the wrong road!

At the time of its publication the students of the Institute of Archaeology in London asked me to talk to them on this same theme, which I did. Gordon Childe took me off to dinner and said, 'Wonderful lecture, lovely slides, do congratulate you. But it's the same old story, isn't it? I suppose we've got it right?'

We hadn't, but meanwhile I went on year after year, generously supported by the Leverhulme Foundation, making an overall survey of the French megaliths. This had never been done before: it seemed worth doing and it was an enjoyable task that took Ruth and me to almost every part of France. It resulted in a few papers and then my book *The Prehistoric Chamber Tombs of France*.

But all the time we were selling a particular model, preaching and practising a special doctrine, namely that all over Europe megalithic monuments were built by people who had come from the East Mediterranean and the Near East. When Thomsen and Worsaae first wrote about the stone monuments of Denmark they accepted the classification: *dysse, jaettester, stenkist*, but believed it a locally originating series. So did Montelius until he began to travel extensively and study the comparative literature. It was passage graves that particularly worried him, and eventually he came to the conclusion that the Danish and Swedish passage graves had come from the Mediterranean via Iberia, Brittany and Ireland. This became the canon in the twenties when proclaimed by Childe, Forde, Peake and Fleure, and it was this that I was preaching in detail.

The complete revision of these views came about in two ways. First by research students who worked in the Mediterranean. John Evans worked both in the East and West Mediterranean and began to have considerable doubts about the East Mediterranean origins of Los Millares in Spain and the Maltese megaliths. Colin Renfrew had more than doubts. Warwick Bray showed me that the *tombe di giganti* in Sardinia could not be ancestors of our British monuments. They were too late, as were the *navetas* of Menorca. Leslie Grinsell, writing in *Antiquity*, 1981, says of the Naveta of Els Tudons: 'It is now clear that Hemp, in visiting Menorca in 1926–32 to search for a possible origin of the British chambered long barrows among the *navetas*, was following a false scent, as it is now known that the *navetas* as a class date from at least a millennium after the British chambered long barrows had mostly fallen out of use.' I was also following a false scent: so was almost everybody at the time.

345

It was the radiocarbon revolution, the greatest breakthrough in the history of archaeology, that brought us to our senses. It was now clear that the megaliths of Portugal, Brittany, Ireland and Malta contained monuments built in 4000 BC and before. Some of the megaliths are older than the ziggurats of Mesopotamia and the pyramids of Egypt – in fact the oldest monumental architecture in the world, a style and craft that originated in that Western Crescent from Scandinavia to South Spain. And it would now appear that megalith building began independently in many parts of Europe. These new views are set out in Colin Renfrew's *Before Civilisation* (dedicated to Ruth and me). They represent a fascinating *volte face* which Gordon Childe did not live to make, or care to make, although he had his doubts.

But enough, or more than enough, about megaliths. My second great interest was in the history of archaeology. I had always been intrigued by how the system of Stone, Bronze, and Iron had come into existence and in the difficulties involved in its detailed application in the second quarter of the twentieth century. I wrote a small book, my first, called *The Three Ages*, which was published in 1942. Looking back on it I see that it showed I was concerned with two things, the history of the development of archaeology, and a dissatisfaction with the three-age system as a chronological and cultural framework for prehistory. I was enormously impressed by Childe's use of periods in his *Prehistoric Communities of the British Isles* and myself worked out a system of periods which was published in *Man*. It was found to be not necessary because of C14 dating but it shows how we were thinking at the time. I still think the old labels should be abolished and people should talk in chronological periods, as does for example the new archaeological gallery in the National Museum of Wales, but I expect we shall always go on using terms like Neolithic and Bronze Age.

But I had not really thought any further about pursuing the history of archaeology until I met Mervyn Horder in India. Mervyn asked me to write the volume on archaeology in his *Hundred Years* series. I agreed: it was published in 1950 – the same year as my *Chambered Tombs of England and Wales*. It was revised and reissued as *A Hundred and Fifty Years of Archaeology* in 1975. Cynical friends and unkind reviewers said how strange it was that archaeology could have aged fifty years in the twenty-five years between 1950 and 1975. What, of course, had happened was that my first volume was cabined and confined by the formula of the *Hundred Years* series. When I came to revise and re-write the book it seemed sensible to fix on the time when archaeology really came into existence as a conscious discipline, which was in the first quarter of the nineteenth century when the Danish National Museum (organized by C.J. Thomsen on the three-age system) was opened to the public, when Champollion announced the decipherment of Egyptian hieroglyphic writing, when the Venus de Milo was discovered and Rich was excavating in Babylon.

When I was asked to give the Josiah Mason Lectures in the University of Birmingham for the year 1956–7 I thought it would be interesting to discuss the development of the idea of prehistory in Western European, and particularly British, thought. I very much enjoyed giving these lectures which were subsequently published in 1962 in The New Thinkers Library under the title of *The Idea of Prehistory*. The Mason Lectures were founded by the Rationalist Press Association. The first series was given by Gordon Childe in 1947–8 and published in his book *Social Evolution* (1951). It was a great compliment, which I much valued, to be asked to give the second archaeological series; I have always thought that Childe's Mason lectures were one of the best things he ever did.

My third great interest in archaeology has been prehistoric art, although I have written very little on the subject. The mural art of the Upper Palaeolithic has been known for just over a hundred years. Now we know that it dates from thirty-four thousand years to ten thousand years ago. We are surprised by its unexpectedness and its naturalism. What was its purpose? The Abbé Breuil had no doubts: to him cave art was the expression of various forms of sympathetic magic and had a practical magical purpose – that the game should be plentiful, that it should increase and that sufficient should be killed. Others have argued for restitutive magic, that is the replacement by magic of an animal killed. Other explanations are house decoration, or art for art's sake.

Leroi Gourhan has been arguing since the mid sixties that each cave is decorated to a pre-determined plan and that the carnival of animals depicts more a mythogram than a catalogue of desirable foodstuffs, and exists only as a vehicle for other concepts. He finds always bison and horse placed in opposition; the bison to him is the female principle, the horse the male principle.

Where does all this get us? I quote from Ann Sieveking's *The Cave Artists*: 'All we know of Palaeolithic art,' she says, 'is its uniformity, its

347

duration, its location, and its content – the content being a very restricted inventory of animals accompanied by groups of schematic signs. It is very probable that we shall never know the meaning of Palaeolithic art for although the naturalistic art is potentially comprehensible, the idiomatic and schematic are not. They are simply a language for which we have no vocabulary.' And yet is this the last word we can say about man's earliest surviving artistic achievement?

There had been for some while a prejudice against prehistoric archaeologists dabbling in the study of art: this is the remains of the conflict between students of the material remains of the classical world, a conflict which unreasonably polarized scholars as archaeologists or art historians. In his *Archaeology and its Problems* (1957) Sigfried De Laet, Professor of Archaeology in the University of Ghent, declared: 'Works of art are not, of course, excluded from the province of archaeology, if they can clarify in any way the history of former civilizations. They remain, however, for archaeology, purely historical documents and archaeology should refrain, *as should the archaeologist*, from forming a subjective judgement on their aesthetic value. The distance which separates archaeology from art-history, moreover, increases every day.'

That was not, and is not, my view. When I was elected Visiting Ferens Professor of Fine Art in the University of Hull in 1969 I entitled my inaugural lecture *Archaeology and the History of Art* (Hull, 1970) and I quoted with approval statements by Seton Lloyd and Terence Powell. Seton Lloyd wrote in the preface to his book *The Ancient Art of the Near East*: 'In a world of equivocal values, art is an acceptable reality and its contemplation one of the greater privileges of our heredity.'

T.G.E. Powell reviewing Nancy Sandars's volume *Prehistoric Art in Europe* said:

The appearance of a volume on European prehistoric art . . . signifies the development of a climate of thought that in art, as in other fields, now begins to recognize the relevance of the works and days of preliterate people belonging to our own far distant past. Ancient art is no longer a matter of passing curiosity to all but a few specialists. . . . The call has gone forth for informed presentation of the great diversity of achievement, its causes for decline as often as for growth, and for some closer understanding of temporal and spiritual situations that find reflection in non-utilitarian creativity of such nature that 'art' is the only available word in modern vocabulary.

Stuart Piggott shared my views that prehistoric art was not studied sufficiently in itself; one evening in Delhi we planned together to do a book on prehistoric art in Britain. The result, published in 1951 by the Cambridge University Press, was *A Picture Book of Ancient British Art*. Since that time excellent books have appeared on this subject, notably Terence Powell's *Prehistoric Art* and Nancy Sandars's volume in the *Penguin History of Art* mentioned above. That 1951 book taught me a curious and sharp lesson. All my foes and most of my friends in Ireland left me in no doubt that they were shocked and furious that objects of prehistoric Irish art were included in a book called *Ancient British Art*. I learnt this salutary lesson and have been very careful ever since never to refer even to British passage graves but the passage graves of Wales, Ireland and Scotland.

I shall never forget my first visit to Dordogne and my first inspection of Palaeolithic cave art. It was not until after the war – I never got that far south as a student. Ruth and I had been looking at megaliths in Poitou and the Vendée and ended our travels in Cognac. Next day we were collected by Dorothy Garrod and Suzanne de Saint-Mathurin and driven to Les Eyzies. We were in the open boot (or rumble seat as Ruth says her father called it) and, in spite of rugs, were frozen all the way! We stopped for lunch at Brantôme where we were joined by Germaine Henri-Martin. Our lunch included, as one might expect in Périgord, an *omelette aux truffes*. Afterwards that vivacious and honest character Minne Henri-Martin said to me: 'Those weren't truffles in the omelette. In my view they were bits of burnt cork.' And of course after the war there were some surprising substitutes offered to the unwary. We once dined in Lapérouse in Paris, then one of the great restaurants. We ordered Chartreuse with our coffee: the usual supposedly correct mixture of $\frac{1}{3}$ green and $\frac{2}{3}$ yellow. I hadn't had any Chartreuse for six years and was a little surprised how sharp and hard it tasted. We slept very badly and felt ill next day. Our friends told us no proper Chartreuse was yet available: we had been fobbed off with some synthetic wood-alcohol substitute.

Despite arriving frozen at the Hôtel Les Glycines at Les Eyzies I fell in love with the place at once, and the next few days with delight we

349

saw Font de Gaume, Les Combarelles, La Mouthe, Cap Blanc and, by special arrangement, Lascaux. Upper Palaeolithic cave art is one of the very great achievements of our ancient past and no one should go through life without seeing some of the caves. Alas, Lascaux is no longer open to the public, but a faithful copy, Lascaux II, is now available and should be visited.

My affection for Dordogne has never left me. I spoke, *en passant*, to Sir Thomas Armstrong, of my 'beloved Dordogne'. Tom knows France well and loves it dearly, especially a little place, Job, in Auvergne, where he has stayed annually at the Hôtel des Voyageurs, for many years. He was moved to write to me from there when I was travelling in Dordogne.

My dear Glyn,

By this time you are perhaps in Brive: I remember it as a fine city, with some wonderful country round it. And you speak of your 'beloved Dordogne'. I could speak of my beloved Auvergne. What is it that makes us able to use such language and to feel love for these places? I know well that there's no exaggeration – no looseness of speech when we speak of love – but understand it or explain it I cannot. Why does one at once feel better when one arrives here? Is it something in the air – in the landscape – in the way of life? I think I feel some wholesomeness and basic integrity in the village life here, which I've known for many years. Of course I know that the well-off people are highly sophisticated and the peasants hard and grasping. I know that in the families who come here to lunch on Sundays there are all sorts of Balzacian horrors. And yet I feel there's a certain quality that I can't analyse or account for. It's a mystery: but it's a reality: and I'm sure you would say, as I do, that I don't know what life would have been if I hadn't as a young soldier in 1916 started a love-affair that has lasted all my life.

When Terence Powell and I began excavating Barclodiad y Gawres in 1952 I drove up to Anglesey from Cambridge and had as passenger Mrs Cyril Rootham whom I was depositing at Bangor Station. She asked me what I expected to find and I said, 'It is a Neolithic grave of Irish type: we may find stones decorated with spirals.' An hour after seeing her on to her train I was being welcomed at Barclodiad by Terence Powell who looked mysterious and excited. 'Come with me,' he said, and led me to see the top half of an orthostat which was being revealed by excavation, and there clearly to be seen were Boyne Valley spirals.

What have enormously interested me are the statue menhirs: the statue from Saint-Sernin has been one of my pin-up girls since my early undergraduate days, and I was most excited when, having inspected the chambered long barrows at Salles-la-Source I was able to see her face-to-face in the Musée Fenaille at Rodez.

My fourth great archaeological interest arose out of giving introductory lectures in Cambridge on the origins of civilization. I first taught the generally accepted thesis that there was, as Childe called it, a Neolithic Revolution that happened in the Near East – in Breasted's Fertile Crescent – and that in the Neolithic societies of the Near East the first civilizations developed, in Sumeria and in Egypt. It was essential to the Childe doctrine that all other civilizations – Crete, the Indus Valley and Shang China – were derived from the first civilizations of the most Ancient Near East. Everyone in the late twenties and thirties taught along these lines. Even Wheeler, until he got to India and to grips with Mohenjodaro and Harappa, repeated this doctrine: the Indus Civilization was a pale reflection of Sumeria.

But all the time I was working out a post-Childe message on the origin of civilization. I became increasingly worried about two areas – China and Central America. It is fascinating that Childe never considered the pre-Columbian American civilizations in his *What Happened in History* because he said they were outside the main stream of history. Similarly when I discussed the Olmecs and Incas with Mortimer Wheeler he pushed them aside saying, 'of only very marginal interest to the history of man,' and added, 'and in any case they were bloodthirsty barbarians'.

There was therefore a highly subjective element in the refusal by the then British archaeological establishment to consider pre-Columbian America. To Gordon Childe the main stream of history was Egypt, Mesopotamia, Palestine, Greece and Rome which led to Western European medieval and modern civilization. The deliberate disregard of American archaeology was one of the really deplorable facets of British prehistoric studies in the first half of the twentieth century. And it still is a neglected subject: there are only two academic posts in the subject among the two hundred archaeological posts in British Universities.

Gradually it became clear to me that the civilizations of the Indus

Valley and Shang China were not diffused from the Near East but were native developments and it seemed clear that this was also true of the civilizations of the New World. I tested out my ideas on my Cambridge pupils, and in a special course of lectures in the University of East Anglia, subsequently published them in my *The First Civilizations: the archaeology of their origins*.

My fifth great interest in archaeology has developed only in the last twenty years; this is in fakes, frauds and forgeries – sparked off by the unmasking of the Piltdown forgery in the fifties, my visit to Glozel, and *l'affaire Rouffignac*.

Whilst there have been endless speculations about Piltdown there is no doubt about three things: first, that the remains canonized as those of *Eoanthropus dawsonii* were announced to the world in December 1912 at a meeting of the Geological Society. I am happy to have known Tresilian C. Nicholas, now in his nineties and senior Fellow of Trinity College, Cambridge, who, as a young geological student, attended that historic meeting when Charles Dawson and Smith Woodward presented their finds.

Secondly, no alleged ancient remains from Piltdown were found by anyone after Dawson's death in 1916. Thirdly, Weiner, Oakley and others demonstrated clearly in the fifties that the remains called *Eoanthropus dawsonii*, the Dawn Man of Sussex, were not very old.

It was the late Professor J.S. Weiner who deduced that the Piltdown remains were not authentic and who took steps to expose the forgery. He worked in close contact with Kenneth Oakley and Sir Wilfred Le Gros Clark and they together published their findings in 1953. Weiner's *The Piltdown Forgery* came out in 1955 and by implication, though not by direct statement, suggested that Dawson was the forger. This I think most people now believe.

Many other candidates have been canvassed: Elliot Smith, W.J. Sollas, Teilhard de Chardin, Sir Arthur Conan Doyle, Horace de Vere Cole (acknowledged as a great hoaxer), Martin Hinton and many another. Both Louis Leakey and Stephen Gould were vigorous supporters of the Teilhard theory: it was difficult to persuade them that a careful study of Teilhard's letters revealed that he was not the culprit. Nevertheless I believe that Teilhard realized early that Piltdown was a hoax and that he had been taken in. Kenneth Oakley and I kept up by letter and discussion for over fifteen years, until his death in 1980, our attempts to get at the real truth of the Piltdown affair. The key issue was, did Dawson plant the canine for Teilhard to find, or, as Dr Harrison Matthews argued in a series of articles in *The New Scientist* from 30 April 1981 onwards, was the canine and, later, the bone implement shaped like a cricket bat, placed there by one or more people from the British Museum (Natural History) to warn Dawson that they knew of his alleged imposture?

Oakley agreed with me that Teilhard's role was that of an innocent accomplice invited on a few occasions to help Dawson in his excavations: and this is the view of Dorothy Garrod and Suzanne de Saint-Mathurin who both knew Teilhard very well. A few years ago I received a letter from a Mr Woodhead, and visited him in his retirement near Brighton, saying how his father, a chemist and public analyst, had been approached by Charles Dawson for advice on how to stain bones so that they looked ancient. I passed this on to Peter Costello who was writing a book on the Piltdown affair. His book is not yet published but he very kindly allowed me to print a summary in the November 1985 issue of *Antiquity*. He believes that the Piltdown hoaxer was Charles Dawson's friend, Sam Woodhead, and until last November I thought he had propounded the most reasonable solution of the affair. But then I received a remarkable letter from a Mrs Pryce of Maidenhead who had watched BBC *Newsnight*'s item on Piltdown, inspired by Costello's article. She told me in her letter that a Professor Hewitt had told her parents in her hearing, in 1952/3, that he and a friend were responsible for the hoax. I have visited Mrs Pryce and her mother, Mrs Hawkins, and find their testimony convincing. I now wonder, and so does Costello, whether the hoax was planned and executed by Hewitt and Woodhead (the 'friend'?), both now dead. I have set out my thoughts on this in a note in *Antiquity* (March 1986, 59–60).

Why was *Eoanthropus dawsonii* so uncritically accepted in the forty years following 1912? It was not accepted by all: some believed the remains were those of two separate individuals, one human and one ape – Louis Leakey was one of these, but he never suggested forgery. There was an unconscious and understandable desire by English scholars to welcome a very ancient fossil found in England; indeed Smith Woodward called his book on Piltdown *The First Englishman*. And they had forgotten the lesson of the Moulin Quignon jaw; and that the English geologist J. Middleton in 1844, and the French mineralogist A. Carnot in 1893, had demonstrated that the amount of fluorine in fossil bones increases with their geological age. Oakley rediscovered the work of these men during the last war. If remembered, the fluorine test could have been applied in 1912 and saved the scientific world a great deal of argument about the true place of these false remains in the ancient history of man's evolution. The whole affair has been a great lesson in the credulity and credibility of scientists.

And yet, and yet, many of us have doubts about Rouffignac and there are *still* some who believe in the genuineness of Glozel. This site, some 30 kilometres south-east of Vichy in Central France, was discovered in 1925 by Emile Fradin, the son of the Fradin family who farmed Glozel. It yielded and went on yielding a strange collection of objects: decorated pots, phallic objects, and inscribed tablets. Fradin was adopted by Dr Morlet, an amateur archaeologist from Vichy, who wrote vigorously advocating the importance of the site. He was supported by Saloman Reinach, then head of the Musée des Antiquités Nationales at Saint-Germain-en-Laye, who had always argued against the origin of the French Neolithic in the Near East – what he called *Le Mirage Orientale* – and found in Glozel the proof of a native French origin of the Neolithic and the arts of writing. But in 1927 an International Committee of which Dorothy Garrod was a member declared Glozel a forgery.

I was eager to see this strange site and when I did so, was flabbergasted. There were one or two genuine objects, polished stone axes that can be found in most places in France, but the rest were fakes of the most blatant kind. I persuaded the BBC to make a film of this curiosity and during a week's filming I got to know Fradin well. One afternoon, after a lot of red wine, he asked me if I would re-excavate the site with him. I said, 'But we would find nothing, unless someone put material there.' He was silent, but has gone on saying there were no fakes and that he had forged nothing.

Then a very curious thing happened: thermoluminescence and C14 dates were obtained which suggested that some of the Glozel objects, obviously made in the twenties, could be dated to the Gallo-Roman period; and this anomaly has not been explained. There was a demand for fresh excavations and this was done a few years ago. Nothing was found. Most French archaeologists want to forget Glozel, but it should not be forgotten: like Piltdown it is an object lesson in the credulity and credibility of archaeologists and scientists. And it still draws the interest of cranks and crackpots on the lunatic fringes of archaeology. The 1982 volume of the *Publications of the Epigraphic Society of America* contains an article by a Mr Donald Buchanan which argues that Glozel was an ancient sex-shop. He claims to have deciphered the Fradin-Morlet forgeries of the twenties and concludes that Glozel was 'some sort of bazaar, whether seasonal or permanent is not known. Since the language was Semitic and the script Iberic, it would appear that Iberian Punic merchants were operating a trading centre and dealing with a predominantly Celtic population. The bazaar dealt in livestock, devices to ensure sexual potency, various salves and ointments, curative charms and amulets.' (See *Antiquity*, 1984.) How much further down the slippery slopes can one go before raving lunacy is certifiable?

While French archaeologists do not wish to mention Glozel, they glory in Rouffignac and regard their colleagues in France, England and America (such as Mademoiselle de Saint-Mathurin, myself and Professor Brian Fagan) who question the authenticity of all the paintings and engravings at Rouffignac, as unbalanced, unkind or even evil persons. Yet this is not so. There remains considerable doubt about Rouffignac and it is to the disgrace of French Palaeolithic archaeology that this issue has not been properly faced.

The facts are straightforward and have been set out by me in Chapter VI of my *The Hungry Archaeologist in France* (1963). The village of Rouffignac is about 15 km north of Les Eyzies: the cave now famous or infamous for its collection of alleged Palaeolithic paintings and engravings has been known for centuries as the Grotte de Miremont and cave explorers have written their names in it for many years. On the 20 July 1956, at the Congrès Préhistorique de France in Poitiers, Professor Robert Nougier of the University of Toulouse and Monsieur R. Robert of Tarascon-en-Ariège announced that on 26 June of that year they had visited the Grotte de Miremont and discovered a fantastic quantity of painted and engraved animals, more than one hundred and forty – mammoths predominate: there are more than twenty-seven painted mammoths and forty-three engraved representations. In between their discovery and the meeting at Poitiers the site was visited by the Abbé Breuil who authenticated the find. He did not spend long there; his sight was failing. He never entertained the possibility that some of the art was a modern forgery. Nor did he at that time recollect that he had visited the site in 1915 but saw no paintings or engravings; later when he remembered this visit he said his visit was a short one and that, with a friend, he was looking for beetles. The one indisputable fact about Rouffignac is that the art is very clear and very obvious.

This discovery of Nougier and Robert, authenticated by Breuil, doyen of Palaeolithic art studies, was published in *Figaro* and *The Times*, where I read of it. I had not heard of the Grotte de Miremont before and idly picked up a book by Bernard Pierret entitled *Le Périgord Souterrain* published in 1953. I had bought it on a visit to Dordogne but had not cut the pages until the *Figaro–Times* announcement in 1956: imagine my surprise when I came across a photograph of Pierret and a friend with their tent and behind them the frieze of rhinoceroses.

Clearly the Rouffignac paintings were known well before the Nougier-Robert 'discovery'. But there was a second shock: as I cut the pages of *Le Périgord Souterrain* and read the text, there was no mention of the paintings so obvious in the photograph or any suggestion that there was Palaeolithic art at Rouffignac. Now we must not forget that Pierret and his *copains* were not only experienced spelaeologists but like every French schoolboy in Dordogne, knew about Palaeolithic art and had been taken on school trips to see Font de Gaume and Les Combarelles. They had spent many days and nights in Rouffignac and produced an accurately surveyed plan of the site which is reproduced by all French archaeologists who write about it.

Why did Bernard Pierret not comment on the paintings? Because, say Nougier and Robert, 'he saw the paintings . . . and did not understand'. Because, says Pierret himself, he knew them to be of recent date! Severin Blanc, schoolmaster at Les Eyzies and subsequently in charge of antiquities in the region, when he heard of the 'discovery' in 1956 said he knew the rhinoceros frieze well and that he examined it at the request of Pierret, who had made detailed visits to the cave for years and was surprised to see these animals appear on a wall hitherto unpainted. This was in 1949. Pierret and his friends explored and surveyed the cave between 1945 and 1949 when the site was closed by its owner. The Pierret photograph dates at least seven years before the discovery.

Much intrigued by all this – and I suppose it is my interest in reading and writing detective stories that rubs off into the study of archaeological forgery – I got in touch with a schoolmaster at

Périgueux by the name of William Martin (French, though admittedly an English sounding name); he told me that he had seen the walls at Rouffignac, now covered with paintings, when they were bare. At my suggestion he wrote a letter to *The Sunday Times* of London who published it on 1 March 1959. Here is part of what Martin wrote:

I assert categorically that in September 1948 there were no paintings or engravings in the Rouffignac cave. In 1946, together with other young men, I founded the Spéléo Club Périgourdin. . . . From the beginning Rouffignac attracted our attention. . . . Our first task was to re-draw and check the plan made by Martel in 1898 and the measurements we had to make for this involved every nook and cranny. In no place at any time did we find traces of paintings or engravings. One day I personally spent from 7 a.m. to 6 p.m. looking specifically for traces of early art and failed to find anything. The last time I visited Rouffignac was September 1948 and on that occasion I spent three days underground. I can confirm that the frieze of rhinoceroses was not there then on the wall of the gallery in which we set up our tents. In December 1949 I learned from Bernard Pierret that two rhinoceroses had been painted on the wall, and by Easter a third. Let us then no longer speak of the authenticity of this rhinoceros frieze.

In the same year in which William Martin last visited Rouffignac, Dr Koby and the Abbé Glory visited the site; both these experienced prehistorians and geologists saw no Palaeolithic art, yet they were studying the site in great detail looking for claw-marks of cave-bears which they found. In March/April 1939 the Cambridge University Spelaeological Society went on a caving expedition to Les Eyzies; after ten days of visiting the known decorated caves they went to Rouffignac. One of its members, Colonel Arthur Walmesley-White, wrote to me (27 September 1956): 'I am fairly certain that we never saw any drawings or paintings and that the owner didn't know of any.'

William Martin mentioned the fact that he, Pierret, and the other members of the Spéléo Club Périgourdin were checking the 1898 Martel plan. Edouard Martel was one of the most famous French spelaeologists and geologists of caves. His plan of Rouffignac took three days to do and he was assisted by French military surveyors. He mentioned no art: Nougier, aware of the damaging effect of the negative evidence of Martel and experienced surveyors, said that they must have seen the paintings but kept silence because of the scepticism aroused by the discovery of Altamira in 1879.

But Martel did not die in the nineties: he lived through the acceptance of Palaeolithic art in 1901/2 and, in 1930 when Palaeolithic cave art was well known and in all archaeological textbooks, he wrote a fine book called *La France Ignorée* in which he described the decorated caves of La Mouthe, Les Combarelles, Font de Gaume and Altamira. In this book he says of Rouffignac: 'Tout l'intérêt . . . est exclusivement d'ordre géologique.'

Yet the French establishment persists in believing Rouffignac to be another Lascaux. In 1982 there was published *L'Art pariétal de Rouffignac: la grotte aux cent mammouths* by Claude Barrière, a large, fully illustrated book costing 400 francs. As a record of what is at present on the walls of Rouffignac it is invaluable. It does nothing to suggest that anything is modern. It is scandalous. But then Rouffignac is a scandal: it is the French Piltdown and there may be one day some scientific tests to show that the paint used is modern. To me there is no way round the testimony of Martel, the Cambridge spelaeologists of 1939, William Martin, Severin Blanc and Bernard Pierret. There may have been one or two genuine engravings at Rouffignac but the major part of the paintings and engravings are from 1948 to 1956. We remember the remark made to us years ago by that perceptive and highly critical and amusing archaeologist, Germaine Henri-Martin, now, alas, dead: 'There are two styles represented at Rouffignac – one is a pastiche copy of other Palaeolithic art, the other is *Babar l'Eléphant*.' I believed her at the time, but now think there *may* have been some original authentic paintings and engravings (yet, all missed by Breuil, Glory, Koby, Martel, Pierret, Martin and Severin Blanc?) but the great majority of what is now passed off as Palaeolithic art can be accurately dated to AD 1948–56.

These words, if read by the Abbé Breuil, would make him turn in his grave. The Abbé died in the fullness of years in 1961, mourned by all who understood the enormous role he had played for so long in the development of Palaeolithic studies and particularly in the discovery and study of Upper Palaeolithic art. But by the time of the Rouffignac discovery and the subsequent controversy he was old, opinionated and his sight and judgment were failing. He refused to consider the reasonable unbiased testimony of those who knew the site well in the forties, dismissing them as ignorant, unobservant schoolteachers and peasants. He declared that there was only one person alive who could make reasonable forged copies of Upper Palaeolithic art and that was himself, and that he had not forged the Rouffignac paintings. It was all sad and painful and his estrangement at the end of his life from Dorothy Garrod and Suzanne de Saint-Mathurin was unhappy. In his obituary notice of Breuil in the *Guardian* (22 August 1961), Darsie Gillie, then its Paris correspondent and himself keenly interested in archaeology, said of the Abbé that he 'failed to carry conviction with many competent prehistorians when he declared authentic all the paintings in the Rouffignac caves. When the *Académie des Inscriptions*, of which he was a member, declined to discuss a communication he made on this subject . . . he swept out in a memorable whirlwind of soutane' and 'did not take his seat again for a long time.'

On 12 September 1956 a special visit to Rouffignac of some thirty archaeologists from various countries was arranged. I was happy to be invited to join this party, which included some distinguished specialists in Palaeolithic art like Professor Martin Almagro of Madrid, Professor Paolo Graziosi of Florence, and Mademoiselle Suzanne de Saint-Mathurin; it also included Severin Blanc, then in charge of the antiquities of the region, general prehistorians like myself, Nougier and Robert, the discoverers, and ten to fifteen Spanish students of Almagro's who were on a field class in France. This ill-assorted gang meeting on 12 September is described, ridiculously, by Barrière in this way:

> Un débat scientifique sur place a lieu en septembre avec tous les grands noms de la Préhistoire, il conclut à l'authenticité des oeuvres pariétales de la grotte de Rouffignac.

What rubbish! How French archaeologists delude themselves! When the visit of the morning of 12 September was over, most of the ill-assorted party signed one of two declarations, the first saying that all was authentic, the second that nothing had been seen to show that Rouffignac was *not* authentic. I myself signed neither declaration and escaped away from the cave as did another non-signatory, Mademoiselle de Saint-Mathurin, whose knowledge of Upper Palaeolithic art was and is certainly wider and deeper than that of most who signed the authenticity document. She remains very doubtful of the authenticity of the paintings and has not minced words on the issue from that day to this.

One very amusing thing happened during our very difficult walk through the cave. Now it is easy to visit it: a little railway transports you from one end to another in seated comfort. In 1956 we tumbled about over thick mud and silt: at one moment Mademoiselle de Saint-Mathurin slipped down into a hole and, as we pulled her up, said something in English to me. The others crowded around to hear what words of wisdom she had pronounced: was she satisfied of the authenticity of the paintings, they asked me. I said: 'Mademoiselle has not yet made up her mind.' What she said to me was: 'Oh hell, I have split my pants.'

When we emerged into the sunshine, having signed no documents, we walked up the hill to our car. An old crone came out of the farm. 'Where do you think we should build the café-restaurant?' she asked us; and as we drove back to Les Eyzies I remembered the pictures from the twenties of the café-restaurants that sprang up around Glozel.

Many people are happy to describe Glozel as a forgery. No one, so far as is recorded, said, before Jo Weiner, that Piltdown was a forgery. I now believe that most of the paintings and engravings at Rouffignac are modern fakes and this infuriates many of my French colleagues, who believe otherwise. In 1959 Vaufrey wrote in *L'Anthropologie*: 'leur authenticité n'est pas douteuse'; but in the very week those words appeared in print Professor Claude Schaeffer, one of the most distinguished French archaeologists, wrote to me: 'You know that Rouffignac is considered a scandalous fake. This will be another Glozel.'

Like Piltdown, Rouffignac has survived. Pierret, Martin, Severin Blanc, the Abbé Breuil, Germaine Henri-Martin, Dorothy Garrod, Claude Schaeffer are all dead. I don't think my views will take me to the guillotine, but I would be happy to mount the steps clutching a few copies of *Antiquity* and perhaps a copy of Isaac de la Peyrère's 1655 *Theological System that there were men before Adam*, which was publicly burnt in Paris in the seventeenth century – the only archaeological/geological treatise ever to be so honoured. I was glad to hear recently an American broadcast in which Professor Brian Fagan made it clear that he believed Rouffignac was a fraud. I am interested to read that *The 'Holiday' Which? Guide to France* (1982) speaks of Rouffignac, 'whose Magdalenian paintings were only recently discovered among fakes and multitudes of graffiti'. The Green Guide Michelin for Dordogne, while it counsels us to wear warm clothing when visiting

Rouffignac, makes no suggestion that the art is other than late Aurignacian to Magdalenian. Here it is on the side of the French establishment – but then *les Guides Michelin* are very much part of the French establishment.

I must not end this chapter on a note of recrimination. The profession of archaeologist is an honourable one, a humanist discipline which, it is now recognized, can truly deepen and extend our knowledge not only of megaliths but also of men.

It has not always been so. A.E. Housman greeted the foundation in 1921 of the Frazer Lectureship with these words:

> The Golden Bough has spread to a spacious forest whose king receives homage from a multitude who find there learning mated with literature and a museum of dark and uncouth superstition invested with the charm of a truly sympathetic magic. You have gathered together, for the admonition of a proud and oblivious race, the scattered and fading relics of its foolish childhood, whether withdrawn from our view among savage folk or lying unnoticed at our doors. The forgotten milestones of the road which man has travelled, the mazes and blind alleys of his progress through time are illuminated by your art and genius.

Labourers in neighbouring fields had come to similar conclusions, expressed more tersely if with less eloquence. Crawford said archaeology was the past tense of anthropology. Lowie said that prehistory was simply the ethnography of extinct social groups; that prehistory reveals only material phenomena and only part of them; it can determine accurately certain phases of technology and nothing else. Adamson Hoebel was even gloomier: 'Archaeology', he said, 'is always limited in the results it can produce: it is doomed always to be the lesser part of anthropology.'

In the face of such scepticism, what can a believing and practising archaeologist say in reply? Even for the historian to claim that he can understand the past – say Athens two thousand years ago – is dubious enough. How then do we approach the task of imagining ourselves among the unimaginably different people who cut the ithyphallic giant at Cerne Abbas; who built the megalithic temples in Malta; who painted the naturalistic masterpieces in the dark caves of Altamira and Lascaux? How do we get behind the material to the behaviour? How do we make the fossil bones and dead cities live?

By controlled imagination inspired by our knowledge of societies technologically parallel to those we are studying. Not most certainly from our knowledge of modern industrial societies – there lies the modern pathetic archaeological fallacy that we must always guard against. Our creative imagination must be inspired by anthropology, history and folk studies.

And we must always remember three things. The inadequacy and incompleteness of the prehistoric record; the subjectivity of the art of historical interpretation; and the necessity of using ethnographical, historical and folk parallels in no deterministic way but as pointers to the possibilities of interpretation. We are still only too painfully aware of the gaps in our knowledge, that we are dealing with the shipwrecks of time. Archaeologists, particularly prehistoric archaeologists like myself, are always labouring with the very imperfectly known prehistoric past.

What, then, does 'creative imagination' mean in the context of the main theme of this chapter, the megaliths? In the first place they must be seen not simply as blocks of stone but as religious monuments, as beliefs made lithic. Their duration is incidentally longer than that of Christianity, Buddhism or Islam. The religion of the megalith builders is, to use Wood-Martin's phrase, one of the elder faiths of Europe. We know, positively and negatively, the purpose of some of these megaliths. Many of the stone chambers were tombs – collective family or communal vaults used over a long period of time – sometimes containing two hundred and more bodies. Tombs and temples are often combined in Christian churches and many of the dolmens and cromlechau may also have been temples. The stone circles, alignments and other structures, like Hal Tarxien and the Gigantija in Malta, were neither tombs nor houses. I believe, with many others, that the Carnac alignments, Stonehenge, Avebury, and Callanish were places where secular and sacred festivals took place rather like the present-day *pardons* in Brittany, which are basically religious occasions but also markets and hiring fairs. Of course to say this is to project into antiquity my personal subjective views based on modern folk parallels and my peasant youth in Wales.

Most archaeologists in their right mind – and many who are not – have always assumed that the complicated and impressive megalithic structures were built by people who possessed very considerable technical and architectural skills: the skill for example to float a capstone weighing a hundred tons and balance it on orthostats six feet high. The megalith builders worked with plans perhaps done on parchments that have not survived, or on sandtables. They must have had units of measurement and a simple knowledge of practical if not theoretical geometry sufficient to lay out a rough ring or a right-angled triangle.

For a very long time it has been clear that many megaliths were oriented, and why not? Christian churches point to the east and mosques to Mecca. The midsummer sunrise happens over the main axis of Stonehenge; at the midwinter solstice the sun rises and shines for a few minutes through the roof box at Newgrange and illuminates the back stone of the far side-chamber. Gerald Hawkins thought that Stonehenge was a giant eclipse predictor, and when I asked my colleague Fred Hoyle for his views on the Hawkins theory he, to my intense surprise, not only thought it was possible and convincing but added that perhaps the doctrine of the Trinity could be based on Stonehenge!

Alexander Thom, his family and his disciples believe that all megalithic monuments point to the stars. They may well do: there are enough stars to go round, but most of us believe that their case, to use a Scottish phrase, is not proven. When I was a young research student working in Brittany I met a remarkable mad doctor called Marcel Baudouin and was taken round his extraordinary museum in the Vendée, his museum of megalithic astronomy. I still have the copy of his book he inscribed to me, *La Préhistoire par les Etoiles*, now happily forgotten by most people. Even then, and certainly now, I prefer my prehistory to be guided *par les étoiles* in le Guide Michelin.

The astroarchaeology of megaliths does not get us very far but it has provided an easy fringe religion for those who demand some certainty in matters megalithic – the certainty of faith rather than fact. In the last few years Colin Renfrew and others have applied ethnographical parallels to the interpretation of prehistoric European megaliths. They have compared the social and religious beliefs of Pacific islanders, like those who set up the great statues of Easter Island, with those of prehistoric Malta, and I shall never forget my talk with John Layard about the Stone men of Malekula. The stone and wooden henge monuments of Britain have been compared with the ritual houses of the Cherokee Indians so well described by Bertram. Renfrew has also argued with cogency that the European megaliths were built by a society with chieftains and priests and even, and this is more speculative, attempted to map the territorial domains of these fourth and third millennia chieftaincies.

So far, so good, and we must pursue and test all these new paradigms; but nothing really gets us nearer to knowing the religious beliefs and non-secular motivations of the megalith builders, or to understanding their society. On the walls of some of their tombs and temples and on small objects we find three representational motifs: a hafted stone axe; snakes or serpents; and the figure of a female, the Déesse Mère, the Earth Mother Goddess. For the rest, megalithic art is schematic and geometrical – spirals, lozenges, ellipses, zigzags. Like Upper Palaeolithic non-representational art these idiomatic and schematic patterns are not comprehensible to us; they too are written in a language for which we have no vocabulary.

You may well think that I am spreading a spirit of archaeological pessimism, scepticism and cynicism. You are right, but I am not alone in this. Many who have studied with care the limitations of archaeological interpretation – Margaret Smith, Christopher Hawkes, Stuart Piggott, to mention three names – have come to the same conclusion. Professor Piggott shares with me what I call a realistically conservative but not defeatist view of the anthropological attempts to interpret the archaeology of the prehistoric past. He says: 'Archaeological evidence alone can inform us of only the broadest aspects of social structure or religious belief, and that in a tentative way. All the prehistorian can really perceive is the history of technology.'

It is not surprising then that the general intelligent reading public are often depressed and defeated by archaeology. When they hope for the history of man they are given the history of tools. They say, and how I sympathize with them: 'We do not wish to know about the types of safety-pin used by the Early Iron Age farmers of northern France; we want to know the essentials of prehistoric societies, how they lived, what they thought, what were their ideals and illusions, how we differ from them, or whether we are the same people. We want the anthropology, not the archaeology of the past.'

Because these answers are not forthcoming there has come into existence what is called by some alternate or alternative archaeology – that is what its practitioners and devotees call it; its opponents and denigrators call it lunatic archaeology. I prefer to call those who dwell on the wilder shores of archaeology and its lush lunatic fringes by the straightforward phrase enshrined in our language since the 1914–18 war; I call them practitioners of bullshit archaeology. These are the people who believe in the lost tribes of Israel, Egypto-centrism, Atlantis, Mu, straight lines; these are the ley-hunters and pyramidiots; these are the people who find the signs of the zodiac in the quiet hedgerows of the English countryside. I sometimes wonder whether it is not something curiously significant that one of the places (apart from Glastonbury, where poor misguided Mrs Maltwood started it all) in which these zodiac signs have been found is the surely appropriately named village of Nuthampstead. Latterly, with the encouragement of Erich von Däniken, visitors from outer space have been added to the already long catalogue of archaeological myths. Von Däniken has added astronautarchaeology to the already dubious semischolarship and semilunacy of astroarchaeology, and everything – Tassili frescoes, Nasca lines, falsely interpreted Maya glyphs – has been pressed into the service of the chariot-riding gods.

Nowhere, alas, does bullshit archaeology flourish so well these days as in America, where foolish fantasies pour from the press every month and sell like hot cakes. When the ordinary New Yorker steps off the pavement of Fifth Avenue and walks into a good bookshop he is faced with nonsense archaeological books all jostling on the same shelves with scholarly books by Gordon Willey, Desmond Clark and Brian Fagan. The sadness to me is that American professors, presumably reputable in their own field, have jumped eagerly on to this bandwagon. Professor Cyrus Gordon of Brown is one such, Sertima of Rutgers another, but the prize must go to Barry Fell, formerly Professor of Marine Zoology at Harvard, whose book *America B.C.* (before Columbus not before Christ) was also published in this country. Fell brings a curious load of Celts from Western Europe to America in prehistoric times; in Spain they met with Libyans, Carthaginians and Berbers, and colonized eastern America, leaving as their clear archaeological traces ogham inscriptions and megalithic monuments. I need not remind my readers that there are no ogham inscriptions or megaliths in America, east, west, north or south.

What can we do about all this? First, by setting out our present-day views in historical perspective, so that we can see how our present views have evolved and how in the past we have ourselves harboured and encouraged misguided enthusiasms.

In the second place we should set out our considered and well argued views about man and his past as clearly, as simply and as cogently as we can in all ways – in books, lectures, broadcasts, museum displays, television programmes. And thirdly we should not shrink from pinpointing and exposing false archaeology in every way we can. It used to be the fashion to brush aside lunatic archaeology: it was bad taste to mention it as it was to mention fakes and forgeries until Kenneth Oakley and Joe Weiner broke open Piltdown. Peter White's *The Past is Human* is an excellent example of what can be done to debunk the false prophets; it is a worthy book to be set alongside Roland Dixon's *The Building of Cultures* and Robert Wauchope's *Lost Tribes and Sunken Continents*. We have for long talked about *haute vulgarisation*; what we need now as well is *haut déboulonnage* and I offer this phrase to the French Academy.

One last word about megaliths. In collecting material for what my pupils and friends amusingly call 'Old Daniel's last megalithic will and testament', I tracked down the origin of Siegfried Sassoon's oft-quoted phrase 'and argued easily round megaliths' which I have been using in lectures for years and which I knew came from his poem *Early Chronology* written in the rooms of W.H. Rivers Rivers on E Staircase, New Court of St John's College.

Rivers was a remarkable man. Born in 1864 he was a Fellow of St John's from 1902 until his sudden early death in 1922. I had two remote connections with him: he was Director of Studies in Archaeology and Anthropology at St John's, the first person to hold such an office in any Cambridge College. I succeeded to this office in 1946 and there was no one holding this post for the quarter century between Rivers and me. In the second place he had made special arrangements for his funeral which so impressed E.A. Benians that, as I have described, he asked for his funeral to be on the same lines and, as acting Junior Bursar, I had to make these arrangements.

In 1897 Rivers had become lecturer in Physiological and Experimental Psychology in the University of Cambridge, a new post which a hostile critic described as a 'ridiculous superfluity'. He made outstanding contributions to physiology, psychology, psychiatry and anthropology as have been well set out by Richard Slobodin in his biography *W.H.R. Rivers* (New York, 1978), a volume in the Leaders of Modern Anthropology Series. He was a pioneer of the study of 'shell-shock' – a term he did not like: 'the unfortunate and misleading

W.H.R. Rivers. from $⌀$.

July. 1919. _____ 'a very wise man'...

EARLY · CHRONOLOGY.

SLOWLY the daylight left our listening faces.

Professor Brown with level baritone
Discoursed into the dusk.
                    Five thousand years
He guided us through scientific spaces
Of excavated History; till the lone
Roads of Research grew blurred; and in our ears
Time was the rumoured tongues of vanished races,
And Thought a chartless Age of 'Ice and Stone'.

The story ended. Then the darkened air
Flowered as he lit his pipe; an aureole glowed
Enwreathed with smoke; the moment's match-light showed
His rosy face, broad brow, and smooth grey hair,
Backed by the crowded book-shelves.
                                In his wake
An archaeologist began to make
Assumptions about aqueducts; (he quoted
Professor Sandstorm's book); and soon they floated
Through dessicated forests; mangled myths;
And argued easily round megaliths.

Beyond the college garden something glinted;
A copper moon climbed clear above the trees.
Some Lydian coin?... Professor Brown agrees
That copper coins were in that culture minted.
But, as her whitening way aloft she took,
I thought she had a pre-dynastic look.

_____

(New Court.
14 - 8 - 19.)

Manuscript of Siegfried Sassoon's poem 'Early Chronology' given to W.H.R. Rivers in 1919.

term "shell shock,"' he wrote, 'which the general public have now come to use for the nervous disturbances of warfare' (*Instinct and the Unconscious*, 1920). He was appointed in 1916 Senior Psychiatrist in the Craiglockhart Hospital for Officers on the outskirts of Edinburgh – the Dottyville of Robert Graves's *Good-bye to All That* and the Slateford War Hospital of Sassoon's memoirs. Siegfried Sassoon was a patient of Rivers and had a tremendous admiration for him: they became firm friends. The first part of Sassoon's *Sherston's Progress* is entitled 'Rivers'. Twelve years after Rivers's death Sassoon wrote 'Revisitation 1934' which begins

> What voice revisits me this night? What face
> To my heart's room returns?

He often visited Rivers after the war in St John's. When the first edition of his *Picture-Show* was published in 1919 it contained a lovely moving poem, 'To a Very Wise Man', which was written to and about Rivers. The copy he gave to Rivers bears the superscription I reproduce here. It also contains, pasted in, the manuscript of his poem 'Early Chronology' (printed in the American edition of *Picture-Show*, 1920) and I reproduce both of these here by kind permission of the Master and Fellows of St John's. It was written during his stay in St John's during a weekend in July 1919 when, after dinner in Hall, a group of Fellows and guests repaired to Rivers's rooms and talked for hours. The Professor Brown of the poem was Elliot Smith and the 'archaeologist' was W.J. Sollas. For all his wisdom Rivers, like Elliot Smith and Perry, did argue easily about megaliths and, like them, went, to use Slobodin's words, 'up the blind alley of heliocentric diffusionism'.

CHAPTER TWELVE

A house in France

MOST MIDDLE-AGED DONS in any university work very hard in term-time – teaching, lecturing, supervising research students, doing administrative work, attending meetings: at an accurate guess a seventy- to eighty-hour week would be quite normal. It is not surprising that they look for places to escape to in vacation or for the odd weekend where they can relax and read and write in peace. Many of my Cambridge colleagues had cottages in Norfolk, the Lake District or Wales.

My native country of Wales seemed the obvious place for us. We had often gone for weekends to that haven of peace, quiet and rest, Llanwrtyd Wells in Central Wales. We thought about a cottage or abandoned farmhouse nearby but we gradually realized that it takes five hours to drive from Cambridge to what was then Radnorshire, that when you get there you are likely to have a lot of rain, and that there are only a very limited number of good eating places in the neighbourhood.

It was Ruth's idea that we might have a house in France rather than Norfolk or Wales: so many of the good things in my life are her idea. It was 1962, we were in our late forties. The house was not to be in the south of France, or Dordogne, or Brittany but in the north of France. We studied Michelin Sheet 51 Boulogne to Arras, not as travellers looking for the road from the Channel ports to Paris or Reims, but as settlers to whom it would be their home map, as it indeed has been for over twenty years.

We consulted the *Guide Michelin*: there was then a one-star hotel in Ardres, 17 kilometres south-east of Calais and 23 kilometres north-east of Saint-Omer. It was the Grand Hôtel Clément and here we were befriended by the then proprietors, M. et Mme Gantelme: and by Mme Gantelme's son Paul Coolen and his Breton wife Monique, who now run the hotel. Ardres is a small country town of just over 3,000 inhabitants, famous in French and English history because it was here that Francis I resided in 1520 during the celebrated encounter of the

369

Field of the Cloth of Gold with Henry VIII, who was in residence at Guines a few miles away. Although I did a paper on the Tudor period at school, I knew nothing of Ardres in relation to Henry VIII. My first conscious knowledge of it was from Wordsworth's poem with its surprising opening. In 1789 he and his friend, Robert Jones, spent a Cambridge vacation walking to Switzerland. They walked all the way from Calais and Wordsworth wrote a sonnet published in 1807 but apparently written on 7 August 1802: and described by him as 'composed near Calais on the road to Ardres'. The published version begins:

> Jones! as from Calais southward you and I
> Went pacing side by side this public way
> Streamed with the pomp of this too-credulous day.

The day was 14 July 1789: the fall of the Bastille.

It is one of his *Poems Dedicated to National Independence*. In that fascinating collection is the poem 'Fair Star of Evening' with the lines written near Calais:

> I with many a fear
> For my dear country, many heartfelt sighs,
> 'Mongst men who do not love her, linger here.

as well as that extraordinary poem (number 42) entitled 'Cathedrals, etc., open your Gates, ye everlasting Piles!', with the line:

> Isis and Cam, to patient science dear!

I would be fascinated to know where Wordsworth and Jones spent their nights on the five-hundred-mile walk from Calais to Switzerland. Where did he linger in the Pas-de-Calais? Not in the Clément at Ardres. This delightful quiet hotel of the early twentieth century, in the middle of the little town, has the air of an English inn and is much frequented by English travellers as their first or last stop in France. Paul Coolen has a high reputation as a chef and so has his son François. I can think with pleasure of many occasions over the last twenty-five years when I have enjoyed their *bar flambé au fenouil*, *andouillettes au genièvre* and *lapin à la moutarde*. Louis Gantelme looked and dressed in every way like an English gentleman: he had once run two outfitters shops in Calais, and spoke good English. He had been an interpreter in the 1914–18 war and it was difficult to fault him – except for an occasional amusing idiom, as when having offered you a drink and lifted up his glass, he would say, with careful emphasis, '*At* your good health'. He was of the greatest help in our early negotiations; we mourned his death in 1971 at the age of 77.

First we went to the British Vice-Consul in Calais, M. Vancoste-noble, explained what we planned to do, and then went on to Maître Ryssen, a *notaire* in Ardres who acted for us throughout. Our plan at this stage was to buy a small plot of land and put up one of the chalet-type prefabricated houses which were being much advertised in the sixties and could be erected in a few days. We visited exhibitions of them in the suburbs of Paris. We had been told *on no account* to buy a house. Together with Maître Ryssen we examined various plots of land south of Ardres. One seemed just what we wanted but the farmer said that if the English found it so nice, then that was just where he was going to build a house for his retirement!

One day, in the summer of 1963, in the pouring rain, having sadly rejected two plots that Ryssen had taken us to, we paused for coffee and cognac in the Café au Bon Accueil on the hill just to the north of the little village of Zouafques, eight kilometres south of Ardres. Ryssen pointed across the road to a house we had not seen before; it was surrounded by trees and looked out over the village and to the hills on the other side of the river Hem. 'I don't suppose you would like to buy that,' said Ryssen. 'It is at present occupied by the postman's widow, Madame Bodelet, and I believe she wants to sell.' We said no, but agreed to examine the house. It had been built in the twenties and consisted of four rooms each four metres square, with a large cellar and a large attic which included one room. We admitted to an interest: the view was lovely and there was a lot of ground. That evening during dinner at the Clément we discussed all possibilities.

Next day, 5 July, was Ruth's birthday and we drove off for a few days' holiday in the Belgian Ardennes, staying in that welcoming hotel, Val Joli, at Celles near Dinant. We went for a walk; I remember the *boudin de truite saumonée* and the *gâteau d'écrevisses* at dinner and our decision not to buy. Next morning at breakfast Ruth said she felt older and time was slipping by: we decided to buy! By the end of July the house was ours, the deeds drawn up by Ryssen and stamped by the Conservation des Hypothèques de Saint-Omer. It was then I realized that Ruth had in all documents to be referred to by her maiden name. The French also had difficulties with my own name, preferring to refer

371

to me as Monsieur Daniel Glyn, and indeed our village postman still lists me as M. Gleen.

We decided that the house had, of course, to be altered and then we had our second stroke of good fortune. The Café au Bon Accueil was run by Elyane Fontaine and we discovered that her husband, Yves, was a builder who then worked with his father, Maurice, now retired. The Fontaines, *père et fils*, said they would willingly undertake the alterations and additions that we wanted, which comprised knocking together the two front rooms into a salon with a large new fireplace (*à grosse poutre*), building a big new bedroom, installing a bathroom and lavatories, and building out a roof over a terrace. We summoned our invaluable adviser, Anne Philippe, from Normandy. We sat round the central café table, Fontaine *père et fils*, Anne, Ruth and I. Anne had said to us that the great thing about employing a small builder was that you need not use an architect, so we had drawn out a fairly careful plan of what we envisaged. Father and son, Maurice and Yves, with Yves' wife Elyane at all times consumed with curiosity, dancing about in the background and regularly refilling our glasses, went over our plan with a fine-tooth-comb, asked many questions and nodded approval of our scale drawing. Our spirits rose. Finally Anne, who was acting as our interpreter in details of *bricolage* new to us, said, 'Eh bien, messieurs, comment prononcez-vous?' All is splendid, they said, but we would like to have an architect. Our hearts sank. But there is the plan and you are experienced builders, we pleaded. 'Pourquoi un architecte?' 'Because,' they said simply, 'we do not know how to join the new roof on to the old. M. Gilbert Platiau of Saint-Omer is a good architect, he will know'. And so it was. Monsieur was charming, drew up a detailed *devis*, and by the time we had removed a few of his fancier (and more expensive) touches it cost us just about the same to extend and sanitize, if that is the right word, the house, as it had done to buy it. (Ruth says that the fact that the bathroom turned out bigger than my dressing room-cum spareroom was the result of an amicable misunderstanding: most of the work, of course, was done in our absence – always a danger – and we count ourselves lucky.) As, indeed, we were lucky in our architect who became a friend: an amiable, cultivated man who turned out to be a royalist and deliberately stuck the stamps upside down on his envelopes. But he was a loyal Frenchman; he never travelled outside the country, saying that France was so large and varied it could give you everything. He lived in one of the old Canons' houses in the 'close' of the Basilica, where he kindly entertained us more than once.

Ruth bought and studied two books, *J'achète et transforme une maison* and *Larousse Ménager*, and set herself rapidly to enlarge her French vocabulary in matters ranging from electric pumps to spanners, pliers, screw-drivers and a whole range of *outillage*.

Local people were employed in the secondary works and we have fond memories of Monsieur Bâle, an elderly bachelor, who did all the carpentry very well, including some beautifully built-in cupboards and drawers in the kitchen. Then M. Rétaux, the electrician, who was very deaf and said, 'S'il vous plaît?' automatically after everything we said, and who fitted us up with the largest electric plugs we had ever seen and have never been able to match anywhere since. When we now show them to electric shops they say 'Très curieux, très drôle.' We believe they are industrial plugs Rétaux got on the cheap! A very minor drawback – more a source of amusement – of having a deaf electrician was that in the passage connecting our bedroom and the *chambre d'amis* with bathroom and lavatory, we decided to have two two-way light switches (*va-et-vient*). Rétaux installed what looked exactly like the front and back door bells, and indeed proved to give off a resounding buzz when pressed! We soon learnt to find our way to the *chalet de nécessité* in the dark!

This work was completed in the spring of 1964 and we prepared for occupation at the end of the summer. The house had to be furnished and we began to assemble a load from England, then bought things locally and in the very good shops in Lille. We found that as we lived in England, French law recognized our house as a *résidence sécondaire* and we could, once and once only, bring over a load of furniture tax free. Ruth collected things together and we bought a lot of unpainted bleached stripped pine in a shop in Beauchamp Place. We had an unhappy adventure driving back to Cambridge from London with a table six feet long strapped on the roof of our car. Between Royston and Bassingbourn the ropes gave way and it flew down the road behind us. It was undamaged but to this day I wonder what horrors would have ensued if it had descended on to a car following us. Fortunately there was none, and with difficulty we strapped the table back on the roof and travelled gingerly home.

Ruth had spent weeks writing to the French Embassy in London and the British Consulate in Paris and built up a formidable dossier with all kinds of permits, signatures and seals. Dorothy Garrod had had the same experience when she built herself a house in Charente in 1952 and transferred to it much of the furniture from her Cambridge house. She gave us a horrific account of how getting her stuff through the customs in Dunkerque took three days, and the meticulous examination they made of the Pickford vans she was accompanying including the plunging of long pointed rods into her mattresses to see whether she was smuggling in undesirable people!

We feared the worst in delays and examination. We had hired a large van in Cambridge and Claudio Vita-Finzi, now Reader in Geography at University College, London, and then a Research Fellow of St John's, agreed to drive the van across with me as passenger. Ruth would drive the car, also stuffed with things, the following day and we would hope to meet in the Hotel Clément. We drove off and took the early evening ferry; when we got to Dunkerque, our vehicle was impounded and we were told to come back in the morning with our papers. I had booked a room in a little hotel in the docks. Next morning the proprietor directed us to a small café where, when we told our story, the chef-patron said he would make us an omelette. 'The English always like my omelettes,' he said, and in front of us at a stove behind the counter he cooked one of the largest and most memorable omelettes I have ever eaten. It was a Spanish-type omelette with bacon, sausages, peppers, tomatoes, potatoes and garlic. 'You need strengthening for your ordeal,' he said, and as we paid and insisted he drank a glass of calvados with us, he said, 'Here is my card. When you get to the customs ask for M. Delsaut.' We gave his card to the man at a desk bearing the name Delsaut and also Ruth's fat dossier of papers. The result was immediate. We were only asked one question: would we mind if the customs officials called on us at six-monthly intervals to make sure we had not sold at great profit the furniture we had imported tax-free? It was all over in half-an-hour and we were in Calais-Marck airport waiting for Ruth long before her aircraft (the splendid old Bristol Carvair) arrived from Southend. And, incidentally, no customs officials have ever called on us.

We were lucky, and we were also lucky when we took up residence in the baking August of '64 surrounded by the gold of those now forgotten corn stooks, to have the assistance of Ruth's godson and nephew, Richard Langhorne, now Junior Bursar at St John's College, and of Pamela Michelmore and her sister Anne. I have already spoken of Pamela's friendship with and encouragement of Ruth in her school and Oxford days. Her sister Anne married a very distinguished French Resistance leader, Armand Philippe, and after the war we often stayed with them in their house, Le Petit Château, at Saint-Just, to the west of Vernon in the valley of the Seine. Armand first ran a garage in Vernon and then had a job with a reconstruction agency in Algeria. He was a colourful and amusing man with good and generous views on food and wine – as one expects a Lyonnais to have. Early one morning I went down to the kitchen in Le Petit Château to find him sitting at the table with a plateful of charcuterie, a selection of cheeses and a bottle of Beaujolais. 'Moi,' he said cheerfully, 'j'aime beaucoup le breakfast anglais.' After his death Anne moved to a small house at Nézé on the other side of the Seine from Vernon. From Le Petit Château and Nézé she provided good counsel and advice and direct help for many years. Indeed we would have been hard put to it to buy and organize our house, which we called La Marnière (because it is on the edge of a marl pit), without the help and advice of the Hôtel Clément, the Fontaines and Anne Philippe.

It happened; and over the years we have continued to make improvements – installed central heating, had the garden organized and planted trees. One of the great charms of the house was its uninterrupted view, which we enjoyed for ten years. The field in front of us sloped down to the village and we looked down on the tiled roofs of the houses and the village church. Then in June 1972 we were set a great problem. The owner of the field in front of us, a farmer called Bouchel, announced that he wished to sell two plots of land as *terrains à bâtir* but as this would inconvenience us he gave us the first offer of buying the land. After endless and complicated discussions with friends and with Maître Ryssen we decided not to buy. Only too soon a very horrible new house was built right in front of us. It blocks part of our main view. We have swallowed our fury and disappointment and planted many more trees. The lovely view still remains either side of the new house and the quiet and beauty of the countryside remain.

Zouafques is not really a village; at most it could be called a small village: it is a hamlet. It has 320 inhabitants, 322 for part of the year when the Daniels are in residence, said the Mayor when we attended the elections in the minute *Mairie*, and he announced with pride, 'We are honoured by the presence of foreign observers'! It has one main street with *Mairie*, church, village primary school, one café-cum-*cabine téléphonique*, a village shop, and an excellent butcher. All the other houses are farms or occupied by retired farmers and widows. A road runs at right angles up the hill through Louches to Ardres and our house and the Café au Bon Accueil, as it was, are above the village on this road called the Leulanne, said to be the Roman road from Sangatte southwards. The village of Louches is immensely long and full of long houses set endwise on to the road – it has a very prehistoric Danubian look.

Zouafques is less than a mile off the main N 43 from Calais through Saint-Omer to Sedan and Metz; another mile further to the west is Tournehem-sur-l'Hem which is a substantial and very attractive village with nearly 1,000 inhabitants, a fine church, a mill, a school, six cafés, a Crédit Agricole, two hairdressers, a butcher, a charcuterie, a baker, and two village shops. The church is dedicated to Saint-Médard, Bishop of Noyon, who died in 560; my French *Dictionnaire des Saints* says, to my shame, that 'as every one knows'[!] the Feast day of St Médard is the 8 June and, 'as this is the anniversary of the Flood, he is naturally the patron-saint of umbrella-sellers.' It has a very fine organ with a splendid *buffet d'orgues*.

The Collines of Boulonnais between Calais, Saint-Omer and Boulogne are really the East Downs of England: they are the extension of our North Downs and South Downs before the English Channel was cut, and to drive from our house the 40 kilometres to Boulogne is to drive over and alongside chalk hills naturally strongly reminiscent of landscapes in Kent and Sussex. The river Aa rises south of the hills and flows past Saint-Omer to the sea at Gravelines. Two rivers rise in the hills: the Liane, which flows westward to Boulogne; and the Hem which rises near Licques (where the annual turkey fair of north France is held on the Sunday before Christmas), and flows north-east to join the Aa between Saint-Omer and Gravelines, curiously enough at a hamlet called Le Ruth. The Hem is a small river but is very beautiful along its length of less than thirty kilometres. We look south over it; in the distance are the hills of Flanders dominated by Mt Cassel. From our terrace looking to the north-east the lights of Dunkerque twinkle in the night, and behind us on the chalk downs at a height of 122 metres is the fifteenth-century chapel of Saint-Louis.

I love being in Zouafques because I am back in the countryside that reared me, and because I am a peasant at heart. My childhood in south Pembrokeshire, Carmarthenshire and the Vale of Glamorgan seemed gone for ever in the academic life of Cambridge and the business life of London. The valley of the Hem has restored to me my youth with the peace and quiet of the country. That, and because, except for secretaries and a few wise friends and business acquaintances, it is thought by so many that when we have left Cambridge 'for abroad' we have vanished from civilization. When we have crossed the Channel we are, if not among the savages of Darkest Africa, at least the barbarians of Darkest France. The Daniels are portrayed as living in some primitive shack in the middle of a forest approached by a long road unsuitable for cars, with no light and primitive heating, wolves howling in the woods. Actually there are wild boar and deer in the woods; the central heating works better than ours in Cambridge, but, true, the electricity is capricious and whenever there are storms and tempests there are blackouts. But I encourage the myth of inaccessibility and lack of comfort lest unwanted acquaintances on their way to and from Switzerland and south France should beg board and lodging. Arthur Shelley who has done so much excellent work for Ruth and me for so many years – his maps and diagrams in *Antiquity* and in *Ancient Peoples and Places* volumes are well known and admired – readily agreed to make a map of our North French neighbourhood. Like Leslie Illingworth's map of the Vale of Glamorgan (see endpapers) it reflects a countryside I love.

And what a tonic it is to find how early everyone still gets up in the countryside in the spring and summer. In high summer we are in the fields at five and the door of the café across the road is being banged on long before six by men wanting a glass of red wine, a beer or a nip of the local gin as they pass from one field to another – for in the Pas-de-Calais we are still very broken up in our holdings.

I find the early morning in summer the most exhilarating time of the year and it suits me best to read and write then, a glass of Perrier – the champagne of the morning – in my hand. 'Vous êtes matinale,' the locals say as I walk along the road to collect the *Voix du Nord* from the café in Tournehem, and take a cup of coffee with the men who are just setting off to jobs in Boulogne, Calais and Dunkerque. But then I am always matinal; in Cambridge I collect the papers from Smith's in the Market Place shortly after six each morning, and as a result have a varied and valued acquaintance with the many who are around in central Cambridge in the early morning – the men who run Smith's, the police, the cleaners of offices and banks, milkmen and postmen, lavatory cleaners and street cleaners (especially Allan who took a degree in history at Sheffield under Ted Miller), and the early market stall-holders.

In my journal in the late sixties I wrote early one perfect July day in Zouafques:

> It is early morning: the birds are busy. A blackbird and his wife are quartering the lawn; a pair of swallows are fussing about the new nest they have been building in the eaves; seven pigeons swoop into the cornfield in front of the house and fly quickly away alerted by some danger unknown to me. There are two rabbits nervously exploring the rough grass at the end of the terrace. A cuckoo hoots in the woods. A lark rises and a partridge crosses the road, its grating cry drowned by the arrival of the morning bus to Ardres – half the passengers are schoolchildren. I wave at the bus driver who gaily toots at me and I look at my watch. It is 6.55; he is on time as usual and he will get some of his passengers to the station in Calais in time to catch the morning train to Paris. And as he drives on up the hill to Ardres, the Curé, Monsieur L'Abbé Couplet, begins ringing his bell for mass.
>
> And now the doors of the Café au Bon Accueil are open: Madame Fontaine busies herself making coffee and cleaning the café. Her husband, Yves, gets the car out and drives to Bonningues to join his father and begin their day's work at house construction.
>
> And coming up the hill is the first of many: one of the very large white Boulonnais horses slowly plods along. Perched on top, sitting sideways – for the backs of these great beasts are too broad for ordinary mounting – is a farmer setting out to his fields. He stops for a moment at the café for *un petit rouge*. I cross the road and join him. The swallows, delighted to be rid of me, redouble their nest-building efforts.

That was written fifteen years ago and much has changed since: the Boulonnais horses have been replaced by tractors, a house has been built in front of us, and the Café au Bon Acceuil has closed its welcoming doors and become a private house. But the agricultural calm remains and I still take (except in dark mid-winter) my matutinal walk along the road to Tournehem.

The Fontaines left the café to the great sadness of Zouafques and the neighbourhood and the Daniels in particular, but their new home

378

further up the valley of the Hem at Bonningues-les-Ardres is only 5 kilometres away and they still look after our house in our absence and regard us as their very special and private property. Indeed the close relationship we have built up with them is one of the most delightful and rewarding aspects of our French life. I feel I know the *famille* Fontaine almost better than I know most English or Welsh families. The four children were all born in the café and have grown up with us, sharing innocent pleasures like playing ping-pong, gathering cherries and walnuts, and going for little tours in our car.

When they were in the café they had two dogs: one, Sheila, a fat mongrel of Sealyham origin who soon distinguished herself by knowing the sound of our car and barking in a special way when she heard it. Then one day a small black-and-white kitten walked into the café and took up residence there. It grew into a fine medium-sized tom cat of great independence and strength of character and got on well with the dogs, the children and the clients. The children, for some reason I have never understood, called it Mouseiou and it readily answered to that name.

I am devoted to cats to the point of idolatry and Ruth likes them too. Mouseiou took to us at once and we became devoted to him. Soon he walked carefully across the road and inspected our house from top to bottom. It was warmer than the café, had comfortable chairs, good food, and, in winter, a bright log fire. Mouseiou decided to take up residence when we were there, returning reluctantly to the café when we were away. We became his *résidence secondaire*. He took part in all our activities, and often slept on or in our bed. He, too, like Sheila, knew the sound of our car and, we are told, heard it before it came into view over the hill. Once, a car like ours drew up by our gate and Mouseiou bounded across the road hopefully. When he saw who got out of the car he was furious and spat at them. The occupants went into the café and said, 'You have a very bad-tempered cat.' 'No', said Elyane. 'It is a very good tempered cat. He was furious with himself for making a mistake. He was looking for his special friends.'

Every time when we returned he was across the road and sitting by the front door. Immediately it was open he made a very extensive and thorough examination of the house. He always knew the sad moment when we were leaving and viewed the growing pile of luggage with disfavour. As we loaded the car he sat on the roof and growled and had to be carried into the café and the door shut.

Mouseiou went hunting in the woods and we were all afraid that one day he would get caught in one of the many traps that farmers set there. But he survived splendidly for five years. Then one day when we came back from England there was no black-and-white cat to greet us. He had eaten some poison in the wood and died. The children insisted on burying him in the garden and put up a little wooden cross with his name on it. Monsieur Daniel would have wanted us to do this, they said, and took us down to see the grave. I wept unashamedly. 'Maman', they said afterwards, 'Monsieur and Madame Daniel were in tears. They must have loved Mouseiou. We know Mouseiou loved them.'

We felt it was the death of a very close friend with whom we had shared part of our lives for many years – and so it was. Five or six years later I was walking home along the road from Tournehem. I had been for a very long walk alone and was looking forward to a cup of tea and to sit down by the fire; it was getting dark. As I got within sight of our house I was suddenly aware that sitting outside our gate and looking towards me was a black-and-white cat. I broke into a run crying, 'Mouseiou, Mouseiou'. I looked to right and left as I crossed the road and then when I looked ahead there was no cat. I went quickly all round the house and garden. There was nobody, nothing anywhere. It is the only time in my life that I have seen a ghost.

There have been other animals in our French life – moles, horses and dormice. Moles surface from time to time in our lawn but the local mole-catcher, M. Tartare *le taupier*, quickly deals with them. A farmer half way to Tournehem keeps Shetland ponies and we have become firm friends with them; we go almost every day to give them sugar and pieces of sugarbeet. This part of northern France is great sugarbeet country and the Begin Say sugar factory at Pont d'Ardres on the road to Calais is said to be the largest of its kind in Europe. I don't think so much chicory is grown here as used to be, but the countryside is dotted with buildings which at first we couldn't understand – places for drying and burning chicory: they are as common around here as oasthouses are in Kent.

Our first encounter with dormice was amusing. One summer we wondered who was taking our cherries. Late one evening I went out with a torch and shone it into the top of our cherry tree and there was a dormouse sitting on his haunches holding a cherry in his fore-paws. We then discovered that the dormice were living in our attic and,

thinking they were dangerous vermin, we put down traps and caught
some of these very pretty creatures with their large liquid eyes, grey-
white bodies and long tails. When we told people what we were doing
they were mildly astonished. 'You must not kill *les loirs*,' they said. 'Ils
ne sont pas méchants.' So we put away our traps and now share our
house with the dormice who do not disturb us much. In the summer
we hear them setting off for their work in the fields and sometimes in
the evening sitting at table at dinner we see and hear them climbing up
the drainpipes on their way to bed. When we are in residence they
keep strictly to their nests in the far dark corners of the attic –
occasionally by accident dropping a pebble or nut on the roof of our
bedroom. When we are away they make themselves comfortably at
home everywhere, eating any bits of soap we have left out; they are
fond of paper and recently I discovered in a cupboard that they had
eaten the greater part of a copy of *The Financial Times*.

Christopher Hawkes, on hearing that we had bought a house in
Pas-de-Calais and only knowing it as a département that you rushed
through on the trains south to Paris or east to Lille, Strasbourg and
Bâle, wrote me a postcard saying: 'Why Pas-de-Calais, une place pas-
de-forêt?' He was wrong: it is a tremendously well-wooded département and the two state forests nearest to us, the Forêt de Tournehem
and the Forêt d'Eperlecques, while beautiful for walks and picnics,
each contain an interesting curiosity. In the middle of the Forêt de
Tournehem is a small chapel; it is always open and almost every day
candles are burning. Mass is celebrated only once a year, on 15
August, the Feast of the Assumption. A very large congregation
attends including, I have been told, many who never go to a normal
parish church. Why is this chapel, Notre Dame de la Forêt, in the
middle of a large forest? In pre-Roman times we are told that people
gathered and worshipped in clearings in forests and some have
thought that the wooden henge monuments of Neolithic times might
have been artificial copies in open country of older circular clearings
in forests. I often wonder if this small Christian church in the Forêt de
Tournehem is a survival from pagan times.

The secrets of the Forêt d'Eperlecques are certain and more sinister.
Early in 1964 we were driving along the road from our house to
Watten and were astonished to see in the lee of the forest what looked
like an enormous ruined château. There was nothing then marked on
the Michelin Sheet 51. We drove down a side road and turned towards

this extraordinary building. At the side of the road was a café, Le Café du Blockhaus, and then Ruth and I remembered. This was the largest bunker in the world ever, built by Hitler to be a V2 firing base against Great Britain. Winston Churchill compared it with a gun pointed at the heart of London. It had been picked up on air photographs and the full story of its construction and destruction are well told in David Irving's *The Mare's Nest*.

Douglas Kendall and I, with our air photographs, had persuaded Lindemann and Churchill that our earlier bombing efforts of 1941 were worthless. Lindemann was also blind to the dangers of the Blockhaus d'Eperlecques. If it had been finished and become operational I do not suppose I should be sitting here now in the peace of the Boulonnais hills writing about its ruins, which are now a tourist attraction with guides and audiovisual aids. Every year there is a memorial service held at the monument near the Blockhaus to those, mostly *déportés*, who perished when it was bombed.

Walking in the woods above Tournehem we came across a launching place for rockets. Relics of the 1914–1918 war are not so obvious. I treasure two. Outside Ruminghem, a few miles west from where the Hem joins the Aa, is a war grave cemetery, planted with cherry trees and beautifully kept, but entirely occupied by Chinese, members of the Hong Kong and Straits Settlement Labour Force who were stationed in these parts. These men did not die in action but were carried away by the 'flu epidemic. There were seventy-five of the simple white stone crosses common to the hundreds of War Grave Commission cemeteries, but only one name: Li Te Cheng. The rest were numbers. Each had an inscription in Chinese with the English translation. It was clear that this could be one of four:

A good reputation endures for ever.
Though dead he still liveth.
Faithful until death.
A noble duty bravely done.

We have often visited this quiet spot and been moved by thoughts of those brave men so far from home.

The second is a small thing. Saint-Omer was well known to the British forces, and on the window of what was formerly a boucherie-charcuterie but is now a private house, one can still read in white glass letters: 'Bacon and English Sausages'. And I remember travelling along what was the old Roman road from Arras to Thérouanne and stopping to see the abbey on Mont St Eloi, partly destroyed during the French Revolution. Only the gateway of the abbey and the two towers of the church remained and they had their tops removed by the German bombardment of May-June 1915. I wanted some postcards and with difficulty found a little shop that had a few: they were sepia cards printed in 1916!

Of course we are not far from the real battlefields of the Great World War. Ypres, Mt Kemmel, Vimy, Notre Dame de Lorette are all within an hour's drive from us. Some of our friends, now necessarily of the older generation, could not understand how one could buy a house in Flanders. Once or twice we invited Mortimer Wheeler to spend a weekend with us at Zouafques. But he made it clear that it was unthinkable that he should deliberately visit for pleasure a country-side that would remind him of the horrors of the First World War and those who have read his *Still Digging* will remember the account of the grim week of action in the Battle of Passchendaele which was to solace him in all future trials because in it he had 'known the worst'.

One of the pleasures of our part of northern France is its nearness to Belgium, with all the architectural and art treasures of Bruges and Ghent and the good restaurants along the dull Belgian coast and inland at Bruges, Ypres, Ghent and Brussels itself. It is nice to be able so quickly to enter another culture and one with such high traditions of eating and drinking. I find the sounding of the Last Post each evening at the Menin Gate a most moving occasion and a reminder of one's good fortune to have been born as late in the century as 1914 and not fifteen or so years earlier. It always reminds me of my conversation with a Senior Intelligence Officer in our Air Photo Unit at Wembley at the height of the blitz. I learned that he had been at Oxford at the outbreak of the 1914–18 war and we talked of those days. I asked what his Oxford friends went on to do after the war. He looked at me sadly. 'None survived,' he said. 'All my friends were killed – all of them.'

All Belgian towns and those in French Flanders have carnivals with giants, masked figures and general merriment. That at Ypres in May is a very special one. I had often wondered why the shops in Ypres were so full of cats and cat motifs everywhere. The May Carnival is concerned with witches and in the olden days cats were thrown down from the roofs, some to die, some to be caught. Nowadays the cats are stuffed toys which rain down on the crowds from on high.

One of the greatest pleasures of living in the countryside between two villages is that you know everybody and meet them in cafés – the postman with the most extraordinary goitre I have ever seen; the man who refused to have his split lip sewn up by a German surgeon in the war and now gives one a hideous Draculesque smile exposing long fangs; the local doctor who is *passionné* of the organ and plays in the basilica at Saint-Omer and at Tournehem; the village idiot; the mad man from Audruicq who arrives on his *vélo* muttering to himself and sings and dances until he is pushed out to weave his unsteady *vélo*-way home; and all the good sound characters – farmers, millers, bakers, butchers.

The doctor, who has tended us a couple of times over the years, revealed that he listened to, and recorded from, the BBC Third Programme, as it then was, because the French programme, France Musique, *never* broadcast organ music. We have lent him many organ records from which he has made tapes, and I am happy to say that his collection of church music now includes several fine examples of the singing of St John's College Choir.

I have naturally maintained a keen interest in the field antiquities of the region. There is only one reputable megalith in the neighbour-hood and that is the Dolmen de Fresnicourt twenty miles north-west of Arras and near the beautiful and enchanting Château d'Olhain, which, with the Château d'Esquelbecq, between Cassel and Bergues, is one of the two most lovely buildings in the Pas-de-Calais. We are in the territory of the Morini, the Celtic tribe whose headquarters were at Thérouanne, and there are several of their hillforts in our neighbourhood. According to Pliny, the Morini were famous for their breeding of geese (I wonder, does this ancient tradition survive in the Licques turkey fairs?) and the geese were walked to Rome where they were much appreciated. When I first drew Paul Johnstone's notice to this curious fact he was incredulous, but then made a TV programme about it with test walks of geese on the Berkshire Ridgeway.

An important Neolithic settlement site on the Montagne de Lumbres is only a few miles south of us. It was investigated by Dom René Prévost, who published a monograph on it in 1962. I discovered he was a monk at the Benedictine Abbaye de Wisques a few miles from us, but learnt that the abbot thought Prévost was spending too much time on archaeology and transferred him to an abbey in Normandy where he is said to be making beeswax. But his successor, Dom

Baudry, a keen collector of surface flints, searched me out and once, when Stuart Piggott was staying with us, invited us both to lunch in the abbey. We were cordially received and our hands washed by the abbot. We moved into the refectory which was organized like a chapel. The abbot sat alone in front of the altar. The monks ate in their stalls and we sat at a small table in the nave with other nonentities, some novitiates or postulants and two or three young men from the village who had come to clear the drains and repair electrical faults. It was a Friday and the main dish was very cheap fish: it was not totally inedible, just very difficult to eat – I have never encountered a fish so full of bones. Stuart Piggott thought it had been especially stuffed with pins and extra bones to chasten us and teach us patience. There was nothing but water to drink. After this exiguous meal we were taken to Dom Baudry's cell which was packed with the results of his field-walking – some genuine implements but many natural objects: it reminded me of the plates in Boucher de Perthes' *Antiquités celtiques et antediluviennes*. He showed us the bent walking-stick that he used on his field trips, to the cry of, 'Je ramasse, toujours je ramasse'. We fled to a café in Saint-Omer and, having restored ourselves, paid homage to Saint-Erkembode. We walked past what had until 1763 been the College of the English Jesuits in the rue Saint-Bertin and went into the magnificent basilica of Notre-Dame, formerly the Cathedral and the seat of a bishopric from 1553 to the Revolution – during those years it was called Marin-la-Montagne, the name Marin perpetuating the Morini.

The basilica dates in its entirety from the thirteenth to the fifteenth centuries; I admire most in it the monumental *buffet d'orgues* of 1717. I always visit the tomb of the monk Audomarus (or Otmar) who came from Luxeuil to evangelize the country and survives as Saint-Omer. But my main target of respect is the tomb of Saint-Erkembode made out of a single large block of brownstone, now black with age, set on the backs of two large lions; it dates from the seventh or eighth centuries AD. The remains of this saint were removed during the Revolution but were restored in the late nineteenth century.

His tomb is a place of great veneration and is always surrounded and covered with votive offerings – shoes, socks, underwear, prayers for favours requested, and thanks for favours granted. It is a piteous, often heart-rending, monument of hope and faith, and a faith which seems to me to go back beyond the sixth century to whatsoever pagan deity was transferred to Erkembode. We lit two candles to this holy man and left.

I have become fascinated not only by the visible antiquities but also by the names of places in the west of the Pas-de-Calais. Zouafques itself is the ancient Roman Zouaficum, and where our road the Leulanne meets in the village the road from Tournehem to the N43 is the crossing of two very important Roman roads – Sangatte to Thérouanne and Boulogne to Cassel. The names ending in -*thun* represent Saxon settlements. The surprising names Salperwick and Craywick between us and St-Omer, are Viking settlements; Audruicq is a French version of Oldwick; while to most peoples' surprise that well-known headland Cap Gris Nez is a French version of Greyness or Craigness. The river Aa is, of course, an early form of the Celtic word for river which survives in England as Avon: and to my astonishment I am told that the curiously named hamlet of Cucq, south of Le Touquet, is one of the oldest place-names in Western Europe, and possibly pre-Indo-European.

Apart from Ardres, our three main towns for shopping are Saint-Omer, Calais and Boulogne. Boulogne is forty minutes away by a beautiful road up the valley of the Hem, over the chalk hills and along the N42. I remember my first surprise on driving one day to Boulogne and seeing over a wall the top of a statue wearing a fez. It was a statue of Mariette, the famous Egyptologist who was born in Boulogne; the Musée Municipal in Boulogne has considerable and interesting Egyptian collections, as well as a fine Napoleonic collection with Napoleon's hat and a remarkable collection of English satirical drawings about Napoleon's projected invasion of England. Boulogne, as most people do not know, is the largest fishing port of France.

And Calais is France's largest passenger port, handling seven million people a year. It is also, with 80,000 inhabitants, the largest town in the département – Boulogne is only 50,000 and so is Arras, the *chef-lieu* of the département. Calais is not as attractive as Boulogne and has suffered more from the terrible bombardments of the 1939–45 war. A traveller of the time of James I described Calais as 'a beggarly extorting town, monstrous dear and sluttish'. Thomas Gray wrote that 'Calais is an exceeding old, but very pretty town,' and Horace Walpole was wildly enthusiastic, calling it 'one of the most surprising cities of the universe'. It is certainly not that now.

Calais, as every schoolboy knows, was English from 1346 to 1558;

he also knows the story of the six burghers and that Mary Tudor, according to Holinshed's *Chronicles*, said, 'When I am dead and opened, you shall find "Calais" lying in my heart.' And most English visitors to Calais very properly go and gaze at the remarkable Rodin bronze of *Les bourgeois de Calais*, cast in 1895, and set up in front of and much diminished by the hideous town hall (not to my mind 'ce bel édifice' of the *Guide Michelin*); it was built between 1914 and 1925, a copy of a fifteenth-century Flemish building with a bell tower seventy-five metres high.

Calais and Boulogne have always been the happy hunting grounds of British day trippers and now, with a reasonable rate of exchange and the quick Channel crossing, the streets and shops are crowded with *les Brits*, particularly in the summer and the weeks before Christmas. The big *hypermarchés*, like Continent in Calais and Auchan just outside Boulogne, have ten English to one native shopper on Saturdays in December; they stagger away with trolleys laden with coffee, wine, beer, Le Creuset casseroles, glasses, mustard, olive oil, *saucisson sec*, *pâtés*, chocolates and liqueurs. 'I live in Chelsea,' said someone to me a few days ago. 'We shop in Calais once a month. The price of the crossing is quickly recovered by the time you have bought a dozen bottles of wine and six dozen cans of beer. We have friends who live in Canterbury who go over every Saturday.'

The people of Calais and Boulogne go out of their way to accommodate their profitable visitors *outre-manche*. 'English money accepted here,' say the notices or, 'Tea here as Mother makes it.' Welsh rabbits have been a feature of north French cuisine for a long time – perhaps a legacy from the 1914–18 war: 'Ici les meilleurs Welsches' says one notice and another counsels, 'Dégustez ses Welshes avec un Stout'. There is a restaurant called Le Welsh Pub in Boulogne; it has nothing to do with my native country – it specializes in toasted cheese, and Cantal and Gruyère make rabbits as good as Caerphilly or Cheshire. Their efforts to translate their menus into English produce some very strange words, like 'Campaign Paté', 'Boss's Plate', 'Fish Make Home', 'Rosty Chiken', 'Veal Seach Gallops', 'Shot Dogs'.

The *Guide Gault-Millau*, in one of its characteristic moments of arrogance and certainty, declares this part of the north of France 'a gastronomic desert'. This is not true: admittedly there are no more than four restaurants with one Michelin rosette within twenty miles of Calais but good eating is not just *haute cuisine*. The restaurants with rosettes in *Michelin* and toques in *Gault-Millau* are for special occasions; the strength of the high culinary traditions of France lies in the excellence of its bourgeois restaurants – its *cuisine familiale*. It has been our pride and joy in the last quarter century to explore, record and test the good cheap cafés and restaurants. They are legion, though there are of course bad ones. Pat Fenn's *French Entrée* is an excellent and reliable guide. Our nearest is the Auberge du Cheval Noir and we often lunch there; it is on the N43, a quarter of an hour's walk away by a lane from us, and is always full of lorry drivers who usually have an aperitif before they sit down to lunch and a cognac with their coffee as they leave. A typical meal consists of soup, a grilled *boudin blanc*, roast pork and sauté potatoes, cheese or fruit or ice-cream; wine *à volonté*, a litre carafe of red on your table. The cost, including wine, service and taxes, is 40 francs, a little over £3 (aperitifs, coffee and liqueurs extra, of course).

There are good regional dishes in this area of northern France extending from Picardy to Belgium: *ficelles picardes* for example (pancakes stuffed with ham and cheese), *lapin à la moutarde*, *flamiche* (leek tart), *tarte à l'oignon* and *pot fleisch* – a galantine of three meats: veal, pork and chicken. And the cheeses are good, notably Maroilles and Vieux Lille – powerful and smelling strongly: they have to be banished to the boot of the car. I am very fond of the *fromage de Bergues*, made in beer, and M. Philippe Olivier, the famous *maître-fromager* of 43 rue Thiers, Boulogne, has an astonishing collection of goat cheeses from the Boulonnais hills – particularly those made in May when goat's milk has all the richness of the lush spring grass. La Fromagerie de Philippe Olivier is a remarkable shop, supplying leading restaurants in France and in England. The cheeses are laid out on wooden storage racks, the timber for which is felled, we are told, when the moon is on the wane because that is when the sap is at its highest!

But of course fish is the great triumph of the Côte d'Opale – mussels, langoustines, crab, lobster, sole – this is not an area for oysters. I still remember my shame when seeing *sole détroit* on a Calais menu and stupidly wondering whether it was served *à l'Américaine* until I realized that *Le détroit* is the French name for the Straits of Dover! There is nowhere better to enjoy the fishy pleasures of the Pas-de-Calais than the Atlantique at Wimereux, that decaying seaside resort once very popular with the English, and memorable today also for the concrete bunker round the corner (now kept firmly locked) where Adolf Hitler was to have taken up residence during the invasion of Britain.

M. Hamiot created L'Atlantique and his son still runs it brilliantly: their *chausson de crabe baie St-Jean*, and their dishes of John Dory and *bar* are outstanding. The Hamiots have a farm in the hinterland, so there is not only fish but chickens and ducks and good meat which is grilled in front of one. Every November the Hamiots run a special fish festival – certainly worth a cross-Channel journey.

Of the many hotels in Calais, the Meurice is the most famous and I am glad to have known Maupin who ran it until his death in the sixties. The Meurice had been founded in 1750 as a coaching inn. Maupin came to Calais in 1894 at the age of 18 to be *maître de cuisine* in the Grand Hôtel which opened that year and which no longer exists. Next year he opened a restaurant of his own and in 1900 took over the Meurice, building it up to international fame as a hotel and restaurant. Before the 1914-18 war it was the home of cock-fighting organized, according to *Le Voix du Nord*, 'par des membres de l'aristocratie anglaise, apparentés à la famille royale.' During the night of 25/26 May 1940, the Meurice was entirely destroyed by German bombardment: only 1,800 bottles from a cellar of 47,000 were saved. Undeterred by this disaster and hopeful for the future, Maupin ran a small restaurant in the salon of his house in the rue du Vauxhall, until in 1956 he was able to move into a new Meurice, rebuilt on a new site. I have the happiest memories of the temporary Meurice in the rue du Vauxhall and of many delicious meals there soon after the war, which began with a superb *terrine maison* and a fine *jambon au gelée de porto*, followed by the little mussels for which the Côte d'Opale is famous done *à la marinière*.

I often saw Jules Maupin in the years before his death, partially blind, walking around Calais with his white stick visiting the shops with which he had traded for so long. He was bedridden for a short while and seemed to be sinking into a coma. One afternoon he awoke in his bedroom in the Meurice overlooking the Jardin Municipal. 'Is there anything you want?' they asked. He paused and said clearly, 'Yes, *moules marinière*, a *sole grillée* and a glass of Muscadet.' He closed his eyes and half an hour later was dead. Good last words. There is still to be found from time to time a Rolls-Royce outside the door of the Meurice. Perhaps the silver ghosts of *l'aristocratie anglaise*?

Alas, there are few architectural survivals of the English occupation, and the meeting place of the Cloth of Gold was in tents. The church of Notre-Dame in Calais was begun in the twelfth century and has many features of English Gothic: perhaps the only Tudor building in France? The Pale of Calais extended 20 km east to Gravelines, 20 km south through the Forêt de Guines to Hermelinghen, and 15 km west to between Cap Blanc-Nez and Wissant. It is amusing to travel along this old frontier (a length of it is still called English Street), and there are fascinating names of inns – the Café de la Muraille at St Inglevert (a flint church that could well be in England) and the Café de France. But beware of easy historical assumptions – the Café de la Barrière de France is not on the frontier of the English Pale and France, but France and Spain (the Spanish had invaded Picardy in the sixteenth century). And everyone with a sense of history must visit the church of Leulinghem, a few kilometres north of Marquise on the N1 from Calais to Boulogne and Paris, the famous church of the two doors, sometimes called *l'église la plus étrange du monde* because it is cut in two by the old frontier. Here for more than twenty years, from 1381 onwards, there met the plenipotentiaries in France of the king of England. Here were signed the truces of 1383, 1389 and 1393. The choir was built for the Count of Guines by English masons, the nave by the Count of Boulogne. The English entered by the north door to the choir, the French by the south door to the nave.

It was on 31 July 1401 that a very remarkable ceremony took place at Leulinghem. Isabella of France had been married at the age of seven in the church of St Nicholas in Calais to Richard II, king of England, aged twenty-nine. Richard was deposed and assassinated and after long negotiations she was returned to her father, the king of France, Charles VI. There disembarked at Calais Queen Isabella, now twelve years old, accompanied by the Duchess of Ireland, the Countess of Hereford, the Duke of Somerset (the Governor of Calais), the Duke of Worcester, and the Bishops of Durham and Hereford: she entered the church by the choir door, crossed the frontier and left by the nave door together with the Comte de Saint Paul, and other representatives of the king of France, who took her the same day to Boulogne where Philippe le Hardi waited with 500 horsemen to escort her to Paris.

There are of course many curious monuments in the countryside between Calais and Boulogne dating between the fall of Calais in 1558 and the First World War. The Colonne de la Grande-Armée is six kilometres north of Boulogne: it is a souvenir of the army which

Napoleon assembled at Boulogne in 1804 to invade England. The column is 53.60 metres high and if you climb up the 265 steps to the top on a good day you have a panorama over the Channel to Dover and inland to Mt Cassel. The original statue of Napoleon was damaged in the 1944 siege of Boulogne and his head and bits of his arms and cloak are in the Musée Municipal in Boulogne. It was restored in 1951–2, still with Bonaparte's back turned firmly towards England.

In the forest of Guines is the Colonne Blanchard commemorating the first aerial crossing of the Channel by Blanchard and Jefferies in a balloon on 7 January 1785 – eight years before Napoleon's attempt to invade Britain. At Blériot-Plage, a kilometre to the west of Calais, is a monument commemorating the first crossing of the Channel by aeroplane by Louis Blériot on 25 July 1909; it took him about half an hour to fly from Calais to Dover, where he landed in a cutting in the chalk cliffs. Further to the south along the lovely N40 coast road, and near the road to Cap Blanc-Nez, is the monument to Henry Latham who tried to cross the Channel at the same time as Blériot but without success. And at Sangatte one can see the trial cuttings for the Channel Tunnel which, as the *Guide Bleu* says so delicately, is an 'entreprise avortée, et qui, de temps à autre, est remise en question'.

Crossing the Channel was not always quick and easy. Thomas Coryat travelled to Calais in 1608 and he wrote in his *Coryat's Crudities* (1611): 'I was embarked at Dover about ten of the clock in the morning, . . . and arrived in Calais about five of the clock in the afternoon, after I had varnished the exterior parts of the ship with the excremental ebullitions of my tumultuous stomach.' Joseph Addison in 1699 took seven hours and as Geoffrey Treast records in his amusing *The Grand Tour* (London, 1967), 'It was unfortunate that he fell straight into the sea as he disembarked at Calais, and that he neither spoke French nor understood a word said to him.' Forty years later Horace Walpole and Thomas Gray, friends at Eton and Cambridge, took five hours.

Now we are down to thirty-five minutes by hovercraft and seventy-five minutes by boat – and boats that are so efficiently stabilized that not once in the scores of crossings I have made in the last quarter century, in all kinds of weather, have I ever been involved in any excremental ebullitions. The development of roads in the last ten years has made Zouafques much closer to Cambridge than it was. It is now just over two hours' drive from Cambridge to Dover and we are only twenty minutes from landing. But I remember that in the early days when there was the air ferry from Calais-Marck to Southend, I once had tea in France, shut up the shutters, drove to the airport and dined in Hall at 7.30 p.m. And Ruth's brilliant organization means that shutting up shop one side and opening business the other is a painless and brief affair.

I shall be sad when old age, infirmity, or some of the thousand natural shocks that flesh is heir to, compel us to give up La Marnière. Having a house in France has been and still is one of the great pleasures of life. I have done a great deal of my writing here, as I am doing now, the sun rising behind the most easterly of the chalk downs, the church tower etched against the blood-red morning sky.

CHAPTER THIRTEEN

Friends and foes

I HAVE BEEN BLESSED by many friends, naturally made a few foes –
though happily not many – and cultivated a small but interesting
group of people whom I call friendly foes, or dear enemies, including
friends who turned into foes, of which the most sad remembrance is
Tom Lethbridge. Alas, many friendships I can no longer enjoy: death
has removed many whose company and advice I so much valued –
Stephen Glanville, Martin Charlesworth, Leslie Illingworth, Sean O
Ríordáin, Dorothy Garrod, Elsie Clifford, Mortimer Wheeler, Terence Powell. Many of them have emerged in earlier chapters. Here I
write about some who have not hitherto appeared except in stray
references. Of men like those I have just mentioned I can only say with
the greatest sincerity and feeling, and using the words George Forrest
Browne said of Henry Bradshaw, they were people 'whom to have
known is a life-long possession, to have lost a life-long regret'.

I remember years ago being arrested by a phrase in Villiers David's
Advice to my Godchildren: 'Friendship is a conspiracy for pleasure.' At
first I thought it was his phrase but he told me that it was said by
Marcus Cheke. Clementine Churchill wrote a very good letter to
Winston protesting mildly that affairs of state kept him away from her.
'My Darling,' she wrote (Mary Soames, *Clementine Churchill*, 1979),
'these grave public anxieties are very wearing. When next I see you I
hope there will be a little time for us both alone. We are still young, but
time flies stealing love away and leaving only friendship which is very
peaceful but not stimulating or warming.' I have all my life cultivated
friendships, constantly conspired for their pleasure, found them
stimulating and warming, and to my great delight have found many
which, to use Tennyson's words, have 'master'd Time'. I have not
with the same assiduity cultivated the gentle art of making enemies
though frequently I have been on the point of doing so and crying out
angrily in Whistler's words: 'I am not arguing with you – I am telling
you.'

First there were friends from my childhood and early upbringing in

393

the Vale of Glamorgan, and of these Leslie Illingworth was para-
mount. Then there were my friends at Barry County School; many of
those early schoolboy friendships have carried on through my life:
Brynmor Lennox (now retired Doctor and MOH for Barry), Gwynfor
Evans, Hrothgar Habakkuk, Bryan Hopkin and Arthur Davies.

My Cambridge friends from the thirties were many, though so
many were tutors, teachers and mentors no longer with us. But many
survive like Deryck Williams, Emeritus Professor of Classics at
Reading, with whom it seems in recollection I played squash every
afternoon for three quarters of an hour every day for years and Pegotty
every night at 11; Bob Marchant, now retired from the Chair of Music
at Hull, and Grace Thornton, also now in retirement after a most
distinguished career in the Foreign Service. The War brought new
vistas which were non-academic and I made many new friends:
Villiers David and Anne Whiteman at Medmenham, Mervyn Horder
and Peter Fleming in India. Back in Cambridge after the war my
friendships became institutionalized through colleagues and pupils in
college or university, through the profession of archaeology and
through writing, editing and broadcasting.

I have already referred to the small group of teenagers in Llantwit
Major who used to go swimming at Colhugh Beach in the summer and
to the senior of this group, W.H. Davies. He was the son of the local
builder, indeed the man who had built our house, Brynawelon, and
was always seriously minded. He and the others taught me to swim,
but he kept an eagle eye on us and severely reprimanded any who
swam out too far into the waters of the Bristol Channel. Bill Davies was
my senior by several years. When I began my train-boy years he was in
the sixth form and then became head prefect, a distant severe figure to
many at school – but not to me. During our train journeys he helped
me with my Latin prep which explains why my masters found in me 'a
surprising aptitude for translation but little understanding of
grammar'.

Whatever competence I may have had in swimming (and it saved
my life in Malta) and in argument is due almost entirely to Bill Davies.
It was his stern fundamentalism, his agile mind and tolerant
conversation that first interested me in the joys of dialectic and debate.
We argued endlessly about the truth of the Bible, the origin of man,
Darwinism, the importance of the Classics, pain and death. These are
the things we thought about when bathing in the Severn Sea in the

very warm summer days and as we lay drying on the beaches between Boverton and St Donat's.

He was clearly destined for a great future. I sometimes thought of him as a successor to Major Edgar Jones and he would have made an excellent headmaster. He went on to University College, Cardiff, took First Class Honours in Classics and was Professor of Classics at Aberystwyth. He remained passionately devoted to Llantwit Major and the Vale and built (or his father and brother Ken did) a house for his retirement. Alas, on the eve of his departure from Aberystwyth he suffered a massive stroke and lives on in Llantwit, able to walk and read, but speechless. After years of strain his wife could bear it no longer and went down to the sunny beaches of our youth and threw herself to her death in the sea.

Bill Davies and Leslie Illingworth were the elder brother figures of my youth. Leslie's friendship remained a close, warm and abiding one from the time I first met him as a schoolboy in 1928 until his death in December 1979. The world will remember him as one of the great political cartoonists and draughtsmen of this century. To me he was a kind and generous friend whom I tried to see on every visit to London.

When he left Barry County School he studied at the Royal College of Art and the Slade School. One day his father was speaking on the Barry golf course to the publisher of the Cardiff *Western Mail* and said: 'What your paper needs is a good political cartoonist and I happen to have a son with a great gift for that sort of stuff.' Leslie got the job at the age of nineteen; then after a period of free-lancing joined the *Daily Mail* in 1939 and *Punch* in 1945. He could not accept that he was a genius. At no time, he said, did he have any feeling of greatness and insisted that anyone could do what he did if they worked hard. He worked very hard but his fingers had the inspiration of genius.

Colin Reed, in his sensitive and generous piece in the Daily Mail when Leslie died, referred to the book by the American historian Draper Hill, *Illingworth on Target*, which accompanied the exhibition of his cartoons and drawings held in the Wiggin Gallery of the Boston Public Library in October 1970. Hill spoke of Leslie's Suez drawings of Dulles as the ostrich who sees no problem and Nasser as the bloated bull-frog of the Nile as ranking 'with the finest political caricature of any era'. There were two outstanding cartoons that will for ever illustrate our history books. *Punch's Almanack* number for 6 November 1939 had, as its central spread, his *The Combat* in which a gigantic bestial Nazi figure, winged and gas masked, crunches on its belly across a flaming Europe challenged by a single Spitfire labelled Freedom. The other was the highly controversial drawing (*Punch*, 3 February 1954) of Churchill, sitting listlessly at his desk, his face showing clearly the effects of the stroke he had suffered the previous summer, the bookcase of his writings full and shut: the caption from Psalm 144 was: 'Man goeth forth unto his work and to his labour until the evening'. This cartoon, suggesting that it was time he went, so obviously true and so frequently remarked among Churchill's closest associates, infuriated a great number of people and there was head-shaking inside the *Punch* office. Clementine Churchill described it as 'exceptionally unchivalrous'.

Yet it was true. Much of Leslie's work had its place in history. As Malcolm Muggeridge has said, much of his work was 'more than cartoons as ordinarily understood. They are more in the vein of a Hogarth or Gillray than of a Low, or Vicky or Bernard Partridge: they belong more to the broad sweep of social history than to the immediacy of politics.'

He was naturally pleased by professional praise and recognition but startled when the University of Kent in its wisdom gave him an honorary degree. 'Help! Help!' he telegraphed me. 'You must come and hold my hand.' He was for a moment jolted out of his deliberately low profile and modest view of himself as a reasonably competent performer in a minor and ephemeral art. For a moment he saw what the world thought of him and rejected it as too embarrassing to live with. This transparently honest and modest man was happiest with his cows and hens on his farm at Robertsbridge in Sussex where he lived with his lifelong companion, Enid Ratcliffe. Happily unmarried ('Who the hell would marry an ugly idiot like me?' he would say) he was devoted to his family – the children of his brother and his sister. He and Enid came to see us in our house at Zouafques a few years before he died. 'Boyo,' he said, 'I know why you like being here. It's like being back in the Vale. Why did we ever leave?' At heart he was a quiet, gentle Welsh country boy.

We did a sound broadcast programme called 'Return to the Vale' and Leslie did an amusing drawing of us both for the *Radio Times* which I reproduce here. I had a plan that we should go back together and spend a fortnight revisiting our childhood haunts, he doing a series of drawings and me wrapping them round with a short text.

Leslie warmly approved of this idea, but I had left it too late and in the summer of 1979 he made it sadly clear to me that he could no longer trust his hand and eye to draw.

Leslie suffered from two sad illusions: that he was ugly and that he was ignorant. Like Gordon Childe, he was conscious that he looked a little odd, with his great chin and remarkable eyebrows; he portrayed himself as a hairy ape – a kind of modern Neanderthal man walking down Fleet Street on his way to El Vino's to drink his favourite tipple, Vosne Romanée. I had great difficulty in getting him down to Cambridge to dine in College, and especially to attend a feast. 'I'm not learned,' he would say. 'I can't talk to dons. They frighten me.' His shyness and self-denigration were obsessive. Yet he was widely read and widely informed.

He had been best man at my wedding and Ruth insisted that he should be at the small lunch we gave in Prunier's in London for my sixtieth birthday. Reluctantly he agreed to come, but as we were waiting to sit down Madame Prunier came with a worried look and told me she had had a curious message from a Mr Illingworth saying he much regretted but that he was too old, too decayed and too obscene to be present.

He was a difficult person to entertain and would sometimes, when asked out to dinner, give the proprietor an open cheque before he sat down. My wife and I would insist he should dine with us and we would meet in El Vino's when he had finished his drawing. He would almost invariably arrive late and with a few unexpected guests. 'You

The author and Leslie Illingworth relaxing over a glass of wine, drawn by Illingworth for 'Radio Times' to illustrate a talk called 'Back to the Vale'.

remember Polly,' he would say, 'haven't seen her myself for twenty years. She used to run the fish and chip shop in Cowbridge.' He had from time to time several flats in different parts of London and we were always welcome to stay in them, and so were many other people. His generous hospitality was such that one never knew what might appear. Eric Keown of *Punch* told how, delayed in London, he asked Leslie if he would put him up. 'Certainly,' was the reply. 'But avoid the bed by the door. There seems to be a Spanish captain in it. Don't know who he is. Been there for some while.'

Stephen Glanville was one of our dearest friends in the ten years following the end of the war, and his sudden death on his 56th birthday in 1956 was a tragic blow. Consulting my journal for that sad time I find I wrote a follow-up piece to his obituary in *The Times*, which was published on 7 May.

Stephen Glanville was, during the brief decade of his Cambridge life, a very close friend of my wife and myself, and, when the cares of state were not to be easily borne, he fled to our small house opposite St John's to eat buttered shrimps and cheese, and anything we had brought back from France, and to drink – and argue about – bourgeois French wines. Then, in the domestic comfort of perfect friendship, we learnt of his plans, his hopes, his fears – and, when he became Provost of King's and Vice-Chancellor designate, his schemes, and his doubts.

Through all these sweet, remembered occasions we talked of many things – Egyptology and prehistory, the relative merits of the educational systems, and of archaeology, at Oxford, London, and Cambridge, travel in France, wine snobbery, our colleagues, whether or not colleges in Oxford and Cambridge should have professional stewards and bursars (we could never agree on this), and whether dons should be made to have a compulsory day a week in London, and then – what gave him the greatest pleasure in his varied career – his unanimous election to be Provost of King's College. How sad that that great foundation should be suddenly deprived of the love, care, and wisdom he had determined to lavish on it with his own characteristic generosity!

Academic society is a lightly sharpened version of the world at large and in this process the scholar and the administrator, the university and the college man, emerge, in small minds, as antitheses. It was always a mystery to the mediocre, who flourish in and around our older universities, that Glanville could be both scholar and administrator. He made himself two studies when he moved into the Provost's Lodge – the one for the Provost, the other for the Demotic scholar. Between these two poles flowed the generous magnetic warmth of his personality and human understanding.

Three days before he died we were trying to fix a date to our mutal convenience. It was difficult – I was going to be away in France, the forward life of high office had already heavily shadowed his life. We could not find a weekend before July and we gave up: as he snapped his diary shut he said, 'Never mind, why worry? We have all our lives in front of us.' He died in the odour of a lively and kindly and warm humanity such as is rare among the people I know.

One very happy memory of Stephen was as his guests at a dinner of The Sette of Odd Volumes at the Savoy, when, with formidable competition, he made one of the best speeches of the evening; and again as his guests in Grocers' Hall when he was Master of the Worshipful Company. Eiddion Edwards, in his obituary in the *Proceedings of the British Academy* for 1958, speaks of his leadership and fairmindedness, and in a happy sentence says: 'His was indeed a life largely devoted to the service of others, and very many are the scholars, pupils and friends who are indebted to him for help and interest which far exceeded what they might have had reason to expect.'

Chadwick and de Navarro introduced me early on in my undergraduate days to Tom Lethbridge, and James Wordie, who was his guardian and trustee, insisted that I should go out on Sunday on his weekly field-cum-excavation trips. Neither Burkitt nor de Navarro was interested in fieldwork and it has always seemed strange that Burkitt, such a good teacher in the lecture room or supervision class, never took us to gravel pits or the beaches at Cromer. We turned quickly and eagerly to Lethbridge who provided us with a fresh open-air view of archaeology.

He was one of the most stimulating, provocative and often controversial figures in British archaeology. Richard Muir in his *Riddles of the British Landscape* described him as 'one of the most colourful characters in British archaeology, an area hardly devoid of such figures.' He was, to use a phrase by which Cyrus Gordon of

399

Brandeis described himself, 'one who throughout his life, kept an open mind and avoided confusing majority opinion with truth.'

He was one of the last of that invaluable band of dilettante scholars and skilled devoted amateurs of whom we have had so many in Britain. The long list begins, if we exclude the antiquaries of the seventeenth and eighteenth centuries, with men like John Frere and William Pengelly and continues through John Evans, Lubbock, Greenwell, Pitt Rivers, Williams Freeman, Alexander Keiller, the Curwens and many another to I.D. Margary, Elsie Clifford and Helen O'Neil.

Lethbridge had read natural sciences at Trinity but was fascinated by field archaeology as an undergraduate and came under the influence of Cyril Fox, himself an amateur who turned professional. He was a man of extensive private means and stayed on in Cambridge as director of excavations for the Cambridge Antiquarian Society and Honorary Keeper of Anglo-Saxon Antiquities in the Museum of Archaeology and Ethnology, as it was then called. He lectured on Anglo-Saxon archaeology and I learnt a great deal from his lectures, particularly about the details of the excavations of Anglo-Saxon cemeteries in the Cambridge region. He was always sharp and critical in his lectures and liked to appear to stand outside the archaeological and university establishment. He viewed professional scholars and unprofessional crackpots with the same critical detachment and amusement, which was to the benefit of both and the advancement of archaeological scholarship, and certainly to the entertainment and inspiration of undergraduates. His lectures, his conversation, and his books had for us a freshness and an eager restless sense of urgency and enquiry. We felt that the carefully stated typologies of Déchelette and Montelius might not really have the divine sanction which some lecturers appeared to give them.

At times, in the formal Cambridge teaching, man's past seemed very academic, very learned, and a matter of taxonomy, typology, artifacts and cross-dating. The tub was there and I laboriously learnt every detail of the staves: but Diogenes was missing. Tom Lethbridge showed my generation of students Diogenes, and brought ordinary man and the ordinary everyday doings of farmers and sailors into what had seemed sometimes, from the time of Montelius onwards, a detailed study of the distribution in time and space of tool types and tomb plans. He was a practical, sensible, down-to-earth countryman.

He took me out of my study, away from my museum cases, to see how life was lived in Fenland farms and Scottish crofts and by fishermen and sailors everywhere. It was Fox, Lethbridge's early mentor, who had taught me that what I had learnt from the years of summer holidays on my grandfather's farm at Alltwalis was very relevant to putting flesh on the dry bones and dead artifacts of Neolithic Europe. Lethbridge and Fox are dead these many years but the breath of fresh country and sea air they blew through academic archaeology fortunately remains.

Sunday after Sunday we set out with our pack of sandwiches and a bottle of beer to dig in Anglo-Saxon and Romano-British cemeteries. Local antiquaries, like Dr Palmer of Linton, or Dr Lucas of Burwell, often joined us and frequently brought with them baskets of provisions to eke out our own fare. On one occasion the kind and genial Dr Palmer announced he had brought with him three quart flagons of what he described as his special mixture: he hinted that it was a concoction of cider, beer, gin and home-made wine. He gave two bottles for undergraduates to open and prepared to open the third for himself. The glasses were ready. 'Right boys, now,' he said. We unscrewed the flagons together, there were three enormous explosions and we were all showered with shattered glass, foam and a sticky evil liquid. Dr Lucas was a small sad-looking man in his early nineties with a drooping moustache and a cultivated melancholy, that vice of which Flaubert had warned Maupassant. He had one simple, all-embracing explanation of anything peculiar we found on our Sunday excavations: 'It was due,' he would say gloomily, 'to the great wind of the resurrection.'

After a day's digging and recording we drove to Cambridge via the Lethbridge house on the Gogs, Mount Blow, designed by Lutyens for a former Master of Trinity Hall. Here we would sit down to an enormous high tea of eggs and bacon, toast, cheese and cakes prepared by his wife, a very attractive blonde who clearly found undergraduates to her taste.

Tom was a lovable, friendly, exciting man, a great pricker of academic pomposity. His books were stimulating if sometimes far-fetched; and their titles indicate his wide interests: *Merlin's Island* (1948), *Herdsmen and Hermits* (1950), *Boats and Boatmen* (1952), *Coastwise Craft* (1952), *The Painted Men* (1954), which was about the Picts, and *Gogmagog: the Buried Gods*.

As I became a postgraduate research student and spent my time looking at megaliths and was no longer a constant weekend digger in Cambridgeshire cemeteries, our relationship became less cordial. This, perhaps, coincided with Tom's disenchantment with archaeology. He described in 1937, although I did not read this until after the war, how at the age of 36 his interest in archaeology began to pall. 'Archaeology was not a big enough subject to occupy one's whole life,' he wrote. 'It was very interesting but it was trivial. An archaeologist was simply a species of public entertainer. He gathered scraps of information about the behaviour of men long ago which occasionally served to liven the tedium of the lives of his fellows for a few minutes at a time. That was all he ever did.'

I didn't know of this change of heart in the years immediately before the outbreak of the War. I thought my relations with this good friend were still frank and cordial, but as I now know he suspected that instead of the young starry-eyed undergraduate interested in everything, I was becoming part of the establishment. James Wordie warned me of this but I did not heed his warning. I invited Tom to dine with me in St John's when I was made a Fellow. He declined. 'These High Table chaps are not for me,' he said, and I was sad.

Tom Lethbridge's health prevented him from being on active service in the war: but he was most active as intelligence officer to the Home Guard in Cambridgeshire. When I got back from India in 1946 there was no mutual warmth or rapprochement. I thought it was part of the natural lack of immediate understanding between those who had slaved away at home and those who had been away, travelling widely, and had achieved field officer rank. But it was more than that, because he was returning to field archaeology and embarking on the strange, sad affair of the Cambridge Giants.

Professor Admiral Sam Morison described Tom Lethbridge's book, *Herdsmen and Hermits: Celtic Seafarers in the Northern Seas* as 'a chatty book by an imaginative archaeologist' and Colin Wilson spoke of his 'lively imagination' and 'continuing curiosity'. This was the essence of Lethbridge, a continuing curiosity and a lively imagination. He was an imaginative archaeologist. Sometimes, and not unnaturally, it seemed to many that he was too imaginative and I slowly moved into that many over the Gog Magog figures.

There is good reason to believe that the low hills to the south of Cambridge were called the Gogmagog hills because there had been chalk-cut figures of giants there – figures like the Cerne Abbas giant or the Long Man of Wilmington. In the eighteenth century a man called Palmer described seeing these figures as he went from Abington to the market in Cambridge. Lethbridge surveyed the hill slopes under the ramparts of the Wandlebury Early Iron Age hillfort and decided where the figures, now grass-covered, must have been. So far, so good. He then surveyed the hillside with a probe and found, to his delight, significant differences in levels. He then surveyed the hillside tracing what he thought were the outlines of the figures. As he went on probing, recording and planning a very strange pattern appeared – or appeared to him. I went out frequently to see him at work. One evening he showed me the strange plan that his soundings were revealing to him. 'Tomorrow,' he said, 'I shall explore this area and expect to find the leg of this figure.' The next day's probings, sure enough, marked in the leg as expected.

I had had for years every faith in Lethbridge as a field archaeologist but I became increasingly doubtful that he was in fact finding the buried outlines of Gog and Magog. This view, gradually, was widely accepted except by kind, too kind, old friends like Cyril Fox and Tom Kendrick. In the end he said to me brutally, 'What's your view?' and I had to say that I did not believe he had found the giants and was unhappily mapping natural features. 'I thought you had joined the shits,' he said. 'You whom I used to think of as a fair and open-minded young man. You disgust me. Let me tell you I am leaving this archaeological hell-hole of Cambridge and will never return.'

He did leave Cambridge in 1957 with Mina, his second wife, and took up residence at Hole House, near Branscombe in Devon where he lived until his death in 1971. As he left he said that he found post-war Cambridge increasingly unpleasant and dreary and that he disliked the 'academic trade unionism'. I believe that his unpublished autobiography *The Ivory Tower* has many interesting and extravagant statements about Cambridge archaeology.

Lethbridge presented his work on the Gog Magog giants for examination by an outside independent body chosen by the Council for British Archaeology who were to make a report to the Cambridge Preservation Society, who owned the site. Two reports were made because the members disagreed: the Society made neither of them public but Sir Henry Willink, Chairman of the Society, later discussed them with me at great length at an Ad Eundem dinner.

Gradually Lethbridge's critics became virtually unanimous that his giant figures were non-existent, and were the result of his wishful thinking. This hurt him enormously and he finally gave up archaeology, while insisting that he was right and everyone else was wrong. He, perhaps fortunately, did not live long enough to hear the results of the magnetometer survey carried out by the warden of Wandlebury which showed that what Tom had been faithfully – perhaps one could say hopefully, using that now much used word in its right sense – recording was the result of solifluction.

When he retreated to Devon and from archaeology, he turned to the study of the paranormal, and wrote on ghosts, ghouls, extra-sensory perception, witches, divining rods, psychometry and the use of pendulums – he even declared that he could detect truffles by the use of the pendulum.

A spate of books flowed from his ready pen. *Ghosts and Ghouls* (1961), *Witches* (1962), *Ghost in Divining Rod* (1963), *E.S.P: Beyond Time and Distance* (1965), *A Step in the Dark* (1967), *The Monkey's Tail: A Study in Evolution and Parapsychology* (1969), *The Legend of the Sons of God* (1972) and *The Power of the Pendulum* (1976) – published five years after his death. All these books sold extremely well and there was, and still may be for a while, a Lethbridge cult. In 1980 there was produced an anthology of his writings called *The Essential T.C. Lethbridge*, badly edited by Tom Graves and Janet Hoult, with a foreword by Colin Wilson (I say badly edited because the provenance of the extracts is not given).

In these writings he didn't entirely abandon archaeology but increasingly wrote nonsense. He declared that up to a hundred years ago only the tops of the stones at Callanish showed above a deep blanket of peat, and that the blue stones at Stonehenge came from Tipperary. He declared that three stone rows on Dartmoor give approximate (!) bearings on Carnac and that stone circles were bio-electronic beacons for aerial navigation. He and his wife Mina found that when they touched the stones of circles in Devon and Cornwall they received electric shocks and they believed that the ritual dances which prehistoric men had carried out in and around these monuments had generated bio-electricity which enabled the stones to act as radar-beacons for the sons of the gods who arrived from outer space. He got to these ideas quite independently of Von Däniken. He always wrote clearly, simply, and persuasively. His line always was: 'These things happened to me, I can't explain them, but I record them.' I can only say that these things have never happened to me and I have touched more megaliths than most people.

After he had left Cambridge for Devon I wrote to him on several occasions but he never replied. I suggested to his wife that we might call one day on our journeys from Cambridge to the West Country but she replied that it would be inadvisable. We had become foes, which was sad. A man of keen intelligence, a practical archaeologist of great· experience, a friend who, disillusioned by archaeology (nothing wrong or strange in that), didn't carry his friendships with him as he voyaged into the mysterious world of the unknown. I know now that he was particularly hurt by my criticism of his mystical interpretation of stone circles.

I have written at length about Tom Lethbridge because he was the only friend who became a foe, the only man I knew well and respected as an archaeologist who moved away into the lunatic fringes and whom I could no longer treat seriously. Others managed to maintain good and friendly relations with him until the end of his life. Such were Sir Cyril Fox and Sir Thomas Kendrick, but they were kinder men than me; from lack of moral courage or intense affection for Lethbridge they never said in print or to his face that they did not believe in the Gog Magog giants, although they both said so to me.

The scholar who goes berserk and especially the scholar immensely distinguished and recognized in one field who writes nonsense in a field far from his own is a fascinating and distressing phenomenon. I never knew Sir Grafton Elliot Smith who was a Johnian: he came up in 1896 from Australia, was one of the first affiliated students (Lord Rutherford was the first in 1895), was made a Fellow in 1899 and an honorary Fellow in 1931. He died in 1937 and during the last few years of his life was seriously incapacitated by a stroke. I would dearly like to have talked to him about his Egyptocentric hyper-diffusionist ideas and argue with him and with W.J. Perry about megaliths, but it was not to be. Here was a great teacher of anatomy, a man who made brilliant contributions to our knowledge of the evolution of the brain, who became besotted – this is not too hard a word – by ancient Egypt and for thirty years darkened scholarship and deluded the public with his extravagant and wrong theories of the origin of man and his culture. Curiously enough in his Huxley Lecture to the Royal Anthropological Institute he said: 'Sometimes the convictions of a scientist are indistinguishable from a delusion.' He was naturally not referring to himself but this is what had happened to him and to Perry. And this is what happened to Tom Lethbridge.

I did know another man who went to the bad in an extravagant way and this was Lord Raglan. He worked steadily and well as an archaeologist and on Welsh vernacular architecture with Cyril Fox (that kind, sweet man who would hear no criticism of Raglan, as he would hear none of Tom Lethbridge). But his views on the origins of civilization were even more extravagant than those of the so-called Manchester School of Elliot Smith and Perry. Raglan published his *How Came Civilization?* in 1939 – two years after the death of Elliot Smith. In this book he substituted Sumeria for Egypt and put forward his Sumerocentric hyperdiffusionist theory that all higher culture started in Mesopotamia. Raglan much disliked my criticism of his work and, after his death, his family protested vigorously at what they thought was my defamation of his character and my misrepresentation of his views.

I have already referred to the deep differences I had with my friend H.A. Harris over Elliot Smith. He could not understand how I could be, as he said, 'so bloodymindedly stupid about that great teacher and scholar.' It meant so much to me to talk to Harris about the Elliot Smith-Perry nonsense: but it was like asking a Roman Catholic to examine the historicity of the Resurrection or the Virgin Birth. It was all history by faith rather than fact. My inability to get a highly intelligent man like H.A.H. to discuss the alleged Egyptian origins of all culture was not only my personal failure but a demonstration of the strength of anti-establishment views among wise men.

I have gently ridiculed a whole procession of these off-prehistorians in my *Antiquity* editorials for the last thirty years and from time to time gentle ridicule has moved to sarcasm and scorn. But there are issues here which no scholars must neglect. We are all dealing with an invented past, and why – because the dark comforts of unreason are easy – should they necessarily be less true than the light uncomfortable statements of reasonable scholars? There is a great issue here which many archaeologists would like to disregard. It is the simple issue: fact, faith or fiction?

I know that, sadly, I made an enemy of Alexander Thom, that nice, kind old man. Thom was Professor of Engineering in Oxford and therefore a scholar: it makes me unhappy to say he was another example of the Elliot Smith syndrome, but he was in that *galère*, alas.

I got him down to talk to my students in Cambridge: his lecture was a disaster. The students took him out to dinner and off to discussion in their rooms. I collected him the next morning and we breakfasted together in the College buttery. He was a shaken man. 'You know my problem, Daniel,' he said. 'It's that the builders of the stone circles knew Pythagorean geometry long before Pythagoras.' This was no time to mince words. 'But Alex,' I said, 'a piece of string on three points and you have the geometry you want.' He was claiming that he had found an exact measurement, the megalithic yard and the megalithic fathom. I said: 'But surely this is just a normal man's pace.' Thom was shocked.

He had worked in England and Scotland and his surveys are of the very highest value and, of course, accuracy. But he wondered what the monuments meant – as we all do – and decided they were lunar observatories. I organized a TV programme in which he set out his views and then it occurred to me that he should go across to France and see what he made of the Carnac alignments. When I had arranged this with the BBC, I approached him and he said: 'No. No. I find it difficult enough getting from Argyll to Oxford. The climate you know. And France, it will be very, very hot.' I assured him that south Brittany would not be much different from Oxford. 'But the food?' he said. 'Snails? Frogs' legs? I'll bring my own food.' And he arrived, together with his family, with buckets of porridge and pounds of haggis. My wife and I persuaded him to come to a *crêperie*: and it was a great success. After a few days he said to me: 'Daniel, I think I like these creeps.'

It was a good idea of mine to get Thom to Brittany and Paul Johnstone warmly approved of it. We all together made a very informative programme. But alas, the Carnac alignments took over Thom. Not only did he and his assistants make the best survey that exists but they created two lunar observatories one of which was based on the Grand Menhir Brisé.

Sir Mortimer Wheeler was certainly one of my closest friend/foes, one of my dearest enemies with whom I had a love/hate relationship for forty years. I was brought up in Cambridge by Chadwick, de Navarro, Burkitt, Grahame Clark and C.W. Phillips to regard him as a shit and a bounder. They all sneered at and raged against this hideous monster who made his excavations prove his theories and went to bed with all the girls who, delightedly, worked for him. We were all advised not to go and dig with him at Maiden Castle.

This was a wrong-headed picture of a man who was, admittedly, an egoist and satyromaniac, and often behaved very badly – who doesn't? It is only half of the Wheeler personality. It was Leslie Murray-Threipland who, in my time in the RAF at Wembley and Medmenham, made me aware of the other side of Wheeler – a brilliant organizer, a born excavator, a dynamic and forceful character, and as I got to know him well in the fifties, sixties and seventies I recognized and appreciated this many-sided character and appreciated warmly its brilliance and scholarship.

Jacquetta Hawkes described him as 'one of the truly heroic figures of the later Heroic Age of British archaeology' (*The Sunday Times*, 25 July 1976), and in the preface to her very good and sympathetic book about him (*Mortimer Wheeler, Adventurer in Archaeology*, 1982) she says that he 'will rise from these pages as a Hero figure'.

Gertrude Caton Thompson in her autobiography, *Mixed Memoirs* (1983), compares Rik Wheeler with Louis Leakey, and it is a good comparison.

> In character they had much in common; an almost pathological physical vitality allied to brilliant perceptive powers which were directed to not dissimilar objectives – History and Prehistory: neither started with a personal penny to help him apart from civilized parents and good education; both had the power to attract money for his own ,impersonal purposes, which, in later life, included the Treasury for Wheeler and the National Geographical Society of Washington for Louis; both were among the first to realise the value of world-wide broadcasting in the rising age of TV; both were showmen.

Wheeler's achievements in the world of British, French and Indian archaeology have been catalogued many times: they are stupendous and of lasting importance. Even the French grudgingly refer to *la méthode Wheeler* in excavation. He was possessed of, and deliberately cultivated, a personality which had *élan vital*, panache and charisma: as a result he was often thought by many to be overbearing, arrogant and authoritarian, as, indeed, he often was. He had cast himself for the part of a handsome, debonair, scholar-cum-man of the world and he acted it well, with flair and growing conviction. Boldness was the key word in his character and it could be said of him, as Jacques Danton said in September 1792 to the Legislative Committee of General Defence, 'De l'audace, et encore de l'audace, et toujours de l'audace'. It was this audacity that distinguished his military careers in the two World Wars, and his archaeological career in Wales, the London Museum, the Institute of Archaeology, the Directorship General of Archaeology in India and the British Academy, not to mention years of television performances.

He was born in the year that Schliemann died; he was ten years old when Pitt Rivers died. He knew well Arthur Evans, Leonard Woolley, Flinders Petrie and Alfred Clapham. He had been taught classics by A.E. Housman. By a series of strange accidents, I was involved in the fifties in the projection of Wheeler to the general public through *Animal, Vegetable, Mineral?* and this amusing period I have described in an earlier chapter. Someone said cruelly of him that he cultivated enemies rather than friends. All I can say now is that from 1950 onwards we built up a friendship – certainly not a mutual admiration society – which survived for a quarter of a century. There were quarrels and disagreements; there were ups and downs, but mainly ups and levels.

And when, largely due to him, I became editor of *Antiquity* in 1957, there were two decades of most fruitful, helpful and nearly always kindly co-operation. We lunched together, he, Ruth and myself, each month alternately in the Athenaeum and our Club, and built up a very close relationship with a man who knew he was outstanding and brilliant. He slightly resented criticisms from someone much younger and more mundane, but often what he decided to say, as he strode at a furious pace from Piccadilly to Pall Mall, was changed by two dry martinis, a bottle of claret, and his ready awareness that there was another point of view.

Certainly he could be unkind, insincere, duplicitous and inhuman. He never visited anyone when they were ill and despised ill-health and death. The day after I had been elected to the Disney Chair of Archaeology in Cambridge, Brian Hope-Taylor was lunching with him and told him the news. His face darkened: 'What,' he said, 'that jumped-up schoolmaster journalist to be Disney Professor? What is Cambridge coming to?' Then he went back to his office that afternoon and dictated a letter of warm and fulsome congratulations concluding: 'Cambridge is honouring itself by electing you.' I do not forget that he was an unsuccessful candidate for the Disney Chair when Minns was appointed in 1927.

I think he was jealous of the easy archaeological and general life I had had. No Passchendaele, an easy Second World War of 'women's work', no grinding away at great excavations, no slaving away at hideous excavational reports, no museum drudgery. It all seemed unfairly easy, an early College Fellowship and a soft don's life in Cambridge.

But it all makes the events of 1956 (as recorded by Jacquetta Hawkes in her *Mortimer Wheeler*) all the more surprising. Wheeler was looking for a successor to Gordon Childe as Director of the Institute of Archaeology, who was retiring early in 1957. In 1955 he wrote to Stuart Piggott and said: 'I should like to see at the Institute a man with the broad vision and the imagination that distinguishes your work, and there is none other than yourself.' Stuart declined this invitation which was to my mind and the minds of most of my friends and contemporaries, sad. Rik was nonplussed, could find no ready alternative: the London University authorities, horrified and infuriated by Childe's administrative incompetence as Director, decided on W.F. Grimes, then Director of the London Museum. Wheeler was violently opposed to this idea; and eventually, perhaps in despair, suggested me. As I knew nothing whatsoever of these ploys and politics until the publication of Jacquetta's book in 1982 it seems appropriate to quote what she said:

> He put forward Glyn Daniel. . . . he mentioned with approval Glyn's promotion to Group-Captain [*sic*] in the non-flying branch of the RAF as a proof of his ability to get on with everybody and to organize: he is indeed outstanding as an administrator and most unusually easy to work with . . . a thoroughly sound archaeologist . . . and a born teacher . . . his judicious use of broadcasting and writing to popularize his subject could be of some value in a Director . . . exceedingly active, lively and personable.

I quote this because, first, it is the only unsolicited testimonial I have ever seen but, second, because at no time did Wheeler tell me he was doing this or ask me if he could do it. I shudder to think what would have happened if London University had accepted Wheeler's advice: I am sure that I would not have accepted the invitation and then we would have become foes for life. Grimes was elected and

Wheeler felt mortified and defeated. Fortunately, as at Aberystwyth many years ago, the fates were with me, and I heard from Wheeler nothing about the affair except continual criticism of the inefficiency and uselessness of Grimes. But it *is* curious that I heard nothing of all this for twenty-seven years. Honesty on this occasion would have been the best policy but that was not one of Wheeler's strong cards – he preferred intrigue and concealment, and his methods often worked, particularly and not surprisingly, in India.

My wife and I were driving from Cambridge to London on 22 July 1976 when we heard on the one o'clock news that Rik had died. That afternoon we had to walk from Thames and Hudson, his publishers and mine, back through Whitcomb Street where he lived for years in a small maisonette, to Piccadilly and on past the Athenaeum to Pall Mall. Memories of the great old man crowded in on us – and then we saw in the streets, everywhere, posters for the evening papers declaring, 'Sir Mortimer Wheeler dies', and we thought for a moment that we heard behind us a ghostly voice saying, 'Well, well, my dears'. His vanity and his sense of humour would have been pleased: his essential good sense would have realized that to have made the placards of the newsboys of central London was a tribute to a great archaeologist who had succeeded more than anyone else in getting archaeology to the public. He is now a part of the history of archaeology and one of the most distinguished and important parts that Britain has ever contributed.

We walked down from Piccadilly into Pall Mall. The flags were flying at half mast on the Society of Antiquaries, the Royal Academy, the British Academy and the Royal Society. Fame had been his spur, and he had died famous.

There were many people who knew Gordon Childe reasonably well but there would be few who would claim him as a close friend. He liked entertaining and talking, eating and drinking, going to the opera and theatre, playing bridge and spending evenings in the Athenaeum. But though he needed friends and to conspire with them for pleasure, he was a man without friends, which made his end in Australia in 1957 all the sadder.

In the mid-sixties Ruth and I drew up our car at the Hôtel Les Glycines in Les Eyzies and walked round the box hedge to find Gordon sitting there alone. 'How splendid,' he said. 'What a delightful surprise,' and turning to the waitress said: 'Trois afternoon teas, s'il vous plaît.' He had come to Dordogne to see Palaeolithic art and we took charge of him for three or four days and showed him everything he should see. He enjoyed himself enormously and was a delightful companion, but it was clear that the French countryside and the life in villages, cafés and restaurants had hitherto passed him by. And it was clear that despite his enjoyment of food and wine he could not understand a regional French wine list. 'Funny thing,' he said. 'They seem to have no good wine in this hotel.' That evening I ordered a Vieux Cahors which we all enjoyed. 'Delicious,' he said. 'Let's have another bottle.'

Next day we all went out to see Lascaux which he naturally found breath-taking. Then we walked up the hill to the farm which does excellent lunches. We ate in the kitchen and afterwards sat on the terrace looking down on the valley of the Vézère. It was their standard menu: *foie gras, omelette aux truffes, confit d'oie* with *pommes salardaises*, a salad *à l'huile de noix*, cheese, *beignets*. The white and red wines were from the farm and with the coffee we had an *eau de vie de noix*. 'I think this is the best meal I have ever had,' said Gordon. 'Do you realize,' I said, 'that everything, except salt and coffee, come from the farm?' 'Wonderful,' he said. 'Do you think I could buy some of their wine?' And we carried down to the car three bottles of white and three red. 'Much better than anything I can get at the Athenaeum,' he declared, as we loaded him and his purchases on the train back to Paris.

We often had meals together and he used to refer constantly to the meal in the farm above Lascaux. 'I must go back there again,' he said, and then shyly, 'We must go back there again.' But we never did. I blame myself for not conspiring more with V.G.C. and yet one felt that he was a great man who didn't want to be bothered with younger colleagues: we were wrong.

My first meeting with him was when Terence Powell invited him to Cambridge to talk to our undergraduate archaeological society on the archaeology of Russia. It was a disastrous occasion because he thought he had arranged his lantern slides but fell asleep in the train from London to Cambridge: they appeared out of order, upside down, back to front. Crossly he blamed the lanternist, then stopped the lecture for ten minutes while he put the slides in order. Ellis Minns said wickedly in a loud whisper, 'Such inefficiency. One might think one was in Russia.' He stayed the night in College and we had a very pleasant breakfast party at which he apologized for the confusion of the night before and asked to be shown the Combination Room and Library.

In 1938 he was President of Section H of the British Association for the Advancement of Science, which was to meet in Cambridge that September, and I was local secretary. He asked me to come to London and lunch with him in the Athenaeum and discuss details of the Cambridge meeting. We went into the dining room and ordered the food. 'Now what shall we have to drink?' he asked. 'Whatever you say,' I replied nervously. He turned to the wine-waiter. 'Two pints of the usual, please,' he said and I went to our table confident that two silver tankards of beer would appear. Silver tankards did appear but they were filled with still champagne.

I reminded him of this when I had dinner with him in the Athenaeum immediately after the end of the war. I had been lecturing to his students in London. This time there was no still champagne so we had a remarkable bottle of Krug. I had been lecturing on the origins of British and French megalithic monuments. 'A very good lecture,' he said. 'But you know,' I replied, 'all I am doing, as I did in my Dual Nature paper several years ago, is repeating and developing what you set out in your Scottish megalith paper to the Glasgow Archaeological Society in 1932.'

It is often forgotten that Childe was at first attracted by the Egyptocentric diffusionist theories of Elliot Smith: and the Givers of Life and the Heliolithic Culture appeared in the earlier editions of *The Dawn of European Civilization*. Childe had established a friendship with C. Daryll Forde and they had travelled together extensively in Eastern Europe. Indeed Forde once told me of a strange encounter in Romania where Gordon came in great distress to his room crying, 'You must rescue me. The patronne is trying to rape me.'

Forde had been a pupil of Elliot Smith's and had written a book in his series proclaiming the Egyptian origins of all things. But Forde and Childe soon realized that the Elliot Smith theory was nonsense and between them they put forward the theory of Aegean/Cycladic origins which dominated European prehistoric thought for half a century.

From those days onwards I knew him reasonably well; we often met, but they were meetings not contrived by ourselves for pleasure, but through the accidents of archaeological gatherings. And it was on one of these archaeological conferences that I had an insight into what was always described as his strong left-wing to Communist leanings. He was in the room next to Ruth and me and I noticed that *The Times* and *The Daily Telegraph* were on his doormat. When we got down to breakfast he said loudly, 'Where are the papers? I cannot begin the day without reading *The Daily Worker*.'

He was a poseur in politics or it might be said more fairly that he wanted a heavily left government and had toyed with membership of the Communist party. And then I think he was a dilettante in archaeological politics. What I mean is that he was happy to put up for consideration any model of the past. *Scotland before the Scots* was such a book. He wrote to annoy the Scots, and he really disliked his nineteen years in Edinburgh, but it was an exercise in a Marxist interpretation of Scottish prehistory. It was not successful: why did he do it? It is not a satisfactory answer to say that V.G.C. disliked the Scots and was having his own back on them as he left. He was interested in new models of the past and this book was one. At the end of the 1939–45 war Wheeler, then Director General of Antiquities in India, and interested in the Deccan megaliths, asked V.G.C. to write him an article for *Ancient India* on the subject in general. This appeared in *Ancient India* and said that all megaliths started in the Caucasus. It was one of the worst things that have been written about megaliths. I asked Childe why he wrote this preposterous article: 'Rik asked for it,' he said, 'and I thought it would amuse him.'

It is clear to me now that though he was the most distinguished and learned scholar of prehistory in Europe in the twenties, thirties and forties, he was sometimes intellectually dishonest: his politics affected his archaeological thinking.

There are, of course, endless stories about V.G.C. and some of them must be part of the mythology of archaeology. He was always driving pupils and friends from London to Edinburgh. Stuart Piggott made one or two, probably more, voyages of this kind. Gordon Childe was a very bad driver and on one occasion his car finished up in a field. The Childe legend says that he then turned to the pupil passenger and said: 'Good heavens! What has happened? I thought you were driving.' It is a good story and probably true, but we have never been able to find who the passenger was on this famous occasion.

When I wrote, at Michael Oakeshott's request, an article for *The Cambridge Journal* called 'In Defence of Prehistory' I described V.G.C. as a Marxist prehistorian. He was not pleased. The great puzzle of Childe at all times was to what extent he was a Marxist (or a Marrist) and to what extent he paid lip-service to an outsider philosophy. Were his love of Russia and his intellectual contortions in *Scotland before the Scots* a pose – an act which he was doing well, and enjoyed doing, and almost believed in? He described his post-Oxford job in Australia as 'a sentimental excursion into Australian politics'. I sometimes think that his Marxism/Marrism was also a sentimental excursion into the use of new archaeological and historical models. It was, most certainly, no conscious pose: he was always deliberately seeking answers to the problems of prehistory and history.

For a while he sought them in the works of Russian prehistorians and he always quoted with delight the passage in Mongait's *The Crisis in Bourgeois Archaeology*:

> Bourgeois archaeology, like history, is distinguished by extreme idealism (Goldenweiser). The English historian Collingwood goes even further . . . and Daniel follows after Taylor. . . . Contemporary bourgeois archaeologists serve the political aims of their governments. . . . Most and more often even the scholars who are hostile to us are obliged to turn to the achievements of Soviet Scholarship. . . . Among bourgeois scholars there are not only our ideological enemies, there are progressive scholars who are friends of our country and who understand very well the universal significance of our science. One of these persons is . . . Gordon Childe. Childe has not yet succeeded in overcoming many of the errors of bourgeois science. But he understands that scientific truth is in the socialist camp and is not ashamed to call himself a pupil of Soviet archaeologists.

Of one thing we can be certain: Childe was never a pupil of Soviet archaeologists; indeed, his attitude to Soviet archaeological scholarship changed markedly during his lifetime. I asked him to write a volume on Russia for the *Ancient Peoples and Places* series; it was perhaps a mistaken suggestion – there ought to be, and perhaps will be one day, three or four volumes dealing with the prehistory and ancient history of that great country. For a year or two Gordon was contemplating the possibility of such a book. He took the possibility with him when he sailed to Australia in 1957 but he had long ago decided not to write that book for me, or, for that matter, any book or anything to do with prehistory again. He sailed away from Tilbury a defeated man, believing he could not make any further contribution to prehistory, and, sadly and mistakenly, that his contribution had not been successful. He ought to have told his friends and acquaintances that he was off to Australia; we could all have been there to wish him a good journey and a safe return.

But did he want a safe return to England, even to the comforts of the Athenaeum and meals and drinks with his friends? He had, it would now appear, planned how he was going to leave this world. Professor W.F. Grimes describes how, shortly after he had succeeded Childe as Director of the Institute of Archaeology, they dined together in Soho:

> We drove back to NW3 in his car. In the hundred or so yards between Primrose Hill station and Chalk Farm (where I was to leave him) the following conversation took place.
> G: What are you going to do when you retire?
> C: I know a 2000-foot cliff in Australia. I intend to jump off it.
> G: Good god! Why are you going to do that?
> C: I have a horror of a prostate operation.
> G: But surely thousands of men have had that and come out of it without difficulty?
> He made no further comment and seconds later I got out of the car. The conversation is verbatim. I saw no point in arguing or remonstrating. Childe knew his own mind, though he rarely – very rarely – revealed it in personal matters.

I published this letter from Grimes in *Antiquity* in 1980. Estyn Evans told me that Childe had had virtually the same conversation with Professor Woolridge; and Sally Green in her excellent book on Childe (1981) says that she has heard this story from many people. I am sure this is so, although he certainly did not speak in this way to Grahame Clark or Stuart Piggott or to me.

But he did deal with his outstanding business affairs in a way which, for a man planning his own death, seems to me tragically, sadly, heroic. He sent a postcard to Crawford from Tilbury as the boat to Australia was sailing. He often signed his name in Cyrillic to his friends. And he wrote to me from Australia saying that he was not going to write me a book on Russia, indeed that no such book could be written. It was a kind of farewell letter although it had no trace of sentiment or of what he was planning to do.

A few days later he took a taxi out to the Blue Mountains, climbed up the two-thousand-foot cliff, took off his hat and spectacles and jumped to his death. To many the idea of his suicide was impossible:

see the letter from Dr Laila Haglund and Mrs Eve Stewart that I published in *Antiquity*, July 1979. These letters were prompted by their reading in *Mallowan's Memoirs* by Sir Max Mallowan that in 1957 Childe 'felt that life for all his interests held but a brief prospect. There is little doubt in my mind that he committed suicide.' Stuart Piggott, one of his close friends, on the other hand wrote in his entry in the *Dictionary of National Biography* that Childe 'met his death accidentally while walking in the Blue Mountains on 19 October 1957'. Many believed this or hoped it was true. It seems it was not.

Childe had written to Grimes, in a letter dated 20 October 1957 (a curious error this, as he died on 19 October), enclosing a statement which he said 'may in time be of historical interest to the Institute. But now it may cause pain and even provoke libel actions. After ten years it will be less inflammable. So I earnestly request that it be deposited in the archives and be not opened till January 1968 supposing that year ever arrives.'

It lay unopened in the archives until 1979 when Grimes and J.D. Evans agreed that it should be published, which I did in *Antiquity* (March, 1980). It was written in the Carrington Hotel, Katoomba, Blue Mountains, New South Wales, and I republish it here in full because it is of the widest interest to anyone concerned with the aged in general and with aged, lonely bachelor scholars in particular.

The Carrington
Katoomba
Blue Mountains, N.S.W.

The progress of medical science has burdened society with a horde of parasites – rentiers, pensioners and other retired persons whom society has to support and even to nurse. They exploit the youth which is expected to produce for them and even to tend them. While many are physically fit to work and some do, others are incapable of looking after themselves and have literally to be kept alive by the exertions of younger attendants who might be more profitably employed otherwise. And in so far as they do work, they block the way to promotion against younger and more efficient successors. For all in all persons over 65 – there are of course numerous exceptions – are physically less capable than their juniors and psychologically far less alert and adaptable. Their reactions are slowed down; they can only gradually and reluctantly, if at all, adopt new habits and still more rarely assimilate fresh ideas. I am doubtful whether they can ever produce new ideas. Compulsory retirement from academic and judicial posts and from the civil services has of course done something to open the rewards of seniority to younger men, and has rescued students and subordinates from inefficient teachers and incompetent administrative chiefs. In British universities the survival of the old system during my lifetime has provided cautionary examples of distinguished professors mumbling lectures ten years out of date and wasting departmental funds on obsolete equipment. These instances probably outweigh better publicized cases of scientists and scholars who in their colleagues' opinion are 'forced to retire at the height of their powers'. But even when retired, their prestige may be such that they can hinder the spread of progressive ideas and blast the careers of innovators who tactlessly challenge theories and procedures that ten or fifteen years previously had been original and fruitful (I am thinking for instance of Arthur Evans).

In fact if the over-age put 'their knowledge, experience and skill at the service of society' as honorary officers or counsellors of learned societies, public bodies, charitable institutions or political parties, they are liable to become a gerontocracy – the worst possible form of leadership. In a changing world their wisdom and maturity of judgment do not compensate for their engrained prejudices and stereotyped routines of behaviour. No doubt the over 65s are competent to carry out routine investigations and undertake compilations of information, and may be helped therein by their accumulated knowledge. Yet after 65 memory begins to fail, and even well-systematized information begins to leak away. My personal experience is confirmed by observations on senior colleagues. And new ideas, original combinations of old knowledge, come rarely if at all. Generally old authors go on repeating the same old theses, not always in better chosen language.

I have always considered that a sane society would disembarrass itself of such parasites by offering euthanasia as a crowning honour or even imposing it in bad cases, but certainly not condemning them to misery and starvation by inflation.

For myself I don't believe I can make further useful contributions to prehistory. I am beginning to forget what I laboriously learned – forget not only details (for these I never relied on memory), but even that there is something relevant to look up in my note-book. New ideas very rarely come my way. I see no prospect of settling the problems that interest me most – such as that of the 'Aryan cradle' – on the available data. In a few instances I actually fear that the balance of evidence is against theories that I have espoused or even in favour of those against which I am strongly biased. Yet at the same time I suspect this fear may be due to an equally irrational desire to overcome my own prejudices. (In history one has to make decisions on inadequate evidence, and, whenever I am faced with this necessity, I am conscious of such opposing tendencies.) I have no wish to hang on the fringe of learned societies or university institutions as a venerable counsellor whose authority may slow down progress. I have become too dependent on a lot of creature comforts – even luxuries – to carry through some kinds of work for which I may still be fitted; I just lack the will-power to face the discomforts and anxieties of travel in the USSR or China. And, in fact, though I have never felt in better health, I do get seriously ill absurdly easily; every little cold in the head turns to bronchitis unless I take elaborate precautions and then I am just a burden on the community. I have never saved any money, and, if I had, inflation would have consumed my savings. On my pension I certainly could not maintain the standard without which life would seem to me intolerable and which may be really necessary to prevent me becoming a worse burden on society as an invalid. I have always intended to cease living before that happens.

The British prejudice against suicide is utterly irrational. To end his life deliberately is in fact something that distinguishes *Homo sapiens* from other animals even better than ceremonial burial of the dead. But I don't intend to hurt my friends by flouting that prejudice. An accident may easily and naturally befall me on a mountain cliff. I have re-visited my native land and found I like Australian society much less than European without believing I can do anything to better it; for I have lost faith in all my own ideals. But I have enormously enjoyed revisiting the haunts of my boyhood, above all the Blue Mountains. I have answered to my own satisfaction questions that intrigued me then. Now I have seen the Australian spring; I have smelt the boronia, watched snakes and lizards, listened to the 'locusts'. There is nothing more I want to do here; nothing I feel I ought and could do. I hate the prospect of the summer, but I hate still more the fogs and snows of British winter. Life ends best when one is happy and strong.

And so, happy (?) and strong, he went up the Blue Mountains, and jumped out into the unknown future of his beloved past. When in 1983 the New American Library re-issued his *Man Makes Himself* (originally published in 1936) I was asked to write a special preface for this new edition, and I quote here what I said, written in August 1982:

> Few men or women are, or can be expected to be, impartial and fair judges of their own achievements and this applies particularly to artists, creative writers, politicians, and scholars. At the end of his life, a life which he was going to end by his own volition, Childe was not a responsible or balanced judge of his own life-work in archaeology. We, who can now look back on what he achieved in those thirty-five years of writing from 1922 to 1957, with detachment and against the developing pattern of twentieth-century archaeology, realize that he was a giant among men, a unique scholar who made one of the greatest contributions to prehistory ever made by one man. *Man Makes Himself* is a classic of archaeological literature, and it is good that it is being reissued in this new edition. We should remember that Childe, the man, made himself a prehistorian. Though influenced by Sir John Myres and Sir Arthur Evans when a student in Oxford, it was by his own travels and studies in museums, his own wide and omnivorous reading, and his constant and continuing exchanges of ideas with colleagues all over Europe, Russia, and the Near East that he achieved that learning and detachment which enabled him to write works of detailed and meticulous scholarship like *The Danube in Prehistory* as well as books of wide and stimulating general interest like *Man Makes Himself*. We owe him a great deal and salute his memory and achievement just over ninety years since he was born in Sydney and fifty since he came, unknown, to be a librarian in London. Now, we remember him, no longer unhonoured and unsung, as one of the great prehistorians of all time.

Much has already been written about Childe's life and work; three books have already appeared: Bruce Trigger, *Gordon Childe: revolutions in archaeology* (1980); Barbara McNairn, *The method and theory of V. Gordon Childe: economic, social and cultural interpretations of prehistory* (1980); and Sally Green, *Prehistorian: a biography of V. Gordon Childe*

420

(1981); and all are very good portraits of his work but not of the man – how could they be?

Peter Gathercole reviewed these three books in a remarkable article in *Antiquity* in 1982 entitled 'Gordon Childe; man or myth?' and I quote some of his concluding words:

> These three books bring us to the grim and cold logic of Childe's suicide. As one who for a long time could not accept that his death was other than an accident, I still find it hard to believe that Childe's letter to Grimes, posted just before his suicide, gives the only reasons for his self-destruction. My own feeling is that the whole letter is a powerful rationalization of his profound and long-lasting sense of loneliness. . . . I think he was personally very lonely all his life, and that he remained to the end quite unreconciled to his bachelorhood. Otherwise there surely must have been another time and another place to die.

CHAPTER FOURTEEN

The last decade 1974-84

I HAVE CALLED THIS CHAPTER 'The last decade'. It deals with the time from my election to the Disney Chair in 1974 to the present day. The phrase is ambiguous; it does not necessarily mean that I no longer exist: there may be, who knows, another decade.

Grahame Clark was due to retire from the Disney Professorship in 1974 and the Electors were to meet in March 1972 to choose a successor. Many of them were friends and colleagues of mine and gossip filtered through that they and their confidential advisers were proposing to elect Desmond Clark or me to this important and prestigious post. Many people put in for the job: neither Desmond nor I did, but not on the principle that Cambridge Chairs very often go to people who don't put in: I think we were both uncertain at sixty whether we wanted the job. Desmond was comfortably placed as a professor at Berkeley and his travels and excavations in Africa well funded. I was by then a Life Fellow of St John's and would retire in a few years and get rid of the burden of teaching, committees and administration.

The Electors first offered the Chair to Desmond and after a few weeks of deliberation he declined. It was then offered to me and after a short period of deliberation I accepted. Looking back on it perhaps I, too, should have declined; I was already sixty, a year which I now recommend for academic retirement. I could have had my sixties free from the chores of academic administration. But it was an honour and a challenge and there were some things I wanted to do and believed that I could.

I received a letter from the University saying it was customary but not compulsory to give an inaugural lecture, and that if one happened it was often the custom to have a party afterwards – but this would be at the expense of the new Professor.

I gave my inaugural on 24 October 1975 and I was delighted that Lord Adrian, as Chancellor, insisted on being there as well as the Marquis Townshend of Raynham as Chairman of Anglia Television, so that I could begin, to my intense amusement, a lecture in the Mill Lane lecture rooms with the preamble: 'Mr Chancellor, Mr Vice-Chancellor, My Lords, Ladies and Gentlemen' which brought the audience to attention. The lecture, entitled *Cambridge and the Back-Looking Curiosity*, was published by the CUP.

I tried to enliven the lecture with some merry tales and in referring to my predecessor said: 'I do find it curiously amusing that the first Cambridge archaeologist was called Daniel Clarke. There were actually three famous Clarkes in Cambridge at the time and Gunning has made us all aware of their amusing nicknames. Tone Clarke was Professor of Music, Bone Clarke was Professor of Anatomy, and Stone Clarke was the great Edward Daniel Clarke, Fellow of Jesus, first Professor of Mineralogy.' There was an appreciable and appreciative titter and for a moment that slide into sleep which happens to so many people at five o'clock lectures was halted.

I concluded, and most of the audience was awake by then, by saying that I believed archaeology:

to be of the very greatest relevance to a modern unversity and a modern society. My predecessor said that he thought that archaeology might be one of the most 'important contributions to thought made by the twentieth century', and he may well be right. There are still those, and there will always be such, who think that the back-looking curiosity in Cambridge and elsewhere is of no value to us today. To them I answer in the words of J.J.A. Worsaae, C.J. Thomsen's successor and the first professional archaeologist: 'It is inconceivable that a nation which cares about itself . . . could rest content without reflecting on the past.'

I don't think that my seven years as Disney Professor and Head of the Department of Archaeology will go down in academic Cambridge history as very remarkable in any way, but I set out to do a few things and was marginally successful in some of these. I tried to humanize the department after the egocentricism of my predecessor: I saw under-graduates and all research students, and even had regular meetings with my staff when we discussed what we were doing and ought to be doing.

I early found that I had the confidence and support of the University and was able to get two more teaching posts and to get two distinguished members of my staff – Charles McBurney and John Coles – made personal professors. In all this and in many other matters I had the warm support and encouragement of Ian Nicol, the Secretary-General of the Faculties.

The Cambridge system is an unusual one. The Secretary-General of the Faculties is probably the most important, certainly the most influential person in the University. Vice-Chancellors come and go every two years and as they leave express their appreciation of the Secretary-General. He, with the Treasurer, runs the University – the Registrary is a protocol figurehead. Noel Annan tried to change all this and introduce a four-to-five-year Vice-Chancellorship so that from time to time one Head of a House was able to devote five years to the proper business of the University. This happened in Oxford and by all accounts Habakkuk did it extremely well. Noel Annan often spoke to me of these matters and, as we have related, himself went away to a full-time job as Provost of University College, London, and then Vice-Chancellor of the University of London, all to the benefit of London, but the loss of Cambridge.

But these are matters of high university politics. I was, as Disney Professor, concerned with the running of a department and was delighted to get new and upgraded posts and the clearest possible indication from the university that archaeology was thought to be a good thing. It has not been otherwise in Cambridge for the last fifty years, which is why I was so astonished, and dismayed, when I went to see Lord Dacre (formerly Professor Hugh Trevor-Roper) as Master of Peterhouse to try to persuade him to have a teaching Fellow in Archaeology in Peterhouse, that College which had such a distinguished archaeological record from John Disney to Grahame Clark and David Clarke. He listened to me with ill-disguised surprise and disfavour and said, 'Is archaeology really an honours subject here in Cambridge? It is not in Oxford, you know.'

It was my ambition to take students abroad but the University couldn't provide enough money. Then in 1974, when I was elected to the Disney Chair, Anglia Television in their generosity and wisdom, asked me how they could celebrate the fact that one of the directors of a TV company had been made a Cambridge professor. 'It almost makes us look respectable,' said George Townshend. I suggested they gave a sum of money to the University the income of which would be inalienably in the personal control of the Disney Professor. I was surprised and overjoyed when the sum was £10,000. Out of this the University founded an Anglia prize for the best candidate in Part II Archaeology of the Tripos and the remainder of the income was mine, as Disney, at my absolute disposal, subject to no committees or faculty boards. This enabled me to start field classes abroad and during my seven years' tenure of the Disney Chair I was able to plan trips to Paris, Normandy, Brittany, one to Scandinavia and another to the Low Countries. I am eternally grateful, as is my successor, to this generous Anglia bequest and in all my activities as Professor I have enjoyed few things so much as setting out with a busload of students from Cambridge to Southampton, where we took on some Southampton students, and driving from Le Havre into Brittany and showing them the sites, wonders and museums which had so excited me as an undergraduate.

We, of course, had adventures and minor disasters. Early one morning on the first day in France a Girton undergraduate asked if we could stop the bus: she felt sick and thought she had diarrhoea. We drew into a lay-by and I concealed her behind a hedge. As we went back to the bus I saw a stout Norman peasant woman getting on to our bus, remonstrated with her and explained what we were at. 'You tell me,' she said, 'that this is not my normal bus to market?' I repeated it was not. 'I always knew,' she said, 'the English could not be trusted.' And on another occasion when we were boarding the boat at Locmariaquer to take us to Gavrinis and I was leaning over the quayside getting the students on, I was struck as though by a very large sack of potatoes and nearly thrown into the sea. A student had had an epileptic fit.

I was surprised and heartened to receive a letter from Gertrude Caton Thompson. We were all a little frightened of this grand intrepid lady and I knew that she held it against me that we had not kept on Ethel John Lindgren. I have since learned to appreciate and know her; her *Mixed Memoirs* is a joy to read. In her letter to me about other matters she added this postscript: 'I hear from a reliable outside source that your handling of the vagaries of Arch and Anth pleases everyone concerned.' It was enormously encouraging.

One day in 1976 Meyer Fortes came to see me in a very conspiratorial mood and said the Council of the Royal Anthropological Institute would like me to be their President – they had not had an archaeological President for a long time – and that it would be a particularly agreeable thing if I would do this while the Prince of Wales was the Royal Patron of the Institute. I agreed and was installed in 1977. The Presidency was for two years and my main job was taking the Chair at Council Meetings and delivering two annual presidential addresses. I was delighted to find that the anthropologist Professor Lucy Mair was a member of the Council and she was amused when I told her that, fifty years before, I had read her pamphlets on drugs and the white slave traffic when swotting for my Welsh League of Nations scholarship that took me to Geneva, and how very good they were.

I can have done little of much help to the Institute during my two years' Presidency: it was so well run by its Director, Jonathan Benthall. It was a personal pleasure to present the Huxley Memorial Medal of the Institute to two of my friends – Meyer Fortes and Gordon Willey. The Huxley Memorial Medal and Lecture was instituted in 1900, five years after the death of T.H. Huxley, 'Darwin's Bulldog', as he called himself: and is the highest honour at the disposal of the Institute. Fortes received the Medal in November 1977 and the provocative title of his lecture was 'Sacrifice, or was your fieldwork really necessary?'

I gave two presidential addresses: both were attended by the Prince of Wales as Patron of the Institute and as a result were given to packed houses. The first on 5 June 1978 was entitled 'Changing Perspectives in Prehistory' and was a survey of the development of prehistoric archaeology from the antiquarianism of the sixteenth, seventeenth and eighteenth centuries to the archaeology, new and old, of the twentieth century. My 1979 presidential was entitled 'The Forgotten Milestones and Blind Alleys of the Past', and I think very few people, when they received their invitations, could place the quotation or know what I was going to talk about. I took a great deal of trouble over this lecture; it was printed in the Royal Anthropological Institute publication *Rain* for August 1979.

I was due to retire from the Disney Professorship in 1981: the year of retirement coincided with the publication of the hundredth volume in the *Ancient Peoples and Places* series. For this centenary volume the publishers, Thames and Hudson, requested me to celebrate the occasion by writing a short history of archaeology, which I did.

The first volume in the *Ancient Peoples and Places* series, *Peru* by Geoffrey Bushnell, was published in 1956. We reached the 100th volume 25 years, 5 million words and 15 thousand illustrations later, and I dedicated it to Walter and Eva Neurath, without whom the series would never have existed.

A special party was arranged in Stationers' Hall on Thursday, 25 June 1981, for the publication of the 100th volume and I was told only a little time before that the Prince of Wales would be there and that I was going to be presented with a *Festschrift*. It was a splendid and, for me and my wife, a very moving occasion. I have always been against *Festschriften* but this one, *Antiquity and Man*, edited by three former pupils, John Evans, Barry Cunliffe and Colin Renfrew, was exceptional – not only because it was personal to me but because it was carefully planned to cover my own special interests: the history of archaeology; megaliths; and archaeology and the public. There is a special section dealing with myself as a person and the chapters are most revealing: they give a much better picture of the author of this book than he here gives of himself!

Antiquity and Man had a preface by the Prince of Wales who made an elegant and generous speech at the party. In his preface he wrote:

> I could not possibly forget the many expeditions I made in my first year to St John's College where I was supervised, entertained, amused and encouraged by Glyn Daniel. There is no doubt that having him as a supervisor made archaeology – and the process of learning – fun. I always remember greatly enjoying his rather irreverent approach to teaching, liberally spiced with anecdotes and numerous stories of encounters with archaeological forgers and confidence tricksters. . . . Well I remember, too, those visits to The Flying Stag in Cambridge, lunches with a definite French influence; some hilarious stories of the joys and tribulations of editing *Antiquity* – and the delight of being entertained by Ruth.

Years ago my pupil and friend, Simon Young, now alas dead, who was the part-architect of the *Ancient Peoples and Places* series when he worked at Thames and Hudson, and who then moved to John Murray, asked me to write a book one day called *Archaeology in my Time* but in conversation with a mutual friend he said, 'I don't think Glyn will ever get down to it until he is eighty'. In this book, as I originally planned it, there was to be a chapter called 'Archaeology in my Time', but as the other chapters developed I realized that I have already set out my views clearly in many books, articles and lectures and that they come out in this book without a heavy and specific treatment.

I retired from the Disney Professorship of Archaeology on 30 September 1981. Ruth and I gave a party in the combination room of St John's to celebrate the departure of the ninth Disney and the arrival of the tenth – both Johnians. Few things have given Ruth and me more pleasure than the election of Colin Renfrew. Colin and Jane have been close friends since their undergraduate days.

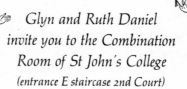

*Glyn and Ruth Daniel
invite you to the Combination
Room of St John's College*
(entrance E staircase 2nd Court)
*from 11.30 to 12.30 on Wednesday 30 September
to drink a farewell glass with the ninth Disney
and to welcome the tenth*

Colin had kept on my staircase for a while and when he moved from the Natural Sciences Tripos to read archaeology I had supervised him and admired his intelligence, vivacity and versatility – he was President of the Union and art correspondent of *Varsity*. I first met Jane when I was giving a talk to the Girls' School at Casterton, Westmorland, and she talked to me at a party the headmistress gave after my lecture. She said she was hoping to go to Cambridge to read archaeology and was already working on the papers of the antiquary, the Reverend Thomas Machell, chaplain to King Charles II. When she came up to Newnham she caused much raising of eyebrows by sitting in the library of the Department of Archaeology correcting the proofs of her book *Antiquary on Horseback* which was published in 1963. Some of my pleasantest memories of the early sixties are those supervision classes in my rooms in St John's looking out over the Backs: one hour had Colin Renfrew and Barry Cunliffe, another Jane and Ruth Whitehouse, now head of the Department of Archaeology in the University of Lancaster. Golden, rewarding, exciting days. I have often been puzzled and disturbed by A.E. Housman's sad characterization of life as 'a long fool's-errand to the Grave': did he not enjoy teaching pupils and seeing them grow and develop into distinguished scholars? Perhaps his standards were so high that he found no one worth encouraging? Teaching and encouraging young men and women and sharing with them one's enthusiasm for archaeology and living, makes life no fool's-errand.

As I grow older I find myself less and less inclined to attend feasts in Cambridge or Oxford colleges, or in London, and look back through my journals with surprise at some of the great meals of the past. But I still attend with pleasure the dinners of the Ad Eundem Club. This is one of the two main Oxford-Cambridge dining clubs: the other is the Arcades. These were founded to keep Oxford and Cambridge dons in touch with each other and they with the outside world. Now when dons flit about so much and are constantly in London the *raison d'être* of these clubs has vanished but they survive as delightful anomalies.

I was happy when I was elected a member of the Ad Eundem and was its Cambridge Secretary for twenty years. The plan of the Club was that there were ten (originally seven) resident and ten non-resident Oxford men, and ten resident and ten non-resident Cambridge men: and that we met three times a year alternately in Oxford and Cambridge in the college of one of the members. We all vied with each other to produce memorable food and wine. I remember many highlights: Corton Charlemagne '53, Leoville Barton and Calon Segur '47, and Chateau d'Yquem '34.

The company over the years was fascinating: Julian Huxley, Thomas Beecham, Nevill Coghill, Bill Williams, John Hale, Tolkien, Peter Fleming, John Sparrow, Philip Howard, Peter Medawar, Lord Devlin, Rab Butler. It brought me Cambridge friends quite outside my college and academic life: Lord Adrian, Frank Adcock, S.C. Roberts, Sir Henry Willink, Sir Lionel Whitby, Tommy Knox-Shaw. The dinners provide endless memories of stories and encounters. Julian Huxley had an inexhaustible supply of strange and amusing anecdotes. Lionel Whitby once told us of a slight difficulty he had one day in the Strand when hurrying to lunch at the Savoy. He had a wooden leg and it came off. 'I picked it up and put it under my arm and hopped into the hotel. The head porter was most understanding and imperturbable: he gave the impression that it was a quite common occurrence, and I was soon restored to bipedality.'

The veneer of generous bonhomie disappeared when, well fed and well wined, we discussed after dinner possible new members to fill vacancies. Names would be mentioned, canvassed, discussed, demolished. 'Over my dead body!' would be the cry. Alas, I am now the senior member of the Cambridge side: there are too many dead bodies to remember.

I particularly remember one sharp overheard conversation. Geoffrey Keynes had just been knighted; he was an astringent, forthright and often ungenerous person, and the scourge of antiquarian booksellers, always looking out for bargains and usually getting them. We were congratulating him: Julian Huxley's voice cut through: 'My dear Geoffrey: what splendid news! My warmest congratulations. I had to wait a long time for my K. You have had to wait much longer. Monstrous. It was long overdue.' 'Yes,' said Keynes, unsmilingly, 'long overdue'.

Tolkien was my opposite number as Oxford Secretary of Ad Eundem: he was great fun, a noisy, ebullient man, and we got on well. I once confessed to him that I was totally unable to read his *The Lord of the Rings*; so was Ruth, whom he much admired, and so were many of our mutual friends and acquaintances, but that I had friends and pupils to whom his writings were among the greatest things that had happened and that many times in America when I said I knew him people came to touch the hem of my garment!

'They were right and you and Ruth are wrong,' he said. 'If you live long enough you will find these books rated as among the major contributions to English literature in the second half of the twentieth century.' He smiled, but behind the smile was a steely look. He believed in himself, which is the surest key to a happy life: I never referred to the Hobbits again in his presence.

His wife's health had been bad for some time: as it failed further he devoted himself to her care and gave up almost all his non-domestic and non-academic activities. This included resigning from Ad Eundem to which club he was devoted. We missed him and tried to entice him back when Mrs Tolkien had died, but he said no: that was a chapter of his life which was closed.

In 1973 it was my turn to give the Cambridge dinner in St John's and I wrote suggesting that although he was not prepared to re-join the club, would he come over as my personal guest on this occasion? I added that Ruth was most anxious to see him again: on all previous Cambridge dinners he had always come to talk to her. To my surprise and great pleasure he said he would come and we got him a guest room in College. I collected him and took him to the Combination Room, more beautiful than ever in the candlelight, fires burning, silver on the tables, waiters handing round glasses of champagne. He was greeted eagerly by friends and was soon deep in animated talk. I noticed after a while he was not drinking and asked him if after all these years he had suffered the fate worse than death – namely, being put on the waterwaggon. 'I have organized such good wines this evening,' I said. 'I know, dear boy,' came his reply in a whisper, 'but my doctors only allow me whisky. Gout, they say.'

I went down to the college bar and brought up a bottle of Bell's and told the butler to see Tolkien had it before, during and after dinner. He blossomed under its influence and was in his best form. When we broke up, others accompanied him to his room. I went round snuffing out the candles in their sconces and locking the doors. The bottle of whisky was empty.

Humphrey Carpenter in his *J.R.R. Tolkien: a biography* takes up the tale:

As the summer of 1973 advanced, some of those close to him thought that he was more sad than usual, and seemed to be ageing faster. Yet the diet had apparently been successful, and in July he went to Cambridge for a dinner of the Ad Eundem, an inter-varsity dining club. On 25 August he wrote a belated note of thanks to his host, Professor Glyn Daniel:

Dear Daniel,

It is a long time since July 20th; but better (I hope) late than never to do what I should have done before being immersed in other matters: to thank you for your delightful dinner in St John's, and especially for your forbearance and great kindness to me person-ally. It proved a turning point! I suffered no ill effects whatever, and have since been able to dispense with most of the diet taboos I had to observe for some six months.

I look forward to the next A.E. dinner, and hope that you will be present.

Yours ever,
Ronald Tolkien

Three days after writing this letter, on Tuesday, 28 August, he travelled down to Bournemouth to stay with friends. Two days later he was taken ill with an acute bleeding gastric ulcer. He died on 2 September 1973, aged eighty-one.

I had fortunately survived to the late sixties with nothing serious the matter with me and my only brief visit to a hospital was for a streptococcal infection of the throat in Delhi. Then one day during my annual visit to Peter Watson to check my eyes, I said to him jocularly, 'How is my cataract getting on?' I had just been reading that almost everyone over fifty had some cataract. 'Rather quickly,' he said, 'but we can easily deal with that.' I had hideous memories of aged relatives and friends who had had cataract operations, weeks of lying still in bed, and months wearing thick-lensed spectacles, and spoke of my alarm. 'All that is a thing of the past,' he said. 'We'll get you into the Hope Nursing Home on a Sunday evening, operate early on Monday morning; you'll be out on Friday seeing as well as ever.' And so it was. This was an amazing introduction to the marvels of modern ophthalmic micro-surgery.

It was a year later when the Prime Minister invited Lord Franks to be Chairman of the Falklands Committee that Tam Dalyell made a cross, unkind speech in the House saying how stupid it was to appoint such an old man who was in fact about to go through the long rigours of cataract surgery. He gave an uncharitable picture of a decaying, partially blind old man who would not be able to read the necessary papers. Now I never had any high opinion of Dalyell during his Cambridge undergraduate days and his performance as an MP, particularly his Belgrano-obsessional complex, has done nothing to change my views. I felt outraged at this attack on Franks, whom I do not know, and the ignorance of modern eye-surgery and wrote angrily to *The Times.*

Falklands scrutiny
From Professor Glyn Daniel

Sir,

You quote in today's paper (Parliament) Mr Tam Dalyell as questioning in the House of Commons the fitness of Lord Franks to lead the enquiry into the Falklands because of his age and the fact that he is faced 'with the appalling burden of going into hospital for a cataract operation'.

Mr Dalyell is obviously not *au fait* with the wonders of modern

432

ophthalmic micro-surgery. On two occasions in the last eighteen months I have been operated on (once for each eye) for cataract removal and acrylic lens implant. On both occasions I entered a Cambridge nursing home on a Sunday evening and the operation took place on Monday morning. I left the nursing home on Friday morning with my sight restored. Each time the process was quick and painless. Admittedly I am an old man of only 68.

I am, Sir, yours faithfully,

Glyn Daniel,
St John's College, Cambridge.
July 16

There was, perhaps understandably, no apology from Dalyell; it is only the most generous and wise and therefore humble men, who are prepared to plead P.B.I.; but I had a very pleasant letter from Lord Franks.

I also had a surprising number of letters and telephone calls from people who knew nothing of micro-eye-surgery and were dreading cataract operations and was able to direct them to hospitals. So some good came out of it all.

My second experience of surgery, while equally successful, was a more extensive and major affair. Several years ago I was sick and had chest pains while preparing breakfast: the doctors were 99 per cent sure I had had a coronary. They were agreeably 100 per cent wrong: it was a pericardial infection caused by a bad flu infection, but from then on my heart was monitored. There was, we were told, a mitral murmur. Then on 29 July 1982 I collapsed on the doorstep of The Flying Stag: I had had a syncope. We were going across to our house in France in a few days but Hugh Fleming, the senior Cambridge cardiologist, when he examined me said, 'On the contrary you are going to Papworth,' and on 1 September 1982 John Wallwork intervened surgically, did a double coronary by-pass and replaced my aortic valve. Papworth was famous when Verrier-Jones developed it as a special TB centre; it has now found new fame as the Heart Surgery unit of Addenbrooke's and a pioneer of heart transplants. I can think of no pleasanter or more efficient hospital in which to live, re-live, or, for that matter indeed, to die.

I had nothing but absolute confidence that all would be well. Open-heart surgery was now an established and reliable thing. Dick

433

Joice and Ruth Fermoy, who had recently been through it, assured me that there was nothing to worry about. But of course there were two worries: pain and possible death. I had been told quite clearly that if I did not have this operation my chances of living much longer were slim. With this grim warning I went happily into Papworth and was amused, as I still am, exteriorizing the whole experience. The night before the operation I was reading *Letters of an Indian Judge to an English Gentlewoman*. The judge wrote before he had an operation: 'I . . . go into the hospital tomorrow morning. I cannot say I greatly care. No man lives for ever, and certainly I have collected a good experience of joys and sorrows, hopes and disappointments to take with me from this world to wherever it is. I must at last go; and through it all friendship runs like a golden thread. When there has been this golden thread, how can we complain?'

I slept well the night before the operation, woke early and wrote in my journal. As the stretcher bearers approached I wrote, 'Farewell, dear journal, for a little while.' And as they wheeled me away, the first anaesthetic beginning to take effect, I remembered what Wingate used to say in his final address to his Chindits before a military operation: 'Gentlemen, life is fleeting. There are many of you who will never come back from this.'

Four days later I was back in my bed and writing in my journal. I have no recollection of the days in the intensive care unit: I am told that a doctor once asked me: 'Do you know where you are?' and I replied, 'Yes, in a hospital'. He persisted and said: 'But where?' to which I apparently replied, 'The Hospital of St John'. Now of course there *was* a Hospital of St John once in Cambridge, out of which St John's College was formed.

A telegram from Buckingham Palace arrived in Papworth; it said:

> Very sorry to hear you have to go into hospital. I hope it isn't due to delayed strain caused by teaching archaeology students 15 years ago. Best wishes for a successful operation and speedy recovery.
>
> (Signed) Charles.

We stuck it up on a board covered with other good wishes and jolly get-well messages. It gave me a new cachet among the nurses and a delightful kind Sister asked mockingly if she should curtsey to it!

I discussed heart-surgery and heart-transplants with my surgeons and doctors in Papworth. They told me there were several kinds of substitute aortic valves, one a metal device made in Sweden, and one (which I had) made of pig-tissue by refugees from Vietnam working in a factory in Minnesota. How long do they last? I asked, knowing that pace-makers can be and are replaced. 'My Miss Piggy valve, how long does that last?' 'For life, dear boy,' said my surgeon, John Wallwork, and when he left me I thought of the oft-repeated remark of ageing dons: 'Time is no longer on our side.'

John Wallwork's deliciously equivocal remark made it clear that I did not know, and would never know, on which side my time was. There were, therefore, two things to do: first to set down, as Walter Neurath had asked me to do a quarter of a century ago, some of the anecdotes and memories of my life. I began writing in Papworth and three years later have finished. In the second place it was prudent, as Ruth and I are connoisseurs of such matters, to arrange the details of my memorial service when, let us hope many years ahead, this will happen, and the College flag will fly at half-mast on the Great Gate for me as it has flown in sorrow on so many occasions for other people in the last fifty years of my life.

I had once asked, in jest, Robin Orr to write an unusual anthem on my invented text, 'Those who do not trust in the Lord are not for ever damned', but, though he was amused, he very properly declined. He did not, however, to the great satisfaction of Ruth and myself, decline our invitation to write an anthem for my memorial service. We were much exercised in choosing the words. I had been affected by two recent memorial services, those of Dorothy Whitelock and Brian Downs. The Whitelock service, devised by her successor, Peter Clemoes, and his successor, Ray Page, used a text from *The Battle of Maldon*. On the cover of the Downs Service were printed these lines from *Hávamál*:

> Cattle die, kin die,
> So too dies the man.
> But a glorious name will never die
> For the man who earns it.
> One thing only never dies
> The good fame of the dead.

In the end, after discussion with Robin, we came to a mixture of *The Battle of Maldon* and *2 Maccabees*:

> O God, ruler of the world,

I thank you for all the joy
I have known in my life.
My work is brought to an end.
If it is found well written,
That is what I hoped for,
If mediocre I could only do my best.

Robin has set this to music in a most beautiful and moving way: one of his loveliest works, and I am a great admirer of him as a composer. The anthem was first performed in St John's College Chapel by the choir under the direction of Dr George Guest at the service for commemoration of benefactors, May 1984, and was much admired.

I, fortunately, cannot say when will be the official performance for which it was intended because, unlike the psalmist (*Psalms*, xxxix.5), I do not say, 'Lord, let me know mine end, and the number of my days: that I may be certified how long I have to live.'

When I had finished writing these ephemeral memoirs I went again through the enormous tell of accumulated letters and papers in my College rooms and found much that I ought, perhaps, to have included. There was one thing that I must now add. When my father died I destroyed his papers and diaries but I kept one or two of his notebooks, and these I looked through a few days ago. They included a strange piece of writing by his dying mother, my grandmother, who died of cancer a few years before I was born. It says simply, sadly, sorrowfully:

You were to call on the 14th of September. I thank you, but I have another call to eternal peace and rest. I have sown my field full but I have reaped no harvest.

My father had kept this moving and disturbing note in his wallet all his life. Attached to it was a scribbled note by him: 'Pray God that when I go there will be some record of something done; some small harvest reaped.'

APPENDICES

Paul Johnstone came to television in 1951. Television, then, was right at the beginning of its development and Paul was 32. I met him soon afterwards, at Alexandra Palace, when I became his trainee assistant. He was a quiet, almost donnish man. It was difficult to believe, as I later found out, that he had ended the war as a young naval lieutenant in command of his own boat, a motor launch in the Coastal Forces. He didn't seem to me to be the sort of bold, decisive man of action that such a job must surely demand. I was, of course, quite wrong. He was just such a man. But I suspect that I wasn't the first or the last of his friends to have been, for a time at least, misled by the quietness and gentleness of his manner.

One of the first glimpses I had of the steel principles that lay behind that mild outward appearance, came soon after the first television programme I saw him direct. All television at that time – and there was only the single limited service of the BBC – was transmitted live. The single-lensed cameras, without zooms or turrets, and mounted on bicycle wheels, required the most complex and ingenious manoeuverings if they were to produce a decent programme. They were also extraordinarily unreliable. One or two breakdowns while the programme was actually on the air were not at all uncommon. So to direct those early programmes you needed nerve, swift reactions, decisiveness, an ability to improvise, and an appearance, at least, of composure so that others in the gallery and on the studio floor remained calm. Your mistakes and disasters were all public ones. It was a tense business. And Paul was a master of it.

When each programme was over, most people went across the road to have a drink and relax. Paul was never the first there. Indeed, he was often the last. It was some time before I discovered what kept him. After each programme, he went back to his office and took out of his drawer what he called his 'Mistakes book'. In it he wrote an analysis of just what had gone wrong with the programme – some of it his fault, some of it nobody's – and what action he could have taken to put it right.

That was typical of him. Practical, constructive, ruthlessly self-honest, and with a deep concern for standards.

At that time, of course, he wasn't just concerned with *maintaining* standards – he was creating them. Standards of visual grammar, of studio discipline, of giving camera directions, of producing unpractised speakers. He had a hand in establishing all these. But they were not the most important of his contributions. Studio equipment was to change fast over the years and so were studio techniques. But what did not and will not change are the

437

standards that should decide what a programme actually says. Documentary honesty, the truth and accuracy of what he put on the screen was of over-riding importance to him. A film shot of one place, but used as though it were taken at another; the reconstruction of an important moment of an excavation but the pretence that it was the actual event – these were issues of great importance to him and ones he would debate rigorously. The pros and cons of those debates were something that those of us who worked for him learned early on in our apprenticeship and have never forgotten.

At that time, in the early fifties, television was dismissed by many serious-minded people as trivial and of no consequence – foolish, mindless. No one did more to abolish that attitude in the academic world than Paul. And he did it by a rigorous attention to the standards that he himself had set and by doggedly insisting – right at that early and difficult stage – on tackling subjects not because they were obviously easy, but because they merited serious consideration. Archaeologists were well ahead of people from other academic disciplines in realising the value and potential of television, of seeing that even a quiz game like *Animal, Vegetable, Mineral?* could provide worthwhile insights. And they were so, entirely because of Paul Johnstone.

Archaeology and history were, of course, his fascination. That was why he read history at Oxford – and took a first class honours degree – and why he came to found and nurture the first television archaeological unit in the world.

Because it was the first in the field, Paul had to invent styles and conventions for handling his subject. The solutions he evolved are now simply taken for granted. His inventions were never merely flashy or fashionable, but they were often of an extraordinary and radical boldness. In 1953, for example, the year of the Coronation, he managed to persuade the Television Service to transmit a whole evening of programmes as they might have been on one evening in the reign of Elizabeth the First, some four hundred years earlier. He wanted Elizabethan news, Elizabethan cookery programmes, music and drama, and he succeeded in convincing his colleagues in other departments that they ought to contribute to this unlikely and extraordinary enterprise. He commissioned a Stone Age play and filmed it inside the Stonehenge circle. And when *Chronicle's* tenth anniversary came up, he decided to mark it by inviting past contributors to the studio and feeding them, before the astonished gaze of millions, with a banquet cooked to prehistoric recipes.

Whatever else these enterprises were, they were spectacular and they stemmed from his delight in the theatrical which had shown itself during his schooldays at Stowe and Oxford. But they also came from the splendid flair he had for making the past vivid. One idea of his, in particular, turned out to be extraordinarily fruitful. How were the bluestones of Stonehenge trans-ported from Wales to Wiltshire? How did people cross the Irish Sea in prehistoric times? How did the Romano-British people manage to smelt iron? To Paul these were excellent subjects for television programmes and he decided that the way to test our hypothetical answers was to try them and see

438

if they worked. The result was that literally millions of people became interested in such questions and answers and what is more, archaeology itself came to accept that such a reconstruction under strict conditions was a proper technique of research. 'Experimental archaeology' they call it now.

Such acceptance by the academic world was always of great consequence to Paul, for he was, in addition to everything else, a scholar. He became an authority on the archaeology of ships and when, in 1973, his contributions to archaeology were recognized by his election as a Fellow of the Society of Antiquaries, it pleased him hugely.

Paul was an unobtrusive man. But he was a true leader, a man who inspired deep loyalties from his friends and his colleagues. When television started to expand swiftly, huge numbers of people with no experience of broadcasting flooded into the BBC. Paul, because of his experience but also because of his patience and his unquenchable concern for people around him, became the person who looked after such recruits to what was then Talks Department. They were very lucky, as I had been earlier. He saw that they got the right sort and variety of experience. He gave them standards of accuracy and responsibility. He praised them with pleasure, corrected them with gentleness and cared for their careers with a reticence that, for most of the time, amounted to invisibility. Many of us, I am sure, do not know even now that what seemed to us to be a lucky chance came our way because of Paul's unseen and benevolent plottings. That care, concern and affection, that was so much a part of his television life was, I know, only a wider extension of his family life – of the affection and concern he had for his relations whom we, his friends, met at his home, and for his immediate family, Barbara, Adam, Rufus and Jemima, to whom he was so devoted.

I have spoken mostly about the programmes that Paul created because I, like so many here, knew him mostly when he was in the process of making them. It may seem, perhaps, that this is therefore only a partial and unbalanced view of him. I doubt it. There was a continuity between Paul and his programmes. They were very much of a piece. Perhaps that was an example of one particularly important meaning of the word 'integrity'. The work revealed the man.

The Elizabethan Evening was marvellously bold and wild, at one and the same time academically correct but shot through with a delicious humour. So was Paul. *The Sky at Night*, which he invented and put on the air nineteen years ago and which has run unobtrusively, through thick and thin every month ever since, is modest, determined, dependable and not easily budged. So was Paul. His archaeological programmes from the early days of *Buried Treasure* right through to today's *Chronicle*, have been quietly adventurous, thorough, filled with a delight in the world – and true.

So was Paul. He gave us standards.

SPEECHES DELIVERED AT STATIONER'S HALL, 25 JUNE, 1981

Thomas Neurath

Your Royal Highness, Master, My Lords, Ladies and Gentlemen, I welcome you most warmly to this glorious hall and to this festive occasion and may I also express the deep honour we feel, and indeed the happiness, that his Royal Highness the Prince of Wales has consented to join us and make the evening an even more special one. The purpose of our being together, as you will know, is to pay tribute to a remarkable man – Professor Glyn Daniel – and to celebrate his many achievements to date.

Glyn's energy, his enthusiasm and ebullience have fostered and championed a multiplicity of causes archaeological, and have inspired literally thousands of individuals. So I find myself comforted by the thought that my own somewhat limited account here of his many talents is being amply supplemented by the essays in his honour which will be published tomorrow. Excluded as I am by publishing etiquette from having my own comments printed in a book issued by the house with which I am associated, I welcome this chance to pay my homage to Glyn publicly before you all, and quickly to recount some of my experiences of Glyn; initially as a pupil, rather soon as a grateful friend and for the last twenty years as his admiring publisher.

The first typically generous act of Glyn's that I encountered was the advice he gave me when, at the age of seventeen, I decided that what I wanted was to read archaeology at Cambridge. He gently suggested that I might care, when sitting the entrance examination, to apply for a place at his own college – St John's. However, when I stubbornly, and no doubt childishly, preferred the college of my best schoolfriend, Glyn, understanding as always, continued to keep an unobtrusively watchful eye on me and on my progress. He invited me to spend time with him in his rooms, at his home and over meals at local inns, where the hospitality met his own high standards. In so many ways, he went out of his way to introduce me to the pleasures and mysteries of life at Cambridge, and to the pleasures and mysteries of archaeology. I, as so many others, benefited enormously from his stimulating company, and his inspired and inspiring teaching, and the eminent archaeological careers of many of his students give testimony to the generosity with which he dispenses his knowledge and help. Of course, his teaching was and, I am certain, still is based on wide reading on his part and serious research, but what is more unusual and what made the process of learning so enjoyable, is his gift for seasoning his scholarship with many bizarre sidelights on a host of subjects, and with fascinating stories of the eccentricities of archaeologists past and present.

Schooled by him in this manner, I entered publishing with an enduring interest in the field of learning that is Glyn's, and have now for twenty years witnessed at first hand not only how much is contributed to that field by his own writing but also his extraordinary proficiency as an editor – that is, someone who recognizes the needs of students for literature on certain topics, and recognizes also the interest on the part of the general public in this literature; who knows which archaeologists have the requisite knowledge; and who can persuade them to commit their knowledge to print. His judgment, his vitality and patience, his tact and good humour as an editor are the envy of me and many another publisher too. And I want to make it clear that all of this activity in the domain of publishing is fuelled by Glyn's vision of the lasting benefit provided by a lively link between the public at large and the professional archaeologists. It is this conviction of Glyn's and his success in communicating it, his ability to coax and cajole numerous scholars from many countries, and indeed all the continents, to undertake the valuable task of recording their own theories and findings that has added so much to the sum of knowledge available in book form.

One series alone for which Glyn is responsible, and it is by no means the only one – I am referring to *Ancient Peoples and Places* – today sees the publication of its 100th volume. That is a volume written by Glyn himself and in my view it is a model of eloquence allied to high-level scholarship.

What I have spoken of so far are those facets and those achievements of Glyn's that I know at first hand. But by no means do they represent the full range of his accomplishments and successes. He is a gifted broadcaster both on radio and on television. He has organized and chaired untold national conferences on prehistory and, together with his wife Ruth, has edited some ninety issues of the premier archaeological journal, *Antiquity*. His investigations of megalithic monuments have become fundamental work – as have his researches and writings on the history of archaeology. As a fellow of St John's he has faithfully served his college and contributed greatly to the academic life of Cambridge University as a whole and for the last seven years he has held the Disney Chair of Archaeology at that university.

All of these diverse interests and many more besides are referred to and recounted in the *Festschrift* that has been prepared for Glyn. And the time has now come for him to receive the first copy of that *Festschrift* from the hands of one of its authors and one whose contribution to it is a special delight – His Royal Highness, the Prince of Wales.

HRH The Prince of Wales

Professor Daniel, ladies and gentlemen, I am enormously honoured to have been asked this evening to say a few words in Professor Daniel's honour – I would have been even more delighted if I hadn't actually had to make a speech! – however, it seems to have fallen to me to say something, although I can't help feeling that really the Queen of Denmark would have been far more appropriate as the *Schrift* speaker, or whatever it is on these occasions, but as she's not here, then as the next most junior or next least senior or whatever it is, I obviously have to say something.

But it does slightly worry me that this evening is almost like a kind of public supervision session – so many professors and other experts in the realms of archaeology – and I hope you will forgive me if it isn't really up to standard. I also thought to myself, 'Why on earth do they want *me* to say anything this evening?' – because I keep reading in various publications that I got a particularly *average* degree at Cambridge. But in fact although I got a 2.2 in history, a lot of people forget that I actually got a 2.1 in archaeology and anthropology. In fact I came to the conclusion that I worked *too hard* in my first year at Cambridge, having come straight from school, rather than as many of my contemporaries had done, spent a year somewhere walking through the desert or whatever before coming to university. So I was still in my A-level mentality and wrote something horrifying, like three essays a week – and as a result it paid off.

But this evening the object of the exercise is just to pay our respects to Professor Daniel and in that sense I would just like to say what an enormous amount I gained through having been taught by him. I can only describe it as the joy of learning through laughter. I always believe that one of the best ways of learning anything is through a sense of humour and Professor Daniel had that, I think, to the nth degree. I always enjoyed his supervisions enormously and as a result learnt a lot more. He had a priceless gift, I think, to make learning fun and what's more to make it different – what Mr Neurath described as a bizarre sense of the ridiculous. And one of the most priceless aspects of my particular time at Cambridge was being taken by Glyn Daniel on a tour of various megalithic monuments in France – and also a tour of various megalithic eating places! That remains firmly in my mind and will do for years and years to come, and in fact it obviously had an effect on the French Press because while I was there, they reported that I was accompanied on visits to, for instance, the palaeolithic caves at Les Eyzies and the megalithic monuments at Carnac by my governess – Mademoiselle Danielle! But we had the most marvellous time, particularly in Brittany I remember, and then when all this was over and my liver had reached bursting point, I was shipped to Jersey and then came under the care of Professor McBurney, where I was used as slave labour digging on a cave site on the beach in Jersey. That was very different indeed. We had to camp and eat a kind of strange stewed rabbit while, as I say, being used as slave labour. And having done my time there, just after I left, they started finding the most interesting finds of all, having found absolutely nothing up until then!

But I would just like to pay my respects to Professor Daniel and to his wife and to say what fun I used to have at Cambridge going to visit them at The Flying Stag and Cambridge won't be the same without Professor Daniel as the professor. But the marvellous thing is he is staying there. He is going to stay on, I believe, at The Flying Stag and will keep some rooms at St John's and will go on entertaining us and stimulating us and provoking thought amongst all of us and no doubt bursting all sorts of bubbles which arise here and there of absolute nonsense talked about archaeology.

Anyway, it is a great pleasure to be here this evening and may I now present you, Professor Daniel, with these essays in your honour.

Your Royal Highness, thank you very much for this book which I accept with the very greatest pleasure, and I look forward later this evening to reading what Philip Howard in *The Times* this morning, called your breezy and affectionate foreword. It was good of you to write it and we are all deeply sensible of the honour you've done us in finding time to be with us this evening in a summer which was full of engagements, and let us warmly and loyally congratulate you on one of them and wish you all happiness.

Master, my lords, ladies and gentlemen, it would be disingenuous of me to say that one of the reasons for this occasion has come as a complete surprise to me. For months I have been aware of hastily terminated telephone conversations and curious references in letters from colleagues in France and Ireland, but when in the end I got my invitation to this party I knew at last what was afoot or rather what had been under the feet of so many kind people for some considerable time. The current issue of that justly successful journal *Popular Archaeology* has a photograph of yourself on the cover and an editorial which warmly and rightly records appreciatively, as we all do, your continuing interest in archaeology and your goodness in being patron of the York Archaeology Trust, the Mary Rose Trust and the Council for British Archaeology. And I know only too well when I was president of the Royal Anthropological Institute and you were patron you kept a very keen and lively interest in the subject. Your great uncle the late King of Sweden, or to give him his proper title, the King of Sweden, the Wends and the Goths, was, as you know, a very keen archaeologist and a very generous one; he paid out of his own privy purse (this is not an improper suggestion) for the first Carbon 14 laboratory in Stockholm and for the lovely Museum of Oriental Art and Archaeology. Now a man who taught me in the '30s and influenced me enormously, J.M. de Navarro, always in his lectures told a story about how King Gustuv Adolphus as a young man was excavating with Oscar Montelius, and Montelius once said to him: 'Young man, if you didn't have another job to go to you would make a good archaeologist'. Once when I was in Stockholm I asked the King whether this story was true. He thought for a while and he then said: 'Daniel, I am an old man and I must confess I don't really remember that occasion, but if I were you I would go on telling the story in your lectures.' Perhaps, and I hope that this is not *lèse-majesté*, I could say the same of you, Sir, as Montelius did of Gustuv Adolphus. (And while we are talking about Scandinavian archaeologists, Countess Armfelt has just handed me a post card from your cousin the Queen of Denmark: 'MY VERY BEST WISHES AND CONGRATULATIONS ON THIS MOST SPECIAL DAY.') May I in the language of the land of my father's and your principality, and for that matter the language of Henry Tudor, say 'Diolch yn fawr iawn bob hywyl a llongyfarchiadau.'

Now I have never made any secret of the fact that I disapprove of *Festschrifts*, and as an editor I find them the most difficult things to get reviewed. But principles are not always carried through to practice, and

443

when I am myself offered a *Festschrift*, I find myself delighted and deeply grateful.

You will recollect, Sir, that one of the most distinguished Fellows of your own college, A.E. Housman, said when he was sent a privately printed list of his writings – and no-one had the temerity to offer him a *Festschrift* – a man who after all had declined seven honorary degrees and the Order of Merit which your great-grandfather proposed to him. 'However deeply I may deplore the misdirection of such energy', wrote the Shropshire Lad, 'it is impossible not to be touched and pleased by the proof of so much kindliness and friendliness.' May I say how touched and pleased I am by the proof of so much kindliness and friendliness and that I welcome the well-intentioned direction of such energy.

But we have what I consider a more important celebration tonight – and this is to the surprise of many of us, and certainly to myself – we are honouring the fact that the *Ancient Peoples and Places* series has eventually reached its century, and what a suitable venue for such an occasion. Five million words have been written in those hundred volumes and this must surely have involved the use of many miles of stationery!

I am still rubbing my eyes in astonishment that this venture which Thames and Hudson embarked on with me so long ago has actually reached its century. There are times when, I will not conceal it from any of you, I thought that for the series to reach a hundred, I would have to turn into Rip Van Winkle myself – and perhaps I have. A century brings to mind my dear wife's favourite game of cricket. Some of my authors may have been said to take a longish time over their innings. A few have even been bowled for a duck and one or two after a quarter of a century are still at the wicket or perhaps deep in the outfield hoping their captain has forgotten all about them. But for the most part, I am happy to say, we have had a succession of fours and some splendid sixes. I don't think, Sir, that you are a keen cricketer, so I will change my metaphor. This course which T&H and I embarked on does bear a certain resemblance to a steeplechase. Some of our authors have completed the course in record time (no need for the whip). Others have fallen at fences and have picked themselves up and gone on cheerfully to the finish. I certainly know that when I myself was commanded by Eva and Thomas Neurath to write this hundredth volume I had masochistically to whip myself over the fences and many fences, but puffing and panting, over-age and overweight, decrepit and decaying, I eventually got there. One of my troubles was that I thought I'd written this hundredth volume before, and more than once.

As one grows older and the series lengthens, we sadly lose friends and colleagues and authors and I think this evening of those, or some of those, who are not with us: Geoffrey Bushnell, who wrote the first volume, Terence Powell, David Talbot-Rice, Sean Ó Ríordáin, Ole Klindt-Jensen. And of course I remember Sir Mortimer Wheeler. I am sure Sir Mortimer on that further shore is still busy writing and lecturing and editing and broadcasting and directing. One might say still digging, if the foundations of the heavens

444

are susceptible to such earthly activities. But to our great good fortune, over half of our hundred authors *are* with us this evening and we welcome them all and thank them for their valued support and cooperation for all these years; and I remember too those who by reason of ill-health, distance or political circumstances can't be with us, like Hugh Hencken from Harvard, Bruce Trigger from Montreal, Jazdzewski from Poland, Merpert from Russia, John Mulvaney from Australia, Aileen Fox from New Zealand, and Brian Fagan who at this moment is sailing his boat from Cornwall to California.

The series owed its origin to a stray conversation between Simon Young, who I'm glad to see is here tonight, and myself, but its execution, to the inspiration and determination of Walter and Eva Neurath and this is why this 100th volume is dedicated to them. It gives me great happiness to declare my devotion, my respect and my profound admiration to Walter Neurath. The fact that the series has got this far is due to his perspicacity and his foresight as a publisher and that too of his wife Eva and of his son Thomas. I recollect with pride at this moment that the Booksellers Association chose Thames and Hudson as the Publisher of the Year for their continued excellence, and this two years ago was the first time that such an award was ever made. Simon Young was succeeded by Eric Peters and now by Colin Ridler and I owe an immense debt of gratitude to these men which I now publicly declare. They are really the people who have created these books and done all the hard work; and it is very nice to have here tonight with us Arthur Shelley who did so much on so many volumes by his skill as a draughtsman to add distinction to these books.

Well, your Royal Highness, it's now my pleasure and privilege on behalf of the publishers, the editors and the authors and the hounded 100th author to present you with this copy of volume 100 with our renewed and appreciative thanks that you could be with us tonight. We hope you will accept it as an earnest of our affection and respect for yourself and for what you do on our behalf in all parts of the world.

INDEX

447

Route of Channel Tunnel

Blériot-
Plage

Cal
Airp

CA

Cap Gris Nez

Guînes

PA

Camp
Drap a
C
St

N1

'THE

N42

Napoleon
Monument

L

BOULOGNE